HUMAN RELATIONS
Interpersonal, Job-Oriented Skills

Seventh Edition

Andrew J. DuBrin

Prentice Hall

Prentice Hall
Upper Saddle River, New Jersey 07458

Library of Congress Cataloging-in-Publication Data

DuBrin, Andrew J.
 Human relations: interpersonal, job-oriented skills / Andrew J. DuBrin. —7th ed.
 p. cm.
 Includes bibliographical references and index.
 ISBN 0-13-010578-3
 1. Industrial sociology. 2. Personnel management. 3. Organizational behavior. I. Title.

HD6955. D82 2000
658.3–dc21
 00-022499

Acquisitions Editor: Elizabeth Sugg
Production Editor: Ann Mohan
Production Liason: Eileen O'Sullivan
Director of Manufacturing
 and Production: Bruce Johnson
Managing Editor: Mary Carnis
Manufacturing Buyer: Ed O'Dougherty
Art Director: Marianne Frasco
Marketing Manager: Shannon Simonsen
Editorial Assistant: Delia Uherec
Cover Design: Bruce Kenselaar
Interior Design and Composition: WordCrafters Editorial Services, Inc.
Printer/Binder: Banta Harrisonburg

Prentice-Hall International (UK) Limited, *London*
Prentice-Hall of Australia Pty. Limited, *Sydney*
Prentice-Hall Canada Inc., *Toronto*
Prentice-Hall Hispanoamericana, S.A., *Mexico*
Prentice-Hall of India Private Limited, *New Delhi*
Prentice-Hall of Japan, Inc., *Toyko*
Prentice-Hall Singapore Pte. Ltd.
Editora Prentice-Hall do Brasil, Ltda., *Rio de Janeiro*

10 9 8 7 6 5 4 3 2 1

ISBN 0-13-010578-3

Once again, to Melanie

Contents

Preface

Welcome to the new and expanded edition of *Human Relations: Interpersonal, Job-Oriented Skills*. Success in any position involving interaction with people requires two broad sets of competencies: functional skills and generic skills. The term *functional skills* refers to knowledge of one's discipline (or organizational function), technical skills, specialty skills, or simply details of the job. *Generic skills* refers to competencies important in a variety of jobs. Among these generic skills are good work habits and time management, computer skills, high ethics, and interpersonal skills.

My purpose in writing this book is to help readers enhance their interpersonal skills in the workplace. By enhancing interpersonal skills, a person has a better chance of capitalizing upon his or her other skills. Two primary approaches are used in this text to achieve the lofty goal of improving interpersonal skills. First, basic concepts are introduced to enhance understanding of key topics in interpersonal relations in organizations.

Second, skill-building suggestions, exercises, and cases are presented that are designed to improve interpersonal skills related to the topic. Chapter 4, for example, presents general information about the nature of teamwork, followed by suggestions for improving teamwork. The chapter also includes several exercises or experiential activities and a case—all designed to improve teamwork skills.

AUDIENCE FOR THE BOOK

The primary audience for this book is people taking courses that emphasize the development of interpersonal skills. Such courses typically include the term *human relations*. Because interpersonal relations contribute so heavily to effective leadership, the text is suited for participants in leadership and supervisory training courses.

FRAMEWORK OF THE BOOK

The book is a blend of current and traditional topics dealing with interpersonal relations in organizations with a heavy component of skill development and self-assessment. The information is organized into chapters, all emphasizing interpersonal relations between two or more people. Chapter 1, "A Framework for Interpersonal Skill Development," sets the stage for improving one's interpersonal skills on the job. Chapter 2, "Understanding Individual Differences," presents information that is the foundation of effective interpersonal relations. Chapter 3, "Interpersonal Communications," deals with skills in sending and receiving messages.

Chapter 4, "Developing Teamwork Skills," sensitizes the reader to a vital set of skills in the workplace. Chapter 5, "Group Problem Solving and Decision Making," provides additional skill in collaborative effort. Chapter 6, "Cross-Cultural Relations and Diversity," is about developing cross-cultural skills in a diverse work force. Chapter 7, "Resolving Conflicts with Others," helps the reader develop skills in finding constructive solutions to differences of opinion and disputes with others.

Four consecutive chapters deal with exerting influence over others: Chapter 8, "Becoming an Effective Leader," presents information relevant to exercising leadership in the workplace; Chapter 9, "Motivating Others," emphasizes skills in getting others to work hard to achieve goals; Chapter 10, "Helping Others Develop and Grow," is about coaching, counseling, and teaching others; and Chapter 11, "Positive Political Skills," describes how to use power and influence for constructive purposes.

Chapter 12, "Customer Satisfaction Skills," describes several approaches to enhancing skills in satisfying customers, and thus lies at the heart of the quality revolution. Chapter 13, "Enhancing Ethical Behavior," translates ethical principles into usable skills. The rationale is that an ethical base is important for achieving career-long effectiveness in interpersonal relations. Chapter 14, "Personal Productivity and Stress Management," supports development of interpersonal skills in showing that productive people who have stress under control can relate more effectively to others. Chapter 15, "Job Search and Career Management Skills," includes information about the application of interpersonal skills (such as networking) to enhance one's career.

CHANGES IN THE NEW EDITION

This new edition of *Human Relations* is expanded and enlarged, in addition to including updated information wherever appropriate. Two new chapters have been added in response to requests by users of the previous edition. Chapter 14 deals with improving productivity and managing stress, and Chapter 15 is

about conducting a job search and career enhancement. Among the new topics in the text are:

- Informal learning by employees (Chapter 1)
- The triarchic theory of intelligence and multiple intelligences (Chapter 2)
- Metacommunication (Chapter 3)
- Virtual teams (Chapter 4)
- Groupware for decision making (Chapter 5)
- 360-degree feedback (Chapter 8)
- Self-efficacy as it contributes to motivation (Chapter 9)
- The integration of information technology into interpersonal skill development (Chapters 3, 6, and 14)

Most chapters contain at least one additional self-assessment quiz and one additional skill-building exercise. Many more references are made to the Internet and information technology, including using the Internet for developing cross-cultural skills (Chapter 6), enhancing personal productivity (Chapter 15), and conducting a job search (Chapter 15).

SUPPLEMENTAL MATERIALS

INSTRUCTOR'S MANUAL

The instructor's manual for this text contains 750 multiple choice and true/false test questions, chapter outlines and lecture notes, answers to discussion questions and case problems, and comments about the exercises.

PRENTICE HALL COMPUTERIZED TEST BANK

This testing software is available on 3.5-inch disk for the Windows platform. The program gives the instructor maximum flexibility in preparing tests. It can create custom tests and print up to 99 different scrambled versions of a test at one time; and build tests randomly by chapter, level of difficulty, or question type. The software also allows on-line testing and record keeping and the ability to add problems to the database.

PRENTICE HALL SELF-ASSESSMENT LIBRARY

A CD-ROM with a computerized assessment program that gives sudents insights into their skills, abilities, and interests. The Library includes 45 exer-

cises to help students learn more about themselves and how they relate to others. It is easy to use and self-scoring.

MEETING WORKPLACE TRAINING GUIDELINES

The U.S. federal government guidelines recommend that postsecondary schools teach five competencies and a three-part foundation of skills and personal qualities needed for job performance. The competencies state that effective workers can productively use resources, interpersonal skills, information, systems, and technology. In addition, the foundation competence requires basic skills (such as reading, writing, and arithmetic), thinking skills (such as thinking creatively), and personal qualities (such as self-management and integrity).

Human Relations provides information and exercises that directly support components of six of the preceding eight requirements—use of resources, interpersonal skills, basic skills, personal qualities, and technology. Information and systems are ordinarily taught outside of an interpersonal skills or human relations curriculum. A guide to meeting the federal guidelines is presented next.

Effective workers can productively use the following:

- *Resources*
 Included are allocating time, money, materials, space, and staff. Chapter 2, about understanding individual differences, provides background information for doing an effective job of allocating staff.

- *Interpersonal Skills*
 Examples are working on teams, teaching others, serving customers, leading, negotiating, and working well with people from culturally diverse backgrounds. Interpersonal skills are taught throughout the book, and each of the skill areas just mentioned is covered by at least one chapter. Chapter 4 is about working on teams; Chapter 10, about helping others develop, covers teaching others; Chapter 12, about customer service skills, deals with serving customers. Leading others is the subject of Chapter 8; negotiating is explained in Chapter 7, about resolving conflicts with others; and Chapter 6, about cross-cultural relations, discusses working well with people from culturally diverse backgrounds.

- *Basic Skills*
 These include reading, writing, arithmetic and mathematics, speaking, and listening. Chapter 3, about communicating with people, provides suggestions for improved writing, speaking, and listening.

- *Thinking Skills*
 These consist of thinking creatively, making decisions, solving problems, seeing things in the mind's eye, knowing how to learn, and reasoning. Chapter 5, about group problem solving, deals directly with cre-

ative thinking, decision making, and problem solving. Chapter 13, about enhancing ethical behavior, deals with ethical reasoning.

- *Personal Qualities*
 These encompass individual responsibility, self-esteem, sociability, self-management, and integrity. Chapter 13, about ethical behavior, discusses individual responsibility in the context of being ethical and having integrity, as well as constructive character traits. Chapter 8, about leadership, contains information about the importance of integrity. Personal qualities are also described in Chapter 2, on individual differences. Chapter 9 describes the role of self-efficacy in being motivated.

- *Technology*
 Frequent mention is made of the Internet, including suggestions for its efficient use (Chapter 14), and using the Internet to enhance cross-cultural skills (Chapter 6).

ACKNOWLEDGMENTS

My appreciation goes to the many people who contributed to the development and production of this book. My primary thanks are due to my editorial and production team: Elizabeth Sugg, Mary Carnis, and Delia Uherec at Prentice Hall and Ann Mohan at WordCrafters Editorial Services. Appreciation is also expressed to the outside reviewers who made suggestions for shaping this edition of the text: H. Frederick Holmes, Ogeechee Technical Institute; Judy Bowie, DeVry Institute of Technology; Gary W. Piggrem, Ph.D., DeVry Institute of Technology; James E. Wetz, Central Florida Community College; Ruth V. Kellar, Ivy Tech State College; Lou Jean Peace, Valdosta Technical Institute; Patricia Lynn Anderson, Valdosta State University; and John Adamski II, Ivy Tech State College.

Andrew J. DuBrin
Rochester, New York

Chapter 1

A Framework for Interpersonal Skill Development

Learning Objectives

After reading and studying this chapter and doing the exercises you should be able to

➤ Explain how interpersonal skills are learned.

➤ Explain the model for interpersonal skill improvement.

➤ Pinpoint your needs for improvement in interpersonal relations.

➤ Describe potential opportunities for developing interpersonal skills on the job.

Sean, a credit analyst, was being considered for promotion to team leader. So far, Sean had not been informed of this development. Alison, Sean's manager, was discussing his pending promotion with his boss, the human resources director.

Alison spoke first: "I'm in Sean's corner. But the guy is just not ready for leadership responsibility. He's a fine credit analyst. Sean has wared off many bad credit risks. But he gets under people's skin. Time and time again, he rubs people the wrong way. If Sean just had better people skills, he would have a great future with our company. The way he deals with people now, he is not ready to manage them."

Scenarios similar to this one take place often in the workplace. Many people are held back from promotions and pay raises, and even lose their jobs, because of poor interpersonal relations. (**Interpersonal relations** is the technical term for relationships with people.) Effective interpersonal relations must be combined with technical knowledge and good work habits to achieve success in any job involving interaction with people. In Sean's case, his potential promotion to team leader was blocked by his poor interpersonal relations.

This chapter explains how people develop interpersonal skills and presents a model that can serve as a foundation for improving your interpersonal skills. In addition the chapter explains how the workplace can be a natural setting for developing interpersonal skills.

PLAN OF THE BOOK

This entire book is devoted to many different ways of improving interpersonal relations in organizations. A three-part strategy is presented for achieving the high level of effectiveness in interpersonal relations required in today's workplace. First, each chapter presents key concepts required for understanding a particular aspect of interpersonal relations, such as resolving conflict. Second, the chapter provides specific suggestions or behavioral guidelines for improvement in the aspect of interpersonal relations under consideration.

Third, a variety of exercises give you the opportunity to work on and improve your skills. Among these exercises are self-assessment quizzes, skill-building exercises, and cases for analysis. In addition, the questions at the end of the chapter give you an opportunity to think through and apply the key ideas in each chapter.

Much of this book is concerned with **interpersonal skill training,** the teaching of skills in dealing with others so they can be put into practice. Interpersonal skill training is referred to as *soft-skills* training to differentiate it from technical training. (Technical skills are referred to as *hard skills*.) Soft-skill training builds interpersonal skills, including communication, listening, group problem solving, cross-cultural relations, and customer service. Soft-skills training is more important than ever as organizations realize that a combination of human effort and technology is needed to produce results.[1] For example, assume that a company establishes an elaborate Intranet system to enable

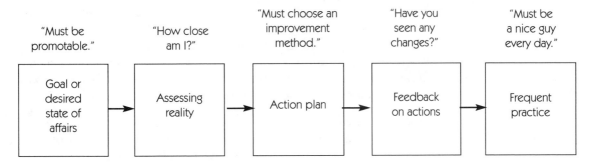

Figure 1-1 A Model for Improving Interpersonal Skills

employees to exchange work-related information with each other. The system will not achieve its potential unless employees are motivated to use it properly and they develop a spirit of cooperation.

A MODEL FOR IMPROVING INTERPERSONAL SKILLS

Acquiring and improving interpersonal skills is facilitated by following a basic model of learning as it applies to changing your behavior. Learning is a complex subject, yet its fundamentals follow a five-part sequence, as shown in Figure 1-1. To change your behavior, and therefore improve, you need a goal and a way to measure your current reality against this goal. You also need a way to affect that reality, and a way to obtain feedback on the impact of your new actions.[2]

Goal or Desired State of Affairs

Changing your behavior, including enhancing your interpersonal relations, requires a clear goal, or desired state of affairs. Your goal can also be regarded as what you want to accomplish as a result of your effort. As a concrete example, let us take the common problem of a person who nibbles his fingernails during tense situations, such as being called on in a meeting. The nibbler might say, "My hopes [a goal] are to be able to sit in a meeting and not nibble my nails even though I know I might be called on." This man's desired state of affairs (his goal) is to avoid putting his nails in his mouth in order to appear calm and professional. Having a goal helps provide motivation and makes it possible to exercise the self-discipline necessary to follow through on your plans. In short, the goal focuses your effort on acquiring the improvements in behavior you seek.

Here we return to Sean, the credit analyst who is being blocked from promotion because his manager perceives him as having poor interpersonal skills. After a discussion with his manager, Sean recognizes that he must improve his interpersonal relations if he wants to become a team leader.

Sean's goal is to be considered promotable to a leadership position. To achieve his goal, he will have to achieve the general goal of improving his interpersonal relations. By conferring with the human resources director, Sean

learns that his broad goal of "improving my interpersonal relations" will have to be supported by more specific goals. Having poor interpersonal relations or "rubbing people the wrong way" includes many different behaviors. To begin, Sean selects one counterproductive behavior to improve: He is exceptionally intolerant of others and does not hide his intolerance. Sean's goal is to become less intolerant and more patient in his dealings with others on the job.

Assessing Reality

The second major requirement for a method of changing behavior is to assess reality. Sean needs a way to assess how far he is from his goal of being eligible for promotion and how intolerant he is perceived to be. Sean has already heard from his manager, Alison, that he is not eligible for promotion right now. Sean might want to dig for more information by finding answers to the following questions:

> "If I were more tolerant, would I be promoted now?"

> "How bad are my interpersonal relations in the office?"

> "How many people in the office think I rub them the wrong way?"

> "How many deficiencies do my manager and coworkers perceive me to have?"

A starting point in answering these questions might be for Sean to confer with Alison about his behavior. To be more thorough, however, Sean might ask a friend in the office to help him answer the questions. A coworker is sometimes in an excellent position to provide feedback on how one is perceived by others in the office. Sean could also ask a confidant outside the office about his intolerance. Sean could ask a parent, a significant other, or both about the extent of his intolerance.

An Action Plan

The learning model needs some mechanism to change the relationship between the person and the environment. An **action plan** is a series of steps to achieve a goal. Without an action plan, a personal goal will be elusive. The person who sets the goal may not initiate steps to make his or her dream (a high-level goal) come true. If your goal is to someday become a self-employed business owner, your action plan should include saving money, establishing a good credit rating, and developing dozens of contacts.

Sean has to take some actions to improve his interpersonal relations, especially his intolerance. The changes should ultimately lead to the promotion he desires. Sean's action plan for becoming more tolerant includes the following:

> ➤ Pausing to attempt to understand why a person is acting the way he or she does. An example would be attempting to understand why a sales representative wants to extend credit to a customer with a poor credit rating.

> ➤ Learning to control his own behavior so he does not make intolerant statements just because he is experiencing pressure.

➤ Taking a course in interpersonal or human relations.

➤ Asking Alison to give him a quick reminder whenever she directly observes, or hears of him being intolerant toward customers or work-mates.

In addition to formulating these action plans, Sean must have the self-discipline to implement them. For example, he should keep a log of situations in which he was intolerant and those in which he was tolerant. He might also make a mental note to attempt to be cooperative and flexible in most of his dealings at work. When a customer does not provide all the information Sean needs to assess his or her creditworthiness, Sean should remind himself to say, "I want to process your credit application as quickly as possible. To do this, I need some important additional information." Sean's reflex in the same situation had been to snap, "I can't read your mind. If you want to do business with us, you've got to stop hiding the truth."

Feedback on Actions

The fourth step in the learning model is to measure the effects of one's actions against reality. You obtain feedback on the consequences of your actions. When your skill-improvement goal is complex, such as becoming more effective at resolving conflict, you will usually have to measure your progress in several ways. You will also need both short- and long-term measures of the effectiveness of your actions. Long-term measures are important because skill-development activities of major consequence have long-range implications.

To obtain short-range feedback, Sean can consult with Alison to see whether she has observed any changes in his tolerance. Alison can also collect any feedback she hears from others in the office. Sean will also profit from feedback over a prolonged period of time, perhaps one or two years. He will be looking to see whether his image has changed from an intolerant person who rubs people the wrong way to a tolerant person who has cordial interactions with others.

Frequent Practice

The final step in the learning model makes true skill development possible. Implementing the new behavior and using feedback for fine-tuning is an excellent start in acquiring a new interpersonal skill. For the skill to be long lasting, however, it must be integrated into your usual way of conducting yourself. In Sean's case, he will have to practice being tolerant regularly until it becomes a positive habit.

After a skill is programmed into your repertoire, it becomes a habit. This is important because a skill involves many habits. For example, good customer service skills include the habits of smiling and listening carefully. After you attempt the new interpersonal skills described in this book, you will need to practice them frequently to make a noticeable difference in your behavior.

A sports analogy is appropriate here. Assume that Marty, a tennis player, takes a lesson to learn how to hit the ball with greater force. The instructor points out that the reason Marty is not hitting with much force is that he is rely-

ing too much on his arm and not enough on his leg and body strength. To hit the ball with more force, Marty is told that he must put one foot out in front of him when he strikes the ball.

Under the watchful eye of the coach, Marty does put a foot out in front when he strikes the ball. Marty is excited about the good results. But if Marty fails to make the same maneuver with his feet during his tennis matches, he will persist in hitting weakly. If Marty makes the effort to make better use of his legs on almost every shot, he will soon integrate the new movement into his game.

In summary, the basics of a model for learning skills comprises five steps: goal or desired state of affairs → assessing reality → an action plan → feedback on actions → frequent practice. You must exercise self-discipline to complete each step. If you skip a step, you will be disappointed with the results of your interpersonal skill-development program.

IDENTIFICATION OF DEVELOPMENTAL NEEDS

An important concept in skill development is that people are most likely to develop new skills when they feel the need for change. The importance of the perceived need for change is reflected in a variation of an old joke:

Question: How many psychologists does it take to change a lightbulb?

Answer: None, if the lightbulb wants to change.

As you read this book and do the experiential exercises, you will probably be more highly motivated to follow through with skill development in areas in which you think you need development. A specific area in which a person needs to change is referred to as a **developmental need.** For instance, some people may be too shy, some too abrasive, some too intolerant, and some may not give others the encouragement they need.

Developmental needs related to interpersonal skills can be identified in several ways. First, if you are candid with yourself you can probably point to areas in which you recognize that change is needed. You might reflect on your experiences and realize that you have had repeated difficulty in resolving conflict. Second, a related approach is to think of feedback you have received. If there has been consistency in asking you to improve in a particular area, you could hypothesize that the feedback has merit. Perhaps five different people have told you that you are not a good team player. "Becoming a better team player" might therefore be one of your developmental needs.

A third approach to assessing developmental needs is to solicit feedback. Ask the opinion of people who know you well to help you identify needs for improvement with respect to interpersonal skills. Present and previous managers are a valuable source of this type of feedback.

A fourth approach to pinpointing developmental needs is closely related to the previous three: feedback from performance appraisals or evaluations. If you have worked for a firm that uses performance appraisals to help people develop, you may have received constructive suggestions during the appraisal. For

example, one manager told his assistant: "You need to project more self-confidence when you answer the phone. You sound so unsure and vague when you talk on the telephone. I have noticed this, and several customers have joked about it." The recipient of this feedback was prompted to participate in assertiveness training where she learned how to express herself more positively.

Self-Assessment Quiz 1-1 gives you the opportunity to identify your developmental needs. The same exercise is a first step in improving your interpersonal relations on the job, because identification of a problem is the first—and most important—step toward change. For example, if you cite improving your relationships with people from cultures different from your own, you have planted the seeds for change. You are then more likely to seek out people from other cultures in the workplace or at school and cultivate their friendship.

Now that you (and perhaps another person) have identified specific behaviors that may require change, you need to draw up an action plan. Proceed with your action plan even though you have just begun studying this text, but peek ahead to relevant chapters if you wish. Describe briefly a plan of attack for bringing about the change you hope to achieve for each statement that is checked. Ideas for your action plan can come from information presented anywhere in this text, from outside reading, or from talking to a person experienced in dealing with people. A basic example would be to study materials about customer service and observe an effective model if you checked "I feel awkward dealing with a customer."

UNIVERSAL NEEDS FOR IMPROVING INTERPERSONAL RELATIONS

We have just described how understanding your unique developmental needs facilitates improving your interpersonal skills. There are also areas for skill improvement in interpersonal relations that are shared by most managerial, professional, technical, and sales personnel. We refer to these common areas for improvement as **universal training needs**. Almost any professional person, for example, could profit from enhancing his or her negotiation and listening skills.

This book provides opportunity for skill development in a number of universal training needs. In working through these universal training needs, be aware that many of them will also fit your specific developmental needs. A given universal training need can be an individual's developmental need at the same time. It is reasonable to expect that you will be more strongly motivated to improve skills that relate closely to your developmental needs.

The major universal training needs covered in this text are as follows:

1. *Understanding individual differences.* To deal effectively with others in the workplace it is necessary to recognize that people have different capabilities, needs, and interests.

2. *Interpersonal communication.* Effective communication with people is essential for carrying out more than 50 percent of the work conducted by most professional and managerial workers.

WHAT ARE YOUR DEVELOPMENTAL NEEDS?

This exercise is designed to heighten your self-awareness of areas in which you could profit from personal improvement. It is not a test, and there is no scoring, yet your answers to the checklist may prove helpful to you in mapping out a program of improvement in your interpersonal relations.

Directions: Below are a number of specific aspects of behavior that suggest a person needs improvement in interpersonal skills. Check each statement that is generally true for you. You can add to the validity of this exercise by having one or two other people who know you well answer this form as they think it describes you. Then compare your self-analysis with their analysis of you.

Place check in this column

1. I'm too shy. _____
2. I'm too overbearing and obnoxious. _____
3. I intimidate too many people. _____
4. I have trouble expressing my feelings. _____
5. I make negative comments about people too readily. ✓
6. I have a difficult time solving problems when working in a group. ✓
7. I'm a poor team player. _____
8. Very few people listen to me. _____
9. My personality isn't colorful enough. _____
10. People say that I'm a clown. _____
11. When I'm in conflict with another person I usually lose. _____
12. I hog too much time in meetings or in class. _____
13. I'm very poor at office politics. _____
14. People find me boring. _____
15. It is difficult for me to criticize others. _____
16. I'm too serious most of the time. _____
17. I feel awkward working with a person from a culture quite different from mine. _____
18. I avoid controversy in dealing with others. ✓
19. It is difficult for me to find things to talk about with others. ✓
20. I don't get my point across well. ✓
21. I feel awkward dealing with a customer. _____
22. I don't get the point of the importance of ethics in business. _____
23. My attempts to lead others have failed. _____
24. Rarely have I been able to get somebody else to work hard on my behalf. _____
25. _____ (Fill in your own statement.) _____

3. *Developing teamwork skills.* The most sweeping change in the organization of work in recent years has been a shift to teams and away from conventional departments. Knowing how to be an effective team player therefore enhances your chances for success in the modern organization.

4. *Group problem solving.* As part of the same movement that emphasizes work teams, organizations now rely heavily on group problem solving. As a consequence, being an above-average contributor to group problem solving is a key part of effective interpersonal relations on the job.

5. *Cross-cultural relations.* The modern workplace has greater cultural diversity than ever before. Being able to deal effectively with people from different cultures, from within and outside your own country, is therefore an important requirement for success.

6. *Resolving conflicts with others.* Conflict in the workplace is almost inevitable as people compete for limited resources. Effective interpersonal relations are therefore dependent upon knowing how to resolve conflict successfully.

7. *Becoming an effective leader.* In today's organizations a large number of people have the opportunity to practice leadership, even if on temporary assignment. Enhancing one's leadership skills is therefore almost a universal requirement.

8. *Motivating others.* Whether you have the title of manager or leader or are working alone, you have to know how to motivate people whom you depend on to get your work accomplished. Given that few people are gifted motivators, most people can profit from skill development in motivation.

9. *Helping others develop.* As power is shared in organizations among managers and individual contributors (nonmanagers) alike, more people are required to help each other grow and develop. To carry out this role, most of us need skill development in coaching and mentoring.

10. *Positive political skills.* Whether you work in a small or large firm, part of having effective interpersonal relations is being able to influence others so your interests are satisfied. Positive political skills help you satisfy your interests without being unethical or devious.

11. *Customer service skills.* The current emphasis on customer satisfaction dictates that every worker should know how to provide good service to customers. Most people can benefit from strengthening their skills in serving both external and internal customers. (**Internal customers** are the people with whom you interact on the job.)

12. *Enhancing ethical behavior.* Although most workers in their heart know right from wrong, we can all sharpen our ability to make ethical decisions. By consistently making highly ethical decisions, people can improve their interpersonal relations.

13. *Personal productivity and stress management.* Having good work habits and time-management skills contributes to relating well to others even though they are not interpersonal skills themselves. By being efficient and productive and having your stress under control, you are in a better position to relate comfortably to others. Coworkers enjoy relating to a person who does not procrastinate and who is not visibly stressed.

14. *Job search and career-management skills.* Finding an outstanding job for yourself, holding onto the job, and moving ahead are not specifically interpersonal skills. However, both finding the right job for yourself and managing your career rely heavily on good interpersonal skills. Two basic examples are conducting yourself well in an interview and developing a network of contacts that can help you advance.

DEVELOPING INTERPERSONAL SKILLS ON THE JOB

The primary thrust of this book is to teach interpersonal skills that can be applied to the job. As part of enhancing your skills, it is essential to recognize that opportunities also exist in the workplace for developing interpersonal skills. This dual opportunity for learning soft skills is similar to the way hard skills are learned both inside and outside the classroom. Studying a text and doing laboratory exercises, for example, will help you learn useful information technology skills. On the job one day you might be asked to send a photo by e-mail. Having never performed this task before, you search a computer manual, ask questions of coworkers, telephone a help desk, and use trial and error. Within a few hours you have acquired a valuable new skill. The information technology skills you learned in the course facilitated learning new computer tasks. Yet the actual learning of how to send the photographs was done on the job.

Here we look at two related aspects of learning interpersonal skills on the job—informal learning and specific developmental experiences.

INFORMAL LEARNING

Business firms, as well as nonprofit organizations, invest an enormous amount of money and time in teaching interpersonal skills. Teaching methods include sending employees to courses, conducting training on company premises, video-conferencing, courses on video tape, and computer-assisted learning programs. (An Internet course, or *distance learning,* is an example of computer-assisted learning.) Workers also develop interpersonal skills by interacting with work associates and observing how other people deal with interpersonal challenges.

Informal learning is the acquisition of knowledge and skills that takes place naturally outside of a structured learning environment. In the context of the workplace, informal learning takes place without being designed by the organization. A study of more than 1,000 employees at seven companies in seven states found that up to 70 percent of learning takes place informally.[3] The director of the study in question emphasizes that formal training includes both

a goal stated by the organization and a defined method or process. Informal learning can occur whether or not a goal is stated or the method defined.

Learning interpersonal skills informally can take place through such means as observing a coworker, manager, or team leader deal with a situation. A newly hired assistant store manager couldn't help seeing and overhearing a customer screaming at the store manager about a defective space heater. The manager said calmly, "It appears you are pretty upset about your heater that caused a short circuit in your house. What can I do to help you?" The customer calmed down as quickly as air being released from a balloon. The assistant store manager thought to herself, "Now I know how to handle a customer who has gone ballistic. I'll state what the customer is probably feeling, and then offer to help."

Informal learning can also occur when another person shows you how to handle a situation. The store manager might have said to the new assistant manager, "Let me tell you what to do in case you encounter a customer who goes ballistic. Summarize in a few words what he or she is probably feeling, and then offer to help. The effect can be remarkable." (This incident is classified as informal learning because it takes place outside of a classroom.)

Formal learning and informal learning of interpersonal skills are useful supplements to each other. If you are formally learning interpersonal skills your level of awareness for enhancing your interpersonal skills will increase. By formally studying interpersonal skills, you are likely to develop the attitude "What hints about dealing more effectively with people can I pick up on the job?" You may have noticed that if you are taking lessons in a sport, you become much more observant about watching the techniques of outstanding athletes in person or on television.

SPECIFIC DEVELOPMENTAL EXPERIENCES

Another perspective on developing interpersonal skills in the workplace is that certain experiences are particularly suited to such development. Coping with a difficult customer, as suggested above, would be one such scenario. Morgan W. McCall, Jr., an industrial psychologist, has studied for many years ways in which leaders develop on the job. Contending with certain challenges is at the heart of these key learning experiences. Several of the powerful learning experiences McCall has identified are particularly geared toward developing better interpersonal skills.[4]

➤ *Unfamiliar responsibilities.* The person has to handle responsibilities that are new, very different, or much broader than previous ones. Dealing with these unfamiliar responsibilities necessitates asking others for help and gaining their cooperation. For example, being assigned to supervise a group doing work unfamiliar to you would put you in a position of gaining the cooperation of group members who knew more about the work than you.

➤ *Proving yourself.* If you feel added pressure to show others that you can deal effectively with responsibilities, you are likely to develop skills in projecting self-confidence and persuading others.

➤ *Problems with employees.* If you supervise employees, or have coworkers, who lack adequate experience, are incompetent, or are poorly motivated, you need to practice such skills as effective listening and conflict resolution in order to work smoothly with them.

➤ *Influencing without authority.* An excellent opportunity for practicing influence skills is being forced to influence coworkers, higher management, company outsiders, and other key people over whom you have no control. Team leaders typically face the challenge of needing to influence workers whom they lack the authority to discipline or grant raises. (The reason is that a team leader usually does not have as much formal authority as a traditional manager.)

➤ *Difficult manager.* If you and your manager have different opinions on how to approach problems, or if your manager has serious shortcomings, you will have to use your best human relations skills to survive. You will need to develop such subtle skills as using diplomacy to explain to your manager that his or her suggestion is completely unworkable.

The general point to be derived from these scenarios is that certain on-the-job challenges require a high level of interpersonal skill. Faced with such challenges, you will be prompted to use the best interpersonal skills you have. Formal training can be a big help because you might remember a skill that should be effective in a particular situation. Assume that you are faced with an overbearing manager who belittles you in front of others. You might be prompted to try a conflict-resolution technique you acquired in class.

SUMMARY

Effective interpersonal relations must be combined with technical knowledge to achieve success in any job involving interactions with people. This book presents a three-part strategy for achieving a high level of interpersonal skill. Each chapter presents concepts related to an area of interpersonal skill, behavioral guidelines, and experiential exercises. Interpersonal skill training is also referred to as *soft-skill training* to differentiate it from technical training.

A five-part model of learning can be applied to improving interpersonal skills. First, state a goal or desired state of affairs. Second, assess the reality of how far you are from your goal. Third, develop an action plan to change the relationship between the person and the environment. Self-discipline is required to implement the action plan. Fourth, solicit feedback on actions to measure the effects of your actions against reality. Fifth, continue to practice your newly learned skill.

People are most likely to develop new skills when they feel the need for change. A developmental need is the specific area in which a person needs to change. Identifying your developmental needs in relation to interpersonal relations can be achieved through self-analysis and feedback from others. You can also solicit feedback and make use of the feedback you have received in performance appraisals.

CAN THE PRESIDENT OF MICROSOFT BE HELPED?

In 1998 Microsoft Corp. chairman and chief executive officer Bill Gates promoted Steven A. Ballmer as president of the software giant. Ballmer, who had been executive vice president of sales and support, filled a position that had been vacant for eight years.

A major purpose of the move was to enable Gates to focus on Microsoft's long-term vision and product strategy. Gates said in an interview, "I decided I wanted to spend more time with our product groups and drive the breakthroughs. Think of Steve as the business leader and customer champion." His formal role is to be in charge of sales and product development.

Ballmer has been a self-appointed cheerleader for Microsoft. During a company sales meeting several years ago, he vaulted on stage and shouted at the top of his lungs: "I love this company! I love this company! I love this company!" The 6,000-member sales team responded with a five-minute standing ovation. Shouting to cheer on employees, discipline them, and express disapproval is characteristic of Ballmer. Another motivational stunt he pulled at one time was to swim across a chilly Microsoft pond on a dare in front of dozens of company employees.

Ballmer, a college chum of Gates, has been copilot of Microsoft since 1980. Gates is thought of as the biggest brain in the company, whereas Ballmer is regarded as the biggest heart and inspiring sales leader. Another contrast is that Gates is seen as the company's technology visionary and Ballmer its top business strategist.

Ballmer's physical presence is imposing. He is six feet tall and built like a football linebacker. His shiny head is disproportionately large, and he has a booming voice. He is intensely devoted to his company and his family. His intensity, however, is often perceived negatively. He can become infuriated when facing conflict. He has been known to bawl out employees so violently that his voice can be heard through the air vents in company headquarters.

Ballmer has become well known for being outspoken with both company insiders and outsiders. During a discussion of the Justice Department's investigation into Microsoft's business tactics, Ballmer blurted out, "To heck with Janet Reno." Later, however, Ballmer said he regretted making the comment. "That's the way I am," he said. "I have to work on being a better version of myself."

Gates, who can be undiplomatic himself, is not much concerned about Ballmer's roughness with people. "He's my best friend," says Gates. "We love working together on very hard problems. We trust each other and understand how the other thinks." Ballmer has equally warm comments about Gates. "Our friendship has grown much stronger as a result of working together. It's like a marriage," says Ballmer. [Both Gates and Ballmer are married with children.]

The Microsoft board deliberated six months before appointing Ballmer president. One concern was his fiery personality. A board member pointed out that "Steve's greatest strength can also be seen as a weakness." Ballmer shouts when he gets excited or angry (as mentioned above). His voice rises so suddenly that it shocks and intimidates many people. Most likely due to his shouting, Ballmer lost his voice during a business trip to Japan in the early 1980s and required vocal chord surgery to regain his speech.

Some of Ballmer's motivational techniques appear heavy handed to employees. When he directed the Microsoft Windows product group, he created fear in engineers by bellowing at them and pounding a baseball bat into his hand. In the last few years, Ballmer has made progress in becoming calmer in demanding business situations.

Gates cleared the way for Ballmer to be promoted by ensuring that each of the executives who would report to him was satisfied with the arrangement. Gates also convinced the board that he could modify Ballmer's behavior.

Despite his rough edges, Ballmer has many supporters. Many people who know Ballmer find

(Continued)

him joyful and refreshing and a good sport. He is willing to engage in publicity stunts such as participating in videos that mock the competition.

Case Questions

1. What needs for interpersonal skill development does Steven Ballmer appear to have?

2. To what extent do you believe that Bill Gates can modify Ballmer's behavior?

3. What positive interpersonal skills does Ballmer appear to have?

4. If it were your decision, would you have approved Steve Ballmer's appointment as president of Microsoft Corp?

Source: "Remaking Microsoft," *Business Week*, May 17, 1999, pp. 106–116; Steve Hamm, "Bill's Co-pilot," *Business Week*, September 14, 1998, pp. 76–90; "Microsoft Names President," http://cnnfn.com/digitaljam/9807/21/ballmer/.

Universal training needs are those areas for improvement that are common to most people. The major topics in this text reflect universal training needs because they are necessary for success in most positions involving interaction with people.

Opportunities exist in the workplace to develop interpersonal skill. A general approach to developing these skills is informal learning, whereby you acquire skills naturally outside of a structured work environment. Informal learning often takes place through such means as observing a coworker, manager, or team leader cope with a situation. Certain workplace experiences are particularly well suited to developing interpersonal skills. These include unfamiliar responsibilities, proving yourself, having problems with employees, influencing without authority, and having a difficult manager.

QUESTIONS FOR DISCUSSION AND REVIEW

1. One of the most prestigious business schools, the Wharton School, now places much more emphasis on "people" skills than previously. What do you suspect are the reasons for this change?

2. In your opinion, do high-ranking business executives rely more on soft skills or hard skills to accomplish their work?

3. Why do people need soft skills in an era of high technology?

4. In your own words, what does "assessing reality" mean in the model for improving interpersonal skills?

5. How does a person know whether or not the feedback he or she receives from another person is accurate?

6. Of the 14 universal training needs listed in this chapter, which two do you think would be the most difficult to improve? Explain. 8, 9

7. Give an example of a skill you might have learned informally at any point in your life. LISTENING

Chapter 2

Understanding Individual Differences

Learning Objectives

After reading and studying this chapter and doing the exercises you should be able to

➤ Take into account the individual differences among people in dealing with them on the job.

➤ Develop insight into how your personality, mental ability, emotional intelligence, and values differ from others.

➤ Respond to personality differences among people.

➤ Respond to mental ability differences among people.

➤ Respond to differences in values among people.

Billy Waxworth and Mary Lou Gold graduated from the Lincoln Institute in the same year, both majoring in business administration. The two met three years later at a class reunion. After exchanging hugs, Billy said, "Mary Lou, it's time we caught up with each other. What kind of work have you been doing?"

Mary Lou responded that she combined her interests in business and technical writing. Her job consisted of preparing technical manuals for electronic consumer products such as VCRs and TVs. She said she worked at her computer about 35 hours per week, preparing copy and diagrams. Billy explained that he sold office furniture and lighting fixtures to business firms.

"How boring that must be, preparing manuals all day long," said Billy. "You must get sick of such a grind." Mary Lou responded, "Quite the opposite, Billy, I intensely like work that requires concentration and produces tangible results. What would make me sick is what you do—knocking on doors and trying to convince strangers they should buy your product."

The exchange that took place between Billy and Mary Lou illustrates one of the most important factors influencing the behavior of people in the workplace. People show substantial **individual differences**, or variations, in how they respond to the same situation based on personal characteristics. Billy, an extrovert, is at his best away from the office, winning people over to his way of thinking. Mary Lou, in contrast, is introverted and analytical. She enjoys working on tasks that require prolonged concentration and attention to detail. In general, individual differences exert a profound effect on job performance and behavior.[1] One of hundreds of possible examples is that some people can concentrate longer and harder on their work, thereby producing more and higher quality work, than others.

This chapter describes several of the major sources of individual differences on the job. It also gives you the chance to measure your standing on several key dimensions of behavior and helps you develop skill in responding to individual differences. Knowing how to respond to such differences is the cornerstone of effective interpersonal relations.

PERSONALITY

"We're not going to promote you to department head," said the vice president to the analyst. "Although you are a great troubleshooter, you've alienated too many people in the company. You're too blunt and insensitive." As just implied, most successes and failures in people-contact jobs are attributed largely to interpersonal skills. And personality traits are important contributors to interpersonal, or human relations, skills. The subject of individual differences in personality must therefore be given consideration in any serious study of interpersonal relations in the workplace.

Personality refers to those persistent and enduring behavior patterns that tend to be expressed in a wide variety of situations. A person who is brash and insensitive in one situation is likely to behave similarly in many other situations.

Your personality is what makes you unique. Your walk, your talk, your appearance, your speech, and your inner values and conflicts all contribute to your personality. Have you ever noticed that when you know a person well you can identify that person by his or her footsteps even though you do not see the individual? This is true because many people have a distinctive gait.

We will illustrate the importance of personality to interpersonal relations in organizations by describing six key personality traits and psychological types related to cognitive styles. In addition, you will be given guidelines for dealing effectively with different personality types.

SIX MAJOR PERSONALITY FACTORS AND TRAITS

Many psychologists believe that the basic structure of human personality is represented by five broad factors, known as the Big Five: extraversion (the scientific spelling of *extroversion*), emotional stability, agreeableness, conscientiousness, and openness to experience. A sixth key personality factor, self-monitoring of behavior, has received much recent attention and is also included here.

Recent evidence has emphasized the contribution of genes, and strips of DNA in particular, in forming personality. The genes do not influence personality traits directly. Instead, they subtly bias the mind so that different individuals react to similar experiences in different ways. Another key speculation is that that genes affect the operation of brain chemicals such as dopamine and serotonin that influence our mood. For example, two experiences that release dopamine are seeing a person you perceive as physically attractive and eating chocolate. As a consequence of either ingesting chocolate or sighting the right person—or a combination of the two—you get a temporary high.

Genes appear to have their biggest impact on temperamental traits such as impulsiveness, openness, conservatism, and hostility. However, genes alone do not control the chemistry of the brain. The environment heavily influences how the genes will express themselves, such as one impulsive person becoming a day trader on the Internet and another becoming a shoplifter. Character helps control our personality traits.[2] A person of good moral character, for example, might channel her aggressiveness into being competitive rather than attacking other people verbally or physically.

All six factors have a substantial impact on interpersonal relations and job performance. The interpretations and meanings of these factors provide useful information because they can help you pinpoint important areas for personal development. Although these factors are partially inherited, most people can improve them providing they exert much conscious effort over a period of time. For example, it usually takes a minimum of three months of effort before a person is perceived to be more agreeable. The six factors, shown in Figure 2–1, are described in more detail in the following list.

1. *Extraversion.* Traits associated with the extraversion factor include being social, gregarious, assertive, talkative, and active. An outgoing person is often described as extraverted, while a shy person is described as being introverted.

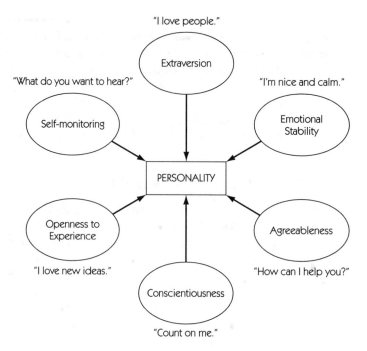

Figure 2-1 Six Major Personality Factors
The six major personality factors are the Big Five factors plus self-monitoring. Research has repeatedly shown that the Big Five factors are related to job performance. The most consistent finding is that job applicants who score high on the trait of conscientiousness perform well on a wide variety of jobs.

2. *Emotional stability.* A person with high emotional stability is calm, relaxed, and secure. Traits associated with the emotional stability factor include being anxious, depressed, angry, embarrassed, emotional, and worried. A person with low emotional stability is often referred to as neurotic or emotionally unstable.

3. *Agreeableness.* An agreeable person is friendly and cooperative. Traits associated with the agreeableness factor include being courteous, flexible, trusting, good-natured, cooperative, forgiving, softhearted, and tolerant.

4. *Conscientiousness.* A variety of meanings have been attached to the conscientiousness factor, but it generally implies being dependable. Traits associated with conscientiousness include being careful, thorough, responsible, organized, and purposeful. Honesty is also closely related to being conscientious. Other related traits include being hardworking, achievement oriented, and persevering.

5. *Openness to experience.* People who score high on the openness-to-experience factor have well-developed intellects. Traits commonly associated with this factor include being imaginative, cultured, curious, original, broad minded, intelligent, and artistically sensitive.

6. *Self-monitoring of behavior.* The self-monitoring trait refers to the process of observing and controlling how we are perceived by others. High self-monitors are pragmatic and even chameleon-like actors in social groups. They often say what others want to hear. Low self-monitors avoid situations that require them to adopt different outer images. In this way their outer behavior adheres to their inner values. Low self-monitoring can often lead to inflexibility. Do Self-Assessment Quiz 2-1 to measure your tendencies toward self-monitoring.

Depending on the job, any one of the preceding personality factors can be important for success. Conscientiousness relates to job performance for many different occupations. Another important research finding is that extraversion is associated with success for managers and sales representatives. The explanation is that managers and salespeople are required to interact extensively with other people.[3] Studies have shown that the Big Five personality factors are related to job performance in the European Community as well as in the United States and Canada. Conscientiousness and emotional stability were shown to be accurate predictors for job success for many different jobs and measures of success in Europe.[4] Different measures of success include objective information such as cost savings and sales figures, as well as ratings of performance by managers.

COGNITIVE STYLES AND PERSONALITY TYPES

COGNITIVE STYLES

Personality also influences a person's **cognitive style**, or the mental processes used to perceive and make judgments from information. A knowledge of these cognitive styles can help you relate better to people because you can better appreciate how they make decisions. According to psychiatrist Carl Jung, how people gather and evaluate information determines their cognitive style. Jung's analysis became the basis for a widely used test of personality and cognitive style called the Myers-Briggs Type Indicator.

Gathering Information

To solve problems it is necessary to gather information. Two different styles of information gathering are sensation and intuition. **Sensation-type individuals** prefer routine and order. They search for precise details when gathering information to solve a problem. Sensation-type individuals prefer to work with established facts rather than search for new possibilities. **Intuitive-type individuals** prefer an overall perspective—the "big picture." Such people enjoy solving new problems. They dislike routine and prefer to look for possibilities rather than work with facts.

Self-Assessment Quiz 2-1

THE SELF-MONITORING SCALE

Directions: Decide whether each of the following statements is more true or false for you. Circle T or F to indicate your answer.

1. I find it hard to imitate the behavior of other people. T (F)

2. My behavior is usually an expression of my true inner feelings, attitudes, and beliefs. (T) F

3. At parties and social gatherings, I do not attempt to say and do things that others will like. T (F)

4. I can only argue about ideas that I already have. T (F)

5. I can make impromptu speeches, even on topics about which I have almost no information. (T) F

6. I guess I put on a show to impress or to entertain people. T (F)

7. When I am uncertain how to act in a social situation, I look to the behavior of others for cues. (T) F

8. I'd make a good actor. (T) F

9. I rarely ask my friends' advice on movies, books, or music. (T) F

10. I sometimes appear to others to be experiencing deeper emotions than I actually am. T (F)

11. I laugh more when I watch a comedy with others than when alone. T (F)

12. In a group I am rarely the center of attention. (T) F

13. In different situations and with different people, I often act like very different persons. (T) F

14. I am not particularly good at making other people like me. T (F)

Scoring and Interpretation: To obtain your score, count one point for each False answer to statements 1, 2, 3, 4, 9, 12, and 14. Count one point for each True response to statements 5, 6, 7, 8, 10, 11, and 13. The higher your score, the stronger your tendencies toward self-monitoring. You are a high self-monitor if your score is 10 or higher; low if it is 5 or less. Refer to the text for the meaning of high and low self-monitoring.

Source: Adapted from Bernard Asbell, *What They Know About You* (New York: Random House, 1993).

When shopping for an automobile, a sensation-type individual would want to gather a large number of facts about such matters as miles or kilometers per gallon, warranty provisions, finance charges, and resale value. In contrast, the intuitive-type individual would be more concerned about the overall style of the car and how proud he or she would be as the owner.

GREGARIOUS

Evaluating Information

The evaluation aspect of problem solving involves judging how to deal with information after it has been collected. Styles of information evaluation range from an emphasis on feeling to an emphasis on thinking. **Feeling-type individuals** have a need to conform and adapt to the wishes of others. Because of these tendencies, they try to avoid problems that might result in disagreements. **Thinking-type individuals** rely on reason and intellect to deal with problems. They downplay emotion in problem solving and decision making.

Assume that a team leader asks group managers their opinion of an idea for a new product. Feeling-type people in the group are likely to look for the good in the proposal and then express approval for the project. Thinking-type team members are likely to be more independent in their evaluation of the new-product idea. As a result they will express their opinion whether or not it is what the manager wants to hear. (Notice that feeling-type people are high self-monitors, and thinking types are the opposite.)

The Four Cognitive Styles

The two dimensions of information gathering and evaluation are combined to produce the following four-way classification of cognitive (or problem-solving) styles.

➤ Sensation/thinking

➤ Intuitive/thinking

➤ Sensation/feeling

➤ Intuitive/feeling

Figure 2-2 lists the four styles and occupations well suited to them.[5] If you take the Myers-Briggs Type Indicator, often available in career centers, you will be presented with a diagnosis of your personality type. You can also study the four types and make a judgment as to your cognitive style. Recognizing your cognitive style can help you identify work that you are likely to perform well. For example, a person who is an intuitive/feeling type is likely to be skillful in resolving customer complaints. The same person might not be well suited by temperament to do bookkeeping.

GUIDELINES FOR DEALING WITH DIFFERENT PERSONALITY TYPES

A key purpose in presenting information about a sampling of various personality types is to provide guidelines for individualizing your approach to people. As a basic example, if you wanted to score points with an introvert, you would approach that person in a restrained, laid-back fashion. In contrast, a more gregarious, lighthearted approach might be more effective with an extravert. The purpose of individualizing your approach is to build a better working relationship or to establish rapport with the other person. To match your approach to dealing with a given personality type, you must first arrive at an approximate

Sensation/Thinking
Decisive, dependable, alert to
details
➤ Accounting and bookkeeping
➤ Computer programming
➤ Manufacturing technology

Sensation/Feeling
Pragmatic, analytical, methodical,
and conscientious
➤ Supervision
➤ Selling
➤ Negotiating

Intuitive/Thinking
Creative, progressive, perceptive
➤ Systems design
➤ Law, paralegal work
➤ Middle management

Intuitive/Feeling
Colorful, people-oriented, helpful
➤ Customer service
➤ Business communications
➤ Human resources

Figure 2-2 Four Problem-Solving Styles and Work Matchup

diagnosis of the individual's personality. The following suggestions are there-fore restricted to readily observable aspects of personality.

1. When relating to an *extraverted* individual, emphasize friendliness, warmth, and a stream of chatter. Talk about people more than ideas, things, or data. Express an interest in a continuing working relationship.

2. When relating to an *introverted* individual, move slowly in forming a working relationship. Do not confuse quietness with a lack of interest. Tolerate moments of silence. Emphasize ideas, things, and data more heavily than people.

3. When relating to a person who appears to be *emotionally unstable* based on symptoms of worry and tension, be laid back and reassuring. Attempt not to project your own anxiety and fears. Be a good listener. If possible, minimize emphasis on deadlines and the dire conse-quences of a project's failing. Show concern and interest in the per-son's welfare.

4. When relating to an *agreeable* person, just relax and be yourself. Reciprocate with kindness to sustain a potentially excellent working relationship.

5. When relating to a *disagreeable* person, be patient and tolerant. At the same time, set limits on how much mistreatment you will take. Disagreeable people sometimes secretly want others to put brakes on their antisocial behavior.

6. When relating to a *conscientious* person, give him or her freedom and do not nag. The person will probably honor commitments without prompting. Conscientious people are often taken for granted, so remember to acknowledge the person's dependability.

7. When relating to a person of *low conscientiousness,* keep close tabs on him or her, especially if you need the person's output to do your job. Do not assume that because the person has an honest face and a pleasing smile he or she will deliver as promised. Frequently follow up on your requests, and impose deadlines if you have the authority. Express deep appreciation when the person does follow through.

8. When relating to a person who is *open to experience,* emphasize information sharing, idea generation, and creative approaches to problems. Appeal to his or her intellect by discussing topics of substance rather than ordinary chatter and gossip.

9. When relating to a person who is *closed to experience,* stick closely to the facts of the situation at hand. Recognize that the person prefers to think small and deal with the here and now.

10. When dealing with a person whom you suspect is a high *self-monitor,* be cautious in thinking that the person is really in support of your position. The person could just be following his or her natural tendency to appear to please others, but not really feel that way.

11. When dealing with a *sensation-type* person, emphasize facts, figures, and conventional thinking without sacrificing your own values. To convince the sensation type, emphasize logic more than emotional appeal. Focus on details more than the big picture.

12. When dealing with an *intuitive-type* individual, emphasize feelings, judgments, playing with ideas, imagination, and creativity. Focus more on the big picture than details.

To start putting these guidelines into practice, do the role plays in Skill-Building Exercise 2-1. Remember that a role player is an extemporaneous actor. Put yourself in the shoes of the character you play and visualize how he or she would act. Because you are given only the general idea of a script, use your imagination to fill in the details.

MENTAL ABILITY

Mental ability, or intelligence, is one of the major sources of individual differences that affects job performance and behavior. **Intelligence** is the capacity to acquire and apply knowledge, including solving problems. Abstract problems can best be solved by intelligent workers. In an exceedingly simple job, such as packing shoes into boxes, having below-average intelligence can be an advantage, because the employee is not likely to become bored.

Understanding the nature of intelligence contributes to effective interpersonal relations in organizations. Your evaluation of a person's intelligence can influence how you relate to that person. For example, if you think a person is intelligent you will tend to seek his or her input on a difficult problem. If you

Skill-Building Exercise 2-1

PERSONALITY ROLE PLAYS

The Extravert: One student assumes the role of a successful outside sales representative who has just signed a $3 million order for the company. The sales rep comes back to the office elated. The other student assumes the role of a member of the office support staff. He or she decides this is a splendid opportunity to build a good relationship with the triumphant sales rep. Run the role play for about 10 minutes. The people not involved in the role play will observe and then provide feedback when the role play is completed. (These directions regarding time, observation, and feedback also apply to the two other role plays in this exercise and throughout the book.)

Open to Experience: One student plays the role of an experienced worker in the department who is told to spend some time orienting a new co-op student. It appears that this new person is open to experience. Another student plays the role of the co-op student who is open to experience and eager to be successful in this new position.

Sensation and Intuitive Types: One student plays the role of a sensation-type individual who is responsible for reviewing the company expense accounts. The other student plays the role of a manager in whose department many expense account abuses (such as lack of documentation and high expenses) have been uncovered. This manager is an intuitive type. The person in charge of the accounts is visiting the manager in the latter's office to discuss this problem.

realize that different types of intelligence exist, you are more likely to appreciate people's strengths. You are thus less likely to judge others as being either good or poor problem solvers.

Here we describe four important aspects of mental ability: (1) the components of traditional intelligence, (2) practical intelligence, (3) multiple intelligences, and (4) emotional intelligence. Knowledge of the four aspects will enrich your understanding of other workers and yourself.

COMPONENTS OF TRADITIONAL INTELLIGENCE

Intelligence consists of more than one component. A component of intelligence is much like a separate mental aptitude. Evidence suggests that intelligence consists of a g **(general) factor** and s **(special) factors** that contribute to problem-solving ability. Scores of tests of almost any type (such as math, aptitude for computer programming, or reading skill) are somewhat influenced by the g factor. The g factor helps explain why some people perform well in so many different mental tasks. Another finding about g is that more intelligent people tend to rely less on g because they also have well-developed s factors. Less intelligent people tend to rely more heavily on g because they have a less diverse set of specific abilities.[6]

Over the years various investigators have arrived at different special factors contributing to overall mental aptitude. The following seven factors have been identified consistently:

1. *Verbal comprehension.* The ability to understand the meaning of words and their relationship to each other and to comprehend written and spoken information.

2. *Word fluency.* The ability to use words quickly and easily, without an emphasis on verbal comprehension.

3. *Numerical acuity.* The ability to handle numbers, engage in mathematical analysis, and to do arithmetic calculations.

4. *Spatial perception.* The ability to visualize forms in space and manipulate objects mentally, particularly in three dimensions.

5. *Memory.* Having a good rote memory for symbols, words, and lists of numbers, along with other associations.

6. *Perceptual speed.* The ability to perceive visual details, to pick out similarities and differences, and to perform tasks requiring visual perception.

7. *Inductive reasoning.* The ability to discover a rule or principle and apply it in solving a problem and to make judgments and decisions that are logically sound.

Being strong in any of the preceding mental aptitudes often leads to an enjoyment of work associated with that aptitude. The reverse can also be true: enjoying a type of mental activity might lead to the development of an aptitude for the activity. Self-Assessment Quiz 2-2 gives you the opportunity to measure your preferences for numerical information.

PRACTICAL INTELLIGENCE

Many people, including psychologists, are concerned that the traditional way of understanding intelligence inadequately describes mental ability. An unfortunate implication of intelligence testing is that intelligence as traditionally calculated is largely the ability to perform tasks related to scholastic work. Thus a person who scored very high on an intelligence test could follow a complicated instruction manual, but might not be street smart.

To overcome the limited idea that intelligence mostly involves the ability to solve abstract problems, the **triarchic theory of intelligence** has been proposed. The theory holds that intelligence is composed of three different subtypes: analytical, creative, and practical. The *analytical* subtype is the traditional intelligence needed for solving difficult problems. Analytical intelligence is required to perform well in most school subjects. The *creative* subtype is the type of intel-

ATTITUDES TOWARD NUMERICAL INFORMATION

Directions: Describe how well you agree with each of the following statements, using the following scale: disagree strongly (DS); disagree (D); neutral (N); agree (A); agree strongly (AS). Circle the number in the appropriate column.

	DS	D	N	A	AS
1. I enjoy work that requires the use of numbers.	1	2	3	4	5
2. I think quantitative information is difficult to understand.	5	4	3	2	1
3. I find it satisfying to solve day-to-day problems involving numbers.	1	2	3	4	5
4. Numerical information is very useful in everyday life.	1	2	3	4	5
5. I prefer not to pay attention to information involving numbers.	5	4	3	2	1
6. I think more information should be available in numerical form.	1	2	3	4	5
7. I don't like to think about issues involving numbers.	5	4	3	2	1
8. Numbers are not necessary for most situations.	5	4	3	2	1
9. Thinking is more enjoyable when it does not involve quantitative information.	5	4	3	2	1
10. I like to make calculations involving numerical information.	1	2	3	4	5
11. Quantitative information is vital for accurate decisions.	1	2	3	4	5
12. I enjoy thinking about issues that involve numerical information.	1	2	3	4	5
13. Understanding numbers is as important in daily life as reading or writing.	1	2	3	4	5
14. I easily lose interest in graphs, percentages, and other quantitative information.	5	4	3	2	1
15. I find numerical information to be relevant to most situations.	1	2	3	4	5
16. I think it is important to learn and use numerical information to make well-informed decisions.	1	2	3	4	5
17. Numbers are redundant for most situations.	5	4	3	2	1
18. It is a waste of time to learn information containing a lot of numbers.	5	4	3	2	1
19. I like to go over numbers in my mind.	1	2	3	4	5
20. It helps me think if I put down information as numbers.	1	2	3	4	5

Total Score _____

Scoring and Interpretation: Add the numbers you circled to obtain your total score.

85–100 You have strong positive attitudes toward numerical information and working with quantitative data.

55–84 You have moderately favorable attitudes toward numerical information and working with quantitative data.

20–54 You have very negative attitudes toward numerical information and working with quantitative data. Your dislike for quantitative solutions to problems is so strong that you are quick to distrust statistical analysis.

Source: Adapted with permission from Madhubalan Viswanathan, "Measurement of Individual Differences in Preference for Numerical Information," *Journal of Applied Psychology,* October 1993, p. 745.

Novel:

ligence required for imagination and combining things in novel ways. The *practical* subtype is the type of intelligence required for adapting your environment to suit your needs.[7]

The idea of practical intelligence helps explain why a person who has a difficult time getting through school can still be a successful businessperson, politician, or athlete. Practical intelligence incorporates the ideas of common sense, wisdom, and street smarts. One major reservation some have about practical intelligence is the implication that people who are highly intelligent in the traditional sense are not practical thinkers. In truth, most executives and other high-level workers score quite well on tests of mental ability. These tests usually measure analytical intelligence.

MULTIPLE INTELLIGENCES

Another approach to understanding the diverse nature of mental ability is the theory of **multiple intelligences**. According to Howard Gardner, people know and understand the world in distinctly different ways and learn in different ways. Individuals possess the following eight intelligences, or faculties, in varying degrees:

1. *Linguistic.* Enables people to communicate through language, including reading, writing, and speaking.

2. *Logical-mathematical.* Enables individuals to see relationships between objects and solve problems, as in calculus and statistics.

3. *Musical.* Gives people the capacity to create and understand meanings made out of sounds and to enjoy different types of music.

4. *Spatial.* Enables people to perceive and manipulate images in the brain and to recreate them from memory, as is required in making graphic designs.

5. *Bodily/kinesthetic.* Enables people to use their body and perceptual and motor systems in skilled ways such as dancing, playing sports, and expressing emotion through facial expressions.

6. *Intrapersonal.* Enables people to distinguish among their own feelings and acquire accurate self-knowledge.

7. *Interpersonal.* Makes it possible for individuals to differentiate among, classify, and utilize various features of the physical external environment.

8. *Naturalist.* Enables individuals to differentiate among, classify, and utilize various features of the physcial external environment.

Your profile of intelligences influences how you best learn and to which types of jobs you are best suited. Gardner believes that it is possible to develop these separate intelligences through concentrated effort. However, any of these intelligences might fade if not used.[8] These separate types of intelligence

might also be perceived as different talents or abilities. Having high general problem-solving ability *(g)* would contribute to high standing on each of the eight intelligences.

EMOTIONAL INTELLIGENCE

Later research has updated and expanded the idea of practical intelligence, suggesting that how effectively people use their emotions has a major impact on their success. **Emotional intelligence** refers to qualities such as understanding one's own feelings, having empathy for others, and regulating one's emotion to enhance living. A person with high emotional intelligence would be able to engage in such behaviors as sizing up people, pleasing others, and influencing them. In recent years, several different versions of emotional intelligence have been proposed. Five key factors included in a well-accepted analysis of emotional intelligence are as follows:[9]

1. *Self-awareness*. The ability to understand your moods, emotions, and needs as well as their impact on others. (A person with good self-awareness knows whether he or she is pushing other people too far.)

2. *Self-regulation*. The ability to control impulsiveness, calming down anxiety and reacting with appropriate anger to situations. (A person with low self-regulation would suddenly decide to drop a project because the work was frustrating.)

3. *Motivation*. A passion to work for reasons in addition to money or status. Also, drive, persistence, and optimism when faced with setbacks. (A person with this type of motivation would make the decision to keep trying when faced with a serious obstacle such as having lost a major account.)

4. *Empathy*. The ability to respond to the unspoken feelings of others. Also, the skill to respond to people according to their emotional reactions. (A manager with empathy would take into account the most likely reaction of group members before making a decision affecting them.)

5. *Social skill*. Competency in managing relationships and building networks of support, and having positive relationships with people. (A worker with social skill would use a method of persuasion that is likely to work well with a particular group or individual.)

Emotional intelligence thus incorporates many of the skills and attitudes necessary to achieve effective interpersonal relations in organizations. Most of the topics in this book, such as resolving conflict, helping others develop, and positive political skills, would be included in emotional intelligence. Self-Assessment Quiz 2-3 gives you an opportunity to measure your emotional intelligence, but you will need persistence to get the information.

WHAT IS YOUR ADVERSITY QUOTIENT (AQ)?

One of the many components to emotional intelligence is resiliency, or the ability to bounce back from adversity. Paul G. Stoltz has developed an Adversity Quotient, designed to measure your capacity to turn obstacles into opportunities.[10] He offers you an opportunity on the Internet to measure your Adversity Quotient. To make this self-assessment, go to www.doogee.com, where you will find complete instructions. If the Web site is not in operation, consult reference number 10 for a print version of the test to measure your AQ. To obtain a broader measure of your emotional intelligence, go to www.utne.com/cgi/bin/eq.

GUIDELINES FOR RELATING TO PEOPLE OF DIFFERENT LEVELS AND TYPES OF INTELLIGENCE

Certainly you cannot expect to administer mental ability and emotional intelligence tests to all your work associates, gather their scores, and then relate to associates differently based on their scores. Yet it is possible to intuitively develop a sense for the mental quickness of people and the types of mental tasks they perform best. For example, managers must make judgments about mental ability in selecting people for jobs and assigning them to tasks. Following are several guidelines worth considering to enhance your working relationships with others:

1. If you perceive another worker (your manager included) to be mentally quick, present your ideas in technical depth. Incorporate difficult words into your conversation and reports. Ask the person challenging questions.

2. If you perceive another worker to be mentally slow, present your ideas with a minimum of technical depth. Use a basic vocabulary, without going so far as to be patronizing. Ask for frequent feedback about having been clear.

3. If you perceive a workmate to relish crunching numbers, use quantitative information when attempting to persuade that person. Instead of using phrases such as "most people," say "about 65 percent."

4. If you perceive a work associate to have high creative intelligence, solicit his or her input on problems requiring a creative solution. Use statements such as "Here's a problem that requires a sharp, creative mind, so I've come to you."

5. If you perceive a work associate to have low emotional intelligence, explain your feelings and attitudes clearly. The person may not get the point of hints and indirect expressions.

Skill-Building Exercise 2-2

ADAPTING TO PEOPLE OF DIFFERENT MENTAL ABILITY

The Mentally Sharp Coworker: One person plays the role of a worker who needs to load a new software package onto the hard drive of his or her computer. You intend to approach a particular coworker who is known for having a sharp mind. You wonder whether this highly intelligent person will be interested in your problem. The other person plays the role of the computer whiz who ordinarily does not like to solve problems for people that they should be able to solve themselves. The first worker meets with the second to discuss loading the software.

The Mentally Average Team Member: One student plays the role of a supervisor who needs to explain to a team member how to calculate discounts for customers. To the supervisor's knowledge, the team member does not know how to calculate discounts, although it will be an important part of the team member's new job. The supervisor and the team member get together for a session on calculating discounts.

To start putting these guidelines into practice, do the role play in Skill-Building Exercise 2-2.

VALUES AS A SOURCE OF INDIVIDUAL DIFFERENCES

Another group of factors influencing how a person behaves on the job is that person's values and beliefs. A **value** refers to the importance a person attaches to something. Values are also tied to the enduring belief that one's mode of conduct is better than another mode of conduct. If you believe that good interpersonal relations are the most important part of your life, your humanistic values are strong. Similarly, you may think that people who are not highly concerned about interpersonal relations have poor values.

Values are closely tied in with **ethics**, or the moral choices a person makes. A person's values influence which kinds of behaviors he or she believes are ethical. An executive who strongly values profits might not find it unethical to raise prices higher than needed to cover additional costs. Another executive who strongly values family life might suggest that the company invest money in an on-premises child-care center. Ethics is such an important part of interpersonal relations in organizations that the topic receives separate mention in Chapter 13.

Differences in values among people often stem from age, or generational, differences. Workers over age 50, in general, may have different values than people much younger. These age differences in values have often been seen as a clash between Baby Boomers and members of Generation X. (Generation Y

is just beginning to enter the workforce.) According to the stereotype, Boomers see Xers as disrespectful of rules, not willing to pay their dues, and being disloyal to employers. Generation Xers see Boomers as worshipping hierarchy (layers of authority), being overcautious, and wanting to preserve the status quo.

HOW VALUES ARE LEARNED

People acquire values in the process of growing up, and many values are learned by the age of four. One important way we acquire values is through observing others, or modeling. Models can be parents, teachers, friends, brothers, sisters, and even public figures. If we identify with a particular person, the probability is high that we will develop some of his or her major values.

> *Derek, a restaurant owner, was known for his ability to offer employment to troubled teenagers and then help them get back on their feet. Asked why he put so much effort into helping youths in trouble, he explained, "I was greatly influenced as a boy by my Uncle Clarence. I was going through troubled times—stealing from Woolworth and getting drunk on beer.*
>
> *"Uncle Clarence took me under his wing and spent hours listening to my problems. He would take me fishing and ask if there was anything he could do to help me. Finally, I straightened out. I decided that I would be like Uncle Clarence if someday I had a chance to help young people."*

Another major way values are learned is through the communication of attitudes. The attitudes that we hear expressed directly or indirectly help shape our values. Assume that using credit to purchase goods and services was considered an evil practice among your family and friends. You might therefore hold negative values about installment purchases.

Unstated but implied attitudes may also shape your values. If key people in your life showed no enthusiasm when you talked about work accomplishments, you might not place such a high value on achieving outstanding results. If, on the other hand, your family and friends centered their lives around their careers, you might develop similar values. (Or you might rebel against such a value because it interfered with a more relaxed life-style.) Many key values are also learned through religion and thus become the basis for society's morals. For example, most religions emphasize treating other people fairly and kindly. To "knife somebody in the back" is considered immoral both on and off the job.

CLARIFYING YOUR VALUES

The values that you develop early in life are directly related to the kind of person you are and to the quality of the relationships you form.[11] A recognition of this fact has led to exercises designed to help people clarify and understand some of their own values. Almost all of these value-clarification exercises ask you, in one way or another, to compare the relative importance you attach to different objects and activities. Self-Assessment Quiz 2-4 gives you an opportunity to clarify your values.

THE MESH BETWEEN INDIVIDUAL AND JOB VALUES

Under the best of circumstances, the values of employees mesh with those required by the job. When this state of congruence exists, job performance is likely to be higher. A national survey of managers investigated the fit between the values of managers and those of their organizations. (One such mesh would be a highly ethical person working for a highly ethical firm.) A major finding was that managers who experienced a good fit were more successful and more likely to believe they could reach their career goals. They were also more confident about remaining with their present firm and more willing to work long hours.[12]

When the demands made by the organization or a superior clash with the basic values of the individual, that person suffers from **person–role conflict.** The individual wants to obey orders, but does not want to perform an act that seems inconsistent with his or her values. A situation such as this might occur when an employee is asked to produce a product that he or she feels is unsafe or of no value to society.

A manager of a commercial weight-reduction center resigned after two years of service. The owners pleaded with her to stay, based on her excellent performance. The manager replied, "Sorry, I think my job is immoral. We sign up all these people with great expectations of losing weight permanently. Most of them do achieve short-term weight reduction. My conflict is that over 90 percent of our clientele regain the weight they lost once they go back to eating normal food. I think we are deceiving them by not telling them up front that they will most likely gain back the weight they lose."

GUIDELINES FOR USING VALUES TO ENHANCE INTERPERSONAL RELATIONS

Values are intangible and abstract, and thus not easy to manipulate to help improve your interpersonal relations on the job. Despite their vagueness, values are an important driver of interpersonal effectiveness. Ponder the following guidelines:

1. Establish the values you will use in your relationships with others on the job, and then use those values as firm guidelines in working with others. For example, following the Golden Rule, you might establish the value of treating others as you want to be treated. You would then not lie to others to gain personal advantage, and you would not backstab your rivals.

2. Establish the values that will guide you as an employee. When you believe that your values are being compromised, express your concern to your manager in a tactful and constructive manner. You might say to your manager, "Sorry, I choose not to tell our customers that our competitor's product is inferior just to make a sale. I choose not to say this because our competitor makes a fine product. But what I will say is that our service is exceptional."

Self-Assessment Quiz 2-4

CLARIFYING YOUR VALUES

Directions: Rank from 1 to 18 the importance of the following values to you as a person. The most important value on the list receives a rank of 1; the least important a rank of 18. Use the space next to "Other" if we have left out an important value in your life.

_____ Having my own place to live

_____ Having one or more children

_____ Having an interesting job and career

_____ Owning a car

_____ Having a good relationship with coworkers

_____ Having good health

_____ Watching my favorite television shows

_____ Participating in sports or other pastimes

_____ Following a sports team, athlete, music group, or other entertainer

_____ Being a religious person

_____ Helping people less fortunate than myself

_____ Loving and being loved by another person

_____ Having physical intimacy with another person

_____ Making an above-average income

_____ Being in good physical condition

_____ Being a knowledgeable, informed person

_____ Completing my formal education

_____ Other

1. Discuss and compare your ranking of these values with the person next to you.

2. Perhaps your class, assisted by your instructor, can arrive at a class average on each of these values. How does your ranking compare to the class ranking?

3. Look back at your own ranking. Does it surprise you?

4. Any surprises in the class ranking? Which values did you think would be highest and lowest?

Skill-Building Exercise 2-3

THE VALUE-CONFLICT ROLE PLAY

One student plays the role of a company president who makes an announcement to the group that the company must soon lay off 10 percent of the workforce in order to remain profitable. The president also points out that the company has a policy against laying off good performers. He or she then asks four of the company managers to purposely give below-average performance ratings to 10 percent of employees. In this way, laying them off will fit company policy.

Four other students play the role of the company managers who receive this directive. If such manipulation of performance evaluations clashes with your values, engage in a dialogue with your manager expressing your conflict. Remember, however, that you may not want to jeopardize your job.

Conduct this group role play for about 10 minutes, with other class members observing and being prepared to offer feedback.

To help you put these guidelines into practice, do Skill-Building Exercise 2-3. Remember, however, that being skilled at using your values requires day-by-day monitoring.

SUMMARY

Individual differences are one of the most important factors influencing the behavior of people in the workplace. Knowing how to respond to such differences is the cornerstone of effective interpersonal relations.

Personality is one of the major sources of individual differences. The six major personality factors described in this chapter are extraversion, emotional stability, agreeableness, conscientiousness, openness to experience, and self-monitoring of behavior. Depending on the job, any one of these personality factors can be important for success, and they also affect interpersonal relations.

Personality also influences a person's cognitive style, or the mental process used to perceive and make judgments from information. How people gather and evaluate information determines their cognitive style. Two different styles of gathering information are sensation and intuition. Sensation-type individuals prefer routine and order. Intuitive-type people prefer an overall perspective and enjoy solving new problems.

Styles for evaluating information tend to place emphasis on either feeling at one extreme or thinking at the other. Feeling-type people are conformists and avoid disagreement, whereas thinking-type individuals rely on intellect more than emotion in problem solving.

The two dimensions of information gathering and evaluation are combined to produce a four-way classification of cognitive styles: sensation/thinking; intuitive/thinking; sensation/feeling; and intuitive/feeling. Cognitive styles have implications for the types of work a person is best suited for (see Figure 2-2).

Mental ability, or intelligence, is one of the major sources of individual differences that affects job performance and behavior. Understanding the nature of intelligence contributes to effective interpersonal relations in organizations. For example, understanding that different types of intelligence exist will help a person appreciate the strengths of others.

Intelligence consists of many components. The traditional perspective is that intelligence includes a general factor along with special factors that contribute to problem-solving ability. A related perspective is that intelligence consists of seven components: verbal comprehension, word fluency, numerical acuity, spatial perception, memory, perceptual speed, and inductive reasoning.

To overcome the idea that intelligence involves mostly the ability to solve abstract problems, the triarchic theory of intelligence has been proposed. According to this theory, intelligence has three subtypes: analytical, creative, and practical (street smarts included). Another approach to understanding mental ability contends that people have multiple intelligences, or faculties, including linguistic, logical-mathematical, musical, spatial, bodily/kinesthetic, intrapersonal, interpersonal, and naturalist.

Emotional intelligence refers to factors other than traditional mental ability that influence a person's success. The five components of emotional intelligence are (1) self-awareness, (2) self-regulation, (3) motivation relating to task enjoyment and resiliency, (4) empathy, and (5) social skill.

Values and beliefs are another set of factors that influence behavior on the job, including interpersonal relations. Values are closely tied in with ethics, the moral choices a person makes. People acquire values in the process of growing up and modeling others. The values a person develops early in life are directly related to the kind of adult he or she becomes and to the quality of relationships formed. Values-clarification exercises help people identify their values. Person–role conflict occurs when the demands made by an organization or a superior clash with the basic values of an individual.

QUESTIONS FOR DISCUSSION AND REVIEW

1. Referring to the lead-in case illustration in the chapter, how effectively were Billy and Mary Lou relating to each other?

2. Why is responding to individual differences considered to be the cornerstone of effective interpersonal relations?

3. How can a knowledge of major personality factors help a person form better interpersonal relations on the job?

4. A coworker of yours who has a high standing on the personality factor "openness to experience" has an upcoming birthday. What would be an appropriate gift for the group to buy this person?

5. Suppose a high-self-monitoring person is attending a company-sponsored social event and that person dislikes such events. How is he or she likely to behave?

6. What kinds of problems would a sensation-type individual prefer to tackle?

7. Which of the seven components of intelligence represents your best mental aptitude? What is your evidence?

8. How could you use the concept of *multiple intelligences* to raise the self-esteem of people who did not consider themselves to be very smart?

9. Why is emotional intelligence so important for success in business?

10. How can you use information about a person's values to help you relate more effectively to him or her?

An Interpersonal Relations Case Problem

BAYER LAYS OUT ITS VALUES

The Bayer Group is a large business firm involved in a variety of businesses including chemicals, health-care (such as the familiar Bayer Aspirin), and photography supplies. Leadership at Bayer decided several years ago that for employees to be successful in their company they must accept company values such as customer loyalty, quality, and productivity.

Senior managers at Bayer wanted to make the message clear: No matter whether a person is a chemist, engineer, manufacturing technician, bookkeeper, salesperson, or customer service representative, the key to success is to embrace the company's values. One implication of this message was that employee performance would be measured against how well the individual's work reflected company values. An executive committee worked hard and long to develop a statement that would communicate company values clearly. Top management hoped that by making these values explicit, employees would have a better understanding of how they should behave on the job. Exhibit 1 presents the Bayer values.

With the new values clearly spelled out for all workers, managers were now expected to guide employees toward behaving in a way consistent with the values. A production supervisor, for example, would devalue high productivity by an employee if he or she sacrificed safety to achieve a high production quota.

Dave Rapp, a packaging design specialist at a Bayer pharmaceutical plant, said to his supervisor, "I thought I was doing a great job helping design packages for medicine. If I designed an attractive package that protected the ingredients, I was rated highly. Now I have to figure out whether what I'm doing matches the company vision statement. Why are you making my job so difficult?"

(Continued)

Exhibit 1

THE VISION AND VALUES OF BAYER CORP., PITTSBURGH

The vision of Bayer Corp. Pittsburgh is to be a leader in the markets it serves and to be a major contributor to its worldwide parent company. The company will achieve its vision through a diversified, highly motivated workforce; by satisfying and retaining loyalties of its external and internal customers with an organization that fosters teamwork and is unencumbered by bureaucracy; by being environmentally responsible; and by being a good corporate citizen in the communities in which its workforce works and lives.

The following are Bayer Corp.'s Value statements:

OUR PEOPLE
➤ Rewarding people with fair and competitive compensation.
➤ Investing in employee professional development and growth.
➤ Achieving management diversity by gender, race and culture.
➤ Encouraging and recognizing outstanding accomplishments.

OUR BUSINESS
➤ Satisfying the requirements of external and internal customers.
➤ Maintaining high ethical standards in all business actions.
➤ Encouraging and supporting among employees, entrepreneurial attitudes, opportunity seeking and applied creativity.
➤ Managing for the long term.

OUR ORGANIZATION
➤ Assuring an organization unencumbered by bureaucracy.
➤ Delegating decision-making authority.
➤ Fostering teamwork and cooperation among organizational units worldwide.

OUR ENVIRONMENT AND COMMUNITIES
➤ Maintaining work environments in which employee health and safety are the highest priorities.
➤ Developing only products that can be manufactured, used, and disposed of in an environmentally friendly way.
➤ Taking an active role in the communities in which we work and live.

Source: Bayer Corp.

(Continued)

Nicole Berkshire, his team leader, responded: "Dave, be careful not to be too narrow-minded, or sell yourself short. Raise your sights. I think there are lots of things you're doing that fit the Bayer value statements. Just to get you started on the right track, think about that latest package you helped design. The one that will be used to hold arthritis medicine. Didn't you tell me the package was environmentally friendly?

"I've got some homework for you Dave. Come back to me next Monday morning with a list of at least five ways in which your work as a package designer fits the Bayer values. And don't forget to include how your personal values match the Bayer values."

"I'll give it a try," said Dave reluctantly. "But why can't I just go back to helping design packages and be evaluated on what I produce?"

Case Questions

1. How realistic is it for Bayer to expect employees to embrace the value statements?

2. Help Dave with his "homework." Describe as best you can how the work of a package designer might fit the value statements of Bayer.

3. What about you? Provide a brief analysis of how your values might fit the Bayer value statements.

Source: Much of the information in this case is based on Bayer Corp.; Jennifer J. Laabs, "Rating Jobs Against New Values," *Workforce,* May 1997, pp. 38–49.

Chapter 3

Interpersonal Communications

Learning Objectives

After reading and studying this chapter and doing the exercises you should be able to

➤ Explain the basic steps in the communication process.

➤ Understand nonverbal communication and improve your nonverbal communication skills.

➤ Understand barriers to communication, including gender differences, and know how to overcome them.

➤ Enhance your listening skills.

"Why isn't this project ready for shipment today?" barked the manager. "I told you to get it done as soon as you could get to it." "That's why it isn't done," replied the group member. "I was too busy to get to it."

The communication problem just described took place because the phrase "as soon as you can get to it" was interpreted differently by the two people involved. The mix-up that took place illustrates that communication breakdowns are responsible for many problems that take place on the job.

Communication is the sending, receiving, and understanding of messages. It is also the basic process by which managers, customer-contact workers, and professionals accomplish their work. For example, a customer service representative cannot resolve a thorny customer problem without carefully receiving and sending information. Communication is also important because communication skills are a success factor for workers in a wide variety of jobs. Figure 3-1 illustrates how important communication skills are to employers.

The information in this chapter is aimed at reducing communication problems among people and helping you enhance your communication effectiveness. The chapter approaches these ends in two ways. First, it explains the nature of a few key facets of interpersonal communication. Second, it presents guidelines for improving your effectiveness, along with skill-building exercises.

STEPS IN THE COMMUNICATION PROCESS

One way to understand how people communicate is to examine the steps involved in transmitting and receiving a message, as shown in Figure 3-2. For

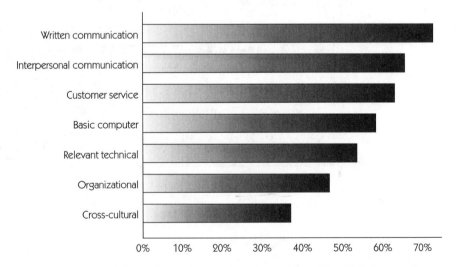

Figure 3-1 Employee Skills Companies Would Most Like to Enhance

Source: Based on data presented in *Human Resource Measurements,* Wonderlic Personnel Test, Inc., December 1991, and updated January 1995. See also Brien N. Smith, Carolee Jones, and Judy Lane, "Employers' Perceptions of Work Skills," *Business Education Forum,* April 1997, pp. 11–17.

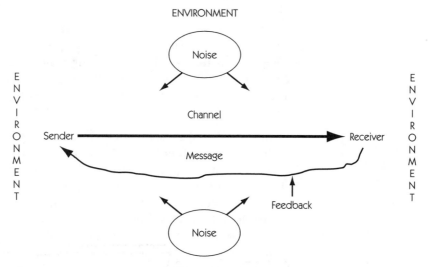

Figure 3-2 A Basic Model of the Communication Process

effective communication to take place, six components must be present: a sender, a message, a channel, a receiver, feedback, and the environment. In addition, the entire communication process is affected by a seventh component, noise. To help understand the communication process, assume that a production manager in a bicycle factory wants to inform a team leader that quality in her department slipped last month.

1. *Sender (or source).* The sender in a communication event is usually a person (in this case the production manager) attempting to send a spoken, written, sign language, or nonverbal message to another person or persons. The perceived authority and credibility of the sender are important factors in influencing how much attention the message will receive.

2. *Message.* The heart of the communication event is the **message**, a purpose or idea to be conveyed. Many factors influence how a message is received. Among them are clarity, the alertness of the receiver, the complexity and length of the message, and how the information is organized. The production manager's message will most likely get across if he says directly, "I need to talk to you about last month's below-average quality figures."

3. *Channel (medium).* Several communication channels, or media, are usually available for sending messages in organizations. Typically, messages are written (usually electronically), spoken, or a combination of the two. Some kind of nonverbal signal such as a smile or hand gesture accompanies most spoken messages. In the production manager's case, he has chosen to drop by the team leader's office and deliver his message in a serious tone.

4. *Receiver.* A communication event can be complete only when another party receives the message and understands it properly. In the example here, the team leader is the receiver. Perceptual distortions of various types act as filters that can prevent a message from being received as intended by the sender. If the team leader is worried that her job is at stake, she might get defensive when she hears the production manager's message.

5. *Feedback.* Messages sent back from the receiver to the sender are referred to as **feedback**. Without feedback it is difficult to know whether a message has been received and understood. The feedback step also includes the reactions of the receiver. If the receiver takes action as intended by the sender, the message has been received satisfactorily. The production manager will know his message got across if the team leader says, "Okay, when would you like to review last month's quality reports?" Effective interpersonal communication therefore involves an exchange of messages between two people. The two communicators take turns being receivers and senders.

6. *Environment.* A full understanding of communication requires knowledge of the environment in which messages are transmitted and received. The organizational culture (attitudes and atmosphere) is a key environmental factor that influences communication. It is easier to transmit controversial messages when trust and respect are high than when they are low.

7. *Noise.* Distractions such as noise have a pervasive influence on the components of the communication process. In this context, **noise** is anything that disrupts communication, including the attitudes and emotions of the receiver. Noise includes such factors as stress, fear, negative attitudes, and low motivation.

NONVERBAL COMMUNICATION IN ORGANIZATIONS

Our discussion so far has emphasized the use of words, or verbal communication. A substantial amount of communication between people, however, takes place at the nonverbal level. **Nonverbal communication** refers to the transmission of messages through means other than words. These messages accompany verbal messages or sometimes stand alone. The general purpose of nonverbal communication is to communicate the feeling behind a message. For instance, you can say no with either a clenched fist or a smile to communicate the intensity of your negative or positive feelings.

A classic study by Albert Mehrabian dramatizes the relevance of nonverbal communication. He calculated the relative weights of three elements of communication with respect to conveying emotion. The words we choose account for only about 7 percent of our emotional impact on others. Our voice tone accounts for 38 percent of the impact, and our facial expressions for 55 percent. Nonverbal behavior therefore accounts for 93 percent of the emotional

impact of a message.[1] Merhabian's study is often interpreted to mean that 93 percent of communication is nonverbal. In truth, the study deals with the emotional impact of a message; it does not mean that the content of the message is unimportant.

The following paragraphs summarize the major modes of transmission of nonverbal communication and provide guidelines for improving nonverbal communication. Chapter 6, about cross-cultural relations, describes cultural differences in nonverbal communication.

MODES OF TRANSMISSION OF NONVERBAL COMMUNICATION

Nonverbal communication can be transmitted in many modes. You may be surprised that certain factors, such as dress and appearance are considered part of nonverbal communication.

ENVIRONMENT

The setting or environment in which you send a message can influence how that message is received. Assume that your manager invites you out to lunch at a fine restaurant to discuss a problem. You will think it is a more important topic under these circumstances than you would if the manager had lunch with you in the company cafeteria.

Other important environmental silent messages include room color, temperature, lighting, and furniture arrangement. A person who sits behind a large, uncluttered desk, for example, appears more powerful than a person who sits behind a small, messy desk.

INTERPERSONAL DISTANCE

The placement of one's body in relation to someone else *(proxemics)* is widely used to transmit messages. (See Figure 3-3.) In general, getting physically close to another person conveys a positive attitude toward that person. Putting your arm around someone is generally interpreted as a friendly act. (Some people, however, recoil when touched by someone other than a close friend. Touching others on the job can also be interpreted as sexual harassment.)

POSTURE

Posture communicates a variety of messages. Standing erect usually conveys the message that the person is self-confident and experiencing positive emotion. Slumping makes a person appear to be lacking in self-confidence or down in the dumps. Another interpersonal message conveyed by posture involves the direction of leaning. Leaning toward the sender suggests that you are favorably disposed toward his or her message; leaning backward communicates the opposite. Openness of the arms or legs serves as an indicator of liking or caring. In general, people establish closed postures (arms folded and legs crossed) when speaking to people they dislike.

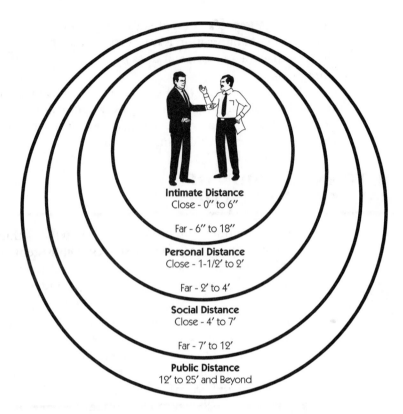

Figure 3-3 Four Circles of Intimacy

GESTURES

Positive attitudes toward another person are shown by frequent hand movements. In contrast, dislike or disinterest usually produces few gestures. An important exception is that some people wave their hands furiously while arguing. Gestures are also said to provide clues to a person's levels of dominance and submission. The gestures of dominant people are typically directed outward toward the other person. Examples include a steady, unwavering gaze and touching one's partner. Submissive gestures are usually protective, such as touching oneself or shrugging one's shoulders.

FACIAL EXPRESSIONS

Using your head, face, and eyes in combination provides the clearest indications of interpersonal attitudes. Looking at the ceiling (without tilting your head), combined with a serious expression, almost always communicates the message "I doubt what you're saying is true." Maintaining eye contact with another person improves communication. To maintain eye contact, it is usually necessary to move your face and eyes *with* the other person. Moving your face and eyes *away* from the other person is often interpreted as defensiveness or a lack of self-confidence.

Facial expressions are also important, because many people rely on them as indicators of whether or not a person is telling the truth. In general, fabrication is suggested by facial tics and nervous mannerisms that reveal how uncomfortable the sender is with telling something false. Looking away from a person is often interpreted as covering up a lie. Computer scientists at the Salk Institute in La Jolla, California, have documented the difference between a truthful smile and a lying smile. An authentic smile is most frequently characterized by crinkly eyes and a generally relaxed expression. A lying smile reveals itself in subtle ways, particularly eye wrinkles that resemble crow's feet more than laugh lines.[2]

VOICE QUALITY

Often more significance is attached to the *way* something is said than to *what* is said. A forceful voice, which includes a consistent tone without vocalized pauses, connotes power and control. Closely related to voice tone are volume, pitch, and rate of speaking. Anger, boredom, and joy often can be interpreted from voice quality. Anger is noted when the person speaks loudly, with a high pitch and at a fast rate. Boredom is indicated by a monotone. Joy is indicated by loud volume. Avoiding an annoying voice quality can make a positive impact on others. The research of voice coach Jeffrey Jacobbi provides some useful suggestions. He surveyed a nationwide sample of 1,000 men and women and asked, "Which irritating or unpleasant voice annoys you the most?" The most irritating was a whining, complaining, or nagging tone.

Jacobbi notes that we are judged by the way we sound. He also notes that careers can be damaged by voice problems such as those indicated in the survey. "We think about how we look and dress," says Jacobbi, "and that gets most of the attention. But people judge our intelligence much more by how we sound than how we dress."[3] Do Self-Assessment Quiz 3-1 to apply Jacobbi's findings to your development.

PERSONAL APPEARANCE

Your external image plays an important role in communicating messages to others. A current analysis confirms what has been known for a long time: A favorable personal appearance enhances a person's ability to persuade others, whether you are dealing with an individual receiver or an audience.[4] Job seekers show recognition of the personal appearance aspect of nonverbal communication when they carefully groom for a job interview. People pay more respect and grant more privileges to those they perceive as being well dressed and neatly groomed. Some research indicates that a favorable personal appearance leads to high starting salaries and later salary increases.[5]

GUIDELINES FOR IMPROVING NONVERBAL COMMUNICATION

Nonverbal communication, like verbal communication, can be improved. Here are six suggestions to consider:

Self-Assessment Quiz 3-1

VOICE-QUALITY CHECKUP

The voice-quality study cited in the text ranked voice quality in decreasing order of annoyance, as follows:

➤ Whining, complaining, or nagging tone—44.0 percent

➤ High-pitched, squeaky voice—15.9 percent

➤ Mumbling—11.1 percent

➤ Very fast talking—4.9 percent

➤ Weak and wimpy voice—3.6 percent

➤ Flat, monotonous tone—3.5 percent

➤ Thick accent—2.4 percent

Directions: Ask yourself and two other people familiar with your voice whether you have one or more of the preceding voice-quality problems. If your self-analysis and feedback from others does indicate a serious problem, get started on self-improvement. Record your voice on tape and attempt to modify the biggest problem. Another avenue of improvement is to consult with a speech coach or therapist.

1. *Obtain feedback on your body language by asking others to comment upon the gestures and facial expressions you use in conversations.* Be videotaped conferring with another individual. After studying your body language, attempt to eliminate those mannerisms and gestures that you think detract from your effectiveness. Common examples include nervous gestures such as moving knees from side to side, cracking knuckles, rubbing the eyes or nose, head scratching, and jingling coins.

2. *Learn to relax when communicating with others.* Take a deep breath and consciously allow your body muscles to loosen. Tension-reducing techniques should be helpful here. A relaxed person makes it easier for other people to relax. You are likely to elicit more useful information from other people when you are relaxed.

3. *Use facial, hand, and body gestures to supplement your speech, but don't overdo it.* A good starting point is to use hand gestures to express enthusiasm. You can increase the potency of enthusiastic comments by shaking the other person's hand, nodding approval, or smiling.

4. *Avoid using the same nonverbal gesture indiscriminately.* If you want to use nodding to convey approval, do not nod with approval when you dislike what somebody else is saying. Also, do not pat everybody on the back. Nonverbal gestures used indiscriminately lose their communication effectiveness.

Skill-Building Exercise 3-1

THE MIRRORING TECHNIQUE

To practice mirroring, during the next 10 days each class member schedules one mirroring session with an unsuspecting subject. An ideal opportunity would be an upcoming meeting on the job. Another possibility would be to ask a friend if you could practice your interviewing techniques with him or her—but do not mention the mirroring technique. A third possibility would be to sit down with a friend and conduct a social conversation.

While holding an interview or discussion with the other party, use the mirroring technique. Imitate the person's breathing pattern, rate of speech, hand movements, eye movements, leg movements, or any other noticeable aspect of behavior.

After the mirroring sessions have been conducted, hold a class discussion about the results. Questions include:

1. Did the other person notice the mirroring and comment on the behavior of the person doing the mirroring?

2. Was the rapport enhanced (or hindered) by the mirroring?

3. How many of the students intend to repeat the mirroring technique in the future?

5. *Use role playing to practice various forms of nonverbal communication.* A good starting point would be to practice selling your ideas about an important project or concept to another person. During your interchange, supplement your spoken messages with appropriate nonverbal cues such as posture, voice intonation, gestures, and so forth. Later, obtain the other person's perception of the effectiveness of your nonverbal communication.

6. *Use mirroring to establish rapport.* Nonverbal communication can be improved through **mirroring**, or subtly imitating someone. The most successful mirroring technique is to imitate the breathing pattern of another person. If you adjust your own breathing rate to match someone else's, you will soon establish rapport with that individual. Another effective mirroring technique is to adopt the voice speed of the person with whom you are communicating. If the other person speaks more slowly than you typically do, slow down to mirror him or her.

You can also use mirroring by imitating a manager to win favor. Many group members have a relentless tendency to copy the boss's mannerisms, gestures, way of speaking, and dress. As a consequence, without realizing why, your manager may think more favorably of you.

Caution: Do not use mirroring to the extent that you appear to be mocking another person, thereby adversely affecting rapport. To get started developing your mirroring skills, do Skill-Building Exercise 3-1.

1. Understand the receiver.
2. Discuss differences in paradigms.
3. Minimize defensive communication.
4. Use multiple channels.
5. Use verbal and nonverbal feedback.
6. Display a positive attitude.
7. Use persuasive communication.
8. Engage in active listening.
9. Engage in complementary transactions with people.
10. Recognize gender differences in communication styles.
11. Engage in metacommunications.

Figure 3-4 Overcoming Communication Problems and Barriers

GUIDELINES FOR OVERCOMING COMMUNICATION PROBLEMS AND BARRIERS

Communication problems in organizations are ever present. Some interference usually takes place between ideation and action, as suggested earlier by the noise factor in Figure 3-2. The type of message influences the amount of interference. Routine or neutral messages are the easiest to communicate. Interference is most likely to occur when a message is complex, emotionally arousing, or clashes with a receiver's mental set.

An emotionally arousing message deals with topics such as money or a relationship between two people. A message that clashes with a receiver's mental set requires the person to change his or her typical pattern of receiving messages. Try this experiment. The next time you visit a restaurant, order dessert first and the entrée second. The server probably will not receive your dessert order, because it deviates from the normal sequence.

Here we will describe strategies and tactics for overcoming some of the more frequently observed communication problems in organizations, as outlined in Figure 3-4.

UNDERSTAND THE RECEIVER

Understanding the person you are trying to reach is a fundamental principle of overcoming communication barriers. The more you know about your receiver, the better able you are to deliver your message effectively. Three important aspects of understanding the receiver are (1) developing empathy, (2) recognizing his or her motivational state, and (3) understanding the other person's frame of reference.

Developing **empathy** requires placing yourself in the receiver's shoes. To accomplish this you have to imagine yourself in the other person's role and assume the viewpoints and emotions of that individual. For example, if a supervisor were trying to communicate the importance of customer service to sales associates, the supervisor might ask himself or herself, "If I were a part-time

employee being paid close to the minimum wage, how receptive would I be to messages about high-quality customer service?" To empathize you have to understand another person. *Sympathy* means that you understand and agree.

The receiver's **motivational state** could include any active needs and interests operating at the time. People tend to listen attentively to messages that show promise of satisfying an active need. Management usually listens attentively to a suggestion framed in terms of cost savings or increased profits.

People perceive words and concepts differently because their vantage points and perspectives differ. Such differences in **frame of reference** create barriers to communication. A frame of reference can also be considered a lens through which we view the world. A manager attempted to chastise a team member by saying, "If you keep up your present level of performance, you'll be a repair technician all your life." The technician replied, "That's good news," because he was proud of being the first person in his family to hold a skilled job. Understanding another person's frame of reference requires empathy.

DISCUSS DIFFERENCES IN PARADIGMS

Another way of understanding differences in frames of reference is to recognize that people often have different **paradigms** that influence how they interpret events. A paradigm is a model, framework, viewpoint, or perspective. When two people look at a situation with different paradigms, a communication problem may occur. For instance, one person may say, "Let's go to Las Vegas for the computer show." The other person may respond, "A ridiculous idea. It costs too much money and takes too much time. Besides, the company would never approve." These objections are based on certain unstated beliefs:

➤ Air travel is the most suitable mode of transportation.

➤ Traveling over 500 miles a day by auto is fatiguing and dangerous.

➤ Traveling over a weekend for business and using vacation days cannot be considered seriously.

➤ Paying for such a trip with personal money is out of the question.

The other person has a different set of unstated beliefs:

➤ It is possible, traveling on interstate highways and using two drivers, to cover 1,000 miles in one day.

➤ Traveling over a weekend and taking vacation days is sensible.

➤ Paying for the trip with personal money is a sound educational investment.

The solution to this communication clash is to discuss the paradigms. Both people live by different rules or guidelines (a major contributor to a paradigm). If the two people can recognize that they are operating with different paradigms, the chances for agreement are improved. Keep in mind that peo-

ple can change their paradigms when the reasons are convincing.[6] For example, the second person in the preceding situation may never have thought about using personal funds for a trip as being an educational investment.

MINIMIZE DEFENSIVE COMMUNICATION

An important general communication barrier is defensive communication—the tendency to receive messages in such a way that our self-esteem is protected. Defensive communication is also responsible for people sending messages to make themselves look good. For example, when being criticized for low production, an investment banker might blame the advertising agency used by his or her firm.

Overcoming the barrier of defensive communication requires two steps. First, people have to recognize the existence of defensive communication. Second, they have to try not to be defensive when questioned or criticized. Such behavior is not easy because of the unconscious or semiconscious process of **denial**—the suppression of information we find uncomfortable. For example, the investment banker just cited would find it uncomfortable to think of himself or herself as being responsible for below-average performance.

USE MULTIPLE CHANNELS

Repetition enhances communication, particularly when different channels are used to convey the same message. Effective communicators at many job levels follow spoken agreements with written documentation. Since most communication is subject to at least some distortion, the chances of a message being received as intended increase when two or more channels are used.

Many firms have a policy of using a multiple-channel approach to communicate the results of a performance appraisal. The group member receives an oral explanation from the manager of the results of the review. The group member is also required to read the form and indicate by signature that he or she has read and understands the meaning of the review. Another useful way of using multiple channels is to follow up a telephone call or in-person conversation with an e-mail message summarizing key facts or agreements.

USE VERBAL AND NONVERBAL FEEDBACK

Ask for feedback to determine whether your message has been received as intended. A frequent managerial practice is to conclude a meeting with a question such as, "Okay, what have we agreed upon?" Unless feedback of this nature is obtained, you will not know whether your message has been received until the receiver carries out your request. If the request is carried out improperly, or if no action is taken, you will know that the message was received poorly.

Obtaining feedback is important because it results in two-way communication in which people take turns being sender and receiver, thereby having a dialogue. Dialogues take time because they require people to speak more slowly and listen more carefully. The results of having employees engage in dialogue are said to include a deeper sense of community (a feeling of belong-

ingness) and greater trust among employees.[7] You might relate this finding to your own experiences. Do you trust people better when you both exchange ideas and listen to each other?

Feedback is also important because it provides reinforcement to the sender, and few people will continue to communicate without any reinforcement. The sender is reinforced when the receiver indicates understanding of the message. When the original receiver indicates that he or she understands the message, that person becomes the sender. A nod of approval would be an appropriate type of nonverbal reinforcement for the sender to receive.

DISPLAY A POSITIVE ATTITUDE

Being perceived as having a positive attitude helps melt communication barriers. This is true because most people prefer to communicate with a positive person. According to Sharon Lund O'Neil, you must establish credibility and trustworthiness if you expect others to listen, let alone get them to react positively to your communication.[8] Being positive helps make you appear more credible and trustworthy, whereas being consistently negative makes you less credible and trustworthy. As one coworker said about a chronic complainer in his office, "Why take Margot seriously? She finds something wrong with everybody and everything."

USE PERSUASIVE COMMUNICATION

A powerful tactic for overcoming communication barriers is to communicate so persuasively that obstacles disappear. *Persuasiveness* refers to the sender's convincing the receiver to accept his or her message. Persuasion thus involves selling to others. Hundreds of articles, books, audiotapes, and videos have been developed to help people become more persuasive. Following are some representative suggestions for becoming a more persuasive communicator, both in speaking and in writing.[9]

1. *Know exactly what you want.* Your chances of selling an idea increase to the extent that you have clarified the idea in your own mind. The clearer and more committed you are at the outset of a selling or negotiating session, the stronger you are as a persuader.

2. *Never suggest an action without telling its end benefit.* In asking for a raise, you might say, "If I get this raise, I'll be able to afford to stay with this job as long as the company likes."

3. *Phrase your proposition in terms of the receiver's interests.* The basic rule of selling is an extension of the communication strategy "understand the receiver." People are far more likely to accept your idea if it is clear how they will benefit. Most receivers want to know "What's in it for me?"

4 *Explore the reasons for people's objections.* Assume a potential customer says, "I like this model but I don't want it in my living room." An effective response would be "What is it that you don't like about it?" Another would be "Which features do you like in this product?"

5. *Get a yes response early on.* It is helpful to give the selling session a positive tone by establishing a "yes pattern" at the outset. Assume that an employee wanted to convince the boss to allow the employee to perform some work at home during normal working hours. The employee might begin the idea-selling questions with "Is it important for the company to obtain maximum productivity from all its employees?"

6. *Use power words.* An expert tactic for being persuasive is to sprinkle your speech with power (meaning *powerful*) words. Power words stir emotion and bring forth images of exciting events. Examples of power words include *decimating* the competition, *bonding* with customers, *surpassing* previous profits, *capturing* customer loyalty, and *rebounding* from a downturn.

7. *Minimize raising your pitch at the end of sentences.* Part of being persuasive is not sound unsure and apologetic. In English and several other languages, a convenient way to ask a question or to express doubt is to raise the pitch of your voice at the end of a sentence or phrase. As a test, use the sentence "You like my ideas." First say *ideas* using approximately the same pitch and tone as with every other word. Then say the same sentence by pronouncing *ideas* with a higher pitch and louder tone. By saying *ideas* loudly, you sound much less certain and are less persuasive.

8. *Talk to your audience, not the screen.* Computer graphic presentations have become standard practice even in small-group meetings. Many presenters rely so heavily on computer-generated slides and transparencies that they basically read the slides and transparencies to the audience. Jean Mausehund and R. Neil Dortch remind us that in an oral presentation, the predominant means of connection between sender and receiver should be eye contact. When your audience is frequently distracted by movement on the screen, computer sounds, garish colors, or your looking at the screen, eye contact suffers. As a result the message is weakened, and you are less persuasive.[10]

9. *Avoid or minimize common language errors.* You will enhance your persuasiveness if you minimize common language errors, because you will appear more articulate and informed. Here are several common language errors:

 a. "Just between you and I" is wrong. "Just between you and me" is correct.

 b. *Irregardless* is not a word; *regardless* is correct.

 c. Avoid double negatives when you want to express the negative, despite the increasing popularity of double negatives. Common examples of double negatives are "I got no *nothing* from my best customer this week" and "We don't have *no money* in the budget for travel." If expressed with the right inflection, a double negative can

be correct. For example to say "We don't have no money" with an emphasis on *no money* means that the budget is not completely depleted. Yet in general, double negatives make the sender appear so ill-informed that they fail to persuade.

d. "We are customer-oriented" is correct. "We are customer-orientated" is wrong.

If you can learn to implement most of the preceding nine suggestions you are on your way toward becoming a persuasive communicator. In addition, you will need solid facts behind you, and you will need to make skillful use of non-verbal communication.

ENGAGE IN ACTIVE LISTENING

Persuasion deals primarily with sending messages. Improving one's receiving of messages is another part of developing better communication skills. Unless you receive messages as they are intended, you cannot perform your job properly or be a good companion. Listening has even been described as our primary communication activity when engaged in face-to-face communication. Listening is a particularly important skill for anybody whose job involves troubleshooting, since one needs to gather information in order to solve problems.

Another reason that improving the listening skills of employees is important is that insufficient listening is extraordinarily costly. Listening mistakes lead to reprocessing letters, rescheduling appointments, reshipping orders, and recalling defective products. Effective listening also improves interpersonal relations because the people listened to feel understood and respected.

A major component of effective listening is to be an **active listener**. The active listener listens intensely, with the goal of empathizing with the speaker. As a result of listening actively, the listener can feed back to the speaker what he or she thinks the speaker meant. Feedback of this type relies on both verbal and nonverbal communication. Active listening also involves **summarization**. When you summarize, you pull together, condense, and thereby clarify the main points communicated by the other person. Here are two examples of summarization statements:

"What I heard you say during our meeting is that . . ."

"As I understand it, your position is that . . ."

Specific suggestions for improving active listening skills are summarized in Figure 3-5. These suggestions relate to good listening in general, as well as active listening. As with any other suggestions for developing a new skill, considerable practice (with some supervision) is needed to bring about actual changes in behavior. One of the problems a poor listener would encounter is the difficulty of breaking old habits in order to acquire new ones. Self-Assessment Quiz 3-2 gives you an opportunity to think about bad listening habits you may have acquired. To practice your listening skills, do Skill-Building Exercise 3-2 on page 56.

➤ *While your target is talking, look at him or her intently.* At the same time, maintain a steady eye contact.
➤ *Be patient about your turn to speak.* A common barrier to effective listening is to mentally prepare an answer while another person is speaking.
➤ *Nod your head in agreement from time to time.*
➤ *Mutter "mmh" or "uh-huh" periodically but not incessantly.*
➤ *Ask open-ended questions to encourage the other person to talk.* For example, you encourage more conversation by saying "What do you think of . . . " rather than asking "Do you agree that"
➤ *Reflect your target's content or meaning.* Rephrase and summarize concisely what the other person is saying.
➤ *Reflect the other person's feelings.* Reflection-of-feeling responses typically begin with "You feel that"
➤ *Keep your ratio of talking to listening down to about 1 to 5.* In other words, spend 20 percent of your time talking, and 80 percent listening to be perceived as a great listener.
➤ *Ask yourself whether anything the other person is saying could benefit you.* Maintaining this perspective will enable you to benefit from most listening episodes and will motivate you to listen intently.

Figure 3-5 Suggestions for Active Listening

ENGAGE IN COMPLEMENTARY TRANSACTIONS WITH PEOPLE

A specific technique for improving communications with people, and thereby breaking down barriers, is to engage in **complementary transactions**. A complementary transaction is an exchange of words between two people that reduces tension and moves the two people toward a positive resolution. The complementary transaction occurs when one person gets the kind of response he or she wants from the other. The skill of using complementary transactions involves adapting your response precisely to the actions and words of the other person, just as a complementary angle completes a circle.

According to the discipline called *transactional analysis,* transactions between people are classified as complementary or noncomplementary (crossed). Complementary transactions lead to effective interaction and *positive strokes,* or ego-building statements. Noncomplementary transactions lead to ineffective interactions and *negative strokes,* or ego-tearing insults.

Finding a complementary response is especially useful when attempting to keep communications running smoothly in a tense situation. You search for the type of response the person is seeking so you can keep the conversation positive. You then stand a reasonable chance of overcoming a communication barrier.

Assume that Dorothy is red in the face with anger because an important file she had been working on is erased from the personal computer she was using. Acting in a childlike manner, she goes into a tirade about how some fool must have been messing around with her computer files. By the tone of her voice, you get the impression she thinks you are the culprit.

One way you can engage in a complementary transaction is by acting in a controlling, parentlike manner in response to her childish state. You might

Self-Assessment Quiz 3-2

LISTENING TRAPS

Communication specialists at Purdue University have identified certain behavior patterns that interfere with effective hearing and listening. After thinking carefully about each trap, check how well the trap applies to you: Not a Problem, or Need Improvement. To respond to the statements accurately, visualize how you acted when you recently were in a situation calling for listening.

	Not a problem	Need improvement
➤ **Mind reader.** You will receive limited information if you constantly think "What is this person really thinking or feeling?"	☐	☐
➤ **Rehearser.** Your mental rehearsals for "Here's what I'll say next" tune out the sender.	☐	☐
➤ **Filterer.** You engage in selective listening by hearing only what you want to hear. (Could be difficult to judge because the process is often unconscious.)	☐	☐
➤ **Dreamer.** You drift off during a face-to-face conversation, which often leads you to an embarrassing "What did you say?" or "Could you repeat that?"	☐	☐
➤ **Identifier.** If you refer everything you hear to your experience, you probably did not really listen to what was said.	☐	☐
➤ **Comparer.** When you get sidetracked sizing up the sender, you are sure to miss the message.	☐	☐
➤ **Derailer.** You change the subject too quickly, giving the impression that you are not interested in anything the sender has to say.	☐	☐
➤ **Sparrer.** You hear what is said, but quickly belittle or discount it, putting you in the same class as the derailer.	☐	☐
➤ **Placater.** You agree with everything you hear just to be nice or to avoid conflict. By behaving this way you miss out on the opportunity for authentic dialogue.	☐	☐

Interpretation: If you checked "Need Improvement" for five or more of the above statements, you are correct—your listening needs improvement! If you checked only two or fewer of the above traps, you are probably an effective listener and a supportive person.

Source: Reprinted with permission from *Messages: The Communication Skills Book* (Oakland, CA: New Harbinger Publications, 1983).

respond, "Please calm down, Dorothy. I am good at finding lost files, and I will do my best to help you." Communication will probably continue, because Dorothy is receiving the type of helping response she wants.

Another way to engage in a complementary transaction with Dorothy is to respond in a childish manner to her childish tirade. You might respond, "Holy

Skill-Building Exercise 3-2

LISTENING TO A COWORKER

Before conducting the following role plays, review the 11 keys to effective listening presented in Figure 3-4. Suggestion 11 about restating what you hear (summarization) is particularly important when listening to a person who is talking about an emotional topic.

The Elated Coworker: One student plays the role of a coworker who has just been offered a promotion to supervisor of another department. She will be receiving a 10 percent raise in pay and be able to travel overseas twice a year for the company. She is eager to describe full details of her good fortune to a coworker. Another student plays the role of the coworker to whom the first worker wants to describe her good fortune. The second worker decides to listen intently to the first worker. Other class members will rate the second student on his or her listening ability.

The Discouraged Coworker: One student plays the role of a coworker who has just been placed on probation for poor job performance. His boss thinks that his performance is below standard and that his attendance and punctuality are poor. He is afraid that if he tells his girlfriend, she will leave him. He is eager to tell his tale of woe to a coworker. Another student plays the role of a coworker he corners to discuss his problems. The second worker decides to listen intently to his problems but is pressed for time. Other class members will rate the second student on his or her listening ability.

cats, what a mess. I bet some fool did mess up your files. Some of the temps we have working in this office are irresponsible. They have no respect for other people's work." Because a person acting like a child will also welcome a childish response in return, communication is likely to continue.

A crossed transaction occurs when a person does not get the type of response he or she sought. In Dorothy's situation, she is not looking for a response that will put her in her place and suggest she take responsibility for her own problems. You would engage in a crossed transaction with Dorothy if you responded, "Hey, Dorothy, don't yell at me in those accusatory tones. It's your responsibility to manage your own computer files. If you want to blame someone, look in the mirror."

In short, if another person is communicating to you in a childish, immature manner, transactional analysis suggests you can salvage the situation two ways. First, you can exert control in a firm, controlling manner, much like a parent. Second, you can respond in an immature manner, thus communicating on the same wavelength. Both responses result in complementary transactions. In a crossed transaction the second party is troubled or irritated by the message sent by the first party. As a result, the second party responds in a way that surprises and troubles the first party.[11] Skill-Building Exercise 3-3 gives you practice in identifying complementary versus crossed transactions.

Skill-Building Exercise 3-3

COMPLEMENTARY VERSUS CROSSED TRANSACTIONS

Following are alternative responses to the same statement. To the left of each response, indicate with a plus sign (+) if the response is a complementary and a minus sign (–) if it is a crossed transaction. Suggested answers may be found at the end of the chapter.

Situation A: A coworker says to you, "Why are you always late coming back from lunch?"

_____ "Look who's talking. You leave work early almost every day."

_____ "You're right. I take care of too many errands during lunch hour. Since it bothers you I will try to get back from lunch more promptly."

Situation B: Out of town on a company-sponsored trip, one worker says to the other, "Why don't we both eat at a sub shop tonight and then charge the company for a fancy dinner?"

_____ "I like the idea of having a little extra cash, but I am concerned that we would be violating company policy. Let's not do it."

_____ "Count me out. I dislike cheating, and I hate cheats."

RECOGNIZE GENDER DIFFERENCES IN COMMUNICATION STYLE

A trend in organizations for many years has been to move toward equality of the sexes. Despite this trend, substantial interest has arisen in identifying differences in communication styles between men and women. A book by linguist Deborah Tannen, *Talking from 9 to 5*, focuses especially on male–female differences in conversational style in the workplace. A book by John Gray, *Men Are from Mars, Women Are from Venus*, explores the same topic.

People who are aware of these differences face fewer communication barriers between themselves and members of the opposite sex. As we describe these differences, recognize that they are group stereotypes. Individual differences in communication style usually are more important than group (men versus women) differences. Here we will describe the major findings of gender differences in communication patterns.[12]

1. *Women prefer to use conversation for rapport building.* For most women, the intent of conversation is to build rapport and connections with people. Women are therefore more likely to emphasize similarities, to listen intently, and to be supportive.

2. *Men prefer to use talk primarily as a means to preserve independence and status by displaying knowledge and skill.* When most men talk they want to

receive positive evaluation from others and maintain their hierarchical status within the group. Men are therefore more oriented to giving a *report* while women are more interested in establishing *rapport*.

3. *Women want empathy, not solutions.* When women share feelings of being stressed out, they seek empathy and understanding. If they feel they have been listened to carefully, they begin to relax. When listening to the woman, the man may feel blamed for her problems or that he has failed the woman in some way. To feel useful, the man might offer solutions to the woman's problems.

4. *Men prefer to work out their problems by themselves, whereas women prefer to talk out solutions with another person.* Women look upon having and sharing problems as an opportunity to build and deepen relationships. Men are more likely to look upon problems as challenges they must meet on their own. The communication consequence of these differences is that men may become uncommunicative when they have a problem.

5. *Women are more likely to compliment the work of a coworker, whereas men are more likely to be critical.* A communication problem may occur when a woman compliments the work of a coworker and expects reciprocal praise.

6. *Men tend to be more directive in their conversation, whereas women emphasize politeness.* Women are therefore more likely to frequently use the phrases "I'm sorry" and "Thank you," even when there is no need to express apology or gratitude. For example, a supermarket manager notices that the store has suddenly become busy. She would therefore say to a store clerk unpacking boxes, "I'm sorry Pedro, but we've become busy all of a sudden. Could you please open up a new lane up front? Thank you." A manager who is a stereotyped male might say, "Pedro, we need you to open a line up front, pronto. Put down the boxes and get up there."

7. *Women tend to be more conciliatory when facing differences, whereas men become more intimidating.* Again, women are more interested in building relationships, whereas men are more concerned about coming out ahead.

8. *Men are more interested than women in calling attention to their accomplishments or hogging recognition.* In one instance a sales representative who had already made her sales quota for the month turned over an excellent prospect to a coworker. She reasoned, "It's somebody else's turn. I've received more than my fair share of bonuses for the month."

9. *Men tend to dominate discussions during meetings.* One study of college faculty meetings found that women's longest turns at speaking were, on the average, of shorter duration than men's shortest turns. A possible explanation here is that women are still less assertive than men in the workplace.

How can the information just presented help overcome communication problems on the job? As a starting point, remember that these gender differences often exist. Understanding these differences will help you interpret the communication behavior of people. For example, if a male coworker is not as effusive with praise as you would like, remember that he is simply engaging in gender-typical behavior. Do not take it personally.

A woman can remind herself to speak up more in meetings because her natural tendency might be toward diffidence. She might say to herself, "I must watch out to avoid gender-typical behavior in this situation." A man might remind himself to be more complimentary and supportive toward coworkers. The problem is that although such behavior is important, his natural tendency might be to skip the praise.

A woman should not take it personally when a male coworker or subordinate is tight-lipped when faced with a problem. She should recognize that he needs more encouragement to talk about his problems than would a woman. If the man persists in not wanting to talk about the problem, the woman might say, "It looks like you want to work out this problem on your own. Go ahead. I'm available if you want to talk about the problem."

Men and women should recognize that when women talk over problems, they might not be seeking hard-hitting advice. Instead, they might simply be searching for a sympathetic ear so they can deal with the emotional aspect of the problem.

A general suggestion for overcoming gender-related communication barriers is for men to improve communication by becoming more empathic (showing more empathy) listeners. Women can improve communication by becoming more direct.

ENGAGE IN METACOMMUNICATIONS

When confronted with a communication problem, one response is to attempt to work around the barrier, perhaps by using one of the methods already described. A more typical response is to ignore the barrier by making no special effort to deal with the problem—a "take-it-or-leave-it" approach to communication. Another possibility is to **metacommunicate**, or communicate about your communication, to help overcome barriers or resolve a problem.[13] If you as a team leader were facing heavy deadline pressures, you might say to a team member, "I might appear brusque today and tomorrow. Please don't take it personally. It's just that I have to make heavy demands on you because the team is facing a gruesome deadline."

SUMMARY

Communication is the basic process by which managers, customer-contact workers, and professionals accomplish their work, yet many communication problems exist in organizations. Communication among people is a complex

JUST CALL ME "KAT"

Katherine Matthews had worked for many years in a variety of retail positions, including a three-year assignment as an assistant manager at a woman's clothing store. Matthews was then involved in an automobile accident as the passenger in a friend's car. Although she was wearing a seat belt, Matthews was severely injured. Her right leg and ankle were broken as the door on her side caved in upon impact with a tree.

After four months of rehabilitation, Matthews walked well with the assistance of a cane. Yet she could not walk for long without enduring pain. Katherine and the team of medical specialists assisting her agreed that an on-the-feet job was not appropriate for her in the foreseeable future. Katherine assessed her financial situation and decided she needed to return to work soon. Her disability payments were ending soon, and her savings were depleted to $450.

To make the transition back to full-time employment, yet in another field, Katherine signed on with OfficeTemps, a well-established temporary placement agency. Katherine explained that she sought work that was mentally challenging but not physically demanding on her right leg and ankle. After carefully assessing Katherine's capabilities and experiences, the employment interviewer, Jack Radison, created a computer file for her. Radison said, "I'll call you as soon as I find a suitable assignment."

One week later Radison called Katherine with good news. He had located a nine-month assignment for her as a telephone interviewer for a market research firm. The market research firm was hiring several people to conduct telephone interviews with dealers and retailers about the acceptability of a relatively new product, a personal air cooler. The cooler is about the size of the central processing unit on a personal computer, and it would easily fit on a desk or adjacent to a television set. The air cooler evaporates water, thereby lowering the temperature by 12° F (6.7° C) in a seven-foot area. Using an air cooler, a person would have less need for air conditioning. With the cooler operating, a person could either eliminate air conditioning or set it at a higher temperature. The manufacturer of the cooler was interested in estimating the potential market for the product, now being sold primarily by mail order.

Katherine's task was to telephone specific people (usually store managers or owners) from a long list of names. Completing an interview would require about 30 minutes, and it involved obtaining answers to 20 separate questions. Each market research interviewer was given a quota of six completed interviews per day.

As the interviewers perceived the task, a major challenge was to keep the interviewee on the line long enough to answer all the detailed questions. Quite often the interviewer had to dig for additional information (such as sales of room air conditioners and fans) or request that the interviewee search his or her files for appropriate information. The several interviewers also agreed that an even bigger challenge was to get the people on the list to cooperate. Among the problems were reaching a voice mail system instead of the actual person, excuses about being too busy to be interviewed, and outright rejection and rudeness.

Following closely the script provided by the market research firm, Katherine began her pitch in this manner: "Hello, this is Katherine from Garson Research Associates in Chicago. I'm asking for your cooperation to participate in an important study about an exciting new product, personal coolers. My interview should only take approximately 30 minutes. May we conduct the interview right now, or would you prefer another time in the next few days?"

Four weeks into the job, Katherine was behind quota by an average of two interviews per day. Feeling fatigued one day, she slipped into introducing herself as "Kat," the name used by family members and close friends. The interviewee prospect responded, "Oh sure, Kat, I can talk now."

(Continued)

Two days later, Katherine made a personal call to a friend and was thus prompted to think of herself as "Kat." She inadvertently introduced herself as "Kat" to the next person on her list. Again, the prospective interviewee responded with enthusiasm: "Hey Kat, I'm ready to talk."

Prompted by the second cooperative response, Katherine then shifted to introducing herself as "Kat." The percentage of prospects willing to be interviewed jumped from 30 percent to 50 percent. Katherine explained this unusual result to her supervisor, who said that using a nickname and achieving good results was probably just a coincidence, that maybe she had simply become more confident. The increased confidence was therefore responsible for the higher success ratio in obtaining interviews.

Katherine responded, "I'm not so sure. There must be some other reasons that Kat gets more interviews than Katherine."

Case Questions

1. How can information about overcoming communication barriers help explain why "Kat" gets more interviews than "Katherine"?

2. How might the sex of the receiver be related to the different success ratios of "Kat" and "Katherine" in obtaining interviews?

3. Based on Kat's good results, what recommendations can you offer the research firm to help them increase the percentage of people who agree to be interviewed?

process that can be divided into six components: sender or source, message, channel (or medium), receiver, feedback, and environment. Noise, or interference, can disrupt communication within any component.

Nonverbal communication plays an important part in sending and receiving messages and is especially important for imparting the emotional aspects of a message. The modes of nonverbal communication include the environment in which the message is sent, interpersonal distance, posture, gestures, facial expressions, voice quality, and personal appearance.

Nonverbal communication can be improved through such means as obtaining feedback, learning to relax, using gestures more discriminately, role playing, and mirroring. The latter refers to subtly imitating someone.

Methods of overcoming communication barriers include the following: (1) understand the receiver, (2) discuss differences in paradigms, (3) minimize defensive communication, (4) use multiple channels, (5) use verbal and nonverbal feedback, (6) display a positive attitude, (7) use persuasive communication, (8) engage in active listening, (9) engage in complementary transactions with people, (10) recognize gender differences in communication styles, and (11) engage in metacommunications (communicate about your communications).

QUESTIONS FOR DISCUSSION AND REVIEW

1. What are the reasons so many workers need improvement in communication skills?

2. How can knowing the steps in the communication process help a person become a more effective communicator?

Skill-Building Exercise 3-4

ENHANCING YOUR NONVERBAL COMMUNICATION E-MAIL SKILLS

Hi readers, The purpose of this assignment is to search the Internet for emoticoms [such as the ;-) for a wink and the :-) for a smile] and acronymns to incorporate nonverbal signals into your e-mail messages. Find a combination of 10 emoticoms and acronymns using the Internet. Compare your list with that of a few classmates, and look for a rare one. •IM [H]O it would be good to do it •ASAP. <G>

P.S. Your Internet search should help you decode the last two acronymns, and the last emoticom.

3. How can people use their automobiles to send nonverbal messages?

4. What type of voice quality do you think would be effective in most work situations?

5. What, if any, ethical problems are involved with mirroring?

6. Suppose your manager does not listen to your suggestions for job improvements. Explain this problem as a paradigm clash.

7. Should a person use power words when he or she is not in a powerful job? Explain.

8. Why is summarization such a powerful communication technique?

9. What are the implications of gender differences in communication for conducting meetings?

10. Describe an example from your work experience or personal life in which it would have been a good idea to metacomunicate.

Suggested Answers to Skill-Building Exercise 3-3

Situation A: The first response will most likely result in a crossed transaction (–) because the second person is revengeful and insulting. The second response will most likely result in a complementary transaction (+) because the second person submits to the parental approach of the first person in a submissive, obedient-child manner.

Situation B: The first response will most likely result in a complementary transaction (+) because the childlike behavior of the first person is being controlled in a parental way. The second response will probably result in a crossed transaction (–) because the first person is insulted by the second.

Chapter 4

Developing Teamwork Skills

Learning Objectives

After reading and studying this chapter and doing the exercises you should be able to

➤ Identify several types of teams in organizations.

➤ Understand the strengths and weaknesses of teams.

➤ Identify various team member roles.

➤ Be ready to apply people-related tactics for effective team play.

➤ Be ready to apply task-related tactics for effective team play.

Wilma Mankiller is principal chief of the Cherokee, the first woman to fill the top position in a major American tribe. While Mankiller has been chief, the tribe has blossomed economically. The Cherokee boast an annual operating budget of $86 million and 1,200 employees. New health centers have been established, along with children's programs and horticultural, motel, electronics, and livestock businesses. Instead of attributing these successes to her individual leadership, Mankiller contends that "the growth is the result of teamwork. Here we call it management by workgroup."[1]

The words of Wilma Mankiller underscore a major shift in the way in which work is accomplished in organizations. Many firms rely more on teamwork than on individuals acting alone to accomplish work. To be successful in the modern organization, it is therefore necessary to be an effective team player. You have to work smoothly with other members of the team to accomplish your goals.

The challenges a team member faces come to light when the true nature of a team is recognized. Two experts on the subject define a **team** as "a small number of people with complementary skills who are committed to a common purpose, set of performance goals, and approach for which they hold themselves mutually accountable."[2] In other words, members of a team work together smoothly, and all pull in the same direction. A workplace team should be more like an effective athletic team than a group of individuals out for individual glory.

This chapter gives you the information, insights, and preliminary practice necessary to develop effective teamwork skills. Self-Assessment Quiz 4-1 will help you assess your current mental readiness to be a contributing team member.

TYPES OF TEAMS

All teams in the workplace have the common element of people working together cooperatively and members possessing a mix of skills. Nevertheless, many specific types of work teams can be identified. Successful people will usually have an opportunity to be a member of several different types of teams.

Three representative work teams are self-managing work teams, cross-functional teams, and virtual teams. Projects, task forces, and committees are similar in design to cross-functional teams, so they do not receive separate mention here. No matter what label the team carries, its broad purpose is contribute to a *collaborative workplace* in which people help each other achieve constructive goals. The idea is for workers to collaborate (a high level of cooperation) rather than compete with or prevent others from getting their work done.

As teams have become more common in the workplace, much effort has been directed toward specifying the skills and knowledge a person needs to function effectively on a team, particularly a self-managing work team. Self-Assessment Quiz 4-2 presents a representative listing of team skills as perceived by employers.

Self-Assessment Quiz 4-1

TEAM PLAYER ATTITUDES

Directions: Describe how well you agree with each of the following statements, using the following scale: Disagree strongly (DS); Disagree (D); Neutral (N); Agree (A); Agree strongly (AS).

	DS	D	N	A	AS
1. I am at my best when working alone.	5	(4)	3	2	1
2. I have belonged to clubs and teams ever since I was a child.	1	2	3	(4)	5
3. It takes far too long to get work accomplished with a group.	5	4	(3)	2	1
4. I like the friendship of working in a group.	1	2	3	(4)	5
5. I would prefer to run a one-person business than to be a member of a large firm.	5	4	3	(2)	1
6. It's difficult to trust others in the group on key assignments.	5	(4)	3	2	1
7. Encouraging others comes to me naturally.	1	2	3	(4)	5
8. I like the give-and-take of ideas that is possible in a group.	1	2	3	(4)	5
9. It is fun for me to share responsibility with other group members.	1	2	3	(4)	5
10. Much more can be accomplished by a team than by the same number of people working alone.	1	2	3	(4)	5

Total Score _____

Scoring and Interpretation: Add the numbers you circled to obtain your total score.

41–50 You have strong positive attitudes toward being a team member and working cooperatively with other members.

(30–40) You have moderately favorable attitudes toward being a team member and working cooperatively with other members.

10–29 You much prefer working by yourself to being a team member. To work effectively in a company that emphasizes teamwork, you may need to develop more positive attitudes toward working jointly with others.

SELF-MANAGING WORK TEAMS

The best-known work team is a group of workers who take over much of the responsibility for managing their own work. The same type of team is referred to as a self-managing work team, a production work team, a work team, or a team. A **self-managing work team** is a small group of employees responsible for managing and performing technical tasks to deliver a product or service to an external or internal customer.[3] According to one survey, about 80 of the largest companies have half of their employees assigned to work teams.[4] Work teams in a wide variety of activities including producing motorcycles, telephone directories, or a major component for a large computer.

TEAM SKILLS

A variety of skills are required to be an effective member of various types of teams. Several different business firms use the skill inventory here to help guide team members toward the competencies they need to become high-performing team members. Review each team skill listed and rate your skill level for each one using the following classification:

S = strong (capable and comfortable with effectively implementing the skill)

M = moderate (demonstrated skill in the past)

B = basic (minimum ability in this area)

N = not applicable (not relevant to the type of work I do)

Communication skills	*Skill level (S, M, B, or N)*
Speak effectively	_____
Foster open communications	_____
Listen to others	_____
Deliver presentations	_____
Prepare written communication	_____

Self-management skills	
Act with integrity	_____
Demonstrate adaptability	_____
Engage in personal development	_____
Strive for results	_____
Display a commitment to work	_____

Thought process skills	
Innovate solutions to problems	_____
Use sound judgment	_____
Analyze issues	_____
Think "outside the box"	_____

Organizational skills	
Know the business	_____
Use technical/functional expertise	_____
Use financial/quantitative data	_____

Strategic (broad business perspective) skills	
Recognize "big picture" impact	_____
Promote corporate citizenship	_____
Focus on customer needs	_____
Commit to quality	_____
Manage profitability	_____

Interpretation: We do not have a scoring key for this questionnaire. Its purpose is to raise your awareness of the types of skills that are required to be a successful team member in business.

Members of a self-managing work team typically work together on an ongoing, day-by-day basis, thus differentiating it from a task force or a committee. The work team is often given total responsibility for or "ownership" of an entire product or service, such as producing a telephone directory. At other times, the team is given responsibility for a major chunk of a job, such as building an airplane engine (but not the entire airplane).

CROSS-FUNCTIONAL TEAMS

It is common practice for teams to be composed of workers from different specialties. A **cross-functional team** is a work group composed of workers from different specialties, and about the same organizational level, who come together to accomplish a task. The purpose of the cross-functional team is to get workers from different specialties to blend their talents toward accomplishing a task that requires such a mix. A typical application of a cross-functional team would be to develop a new product such as a Net TV. Among the specialties needed on such a team would be computer science, engineering, manufacturing, industrial design, marketing, and finance. (The finance person would help guide the team toward producing a Net TV that could be sold at a profit.) When members from different specialties work together, they can take into account each other's perspectives when making their contribution. For example, if the manufacturing representative knows that a Net TV must sell for about one-half the price of a personal computer, then he or she will have to build the device inexpensively. A major advantage of cross-functional teams for product development is that they enhance communication across groups, thereby saving time.

In addition to product development, cross-functional teams are used for such purposes as improving quality, reducing costs, and running a company (in the form of a top management team).

To perform well on a cross-functional team a person would have to think in terms of the good of the larger organization, rather than in terms of his or her own specialty. For example, a manufacturing technician might say, "If I proposed using expensive components for the Net TV, would the product cost too much for its intended market?"

VIRTUAL TEAMS

Some teams conduct most of their work by sending electronic messages to each other rather than conducting face-to-face meetings. A **virtual team** is a small group of people who conduct almost all of their collaborative work by electronic communication rather than face-to-face meetings. In the language of information technology, they engage in "cybercollaboration" by conducting "cybermeetings." E-mail is the usual medium for sharing information and conducting meetings. *Groupware* is another widely used approach to conducting a cybermeeting. Using groupware, several people can edit a document at the same time, or in sequence. Desktop videoconferencing is another technological advance that facilitates the virtual team.[5] Electronic brainstorming, as described in Chapter 5, is well suited for a virtual team.

Most high-tech companies make some use of virtual teams and cybermeetings. Strategic alliances in which geographically dispersed companies work with each other are a natural for virtual teams. It is less expensive for the field technician in Iceland to hold a cybermeeting with her counterparts in South Africa, Mexico, and California than it is to bring them all together in one physical location. IBM makes some use of virtual teams in selling information-technology systems, partially because so many IBM field personnel work from their homes and vehicles.

Despite the efficiency of virtual teams, there are times when face-to-face interaction is necessary to deal with complex and emotional issues. Negotiating a new contract between management and a labor union, for example, is not well suited to a cybermeeting.

THE ADVANTAGES AND DISADVANTAGES OF TEAMS AND TEAMWORK

Groups have always been the building blocks of organizations. Yet groups and teams have recently grown in importance as the basic unit for organizing work. In an attempt to cope with numerous changes in the outside world, many organizations have granted teams increased independence and flexibility. Furthermore, teams are often required to work more closely with customers and suppliers.

The increased acceptance of teams suggests that group work offers many advantages. Nevertheless, it is useful to specify several of these advantages and also examine the potential problems of groups. Being aware of these potential pitfalls can often help a person avoid them. These same advantages and disadvantages also apply to group decision making, to be described in Chapter 5.

ADVANTAGES OF GROUP WORK AND TEAMWORK

Group work and group decision making offer several advantages over individual effort. If several knowledgeable people are brought into the decision-making process, a number of worthwhile possibilities may be uncovered. It is also possible to gain **synergy**, whereby the group's total output exceeds the sum of each individual's contribution. For example, it would be a rare person working alone who could build a racing car. Dozens of case histories have been collected about successes with work teams, as illustrated next.

> Teams at Monarch Marking Systems, a Dayton, Ohio, manufacturer of labeling, identification and tracking equipment, trimmed the square footage of an assembly area by 70 percent, reduced past-due shipments 90 percent and doubled productivity. In one year alone, they identified 1,400 areas of waste in the organization.[6]

Group decision making is also helpful in gaining acceptance and commitment. The argument is that people who contribute to making a decision will feel some ownership about implementing the decision. Team members often evaluate each other's thinking, so the team is likely to avoid major errors. An

advertising specialist was developing an advertising campaign to attract seniors to live in a retirement community. The proposed ads had photographs of senior citizens engaged in playing shuffleboard, visiting the pharmacy, and sleeping in a hammock. Another team member on the project pointed out that many seniors perceive themselves to be energetic and youthful. Ads emphasizing advanced age might therefore backfire. A successful advertising campaign was then developed that featured seniors in more youthful activities such as jogging and dancing.

Working in teams and groups also enhances the job satisfaction of members. Being a member of a work group makes it possible to satisfy more needs than working alone. Among these needs are affiliation, security, self-esteem, and self-fulfillment. (See Chapter 9 for details about psychological needs.)

DISADVANTAGES OF GROUP WORK AND TEAMWORK

Group activity has some potential disadvantages for both individuals and the organization. Teams and other groups often waste time because they talk too much and act too little. Committees appear to suffer from more inaction than teams. Abigail Johnson, a top executive at Fidelity Corp., the financial services giant, says that committees are not effective decision makers. "They have tended to be slow and overly risk averse. Even worse, I believe, they can drain an organization of talent, because the group can only be as good as the average."[7]

A major problem is that members face pressures to conform to group standards of performance and conduct, as just implied. Some teams might shun a person who is much more productive than his or her coworkers. Shirking of individual responsibility is another problem frequently noted in groups. Unless work is assigned carefully to each team member, an undermotivated person can often squeeze by without contributing his or her fair share to a group effort.

Social loafing is the psychological term for shirking individual responsibility in a group setting. The social loafer risks being ostracized (shunned) by the group but may be willing to pay the price rather than work hard. Loafing of this type is sometimes found in groups such as committees and project teams. Have you ever encountered a social loafer on a group project at school?

At their worst, teams and other groups foster conflict on the job. People within the work group often bicker about such matters as doing a fair share of the undesirable tasks within the department. Cohesive work groups can also become xenophobic (fearful of outsiders). As a consequence, they may grow to dislike other groups and enter into conflict with them. A customer service group might put considerable effort into showing up a sales group because the latter makes promises to customers that the customer service group cannot keep. For example, a sales representative might promise that a customer can get a loaner if his or her equipment needs repair, although customer service has no such policy.

A well-publicized disadvantage of group decision making is **groupthink**, a deterioration of mental efficiency, reality testing, and moral judgment in the interest of group solidarity. Simply put, groupthink is an extreme form of consensus. The group atmosphere values getting along more than getting things

➤ The team has clear-cut goals linked to organizational goals so that group members feel connected to the entire organization.
➤ Members learn to think for themselves rather than expecting a supervisor to solve all the difficult problems.
➤ Members learn to think "outside of the box" (be creative).
➤ Members receive extensive training in technical knowledge, problem-solving skills, and interpersonal skills.
➤ Members inspect their own work for quality.
➤ Members receive part of their pay related to team or group incentives rather than strictly based on individual performance.
➤ Group size is generally about 6 people, rather than 10 or more.
➤ Team members have good intelligence and personality factors, such as conscientiousness and pride, that contribute to good performance.
➤ There is honest and open communication among group members and with other groups in the organization.
➤ Members have the philosophy of working as a team—25 brains, not just 50 hands.

Figure 4-1 Key Characteristics of Effective Teams and Work Groups

Source: Ben Nagler, "Recasting Employees into Teams," *Workforce,* January 1998, p. 104; Carla Johnson, "Teams at Work," *HR Magazine,* May 1999, pp. 30–36; Dale E. Yeatts and Cloyd Hyten, *High-Performing Self-Managed Work Teams: A Comparison of Theory and Practice* (Thousand Oaks, CA: Sage, 1998).

done. The group thinks as a unit, believes it is impervious to outside criticism, and begins to have illusions about its own invincibility. As a consequence, the group loses its powers of critical analysis.[8]

Groupthink took place at one of the failed savings and loan associations. The senior management group voted themselves extraordinary salaries and bought art collections that they frequently borrowed for personal use. In addition, they purchased corporate jets to fly around the country looking for investments and to use for vacations for themselves and their families. Not one of the savings and loan association executives expressed a dissenting opinion.

Two conditions are important for overcoming the potential disadvantages of teams and groups. First, the members must strive to act like a team,[9] following some of the suggestions given in the pages ahead. Second, the task given to the group should require collective effort instead of being a task that could better be performed by individuals. For example, an international business specialist would probably learn to conjugate verbs in a foreign language better by working alone than in a team. What is your opinion on this issue?

Figure 4-1 presents more information about key factors associated with effective work teams and groups. The more of these factors present, the more likely it is that a given team or groups will be productive.

TEAM MEMBER ROLES

A major challenge in learning to become an effective team member is to choose the right roles to occupy. If you carry out positive roles, you will be per-

ceived as a contributor to team effort. If you neglect carrying out these roles, you will be perceived as a poor contributor. Self-Assessment Quiz 4-3 will help you evaluate your present inclinations toward occupying effective roles as a team member. In this section we describe a number of the most frequently observed positive roles played by team members.[10] The description will be followed by an activity in which the roles can be practiced.

KNOWLEDGE CONTRIBUTOR

A technically knowledgeable team member, the *knowledge contributor,* gravitates toward the role of providing the group with useful and valid information. (In this sense, *technical* refers to knowledge about the group task.) He or she is a facts-and-figures person who is intent upon helping the team with task accomplishment. The knowledge contributor believes it is important to share technical expertise with team members. He or she does not ignore the human element in a team setting but pays attention to it primarily to help get the task accomplished. Being a knowledge contributor is especially important for virtual teams, because much of the activity in such teams consists of sharing information. A financial specialist on a cross-functional team explains how the human factor can enter into working with facts and figures:

> As the financial expert on the team, I had to explain the reasoning behind a sales forecast I developed. To really understand this forecast, a person has to know basic calculus. Unfortunately, the person I was explaining the forecast to had zero knowledge of calculus. I had to calm him down enough so he could listen to me. I explained that very few people in customer service understood calculus. He then stopped being so defensive, and I was able to explain the value of my forecast.

PROCESS OBSERVER

Dealing with knowledge, technology, and methodology is indispensable for group achievement—the *hard side* of collective effort. Another key aspect of a team's work is the processes within the group. This *soft side* of teamwork includes the transactions that take place among and between members of the team. Among the many processes within a team are soothing each other's feelings, forming coalitions, communicating problems, and complimenting each other.

The *process observer* forces the group to look at how it is functioning with a statement such as: "Look, gang. We've been at it for two and one-half hours, and we have only taken care of one agenda item. Shouldn't we be doing better?" The process observer might point to excellent progress that the team has made.

COLLABORATOR

Another key role is the person who pitches in to do whatever is necessary to achieve team goals and is not constrained by his or her official statement of responsibilities. The *collaborator* keeps the team focused on its goal and fre-

TEAM PLAYER ROLES

Directions: For each of the following statements about team activity, check Mostly agree or Mostly disagree. If you have not experienced such a situation, imagine how you would act or think if placed in that situation. In responding to the statements, assume that you are taking the questionnaire with the intent of learning something about yourself.

	Mostly agree	Mostly disagree
1. It is rare that I ever miss a team meeting.	✓	
2. I regularly compliment team members when they do something exceptional.	✓	
3. Whenever I can, I avoid being the notetaker at a team meeting.	✓	
4. From time to time, other team members come to me for advice on technical matters.	✓	
5. I like to hide some information from other team members so I can be in control.		✓
6. I welcome new team members coming to me for advice and learning the ropes.	✓	
7. My priorities come first, which leaves me with very little time to help other team members.		✓
8. During a team meeting, it is not unusual for several other people at a time to look toward me for my opinion.		✓
9. If I think the team is moving in an unethical direction, I will say so explicitly.	✓	
10. Rarely will I criticize the progress of the team even if I think such criticism is deserved.	✓	
11. It is not unusual for me to summarize the progress in a team meeting, even if not asked.		✓
12. To conserve time, I attempt to minimize contact with my teammates outside of our meetings.		✓
13. I intensely dislike going along with a consensus decision if the decision runs contrary to my thoughts on the issue.	✓	
14. I rarely remind teammates of our mission statement as we go about our work.		✓
15. Once I have made up my mind on an issue facing the team, I am unlikely to be persuaded in another direction.		✓
16. I am willing to accept negative feedback from team members.	✓	.
17. Just to get a new member of the team involved, I will ask his or her opinion.	✓	

(Continued)

18. Even if the team has decided on a course of action, I am not hesitant to bring in new information that supports another position. ___✓___ _____

19. Quite often I talk negatively about one team member to another. ___✓___ ___✗___

20. My teammates are almost a family to me, because I am truly concerned about their welfare. ___✓___ _____

21. When it seems appropriate, I joke and kid with teammates. ___✓___ _____

22. My contribution to team tasks is as important to me as my individual work. ___✓___ _____

23. From time to time I have pointed out to the team how we can all improve in reaching our goals. _____ ___✓___

24. I will fight to the last when the team does not support my viewpoint and wants to move toward consensus. ___✗✗___ ___✓___

25. I will confront the team if I believe that the members are thinking too much alike. _____ ___✓___

Total Score ___15___ ___10___

Scoring and Interpretation: Give yourself one point (+1) for each statement you gave in agreement with the keyed answer. The keyed answer indicates carrying out a positive, as opposed to a negative, role.

Question number	Positive role answer		Question number	Positive role answer
1.	Mostly agree ✓		14.	Mostly disagree
2.	Mostly agree		15.	Mostly disagree
3.	Mostly disagree		16.	Mostly agree
4.	Mostly agree ✓		17.	Mostly agree
5.	Mostly disagree ✓		18.	Mostly agree
6.	Mostly agree ✓		19.	Mostly disagree
7.	Mostly disagree ✓		20.	Mostly agree ✓
8.	Mostly agree		21.	Mostly agree
9.	Mostly agree ✓		22.	Mostly agree ✓
10.	Mostly disagree		23.	Mostly agree
11.	Mostly agree		24.	Mostly disagree
12.	Mostly disagree ✓		25.	Mostly agree
13.	Mostly disagree			

20–25 You carry out a well above average number of positive team roles. Behavior of this type contributes substantially to being an effective team player. Study the information in this chapter to build upon your already laudable sensitivity to occupying various positive roles within the team.

10–19 You carry out an average number of positive team roles. Study carefully the roles described in this chapter to search for ways to carry out a greater number of positive roles.

0–9 You carry out a substantially above average number of negative team roles. If becoming an effective team player is important to you, you will have to assiduously search for ways to play positive team roles. Study the information in this chapter carefully.

quently reminds the group to do whatever is necessary to stay on track. A collaborator's typical behavior during a team meeting would be to indicate how much progress the team has made toward goal attainment. A representative comment would be, "We are halfway through our time budget, and we have achieved one-fourth of our goals. We are behind schedule, but catching up is doable."

The collaborator works for the good of the group and does not care who gets recognition as long as the job gets done. He or she often works quietly behind the scenes and does not look for individual recognition.

PEOPLE SUPPORTER

The *people supporter* on the team assumes some of the leader's responsibility for providing emotional support to teammates and resolving conflict. He or she serves as a model of active listening when others are presenting. The people supporter helps others relax by smiling, making humorous comments, and appearing relaxed. However, the people supporter is not the team clown who attempts to defuse the seriousness of a situation. In contrast, he or she is a model of etiquette and professionalism.

The people supporter reinforces the views of other team members with whom he or she agrees. Most team players find this to be a comfortable role. What distinguishes people supporters is their willingness to also support and encourage team members with whom they disagree. The people supporter believes that anybody who is serious about his or her position on an issue deserves encouragement. By receiving encouragement now, the person is more likely to contribute ideas in the future.

CHALLENGER

To prevent complacency and groupthink, a team needs one or more members who confront and challenge bad ideas. The *challenger* fills this role if he or she has effective enough interpersonal skills to fill the role successfully. Antagonistic, attack-style people who attempt the challenger role lose their credibility quickly. A challenger will criticize any decision or preliminary thinking of the team that is deficient in any way, including being ethically unsound. An accomplished challenger will even criticize the methods and decision-making process of a team.

Here is a transcript of a portion of a team meeting in which Ruth is the challenger. Carlos is the team leader. The team was formed within a service organization to develop suggestions for reducing costs throughout the organization.

Carlos: We've been gathering information for a month now. It's about time we heard some of the specific suggestions.

Jack: At the top of my list is cutting pension benefits. Our pension payments are higher than those required by law. Our medical benefits are way above average. If we cut back on pension benefits, no current employees would be adversely affected.

Melissa: I like your analysis, Jack. No sense risking laying off employees just to keep retirees happy.

Jordan: We should first make absolutely certain there are no legal complications here. Then we can sharpen our cost-cutting knives and dig right in.

Gunther: I'll support cutting pension benefits. It will probably reduce expenses more dramatically than the smaller ways to reduce expenses that I have uncovered.

Carlos: There seems to be consensus so far that we should look toward making recommendations about cutting pension benefits. Ruth, what do you think?

Ruth: I think it is much too early to reach consensus on such a sensitive issue. Cutting pension benefits would create panic in our retirees. Our older employees would also be screaming. We'll have an avalanche of negative publicity in the media.

Jordan: Hold on, Ruth. I said the team would first check out this idea with the legal department.

Ruth: Just because cutting pension benefits could squeeze by legally doesn't mean it's a good idea. We haven't studied enough of the negative ramifications of cutting pension benefits. Let's study this issue further before word leaks out that we're taking away the golden egg.

Carlos: Maybe Ruth has a point. Let's investigate this issue further before making a recommendation.

LISTENER

Listening to others is an important aspect of several team-player roles, including the people supporter. Nevertheless, listening contributes so substantially to team success that it comprises a separate role. If other people are not heard, the full contribution of team effort cannot be realized. Listening takes hard work and commitment, with the *listener* serving as a model for the rest of the group.

Some people neglect slipping into the listener role when appropriate and required because they are so preoccupied with their own points of view and agendas. Think back to recent meetings you have attended. Do you remember how some people start their counterargument before the speaker has finished his or her sentence? Another reason some team members do not listen is that they become closed-minded and defensive when their views are challenged.

The team leader must shift frequently into the listener role, as did Carlos when he listened carefully to Ruth's concerns about cutting the pension benefits. Other members of the team also must seize the opportunity to occupy the role of listener—one who listens intently to elicit information, understand the opinion or data being presented, and increase the satisfaction of another member.

As a result of being a listener, a team member or team leader is able to summarize discussion and progress for the team. So many details and varied points

arise during team meetings that confusion may result. Members may ask themselves *"Where are we?"* or *"What's going on here?"* At other times, several group members may forget the purpose of the meeting.

MEDIATOR

Despite the good intentions of team effort, disputes within the group may become so intense or prolonged that two people no longer listen or respond to each other. The two antagonists develop such polarized viewpoints that they are unwilling to move toward each other's point of view. In addition, they have moved beyond the point that conciliation is effective. Instead, it becomes necessary for the team leader or a team member to mediate the dispute. The *mediator* attempts to resolve the conflict following (approximately) these steps:

1. Ask permission to interpret each position.

2. Interpret each side, and then ask both parties whether the interpretation is accurate.

3. Give each side the opportunity to edit or correct the statement of his or her position.

The mediator's intervention helps clarify for each side what the other side has said. In the heat of the dispute, each side may not have listened carefully to the other side. After the three-point intervention is completed, other members of the team can discuss the differences in viewpoints. Mediation makes a contribution because it can move a group away from being stuck and on to more productive activity.

GATEKEEPER

A recurring problem in group effort is that some members may fail to contribute because most of the time has been taken up by dominant team members. Even when the viewpoints of the timid team members have been expressed, they may not be remembered because one or two other members contribute so frequently to discussion. When the opportunity gate is closed to several members, the *gatekeeper* in the group intentionally opens the gate. The gatekeeper requests that a specific team member be allowed to contribute, or that his or her past contribution be recognized, with comments such as the following:

➤ "Alice has been trying for 15 minutes to make a point. We've all been talking so much that she hasn't found room to talk. I think it's Alice's turn."

➤ "Tom, you've been using much more than your share of our discussion time. Since this is a team effort, we need to hear from other people on the team also."

The many roles just presented overlap somewhat. For example, the process observer might engage in gatekeeper activities. Do not be concerned about the overlap. Instead, pick and choose from the many roles as the situation dictates—whether or not overlap exists. Skill-Building Exercise 4-1 gives you an opportunity to observe these roles in action.

The behavior associated with the roles just described is more important than remembering the labels. For example, remembering to help others resolve conflict in meetings is more important than remembering the specific label *mediator role.*

GUIDELINES FOR THE INTERPERSONAL ASPECTS OF TEAM PLAY

The purpose of this and the following section is to help you enhance your effectiveness as a team player by describing the skills, actions, and attitudes required to be an effective team player. You can regard these *behaviors* (the collective term for skills, actions, and attitudes) as goals for personal improvement. Identify the actions and attitudes for which you need the most improvement, and proceed accordingly with self-development. Apply the model for skill-development presented in Chapter 1.

One convenient method for classifying team activities in pursuit of goals is to categorize them as people-related or task-related. Remember, however, that the categorization of people- versus task-related activities is not entirely accurate. For example, if you are challenging your teammates with a difficult goal, are you focusing more on the people (offering them a motivational challenge) or the task (achieving the goal)? We begin first with people-related actions and attitudes, followed in the next section by task-related actions and attitudes.

TRUSTING TEAM MEMBERS

ANALOGO, SEMEJANTE

The cornerstone attitude of an outstanding team player is to trust team members, including the leader. Working on a team is akin to a small-business partnership. If you do not believe that the other team members have your best interests at heart, it will be difficult for you to share opinions and ideas. You will fear that others will make negative statements behind your back.

Trusting team members also includes believing that their ideas are technically sound and rational until proven otherwise. Another manifestation of trust is taking risks with others. You can take a risk by trying out one of their unproved ideas. You can also take a risk by submitting an unproved idea and not worrying about being ridiculed. Skill-Building Exercise 4-2 is a widely used trust-building exercise.

DISPLAYING A HIGH LEVEL OF COOPERATION AND COLLABORATION

Cooperation and collaboration are synonymous with teamwork. If you display a willingness to help others by working cooperatively with them, you will be

TEAM MEMBER ROLES

A team of approximately six people is formed to conduct a 20-minute meeting on a significant topic of their choosing. Possibilities include (a) a management team deciding on whether to lay off one-third of the workforce in order to increase profits, (b) a group of fans who have volunteered to find a new team mascot name to replace "Redskins," and (c) a community group attempting to launch an initiative to help battered adults and children.

While the team members are conducting their heated discussion, other class members make notes on which team members carry out which roles. Watching for the eight different roles can be divided among class members. For example, the people in the first row might look for examples of knowledge contributor. Use the role worksheet that follows to help make your observations. Summarize the comment that is indicative of the role. An example would be noting in the challenger category: "Linda said naming the team the 'Washington Rainbows' seems like too much of an attempt to be politically correct."

Knowledge contributor: _____

Process observer: _____

Collaborator: _____

People supporter: _____

Challenger: _____

Listener: _____

Mediator: _____

Gatekeeper: _____

Skill-Building Exercise 4-2

THE TRUST FALL

A standard part of outdoor training for team building and leadership is for people to experience being dependent upon other team members for their physical safety. One such trust builder is for a person to fall backward into the arms of teammates. If the person is not caught, he or she will sustain serious physical injury. (*Caution:* Excuse yourself from this exercise if you are currently injured, are suffering from circulatory or eye disease, or are pregnant.)

The class organizes into groups of six. Each group member takes a turn standing on a chair (a blindfold is optional). At the appropriate signal from a team member, the person falls backward into the arms of teammates. The fall can take place outdoors on a lawn, on the beach, or in the snow, or inside the classroom. After each person has taken a turn, discuss among yourselves the impact of this exercise on the development of trust. If time allows, conduct a class discussion of the advantages and disadvantages of the trust fall.

regarded as a team player. If you do not cooperate with other team members, the team structure breaks down. Collaboration at a team level refers to working jointly with others to solve mutual problems. Although working with another person on a given problem may take longer than working through a problem yourself, the long-term payoff is important. You have established a climate favorable to working on joint problems where collective action is necessary.

Achieving a cooperative team spirit is often a question of making the first move. Instead of grumbling about poor teamwork, take the initiative and launch a cooperative spirit in your group. Target the most individualistic, least cooperative member of the group. Ask the person for his or her input on an idea you are formulating. Thank the person, then state that you would be privileged to return the favor.

RECOGNIZING THE INTERESTS AND ACHIEVEMENTS OF OTHERS

A fundamental tactic for establishing yourself as a solid team player is to actively recognize the interests and achievements of others. Let others know you care about their interests. After you make a suggestion during a team meeting, ask: "Would my suggestion create any problems for anybody else?" or "How do my ideas fit into what you have planned?"

Recognizing the achievements of others is more straightforward than recognizing interests. Be prepared to compliment any tangible achievement. Give realistic compliments by making the compliment commensurate with the achievement. To do otherwise is to compromise your sincerity. For example, do

not call someone a genius just because he or she showed you how to compute an exchange rate from one currency to another. Instead, you might say, "Thank you. I am very impressed by your knowledge of exchange rates."

GIVING HELPFUL CRITICISM

The outstanding team player offers constructive criticism when needed, but does so diplomatically. To do otherwise is to let down the team. A high-performance team demands sincere and tactful criticism among members. No matter how diplomatic you are, keep your ratio of criticism to praise small. Keep two time-tested principles in mind. First, attempt to criticize the person's work, not the person. It is better to say, "The conclusion is missing from your analysis" than "You left out the conclusion." (The latter statement hurts because it sounds like your teammate did something wrong.)

Another key guideline for criticism is to ask a question rather than to make a declarative statement. By answering a question, the person being criticized is involved in improving his or her work. In the example at hand, it would be effective to ask, "Do you think your report would have a greater impact if it contained a conclusion?" In this way, the person being criticized contributes a judgment about the conclusion. The person has a chance to say, "Yes, I will prepare a conclusion."

SHARING THE GLORY

An effective team player shares praise and other rewards for accomplishment even if he or she is the most deserving. Shared praise is usually merited to some extent because teammates have probably made at least some contribution to the achievement that received praise. For example, if a team member comes up with a powerful suggestion for cutting costs, it is likely that somebody else in the group sparked his or her thinking. Effective examples of sharing glory are easy to find. Think back to watching athletes and other entertainers who win a title or an award. Many of them are gracious enough to share the glory. Shortly after he retired, hockey legend Wayne Gretzky told a television reporter, "I never would have accomplished what I did if I hadn't played with such a great group of guys."

TAKING CARE NOT TO RAIN ON ANOTHER PERSON'S PARADE

As teamwork specialist Pamela Lovel observes, we all have achievements and accomplishments that are sources of pride. Belittling the achievements of others for no legitimate reason brings about tension and anger. Suppress your feelings of petty jealousy.[11] An example would be saying to someone who is proudly describing an accomplishment, "Don't take too much credit. It looks to me like you were at the right place at the right time." If you support teammates by acknowledging their accomplishments, you are more likely to receive their support when needed.

GUIDELINES FOR THE TASK ASPECTS OF TEAM PLAY

The task aspects of team play also make a key contribution to becoming an effective team player. Here we describe five major task-related tactics. As mentioned earlier, a task aspect usually has interpersonal consequences.

TECHNICAL EXPERTISE (OR KNOWLEDGE OF THE TASK)

Most people are selected for a work team primarily because of their technical expertise. *Technical* refers to the intimate details of any task, not just tasks in engineering, physical science, and information technology. The sales promotion specialist on a product development team has technical expertise about sales promotion, whether or not sales promotion requires knowledge of engineering or computers.

As team consultant Glenn Parker observes, to use your technical expertise to outstanding advantage you must have the willingness to share that expertise.[12] Some experts perceive their esoteric knowledge as a source of power. As a consequence, they are hesitant to let others share their knowledge for fear of relinquishing power. It is also necessary for the technical expert to be able to communicate with team members in other disciplines who lack the same technical background. The technical person who cannot explain the potential value of his or her contribution may not receive much attention.

ASSUMING RESPONSIBILITY FOR PROBLEMS

The outstanding team player assumes responsibilities for problems. If a problem is not yet assigned to anybody, he or she says, "I'll do it." One team member might note that true progress on the team's effort is blocked until the team benchmarks (compares itself) with other successful teams. The effective team player might say, "You are right, we need to benchmark. If it's okay with everybody else, I'll get started on the benchmarking project tomorrow. It will be my responsibility." Taking responsibility must be combined with dependability. The person who takes responsibility for a task must produce, time after time.

SEEING THE BIG PICTURE

Effective team players need to think conceptually, or see the big picture. A trap in team effort is that discussion can get bogged down in small details and the team might lose sight of what it is trying to accomplish. The team player (including the team leader) who can help the group focus on its broader purpose plays a vital role. The following case history illustrates what it means to see the big picture.

A sales process improvement team was asked to make it easier for customers to purchase office equipment when they visited the company's retail center. Under the existing process, five different people had to handle the sales transaction. The customer was often kept waiting for up to an hour. During its second meeting, the team vented its hostility toward the

warehouse specialists. As the conversation became more heated, several team members discussed documenting all the problems created by the warehouse personnel and then reporting them to the vice president of marketing. As emotions intensified, several team members ridiculed the warehouse workers.

Beth, the store manager and one of the team members, helped the group step back and see the big picture. She challenged the group in these words: "Hold on. Why are we here? Is our purpose to improve the sales process or to attack the very people who keep items for sale in stock?" The team accepted the suggestion and praised Beth for her contribution. The team then refocused its effort on reducing the paperwork required to complete a sales transaction.

BELIEVING IN CONSENSUS

A major task-related attitude for outstanding team play is to believe that consensus has merit. **Consensus** is general acceptance of a decision by the group. Every member may not be thrilled about the decision, yet they are not opposed and are willing to support the decision. Believing that consensus is valuable enables you to participate fully in team decisions without thinking that you have sacrificed your beliefs or the right to think independently. To believe in consensus is to believe that the democratic process has relevance for organizations and that ideal solutions are not always possible.

HELPING TEAM MEMBERS DO THEIR JOBS BETTER

Your stature as a team player will increase if you take the initiative to help coworkers make needed work improvements. Helping other team members with their work assignments is a high-level form of cooperation. Make the suggestions in a constructive spirit rather than displaying an air of superiority. Identify a problem that a coworker is having, and then suggest alternatives he or she might be interested in exploring. Avoid saying to team members that they "should" do something, because many people become defensive when told what they should do. The term *should* is usually perceived as a moral judgment given to one person by another, such as being told that you should save money, should learn a second language, or should improve your math skills.

Skill-Building Exercise 4-3 will help you integrate the many suggestions presented here for developing teamwork skills.

SUMMARY

To be successful in the modern organization it is necessary to be an effective team player. Team members have complementary skills and are committed to a common purpose. All teams have some elements in common, but three key types of teams are self-managing work teams, cross-functional teams, and virtu-

Consensus: Acuerdo General — Opinión General

Skill-Building Exercise 4-3

HABITAT FOR THE HOMELESS

Organize the class into teams of about six people. Each team takes on the assignment of formulating plans for building temporary shelters for the homeless. The task will take about one hour and can be done inside or outside of class. The dwellings you plan to build, for example, might be two-room cottages with electricity and indoor plumbing.

During the time allotted to the task, formulate plans for going ahead with Habitat for the Homeless. Consider dividing up work by assigning certain roles to each team member. Sketch out tentative answers to the following questions:

1. How will you obtain funding for your venture?
2. Which homeless people will you help?
3. Where will your shelters be located?
4. Who will do the actual construction?

After your plan is completed, evaluate the quality of the teamwork that took place within the group. Specify which teamwork skills were evident and which ones did not surface. Search the chapter for techniques you might use to improve teamwork.

al teams. (A virtual team does most of its work electronically instead of in face-to-face meetings.)

Groups and teams offer such advantages as synergy, avoiding major errors, and increased acceptance of and commitment to decisions. Working in groups can also enhance job satisfaction. Groups and teams also have disadvantages, such as more talk than action, conformity in thinking and action, social loafing, and the creation of conflict. A serious potential problem is groupthink, whereby bad decisions are made as a by-product of strong consensus. Key characteristics of effective work groups are outlined in Figure 4-1.

An important part of being an effective team player is to choose effective roles. The roles studied here are knowledge contributor, process observer, collaborator, people supporter, challenger, listener, mediator, and gatekeeper.

Guidelines for effectively contributing to the interpersonal aspects of team play include (a) trusting team members, (b) displaying a high level of cooperation and collaboration, (c) recognizing the interests and achievements of others, (d) giving helpful criticism, (e) sharing the glory, and (f) taking care not to rain on another person's parade.

Guidelines for effectively contributing to the task aspects of team play include (a) providing technical expertise, (b) assuming responsibility for problems, (c) seeing the big picture, (d) believing in consensus, and (e) helping team members do their jobs better.

QUESTIONS FOR DISCUSSION AND REVIEW

1. Part of being a good team player is helping other members. How can members of a workplace team help each other?

2. How do team members know when they have achieved synergy?

3. What should the other team members do when they uncover a social loafer?

4. What is the potential downside of heavily emphasizing the knowledge contributor role?

5. Explain the difference between the hard side and soft side of contributing to team effort.

6. How can the challenger role backfire for a person?

7. Why is it important for the team leader to frequently occupy the listener role?

8. How effective do you think the "trust fall" really is in building trust among team members?

9. The "little picture" in studying this chapter is learning details about teamwork skills. What is the "big picture"?

10. How can a person achieve individual recognition yet still be a team player?

THE UNBALANCED TEAM

Fidelity Protection Systems is one of the largest home and small-business security system distributors in its city, with annual sales of $18 million. Two years ago, Jim Maxwell, the vice president of marketing and sales, reorganized the sales force. Previously the sales force consisted of inside sales representatives (who took care of phone-in orders) and outside sales representatives (who called on accounts). The reorganization divided the outside sales force into two groups: direct sales and major accounts. The direct-sales representatives were made responsible for small commercial customers and individual homeowners. As before, they would service existing customers and prospect for new accounts. Servicing existing customers usually involves adding fire protection to burglary protection and upgrading the burglary systems.

Three of the people who were direct-sales representatives were promoted to major account executives. The account executives would service Fidelity's largest accounts, including prospecting for new business within those accounts. An example would be expanding the security system to other stores of a retailer. To promote teamwork and cooperation, Maxwell assigned group sales quotas to the account representatives. Collectively, their goal was to bring in 21 new large accounts per month.

Given that the sales quota was a group quota, the account representatives were supposed to work together on strategy for acquiring new accounts. If a particular account executive did not have the expertise to handle his or her customer's problems, another account executive was supposed to offer help. Brian Jones, for example, was the resident expert on the unique security problems of warehouses. If invited, Brian would join one of the two other account executives to call on a customer who owned a warehouse.

After the new sales organization had been in place 19 months, Karen Klein, an account executive, was having lunch with Larry Starks, the manufacturing director at Fidelity. "I've about had it," said Karen, "I'm tired of single-handedly carrying the team."

"What do you mean you are single-handedly carrying the team?" asked Larry.

"You're a trusted friend, Larry. So let me lay out the facts. Each month the group is supposed to bring in 21 new sales. If we don't average those 21 sales per month, we don't get our semi-annual bonus. That represents about 25 percent of my income. So a big chunk of my money comes from group effort.

"My average number of new accounts brought in for the last 12 months has been 11. And we are averaging about 18 new sales per month. This translates into the other account execs averaging about 7 sales among them. I'm carrying the group, but overall sales are still below quota. This means I didn't get my bonus last month.

"The other account execs are friendly and helpful in writing up proposals. But they just don't bring in their share of accounts."

Larry asked, "What does your boss say about this?"

"I've had several conversations with him about the problem. He tells me to be patient and to remember that the development of a fully balanced team requires time. He also tells me that I should develop a stronger team spirit. My problem is that I can't pay my bills with team spirit."

Case Questions

1. What does this case illustrate about teamwork?

2. What role or roles is Karen Klein occupying in the group?

3. What teamwork behaviors is Karen demonstrating?

4. What teamwork behaviors is Karen not demonstrating?

5. To what extent are Karen's complaints justifiable?

Chapter 5

Group Problem Solving and Decision Making

Learning Objectives

After reading and studying this chapter and doing the exercises you should be able to

➤ Understand the difference between rational and political decision making.

➤ Use the general approach to problem-solving groups.

➤ Make effective use of brainstorming.

➤ Recognize the potential contribution of electronic brainstorming.

➤ Make effective use of the nominal group technique.

➤ Understand how to increase the efficiency of group problem solving through e-mail and groupware.

The vice president of human resources at a consumer products company announced to the human resources staff that they would be receiving an average raise of 5 percent for the year. "Sounds great," said Melissa Olsten, the director of training. "But how is management deciding who gets how much? I take it we are not all going to receive the same 5 percent raise."

With an excited expression, the vice president replied, "You people are an empowered group of professionals. You will decide how to divide up the pool of money available for raises." Surprised but delighted with the answer to her question, Melissa took the initiative to ask the group to set aside time for a three-hour meeting. The goal of the problem-solving session would be to decide how to divide up the money allocated for the raises. Several of the group members were apprehensive, but they realized that here was a chance to engage in meaningful group decision making.

The case example just presented illustrates an increasingly important aspect of interpersonal relations in organizations: Many key problems are solved by groups. Part of having high-level interpersonal skills is the ability to work closely with others in solving problems and making decisions. This chapter will enhance your group problem-solving and decision-making skills. You will receive guidelines for applying several major group problem-solving methods. As a starting point in studying these techniques, first think through your present level of receptiveness toward group problem solving by doing Self-Assessment Quiz 5-1.

RATIONAL VERSUS POLITICAL DECISION MAKING IN GROUPS

Group decision making is the process of reaching a judgment based on feedback from more than one individual.[1] Most people involved in group problem solving may share the same purpose in agreeing on a solution and making a decision. Nevertheless, they may have different agendas and use different methods. Two such different approaches to group decision making are the rational model and the political model.

The *rational decision-making model* is the traditional, logical approach to decision making, based on the scientific method. It is grounded in establishing goals, establishing alternatives, examining consequences, and hoping for optimum results. The search for optimum results is based on an economic view of decision making—the idea that people hope to maximize gain and minimize loss when making a decision. For example, a work team would choose the lowest cost/highest quality supplier even though the team leader was good friends with the sales representative of a competitor.

The rational model also assumes that each alternative is evaluated in terms of how well it contributes to reaching the goals involved in making the decision. For example, if one of the goals in relocating a factory was to reduce energy costs and taxes, each alternative would be carefully examined in terms of its

Self-Assessment Quiz 5-1

MY PROBLEM-SOLVING TENDENCIES

Directions: Describe how well you agree with the following statements. Use the following scale: Disagree strongly (DS); Disagree (D); Neutral (N); Agree (A); Agree strongly (AS).

	DS	D	N	A	AS
1. Before reaching a final decision on a matter of significance, I like to discuss it with one or more other people.	1	2	3	4	(5)
2. If I'm facing a major decision, I like to get away from others to think it through.	5	(4)	3	2	1
3. I get lonely working by myself.	1	(2)	3	4	5
4. Two heads are better than one.	1	2	3	4	(5)
5. A wide range of people should be consulted before an executive makes a major decision	1	2	3	4	(5)
6. To arrive at a creative solution to a problem it is best to rely on a group.	1	2	3	4	(5)
7. From what I've seen so far, group decision making is a waste of time.	(5)	4	3	2	1
8. Most great ideas stem from the solitary effort of great thinkers.	5	(4)	3	2	1
9. Important legal cases should be decided by a jury rather than by a judge.	(1)	2	3	4	5
10. Individuals are better suited than groups to solve technical problems.	5	4	3	2	(1)

Total Score _____

Scoring and Interpretation: Add the numbers you circled to obtain your total score.

46–50 You have strong positive attitudes toward group problem solving and decision making. You will therefore adapt well to the decision-making techniques widely used in organizations. Be careful, however, not to neglect your individual problem-solving skills.

30–45 You have neutral attitudes toward group problem solving and decision making. You may need to remind yourself that group problem solving is well accepted in business.

10–29 You much prefer individual to group decision making. Retain your pride in your ability to think independently, but do not overlook the contribution of group problem solving and decision making. You may need to develop more patience for group problem solving and decision making.

tax and energy consequences. A team member might say, "Setting up a factory in the Phoenix area sounds great. It's true that taxes are low, the labor market is wonderful, and we won't lose any days to snow emergencies. But did you know that the energy costs are very high because of the amount of air conditioning required?"

EMPOWER: AUTORIZAR, FACULTAR, COMISIONAR, DAR PODER, Habilitar.

The *political decision-making model* assumes that people bring preconceived notions and biases into the decision-making situation. Because the decision makers are politically motivated (a focus on satisfying one's own interests), the individuals often do not make the most rational choice. In the relocation example at hand, two of the members may say "Thumbs up to Phoenix" for reasons that satisfy their own needs. One team member might be fascinated with the American Indian culture so prevalent in Arizona and therefore want to move to Phoenix. Another member might have retired parents living in Phoenix and be interested in living near them.

People who use the political model may operate on the basis of incomplete information. Facts and figures that conflict with personal biases and preferences might get blocked out of memory or rationalized away. A team member might say, "Those air conditioning costs are exaggerated. I have heard that if you use thermal pumps in a factory, the cooling costs go way down."

In practice, it is sometimes difficult to determine whether a decision maker is being rational or political. Have you ever noticed that many hotels do not have a 13th floor? The reason is both rational and political. The hotel manager might say rationally, "Many people are superstitious about the number 13, so they will refuse to take a room on the 13th floor. So if we want to maximize room use, the rational decision for us is to label the 13th floor as 14. In this way we will avoid the irrational (political) thinking of guests."

Whether groups approach their decisions rationally or politically, it is helpful to look at a sampling of the problems work groups tackle. Figure 5-1 presents a list of the specific types of decisions often made by self-managing work teams. Group problem solving is the rule in carrying out these activities, because work teams are designed to be democratic. For example, a highly empowered work team might decide which one of its members should be the next team leader.

GUIDELINES FOR USING GENERAL PROBLEM-SOLVING GROUPS

RELY ON: - CONFIAR EN o
- FIAR EN
- CONTAR CON

When team members get together to solve a problem, they typically hold a discussion rather than rely on formal problem-solving techniques. Several team members might attempt to clarify the true nature of the problem, and a search then begins for an acceptable solution. Although this technique can be effective, the probability of solving the problem well (and therefore making the right decision) increases when the team follows a systematic procedure. The following guidelines represent a time-tested way of solving problems and making decisions within a group.[2] You may recognize these steps as having much in common with the scientific method. The same steps are therefore ideal for following the rational decision making.

Assume that you are a team member of a small business that distributes food supplies to hospitals, nursing homes, and schools. Your business volume is adequate, but you have a cash-flow problem because some of your customers

ULTIMATE: ADJ. ULTIMO, FINAL, FUNDAMENTAL, ESENCIAL, ELEMENTAL.

Figure 5-1 Problem-Solving and Decision-Making Topics for Work Teams

Source: Based on information in Richard S. Wellins, William C. Byham, and Jeanne M. Wilson, *Empowered Teams: Creating Self-Directed Work Groups That Improve Quality, Productivity, and Participation* (San Francisco: Jossey-Bass, 1991), p. 26; Carla Johnson, "Teams at Work," *HR Magazine,* May 1999, pp. 30–36.

take over 30 days to pay their bills. Here is how problem solving would proceed following the steps for effective group problem solving and decision making:

1. *Identify the problem.* Describe specifically what the problem is and how it manifests itself. The surface problem is that some customers are paying their bills late. Your company's ultimate problem is that it does not have enough cash on hand to pay expenses.

2. *Clarify the problem.* If group members do not see the problem the same way, they will offer divergent solutions to their own individual perceptions of the problem. To some team members, late payments may simply mean the company has less cash in the bank. As a result, the company earns a few dollars less in interest. Someone else on the team might perceive the problem as mostly an annoyance and inconvenience. Another person may perceive late payers as being immoral and therefore want to penalize them. The various perceptions of the problem solvers contribute to their exercising a political model of decision making. It is important for the group to reach consensus that the ultimate problem is not enough cash on hand to run the business, as explained in Step 1.

3. *Analyze the cause.* To convert what exists into what they want, the group must understand the cause of the specific problems and find ways to overcome the causes. Late payment of bills (over 30 days) can be caused by several factors. The customers may have cash-flow problems of their own, they may have slow-moving bureaucratic procedures, or they may be understaffed. Another possibility is that the slow-paying customers are dissatisfied with the service and are holding back on payments in retaliation. Research, including interviewing customers, may be needed to analyze the cause or causes.

4. *Search for alternative solutions.* Remember that multiple alternative solutions can be found to most problems. The alternative solutions you choose will depend on your analysis of the causes. Assume that you did not find customers to be dissatisfied with your service, but that they were slow in paying bills for a variety of reasons. Your team then gets into a creative mode by developing a number of alternatives. Among them are offering bigger discounts for quick payment, dropping slow-paying customers, sending out your own bills more promptly, and using follow-up phone calls to bring in money. Another possibility would be to set up a line of credit that would enable your firm to make short-term loans to cover expenses until your bills were paid.

5. *Select alternatives.* Identify the criteria that solutions should meet; then discuss the pros and cons of the proposed alternatives. No solution should be laughed at or scorned. Specifying the criteria that proposed solutions should meet requires you to think deeply about your goals. For example, your team might establish the following criteria for solutions: that they (a) improve cash flow, (b) do not lose customers, (c) do not cost much to implement, and (d) do not make the company appear desperate. The pros and cons of each proposed alternative can be placed on a flip chart, chalkboard, or computer screen.

6. *Plan for implementation.* Decide what actions are necessary to carry out the chosen solution to the problem. Suppose your group decides that establishing a bank line of credit is the most feasible alternative. The company president or the chief financial officer might then meet with a couple of local banks to apply for a line of credit at the most favorable rate. Your group also chooses to initiate a program of friendly follow-up telephone calls to encourage more rapid payment.

7. *Clarify the contract.* The contract is a restatement of what group members have agreed to do and deadlines for accomplishment. In your situation, several team members are involved in establishing a line of credit and initiating a system of follow-up phone calls.

8. *Develop an action plan.* Specify who does what and when to carry out the contract. Each person involved in implementing alternatives develops an action plan in detail that stems logically from the previous step.

FEASIBLE: FACTIBLE, HACEDERO, PRACTICABLE, POSIBLE, VIABLE - A PROPÓSITO, APROPIADO.

A GENERAL PROBLEM-SOLVING GROUP

The class is divided into groups of about six people. Each group takes the same complicated problem through the nine steps for effective group decision making. Several of the steps will be hypothetical, because this is a simulated experience. Pretend you are a task force composed of people from different departments in the company. Choose one of the following possibilities:

Scenario 1: Your company wants your task force to decide whether to purchase a corporate jet for members of senior management or require them to continue to fly on commercial airlines.

Scenario 2: You are employed by Eastman Kodak Company, the film and digital imaging giant. Data supplied by the marketing research department indicates that the consumption of film by consumers worldwide is declining slightly. At the same time, digital photography is increasing. Your task force is asked to recommend a plan for increasing the consumption of film.

9. *Provide for evaluation and accountability.* After the plan is implemented, reconvene to discuss progress and to hold people accountable for results that have not been achieved. In the situation at hand, progress will be measured in at least two objective ways. You can evaluate by accounting measures whether the cash-flow problem has improved and whether the average cycle time on accounts receivable has decreased.

The steps for effective group problem solving are best applied to complex problems. Straightforward problems of minor consequence (such as deciding on holiday decorations for the office) do not require all the steps. Nevertheless, remember that virtually every problem has more than one feasible alternative. For practice in using the steps just described, do Skill-Building Exercise 5-1.

GUIDELINES FOR BRAINSTORMING

In many work situations, groups are expected to produce creative and imaginative solutions to problems. When the organization is seeking a large number of alternatives for solving the problems, **brainstorming** is often the technique of choice. Brainstorming is a group problem-solving technique that promotes creativity by encouraging idea generation through noncritical discussion. The basic technique is to encourage unrestrained and spontaneous participation by group members. The term *brainstorm* has become so widely known that it is often used as a synonym for a clever idea.

Brainstorming is used both as a method of finding alternatives to real-life problems and as a creativity-training program. In the usual form of brain-

storming, group members spontaneously call out alternative solutions to a problem facing them. Any member is free to enhance or "hitchhike" upon the contribution of another person. At the end of the session, somebody sorts out the ideas and edits the more unrefined ones.

Brainstorming is widely used to develop new ideas for products, find names for products, develop advertising slogans, and solve customer problems. For instance, the idea for luxury sport utility vehicles (SUVs) emerged from a brainstorming session. Brainstorming has also been used to develop a new organization structure in a government agency, and it is now widely used in developing software.

Adhering to a few simple rules or guidelines helps ensure that creative alternative solutions to problems will be forthcoming. The brainstorming process usually falls into place without frequent reminders about guidelines. Nevertheless, here are eight rules to improve the chances of having a good session:

1. *Group size should be about five to seven people.* If there are too few people, not enough suggestions are generated; if there are too many people, the session becomes uncontrolled. However, brainstorming can be conducted with as few as three people.

2. *Everybody is given the chance to suggest alternative solutions.* Members spontaneously call out alternatives to the problem facing the group. (Another approach is for people to speak in sequence.)

3. *No criticism is allowed.* All suggestions should be welcome; it is particularly important not to use derisive laughter.

4. *Freewheeling is encouraged.* Outlandish ideas often prove quite useful. It's easier to tame a wild idea than to originate one.

5. *Quantity and variety are very important.* The greater the number of ideas put forth, the greater the likelihood of a breakthrough idea.

6. *Combinations and improvements are encouraged.* Building upon the ideas of others, including combining them, is very productive. "Hitchhiking" or "piggybacking" is an essential part of brainstorming.

7. *Notes must be taken during the session by a person who serves as the recording secretary.* The session can also be taped, but this requires substantial time to retrieve ideas.

8. *Do not overstructure by following any of the seven ideas too rigidly.* Brainstorming is a spontaneous group process.

Brainstorming is an effective technique for finding a large number of alternatives to problems, particularly when the list of alternatives is subsequently refined and edited. Brainstorming in groups is also valuable, because it contributes to job satisfaction for many people. Skill-Building Exercise 5-2 gives you an opportunity to practice a commercially useful application of brainstorming.

Skill Building Exercise 5-2

1-800-INSIGHT

Using conventional brainstorming, huddle in small groups. Your task is to develop 800, 888, or 900 numbers for firms in various enterprises. Keep in mind that the best 800, 888, or 900 numbers are easy to memorize and have a logical connection to the goods or services provided. After each group makes up its list of telephone numbers (approximately five for each firm on the list), compare results with the other groups. Here is the list of nationwide enterprises:·

➤ A chain of funeral homes (RIP-)(FOR-EVER)(FUN-HOME)(

➤ A heating and air-conditioning firm (COOL IT)(CHIL OUT)(COMFORT)

➤ A software problem help line for Microsoft Corp.

➤ A used-car chain (OLD-CARS)

➤ A dial-a-laugh service (a 900 number)

➤ An introduction (dating) service (a 900 number)

A curious feature of brainstorming is that individuals working alone typically produce more useful ideas than those placed in a group. Brainstorming by individuals working alone is referred to as **brainwriting**. When electronic brainstorming is described in the next section, we will analyze why some people generate fewer ideas in a group setting. Skill-Building Exercise 5-3 gives you a chance to compare brainstorming with brainwriting.

GUIDELINES FOR ELECTRONIC BRAINSTORMING

A promising electronic procedure has been developed to overcome the limitations of conventional brainstorming in groups. First, we will examine problems with brainstorming more carefully; then we will describe electronic brainstorming.

LIMITATIONS TO VERBAL BRAINSTORMING

The full potential of brainstorming has been held back by three forces that block production of ideas: evaluation apprehension, free riding, and inhibiting procedures.[3] Being aware of these production-blocking mechanisms can help you improve your skill in brainstorming.

Evaluation apprehension means that many people are unwilling to come forth with some of their ideas because they fear being critically evaluated. This fear may be intensified when people are told that the group is being observed and rated or that experts are in the group. (Did you notice any evaluation apprehension in the brainstorming exercise?) When people work by themselves—and do not have to present their ideas to the larger group—they will have less evaluation apprehension.

Skill Building Exercise 5-3

BRAINSTORMING VERSUS BRAINWRITING

Half the class is organized into brainstorming groups of about six people. The rest of the class work by themselves. Groups and individuals then work on the same problems for 10 minutes. The brainstorming groups follow the aforementioned guidelines. Individuals jot down as many alternatives as come to mind without interacting with other people. After the problem-solving sessions are completed, compare the alternatives developed by the groups and individuals.

Groups and individuals choose one of the following problems so that solutions can be compared to the same problems:

1. How might we effectively utilize the senior citizens in our community?

2. How can we earn extra money, aside from holding a regular job?

3. How can we find new people to date?

4. How can we save money on food costs?

5. How can we save money on gasoline?

Free riding is just about the same behavior as social loafing. Free riders do not work as hard in a group as they would if they worked alone. They are willing to let the next person do the heavy thinking. A reason offered for free riding is that being an outstanding contributor in a group carries no larger reward than being a noncontributor. A person generating ideas alone would not have the opportunity to free ride.

An *inhibiting procedure* in verbal brainstorming is that only one person can speak at a time. This limits the idea generation and production time available to group members. As a result some people forget what they wanted to say because they were listening to others. They might also ignore the ideas of others because they are rehearsing what they want to say. Furthermore, they will hold back on ideas that are redundant.

THE ELECTRONIC BRAINSTORMING PROCEDURE

A recent development designed to overcome the problem of production blocking in brainstorming is **electronic brainstorming**. Using this method, group members simultaneously enter their suggestions into a computer, and the ideas are distributed to the screens of other group members. Although the group members do not talk to each other, they are still able to build on each other's ideas and combine ideas.

Electronic brainstorming allows members to enter their ideas whenever they want, while sending along their ideas anonymously. These two features reduce the inhibitions caused by waiting for other people and by fear of negative evaluations.

During electronic brainstorming, individuals work in face-to-face groups, typically seated around a U-shaped table. Each group member has a computer terminal connected to all the other terminals and a monitor. *Electronic Brainstorming* is the title of representative software for this activity. The software enables individuals to enter their ideas anonymously as those ideas occur to them. (Good keyboarding skills are essential to keep up with the group.)

Every time an individual enters an idea, a random set of the group's ideas is entered on the individual's monitor. Individuals can access other random sets of ideas by pressing a specified function key. Accessing the other ideas can stimulate the person's own generation of new ideas and also allows for piggybacking.

An experiment with electronic brainstorming indicated that, with large groups, the method produces more useful ideas than does verbal brainstorming (the usual type). In the study, a four-person electronic brainstorming group produced more nonredundant ideas than verbal groups (traditional brainstorming). The group also produced more ideas than nonelectronic groups who did not interact with people.[4]

Electronic brainstorming researcher Keng L. Siau suggests that brainstorming via e-mail can increase both the quantity and quality of ideas. When participants do not face each other directly, they can concentrate more on the creativity task at hand and less on the interpersonal aspects of interaction.[5]

If your school or employer is equipped with an electronic brainstorming capability, you are encouraged to try the procedure. Setting up such a capability is costly, however. Next, we describe a low-cost manual (nonelectronic) procedure that offers many of the advantages of electronic brainstorming. In addition, you will be able to test the procedure yourself.

GUIDELINES FOR THE NOMINAL GROUP TECHNIQUE

A team leader or other manager who must make a decision about an important issue sometimes needs to know what alternatives are available and how people would react to them. In such cases, group input may be helpful. Verbal brainstorming is not advisable, because the problem is still in the exploration phase and requires more than a list of alternative solutions.

A problem-solving technique called the **nominal group technique (NGT)** has been developed to fit the situation. The NGT is a group problem-solving technique that calls people together in a structured meeting with limited interaction. The group is called *nominal* (in name only) because people first present their ideas without interacting with each other, as they would in a *real* group. (This aspect of the nominal group technique is incorporated into electronic brainstorming.) However, group discussion does take place at a later stage in the process.

A problem that is an appropriate candidate for NGT is a decision about which suppliers or vendors should be eliminated. Many companies are shrinking their number of suppliers because they believe that working with a smaller number of suppliers can lead to higher quality components. It is easier to train

a small number of suppliers, and it is also possible to build better working relationships when fewer people are involved.

A decision of this type can lead to hurt feelings and breaking up of old friendships. Suppose Pedro Ortiz, the team leader, is empowered to make this decision about reducing the number of suppliers. The nominal group technique is followed by using a six-step decision process.

1. Work-team members are assembled because they will all participate in the decision to reduce the number of companies that serve as suppliers to the team. All team members are told in advance of the meeting and the agenda. The meeting is called, and an office assistant is invited to help take care of the administrative details of the meeting.

2. The team leader presents a specific question. Ortiz tells the group, "Top management says we have to reduce our number of suppliers by two-thirds. It's too difficult to keep track of all these different suppliers and train them to meet our quality specs. I dislike terminating a supplier as much as anybody, but I can understand the logic of top management. Right now our team is doing business with 12 suppliers, and we should shrink that number to 4. Your assignment is to develop criteria for choosing which suppliers to eliminate. I also need to know how you feel about the decision you make on supplier reduction and how it might affect the operations of our team."

3. Individual team members write down their ideas independently, without speaking to other members. Using notepads, the five team members write down their ideas about reducing the number of suppliers by two-thirds.

4. Each team member in turn presents one idea to the group. The group does not discuss the ideas. The office assistant summarizes each idea by writing it on a flip chart. Here are the ideas submitted by each team member:

Alternative A. We'll carefully study the prices offered by all 12 suppliers. The 8 suppliers with the highest average prices for comparable goods are given the boot. I like this idea because our team will save the company a bundle of money.

Alternative B. Let's keep the 4 suppliers who have the best quality record. We'll ask each supplier if they have won a quality award. If a supplier has won a quality award, the company is put on the retained list. We'll include awards from their customers or outside standards such as ISO 9000. If we find more than 4 of the suppliers have won awards, we'll retain those with the most impressive awards.

Alternative C. I say we reward good service. We keep the 4 suppliers among the 12 who have been the most prompt with deliveries. We'll also take into account how good the suppliers have been about accepting returns of damaged or defective merchandise.

Alternative D. Here's an opportunity to get in good with top management. Stop kidding each other. We know that the plant's general manager [Jake] has his favorite suppliers. Some of them are his fishing and golfing buddies. The suppliers who are friends with Jake get our vote. In this way, Jake will think our team shows really good judgment.

Alternative E. Let's reward the suppliers who have served us best. We'll rate each supplier on a 1 to 10 scale on three dimensions: the quality of goods they have provided us, price, and service in terms of prompt delivery and returns policy. We could do the ratings in less than one hour.

5. After each team member has presented his or her idea, the group clarifies and evaluates the suggestions. The length of the discussion for each of the ideas varies substantially. For example, the idea about rating suppliers on three criteria might precipitate a 30-minute discussion. The discussion about retaining the plant manager's political connections might last only 5 minutes.

6. The meeting ends with a silent, independent rating of the alternatives. The final group decision is the pooled outcome of the individual votes. The team members are instructed to rate each alternative on a 1 to 10 scale, with 10 being the most favorable rating. The ratings that follow are the *pooled ratings* (the sum of the individual ratings) received for each alternative. The maximum score is 50 (10 points × 5 raters).

Alternative A, price alone: 35

Alternative B, quality-award record: 30

Alternative C, good service: 39

Alternative D, plant manager's favorites: 14

Alternative E, combination of quality, price, and service: 44

Team leader Ortiz agrees with the group's preference for choosing the four suppliers with the best combination of quality, price, and service. He schedules a meeting to decide which suppliers meet these standards. Ortiz brings the team's recommendations to the plant manager, and they are accepted. Although the team is empowered to make the decision, it is still brought to management for final approval. To practice the nominal group technique, do Skill-Building Exercise 5-4.

USING STAND-UP MEETINGS TO FACILITATE PROBLEM SOLVING

Problem solving and decision making can sometimes be improved by conducting meetings while standing up instead of sitting down. The general idea is that participants standing up in the problem-solving group are likely to be more alert and will come to a decision more quickly. Some people solve problems bet-

Skill Building Exercise 5-4

THE NOMINAL GROUP TECHNIQUE

With a clear understanding of the mechanics of the NGT as described in the text, the technique can be demonstrated in about 30 minutes. The class is divided into groups of about seven. One person plays the role of the team leader, who can also assume the responsibility of the office assistant (recording information on flip charts).

You are the key members of a motion picture and television film production company. You have a contract to produce a series of four action films. The problem you face is which North American (U.S., Canadian, or Mexican) city to choose as the film site. The president has ruled out Hollywood because expenses are too high. Solve this problem using the NGT, and make a decision about which city to choose for your film site.

ter when standing because they literally "think well on their feet." Few people would be willing to stand for several hours, so they reach a decision quickly.

Many meeting leaders who use stand-up meetings are pleased with the results in terms of reaching high-quality decisions rapidly. For example, a team of researchers decided to investigate the validity of their observations.[6] Study participants were 555 students in an introduction to management course who were offered extra credit for participating in the study. The students were randomly assigned to five-person groups, producing 111 groups. They were divided almost equally into stand-up and sit-down groups.

All groups were assigned the Lost on the Moon exercise, which presents a scenario involving a crash on the moon. Participants were asked to rank 15 pieces of equipment that survived the crash in terms of their importance for survival. Correct answers to the problem were the ranking of the equipment given by NASA astronauts and scientists. The major results of the experiment were as follows:

1. Sit-down meetings lasted about 34 percent longer than the stand-up meetings (788 seconds versus 589 seconds).

2. Sit-down and stand-up meetings made decisions of equal quality.

3. More suggestions about task accomplishment were used by groups in the sit-down than in the stand-up meetings.

4. Participants in the sit-down meetings were more satisfied than participants in the stand-up meetings.

One implication for this study is that people make decisions more quickly when standing up, without sacrificing decision quality. However, people prefer to sit down. In general, if you think that a task can be performed in 30 minutes or less, a stand-up meeting is likely to be effective.

USING E-MAIL AND GROUPWARE TO FACILITATE GROUP DECISION MAKING

The presence of so many teams in the workplace means that people must work collectively and that they must make decisions together. An obvious requirement of group decision making is that group members have to engage in collective effort. Collective effort usually translates into meetings. Without any meetings, people are working primarily on their own and thus are not benefiting from working in teams. Yet with too many meetings it is difficult to accomplish individual work such as making telephone calls, analyzing information, and preparing reports.

Appropriate use of e-mail and groupware can facilitate interaction among team members and group decision making, while at the same time minimizing the number of meetings. (**Groupware** is technology designed to facilitate the work of groups.) Such use of e-mail and other electronic tools makes possible the virtual teams described earlier in the chapter.

USING E-MAIL TO FACILITATE MEETINGS

By using e-mail, team members can feed important information to all other members of the team without the ritual of entering a meeting and passing around handouts.[7] The typical use of e-mail is to send brief memos to people on a distribution list. A more advanced use of e-mail is to distribute word processing documents as well as spreadsheets and graphics, including photographs, as attachments.

Think back to the decision reached by the team using the nominal group technique. As a follow-up to the meeting, the team was to get together to rate all 12 suppliers on quality, price, and service. Using e-mail, the group could cut down substantially on the amount of time they would have to spend in a group meeting. They might even be able to eliminate a group meeting. Pedro Ortiz might instruct the team members to send their ratings and explanations to each other within 10 working days.

Each team member would then rate all 12 suppliers on quality, service, and price. The ratings would then be sent to all other team members by e-mail. Pedro could tally the results and report the final tally to each team member by e-mail. Since all team members could have performed the same calculation themselves, there would be no claims of a biased decision. A team meeting could be called to discuss the final results if Pedro or the other team members thought it was necessary.

Pushing the use of e-mail too far can inhibit rather than enhance group decision making and teamwork. If people communicate with each other almost exclusively by e-mail, the warmth of human interaction and facial expressions is lost. Piggybacking of ideas is possible by reading each other's ideas on a computer monitor. Nevertheless, the wink of an eye, the shared laughter, and the encouraging smiles that take place in a traditional meeting make an important contribution to team effort, including group problem solving.

USING GROUPWARE TO FACILITATE GROUP PROBLEM SOLVING

The application of e-mail just described can be considered part of groupware because e-mail was used to facilitate work in groups. Electronic brainstorming also relies on groupware because software is applied to facilitate group decision making. At its best, groupware offers certain advantages over single-user systems. Some of the most common reasons people use groupware are as follows:[8]

➤ To facilitate communication by making it faster, clearer, and more persuasive.

➤ To communicate when it would not otherwise be possible.

➤ To enable telecommuting (working from home).

➤ To reduce travel costs.

➤ To bring together multiple perspectives and expertise.

➤ To assemble groups with common interests where it would not be possible to gather a sufficient number of people face to face.

➤ To facilitate group problem solving.

Another example of groupware is a *shared whiteboard* that allows two or more people to view and draw on a shared drawing surface even when they are at a distance. The link to group decision making is that drawing sketches and diagrams might be an important part of the decision making. An example would be a sales team suggesting ways of dividing a geographic territory for selling.

A shared whiteboard can be used during a telephone call, with each person jotting down notes or several participants working together on a visual problem. Typical shared whiteboards are designed for informal conversation, but they can also service more technical applications such as collaborative graphic design and working out a manufacturing problem. The various drawings, or modifications of an existing drawing, submitted by group members are indicated by telepointers, color-coded to identify each person.

Despite all these potential applications and benefits of groupware, the system will break down unless almost all the parties involved use the software successfully. For example, all members of the virtual team must be willing to get online at the same time to have a successful meeting.

SUMMARY

An important aspect of interpersonal relations in organizations is that many key problems are solved by groups. Group problem solvers and decision makers often use the rational model or the political model. The rational decision-making model is the traditional, logical approach to decision making based on the

scientific method. The model assumes that each alternative is evaluated in terms of how well it contributes to reaching the goals involved in making the decision.

The political decision-making model assumes that people bring preconceived notions and biases into the decision-making situation. Because the decision makers are politically motivated, the individuals often do not make the most rational choice. Instead, the decision makers attempt to satisfy their own needs.

General problem-solving groups are likely to arrive at better decisions when they follow standard guidelines for group problem solving. The guidelines are as follows: (a) identify the problem; (b) clarify the problem; (c) analyze the cause; (d) search for alternative solutions; (e) select alternatives; (f) plan for implementation; (g) clarify the contract; (h) develop an action plan; and (i) provide for evaluation and accountability.

When the organization is seeking a large number of alternatives to problems, brainstorming is often the technique of choice. Brainstorming is used as a method of finding alternatives to real-life problems and as a creativity-training program. Using the technique, group members spontaneously call out alternative solutions to the problem. Members build on the ideas of each other, and ideas are not screened or evaluated until a later stage. Brainstorming by working alone, or brainwriting, is also effective in generating alternative solutions.

Electronic brainstorming is a recent development designed to overcome the problem of production blocking in brainstorming, such as free riding. Using electronic brainstorming, group members simultaneously enter their suggestions into a computer, and the ideas are transmitted to the screens of other group members. Building on each other's ideas is allowed. Experiments with electronic brainstorming have been favorable.

The nominal group technique (NGT) is recommended for a situation in which a leader needs to know what alternatives are available and how people will react to them. In the NGT, a small group of people contribute written solutions to the problem. Other members respond to their ideas later. Members rate each other's ideas numerically, and the final group decision is the sum of the pooled individual votes.

Problem solving and decision making can sometimes be improved by conducting meetings while standing up instead of sitting down. The general idea is that participants who are standing up are more likely to be alert and come to a decision quickly. An experiment with management students indicated that stand-up groups made decisions more quickly, but that decision makers who sat down were more satisfied.

Electronic mail can be used to facilitate group decision making because members can feed information to each other without having to meet as a group. Memos, spreadsheet analyses, and graphics can be distributed through the network. Too much emphasis on e-mail, however, results in losing the value of face-to-face human interaction.

Various types of groupware, including e-mail and electronic brainstorming, can facilitate group decision making. Also, a shared whiteboard allows two or more people to view and draw on a shared drawing surface even when they are at a distance.

An Interpersonal Relations Case Problem

THE GREAT WIPER BLADE MYSTERY

It was a mystery—a mystery with millions of dollars and hundreds of jobs riding on the answer. A huge 6.5 percent of the windshield wiper systems being manufactured at an ITT automotive plant in upstate New York for DaimlerChrysler's minivans were defective. Nobody could figure out why the defect existed. All the parts met specifications; they were assembled correctly, and engineers found no fault with the design. Yet, in a test run, many wipers failed to make a complete sweep across the windshield—a potential disaster for Chrysler and for the 3,800 automotive workers in the upstate plant.

Plant management assembled a six-person team including engineers, union members, and manufacturing experts to become a detective force to find the answers. The team felt a lot of pressure to resolve the problem because the livelihood of the plant was threatened. If its major product was defective, the plant might be shuttered.

Technical Aspects of the Problem

The new wiper system was the biggest and most complex ever assembled in the plant. Instead of just delivering wiper blades, the local plant was given "black box responsibility" to deliver a perfectly functioning windshield system that Chrysler workers could just snap into place.

The blades, instead of moving right and left in tandem, came together in the center of the windshield and spread apart again, making timing a crucial issue. "The number of things that could go wrong was exponentially greater than for anything we had ever done before," said Rob Price, manufacturing general supervisor. Just one thing did go wrong, but it was enough to threaten the project.

In 6.5 percent of the wipers, the blade's swing was up to 2.5 degrees short. That's equivalent to less than half a second on the face of a clock. But it was enough to make the blade fall short of sweeping the full area in front of the driver's face—an area that federal regulators insist be kept clear of rain and ice.

The Cross-Functional Team Tackles the Problem

Responsibility for solving the problem fell to the Chrysler cross-functional team: leader of the plant's Chrysler team Craig Hysong, manufacturing general supervisor Rob Price, quality technician Rick Fisher, quality analyst Jeannine Marciano, engineer Mike Kinsky, and Ron Maor, an engineer from a sister plant in Ontario, Canada. Each new ITT automotive product has its cross-functional team, drawn from the different departments. The team's goal was to make sure the product was launched flawlessly.

The Chrysler team picked the best and worst of the wipers—called "Bob" and "Wow" for the best of the best and the worst of the worst. They thought that by comparing the best with the worst, they might somehow isolate and fix the problem.

The team felt the pressure to perform, because unless they solved the mystery Chrysler would have to find a new supplier for windshield wiper systems. Finally, Fisher, the technician, and Maor, the engineer from the plant that supplies the motors, found the answer. It was in the serrations (rough marks, like those on a serrated knife) on the motor's drive shaft that are meant to hold the crank in place.

Case Questions

1. Which approach to (or method of) group problem solving did the plant team use?
2. To what extent did management make the right move in assigning the flawed windshield wiper problem to a team instead of to one engineer or technician?

(Continued)

3. Where would the windshield wiper problem fit on Figure 5-1 of this chapter in terms of degree of empowerment?

4. If by chance you happen to have the right expertise, what would you guess was the problem with the windshield wiper system?

Case excerpted and paraphrased from Phil Ebersole, "ITT Automotive Sleuths Solve a Design Mystery," Rochester, New York, *Democrat and Chronicle*, May 4, 1997, pp. 1E, 4E.

QUESTIONS FOR DISCUSSION AND REVIEW

1. Why are group decision-making skills so important for members of a work team?

2. Based on any experience you have had at school or at work, what process or method is usually followed in making group decisions?

3. Most textbook mentions of brainstorming are neutral to unfavorable. What do you suppose the textbook authors tend to dislike about brainstorming?

4. Identify several problems on or off the job for which you think brainstorming would be effective.

5. What, if any, accommodations should be made in electronic brainstorming for group members who have poor keyboarding skills?

6. Identify two work-related problems for which the nominal group technique is particularly well suited?

7. Companies have known about stand-up meetings for many years, and the results have been favorable in terms of productivity. Why, then, are stand-up meetings still not very popular?

8. What advantage does e-mail offer over paper memos and telephone calls as a contributor to group decision making?

9. How can a team leader apply groupware to help the group become more productive?

10. Which group decision-making technique described in this chapter do you think members of top management are the most likely to use? Why?

Chapter 6

Cross-Cultural Relations and Diversity

Stella, who is Puerto Rican, receives excellent performance reviews as a teller at an East Harlem branch of a major bank. East Harlem is a Latino section of New York City. Stella has been taking college courses and continuing education courses offered by the bank, which will qualify her for a position in the bank's central operations department in midtown Manhattan.

Her boss, John, is surprised and annoyed when Stella asks to be recommended for the operations job. He tells Stella that she won't fit in with others and that her style of dress is too flamboyant for the bank's midtown customers. He also encourages Stella to stay at the branch where her Spanish skills are helpful with Latino customers. He says, "Stella, we really need you here to work with our customers. Don't you want to help serve your people? They need you, and I don't think you should let them down."

Stella is discouraged about her career and resents the comments about the community. She knows many other bank people who could do her job as a teller and also speak Spanish.[1]

The brewing conflict between Stella and her manager, John, points out the need for better cross-cultural understanding. John appears to be stereotyping Stella in terms of what he thinks her role should be. Stella wants to break through the limited view of her potential contribution to the bank. Conflicts based on misunderstandings of this nature are frequent because today's workplace is so diverse. Minority group members in the United States are growing seven times as fast as the majority population. According to the Bureau of Labor Statistics, women make up about 47 percent of the workforce. Minorities and workers from other countries occupy 26 percent of jobs. Furthermore, white males constitute only 15 percent of new entrants to the workforce.

Not only is the workforce becoming more diverse, but business has become increasingly international. Small- and medium-size firms, as well as corporate giants, are increasingly dependent on trade with other countries. An estimated 10 to 15 percent of jobs in the United States depend on imports or exports. Furthermore, most manufactured goods contain components from more than one country.

All this workplace diversity has an important implication for the career-minded individual. To succeed in today's workplace a person must be able to relate effectively to people from different cultural groups from within and outside his or her country. Being able to relate to a culturally diverse customer base is also necessary for success.

This chapter presents concepts and techniques you can use to sharpen your ability to work effectively with people from diverse backgrounds. To get you started thinking about your readiness to work in a culturally diverse environment, take Self-Assessment Quiz 6-1.

THE DIVERSITY UMBRELLA

Improving cross-cultural relations includes understanding the true meaning of appreciating diversity. To appreciate diversity a person must go beyond toler-

Self-Assessment Quiz 6-1

CROSS-CULTURAL SKILLS AND ATTITUDES

Listed below are various skills and attitudes that various employers and cross-cultural experts think are important for relating effectively to coworkers in a culturally diverse environment.

	Applies to me now	Not there yet
1. I have spent some time in another country.	✓	
2. At least one of my friends is deaf, blind, or uses a wheel chair.	✓	✓
3. Currency from other countries is as real as the currency from my own country.	✓	
4. I can read in a language other than my own.	✓	
5. I can speak in a language other than my own.	✓	
6. I can write in a language other than my own.	✓	
7. I can understand people speaking in a language other than my own.	✓	
8. I use my second language regularly.	✓	
9. My friends include people of races different from my own.	✓	
10. My friends include people of different ages.	✓	
11. I feel (or would feel) comfortable having a friend with a sexual orientation different from mine.	✓	
12. My attitude is that although another culture may be very different from mine, that culture is equally good.	✓	
13. I would be willing to (or already do) hang art from different countries in my home.	✓	
14. I would accept (or have already accepted) a work assignment of more than several months in another country.		✓
15. I have a passport.	✓	

Interpretation: If you answered "Applies to me now" to 10 or more of the preceding questions, you most likely function well in a multicultural work environment. If you answered "Not there yet" to 10 or more of the questions, you need to develop more cross-cultural awareness and skills to work effectively in a multicultural work environment. You will notice that being bilingual gives you at least five points on this quiz.

Source: Several ideas for statements on this quiz are derived from Ruthann Dirks and Janet Buzzard, "What CEOs Expect of Employees Hired for International Work," *Business Education Forum*, April 1997, pp. 3–7; and Gunnar Beeth, "Multicultural Managers Wanted," *Management Review*, May 1997, pp. 17–21.

ating and treating people from different racial and ethnic groups fairly. The true meaning of valuing diversity is to respect and enjoy a wide range of cultural and individual differences. To be diverse is to be different in some measurable way.

Eva Hall, a diversity consultant, helps employees recognize that everybody is different. As she mentions in her seminars, "I'm different in many ways. I'm a middle-aged woman of color, and everyone in this room is different in at least one important way."[2] To be highly skilled in interpersonal relations, one must recognize and appreciate these differences. Some people are more visibly diverse than others because of physical features or disabilities. Yet the diversity umbrella is supposed to include everybody in an organization. To value diversity is therefore to appreciate individual differences among people.

The diversity umbrella continues to include more people as the workforce encompasses a greater variety of people. The goal of a diverse organization is for persons of all cultural backgrounds to achieve their full potential, not restrained by group identities such as sex, nationality, or race.[3]

Figure 6-1 presents a broad sampling of the ways in which workplace associates can differ from one another. Studying this list can help you anticipate the types of differences to understand and appreciate in a diverse workplace. The differences include cultural as well as individual factors. Individual factors are also important because people can be discriminated against for personal characteristics as well as group factors. Many people, for example, believe they are held back from promotion because of their weight-to-height ratio.

UNDERSTANDING CULTURAL DIFFERENCES

The groundwork for developing effective cross-cultural relations is to understand cultural differences. The information about different communication patterns between men and women presented in Chapter 3 is relevant here. Some researchers think that men and women represent different cultures! One cultural difference between the two groups is that women tend to speak indirectly and soften criticism. Men, in contrast, tend to be more direct in giving criticism. Here we feature three aspects of understanding cultural differences: (1) competency goals, (2) dimensions of differences in cultural values, and (3) cultural bloopers.

COMPETENCY GOALS METAS COMPETENCIALES

Setting competency goals will improve your chances of understanding cultural differences. As shown in Figure 6-2, three such goals are cultural sensitivity, respect for diverse groups, and cultural fluency. All three goals are closely related.

Cultural Sensitivity

In order to relate well to someone from a foreign country, a person must be alert to possible cultural differences. When working in another country a person must be willing to acquire knowledge about local customs and learn how

- Race
- Sex (or gender)
- Religion
- Age (young, middle-aged, and old)
- Ethnicity (country of origin)
- Education
- Abilities
- Mental disabilities (including attention deficit disorder)
- Physical disabilities (including hearing status, visual status, able-bodied, wheelchair user)
- Values and motivation
- Sexual orientation (heterosexual, homosexual, bisexual)
- Marital status (married, single, cohabitating, widow, widower)
- Family status (children, no children, two-parent family, single parent, grandparent)
- Personality traits (RASGOS DE PERSONALIDAD.
- Functional background (area of specialization)
- Technology interest (high-tech, low-tech, technophobe)
- Weight status (average, obese, underweight, anorexic)
- Hair status (full head of hair, bald, wild hair, tame hair, long hair, short hair)
- Tobacco status (smoker versus nonsmoker, chewer versus nonchewer)
- Styles of clothing and appearance (dress up, dress down, professional appearance, casual appearance)

Figure 6-1 The Diversity Umbrella

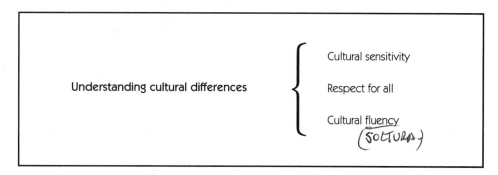

Understanding cultural differences { Cultural sensitivity

Respect for all

Cultural fluency
(SOLTURA)

Figure 6-2 Competency Goals for Understanding Cultural Differences

to speak the native language at least passably. When working with people from different cultures, even from his or her own country, the person must be patient, adaptable, flexible, and willing to listen and learn. The characteristics just mentioned are part of **cultural sensitivity**, an awareness of and willingness to investigate the reasons why people of another culture act as they do.[4] A person with cultural sensitivity will recognize certain nuances in customs that will help build better relationships from cultural backgrounds other than his or her own.

Respect for All Workers and Cultures

An effective strategy for achieving cross-cultural understanding is to simply respect all others in the workplace, including their cultures. An important component of respect is to believe that although another person's culture is different from yours, it is equally good. Colgate-Palmolive Company, the consumer products giant, conducts a program for managers called "Valuing Colgate People." The program's key objective is to teach managers to respect all workers. Respect comes from valuing differences.

Respecting other people's customs can translate into specific attitudes, such as respecting one coworker for wearing a yarmulke on Friday or another for wearing an African costume to celebrate Kwanza. Another way of being respectful would be to listen carefully to the opinion of a senior worker who says the company should never have converted to voice mail in place of assistants answering the phone (even though you disagree).

An aspect of respecting all workers that has achieved attention recently is the importance of respecting the rights of majorities, particularly white males. Gillian Flynn, a human resource professional, states the problem in this way: "These days things aren't so easy for white males. They've been under attack for a long time, en masse, for the problems of women and minorities. And some should be, certainly. But it's ironic that a movement that demands equal treatment for individuals often lumps all men into one troublesome bundle."[5] Following this logic, a true multicultural person would not have negative attitudes toward a person just because that person is a white male.

Cultural Fluency

A high-level goal in understanding cultural differences is to achieve **cultural fluency**, the ability to conduct business in a diverse, international environment.[6] Achieving cultural fluency includes a variety of skills, such as relating well to people from different cultures and knowing a second language. Cultural fluency also includes knowledge of the international business environment, such as how the exchange rate can affect profits.

Skill-Building Exercise 6-1 is a warm-up activity for achieving cultural sensitivity, and perhaps respect for all workers.

DIMENSIONS OF DIFFERENCES IN CULTURAL VALUES

One way to understand how national cultures differ is to examine their values. Table 6-1 presents an introduction to the subject by comparing values in the United States to the collective values of many Western and Eastern countries.

Skill-Building Exercise 6-1

DEVELOPING CULTURAL SENSITIVITY

Carefully observe products and services such as tennis shoes, notebooks, bicycles, and banking services, and attempt to find out how they are marketed and sold in other countries. For a convenient reference source, interview foreign students and foreigners outside of class about these products and services. Your digging for information might uncover such nuggets as the following:

➤ In India, cricket champions are celebrities comparable to U. S. basketball stars who endorse soft drinks like Coca-Cola and Pepsi.

➤ In Hungary, peanut butter is considered a luxury food item.

➤ In some countries in warm climates, meat is freshly killed and hung on hooks for sale—without refrigeration or freezing.

After conducting these product and service interviews, arrive at some kind of interpretation or conclusion. Share your insights with other class members.

Source: "Teaching International Business," *Keying In* (The Newsletter of the National Business Education Association), January 1999, p. 1.

You can use this information as a general stereotype of how Americans are likely to differ from people in many other countries.

The focus of our attention is a more detailed look at eight different values and how selected nationalities relate to them, based on the work of several researchers.[7] A summary of these values follows.

1. *Individualism versus collectivism.* At one end of the continuum is **individualism**, a mental set in which people see themselves first as individuals

TABLE 6-1 Comparison of United States Values with Those in Many Other Countries

In the United States	In many other countries
Time is to be controlled	Time is fluid, malleable
Emphasis on change	Tradition, continuity
Individualism	Group orientation
Personal privacy	Openness, accessibility
Informality	Formality
Individual competition	Cooperation
Equality/egalitarianism	Hierarchy/authority
Short-term emphasis	Long-term emphasis
Work emphasis ("One lives to work.")	Leisure + work emphasis ("One works to live.")
Task emphasis	People emphasis
Direct/explicit communication style	Indirect/implicit communication style
Action bias or emphasis	Planning and preparation emphasis

Source: Adaptation of chart prepared by International Orientation Resources.

and believe that their own interests take priority. **Collectivism**, at the other end of the continuum, is a feeling that the group and society receive top priority. Members of a society who value individualism are more concerned with their careers than with the good of the firm. Members of a society who value collectivism, in contrast, are typically more concerned with the organization than with themselves.

Highly individualistic cultures include the United States, Canada, Great Britain, Australia, and the Netherlands. Japan, Taiwan, Mexico, Greece, and Hong Kong are among the countries that strongly value collectivism.

> An example of collectivistic thinking took place during South Korea's economic crisis in 1997. Worried about the crisis, employees in a Seoul government office gathered up spare change from their desk drawers and donated it to their country. Banks encouraged people to open accounts with their hoarded foreign currencies. Furthermore, collection boxes were placed on the streets for donation of spare bills and coins. Many citizens brought foreign currency to banks to exchange it for Korean currency.[8]

2. *High power distance versus low power distance.* The extent to which employees accept the idea that members of an organization have different levels of power is referred to as **power distance**. In a high-power-distance culture, the boss makes many decisions simply because he or she is the boss. Group members readily comply because they have a positive orientation toward authority. In a low-power-distance culture, employees do not readily recognize a power hierarchy. They accept directions only when they think the boss is right or when they feel threatened. High-power-distance cultures include France, Spain, Japan, Mexico, and Brazil. Low-power-distance cultures include the United States, Israel, Germany, and Ireland.

3. *Low uncertainty avoidance versus high uncertainty avoidance.* People who accept the unknown and tolerate risk and unconventional behavior are said to have low **uncertainty avoidance**. In other words, these people are not afraid to face the unknown. A society ranked high in uncertainty avoidance contains a majority of people who want predictable and certain futures. Low-uncertainty-avoidance cultures include the United States, Canada, Australia, and Singapore. Workers in Israel, Japan, Italy, and Argentina are more motivated to avoid uncertainty in their careers.

4. *Materialism versus concern for others.* In this context, **materialism** refers to an emphasis on assertiveness and the acquisition of money and material objects. It also means a deemphasis on caring for others. At the other end of the cotinuum is **concern for others**, an emphasis on personal relations and a concern for the welfare of others. Materialistic countries include Japan, Austria, and Italy. The United States is considered to be moderately materialistic. Scandinavian nations all emphasize caring as a national value. (In the original, the same dimension was referred to as *masculinity* versus *femininity*. Such terms are considered to be sexist today.)

5. *Long-term orientation versus short-term orientation.* Workers from a culture with a **long-term orientation** maintain a long-range perspective, thus being thrifty and not demanding quick returns on their investments. A **short-term orientation** is characterized by a demand for immediate results and a propensity not to save. Pacific Rim countries are noted for their long-term orientation. In contrast, the cultures of the United States and Canada are characterized more by short-term orientation.

6. *Formality versus informality.* A country that values **formality** attaches considerable importance to tradition, ceremony, social rules, and rank. At the other extreme, **informality** refers to a casual attitude toward tradition, ceremony, social rules, and rank. Workers in Latin American countries highly value formality, such as lavish public receptions and processions. Americans, Canadians, and Scandinavians are much more informal.

7. *Urgent time orientation versus casual time orientation.* Individuals and nations attach different importance to time. People with an **urgent time orientation** perceive time as a scarce resource and tend to be impatient. People with a **casual time orientation** view time as an unlimited and unending resource and tend to be patient. Americans are noted for their urgent time orientation. They frequently impose deadlines and are eager to get started doing business. Asians and Middle Easterners, in contrast, are patient negotiators.

8. *High-context versus low-context cultures.* Cultures differ in how much importance they attach to the surrounding circumstances, or context, of an event. **High-context cultures** make more extensive use of body language. Some cultures, such as the Asian, Hispanic, and African-American cultures, are high context. In contrast, northern European cultures are low context and make less use of body language. The Anglo-American culture is considered to be medium-low context. People in low-context cultures seldom take time in business dealings to build relationships and establish trust.

How might a person use information about cultural differences to improve his or her interpersonal relations on the job? A starting point would be to recognize that a person's national values might influence his or her behavior. Assume that you wanted to establish a good working relationship with a person from a high-context culture. An effective starting point would be to emphasize body language when communicating with the individual. Self-Assessment Quiz 6-2 will help you think about how values might be influencing your interpersonal relations in the workplace.

CULTURAL BLOOPERS

An effective way of being culturally sensitive is to minimize actions that are likely to offend people from another culture based on their values. Cultural bloopers are most likely to take place when you are visiting another country. The same bloopers, however, can also be committed with people from a different

Self-Assessment Quiz 6-2

CHARTING YOUR CULTURAL VALUE PROFILE

Directions: For each of the eight value dimensions, circle the number that most accurately fits your standing on the dimension. For example, if you perceive yourself to be "highly formal," circle 7 on the sixth dimension (item 6).

1. Individualism Collectivism
 1 2 3 4 5 6 7

2. High power distance Low power distance
 1 2 3 4 5 6 7

3. High uncertainty avoidance Low uncertainty avoidance
 1 2 3 4 5 6 7

4. Materialism (masculinity) Concern for others (femininity)
 1 2 3 4 5 6 7

5. Long-term orientation Short-term orientation
 1 2 3 4 5 6 7

6. Informality Formality
 1 2 3 4 5 6 7

7. Urgent time orientation Casual time orientation
 1 2 3 4 5 6 7

8. High context Low context
 1 2 3 4 5 6 7

Scoring and Interpretation: After circling one number for each dimension, use a felt-tipped pen to connect the circles, thereby giving yourself a *profile of cultural values*. Do not be concerned if your marker cuts through the names of the dimensions. Compare your profile to others in the class. Should time allow, develop a class profile by computing the class average for each of the eight points and then connecting the points.

culture within your own country. To avoid these bloopers, you must carefully observe persons from another culture. Studying another culture through reading is also helpful.

E-commerce and other forms of Internet communication have created new opportunities for creating cultural bloopers. The Web site developers and the workers responsible for adding content must have good cross-cultural literacy, including an awareness of how the information might be misinterpreted. Here is a sampling of potential problems:

➤ Numerical date formats can be readily misinterpreted. To an American, 4/9/01 would be interpreted as April 9, 2001 (or 1901!). However,

many Europeans would interpret the same numerical expression as September 4, 2001.

➤ Colors on Web sites must be chosen carefully. For example, in some cultures purple is the color of royalty, whereas in Brazil purple is associated with death.

➤ Be careful of metaphors that may not make sense to a person for whom your language is a second language. Examples include "We've encountered an ethical meltdown" and "Our biggest competitor is over the hill."

International business specialist Rick Borelli recommends that being able to communicate your message directly in your customer's mother tongue provides a competitive advantage.[9] The translator, of course, must have good knowledge of the subtleties of the language to avoid a blooper. An English-to-French translator used the verb *baiser* instead of *baisser* to describe a program of lowering prices. *Baisser* is the French verb "to lower" whereas *baiser* is the verb "to kiss." Worse, in slang *baiser* is a verb that refers to having intimate physical relationships!

Keep two key facts in mind when attempting to avoid cultural mistakes. One is that members of any cultural group show individual differences. What one member of the group might regard as an insensitive act, another might welcome. Recognize also that one or two cultural mistakes will not peg you permanently as a boor. Skill-Building Exercise 6-2 will help you minimize certain cultural bloopers.

OVERCOMING CROSS-CULTURAL COMMUNICATION BARRIERS

We have already discussed the importance of overcoming communication barriers in Chapter 3. Cultural differences create additional barriers. Here are some guidelines for overcoming cross-cultural communication barriers.

1. *Be sensitive to the fact that cross-cultural communication barriers exist. If you are aware of these potential barriers, you will be ready to deal with them.* When you are dealing with a person in the workplace with a different cultural background than yours, solicit feedback in order to minimize cross-cultural barriers to communication. Being aware of these potential barriers will help you develop cultural sensitivity.

2. *Show respect for all workers.* The same behavior that promotes good cross-cultural relations in general helps overcome communication barriers. A widely-used comment that implies disrespect is to say to another person from another culture, "You have a funny accent." Should you be transposed to that person's culture, you, too, might have a "funny accent."

3. *Use straightforward language and speak slowly and clearly.* When working with people who do not speak your language fluently, speak in an easy-

Skill-Building Exercise 6-2

CULTURAL MISTAKES TO AVOID
WITH SELECTED CULTURAL GROUPS

EUROPE

Great Britain
- Asking personal questions. The British protect their privacy.
- Thinking that a businessperson from England is unenthusiastic when he or she says, "Not bad at all." English people understate positive emotion.
- Gossiping about royalty.

France
- Expecting to complete work during the French two-hour lunch.
- Attempting to conduct significant business during August—*les vacances* (vacation time).
- Greeting a French person for the first time and not using a title such as "sir" or "madam" (or "monsieur," "madame," or "mademoiselle").

Italy
- Eating too much pasta, as it is not the main course.
- Handing out business cards freely. Italians use them infrequently.

Spain
- Expecting punctuality. Your appointments will usually arrive 20 to 30 minutes late.
- Making the American sign for "okay" with your thumb and forefinger. In Spain (and many other countries) this is vulgar.

Scandinavia (Denmark, Sweden, Norway)
- Being overly rank conscious. Scandinavians pay relatively little attention to a person's place in the hierarchy.

ASIA

All Asian countries
- Pressuring an Asian job applicant or employee to brag about his or her accomplishments. Asians feel self-conscious when boasting about individual accomplishments; they prefer to let the record speak for itself. In addition, they prefer to talk about group rather than individual accomplishment.

Japan
- Shaking hands or hugging Japanese (as well as other Asians) in public. Japanese consider these practices to be offensive.
- Not interpreting "We'll consider it" as a no when spoken by a Japanese businessperson. Japanese negotiators mean no when they say "We'll consider it."
- Not giving small gifts to Japanese when conducting business. Japanese are offended by not receiving these gifts.
- Giving your business card to a Japanese businessperson more than once. Japanese prefer to give and receive business cards only once.

China
- Using black borders on stationary and business cards, because black is associated with death.

(Continued)

- Giving small gifts to Chinese when conducting business. Chinese are offended by these gifts.
- Making cold calls on Chinese business executives. An appropriate introduction is required for a first-time meeting with a Chinese official.

Korea
- Saying no. Koreans feel it is important to have visitors leave with good feelings.

India
- Telling Indians you prefer not to eat with your hands. If the Indians are not using cutlery when eating they expect you to do likewise.

MEXICO AND LATIN AMERICA

Mexico
- Flying into a Mexican city in the morning and expecting to close a deal by lunch. Mexicans build business relationships slowly.

Brazil
- Attempting to impress Brazilians by speaking a few words of Spanish. Portuguese is the official language of Brazil.

Most Latin American countries
- Wearing elegant and expensive jewelry during a business meeting. Most Latin Americans think people should appear more conservative during a business meeting.

Note: A cultural mistake for Americans to avoid when conducting business in most countries outside the United States and Canada is to insist on getting down to business quickly. North Americans in small towns also like to build a relationship before getting down to business. The preceding suggestions will lead to cross-cultural skill development if practiced in the right setting. During the next 30 days, look for an opportunity to relate to a person from another culture in the way described in these suggestions. Observe the reaction of the other person for feedback on your cross-cultural effectiveness.

to-understand manner. Minimize the use of idioms and analogies specific to your language. A computer analyst from Greece left confused after a discussion about a software problem with her manager. The manager said, "Let's talk about this another time because *I can't seem to get to first base with you.*" (The manager was referring to the fact that the conversation was headed nowhere because he couldn't come to an agreement with the analyst.) The computer analyst did not ask for clarification because she did not want to appear uninformed.

4. *Observe cultural differences in etiquette.* Violating rules of etiquette without explanation can erect immediate communication barriers. A major rule of etiquette in many countries is that people address each other by last name unless they have worked together for a long time. Letitia Baldrige recommends that you explain the difference in custom to prevent misunderstanding. Imagine this scenario, in which you are working with a man from Germany and you are speaking:

Herr Schultz, in my country by now I would be calling you Heinrich and you would be calling me Charlie. Would you be comfortable

with that? Because if you wouldn't, I would be glad to call you Herr Schultz until you tell me it is time to call you Heinrich.[10]

5. *Be sensitive to differences in nonverbal communication.* Stay alert to the possibility that your nonverbal signal may be misinterpreted by a person from another culture. An engineer for a New Jersey company was asked a question by a German coworker. He signaled OK by making a circle with his thumb and forefinger. The German worker stormed away, because in his country the same gesture is a personal insult and a vulgar gesture.

6. *Do not be diverted by style, accent, grammar, or personal appearance.* Although these superficial factors are all related to business success, they are difficult to interpret when judging a person from another culture. It is therefore better to judge the merits of the statement or behavior.[11] A brilliant individual from another culture may still be learning your language and thus make basic mistakes in speaking your language. Also, he or she might not yet have developed a sensitivity to dress style in your culture.

BUSINESS IMPLICATIONS OF UNDERSTANDING CULTURAL DIFFERENCES

Top-level management at many companies emphasizes cross-cultural understanding, including overcoming communication barriers, because such activities improve profits. If you establish rapport with people from other cultures—and avoid antagonizing them—they will most likely become and remain your customers. Similarly, if you establish good rapport with valuable employees from other cultures, they are more likely to stay with the company. Following are two examples of how cross-cultural understanding has improved profits or reduced costs:

➤ A marketing firm specializing in targeting cultural groups developed a concept for a JCPenney ad campaign based on an intimate knowledge of African-American culture. African-American women have a tradition of wearing white dresses to church on the fifth Sunday of the month. The marketing firm created an elegant photo layout of black churchgoers wearing white dresses from JCPenney. The ad led to brisk sales of white dresses at JCPenney in top markets.[12]

➤ Xerox Corp. has a longstanding reputation of reaching out to minorities and appreciating the contributions of people from diverse cultures. As a result, Xerox has been able to recruit and retain talented people from many cultural groups. One of many examples is Ursula Burns, the head of worldwide manufacturing, who is helping the company find ways to cut per-unit manufacturing costs by 15 to 20 percent. Burns is the highest placed black woman in American manufacturing.

➤ Several large automobile dealerships across the United States and Canada have deliberately cultivated a culturally diverse sales force. This type of cultural diversity often leads to much improved sales to the diverse cultural groups. A Cadillac dealer in New York City reported that sales to Asiatic Indians have quadrupled since he hired a sales representative raised in India. The same dealer reports that more cultural diversity in the service end of the business has also boosted sales to diverse ethnic and racial groups.

TECHNIQUES FOR IMPROVING CROSS-CULTURAL RELATIONS AND VALUING DIFFERENCES

Many training programs have been developed to improve cross-cultural relations and to help employees value diversity. All of the information presented so far in this chapter is likely to be included in such programs. In this section we describe programs for improving cross-cultural relations, language training, and valuing diversity. A skill-building exercise accompanies a description of each program. We will also describe some precautions regarding how valuing differences can sometimes backfire.

CULTURAL TRAINING

For many years companies and government agencies have prepared their workers for overseas assignments. The method most frequently chosen is **cultural training**, a set of learning experiences designed to help employees understand the customs, traditions, and beliefs of another culture. In today's diverse business environment and international marketplace, learning about individuals raised in different cultural backgrounds has become more important. Many industries therefore train employees in cross-cultural relations. Here we describe one such program geared to a particular industry—real estate sales.

Cross-cultural training is taken seriously in the home-building and real estate industries. Workers in these industries are learning the Asian cultural language.[13] Such training does not necessarily involve taking crash courses in Chinese or Japanese. Instead, it means the workers have been learning about subtle cultural differences between Eastern and Western people. (Some forms of cross-cultural training do emphasize learning another language, as described in the next section.)

One justification for this training is that Asians represent 3 percent of the population in the United States, totaling 7.3 million people. Also, because the fast-expanding Asian population is affluent, they are a target market for home builders and sellers. In California, for example, Asians and Asian-Americans account for 30 to 40 percent of the first-time buyers' market.

Builders and Realtors hire cultural diversity specialists to help them learn how to communicate with and accommodate their customers from China, Japan, Taiwan, Korea, Vietnam, and the Philippines. (*Realtor* is a trademark name for a certified real estate broker.) Home builders and Realtors receive cultural training in issues such as the following:

➤ Negotiating styles

➤ Money-matter discussions

➤ Use of body language such as eye contact

➤ Business etiquette

➤ Design preferences in a home, such as *feng shui* (term referring to the ancient Chinese philosophy of creating a harmonious home environment, leading to good luck and prosperity for the inhabitants)

One cultural training seminar teaches participants to examine the mind-set of Asian people in order to understand their actions. Real estate personnel are taught the dynamics of an Asian family who might look at model homes as a group. A home-buying decision involves the entire family. As a trainer notes, "So when a professional couple comes in with Grandma, Grandpa, and the kids, be very respectful to everyone. Probably the older couple will be making the down payment."

Participants are also taught that carefully observing body language will help the seller determine who is the boss in the family. The trainer explains as follows: "In the United States, we always can tell who's the decision maker. It's usually the one who talks the most. But in Asian cultures, very often the one who doesn't talk is the one who has the power."

Realtors are also taught how to sell to Asian customers. Asians frown on familiarity, so sales representatives are urged not to be aggressive. Patience is a virtue in selling to Asians. Chinese, in particular, prefer to develop a relationship gradually rather than close a deal quickly. A point established early in the seminar is that the worst error is to mistake a person of one Asian extraction for one of another (such as a Vietnamese for a Japanese). The Asian continent comprises 41 countries, with 19 in the Pacific Rim.

Dozens of other small, yet important, details are presented in the seminar to improve relationships with Asian clients. Participants learn different types of handshakes, how to bow the correct ways, and how to exchange business cards. Participants even learn about the significance of colors and certain numbers to Asians. For example, Asians consider white, blue, and yellow to be funeral colors and might reject a house lavishly decorated with these colors. Some Asians might choose a house based on whether the numbers in the address are thought to bring good or bad luck.

To practice improving your cross-cultural relations, do Skill-Building Exercise 6-3. Asian and Asian-American class members may have a natural advantage in playing the roles in the exercise.

LANGUAGE TRAINING

Learning a foreign language is often part of cultural training, yet it can also be a separate activity. Knowledge of a second language is important because it builds better connections with people from other cultures than does relying on a translator. Many workers, aside from international business specialists, also

Skill-Building Exercise 6-3

CROSS-CULTURAL RELATIONS ROLE PLAY

To get started applying cross-cultural sensitivity, a group of students engage in the following role play. One person plays the role of a Realtor who is showing a single-family dwelling to the Wong family (Chinese Americans). The Realtor recognizes that the family is a hot prospect, because they are affluent, headed by two business professionals. Six students play the role of the Wong family: two parents, two grandparents, and two elementary-school-age children. The Wong family would like to purchase this luxurious home at a fair price. The grandparents in particular think that they should buy only from a Realtor who respects their culture.

The Realtor and the Wong family engage in the selling transaction for about 10 minutes. The balance of the class will critically observe the interaction and then provide feedback.

choose to develop skills in a target language. Speaking another language can help build rapport with customers and employees who speak that language.

Almost all language training has elements similar to taking a course in another language or self-study. Companies invest heavily in helping employees learn a target language because it facilitates conducting business in other countries. Medical specialists, police workers, and fire fighters also find second language skills to be quite helpful because clients under stress, such as an injured person, are likely to revert to their native tongue. Here is a sampling of the range of activities and costs for language training used in business:[14]

$50—A language training CD-ROM and a microphone for speech recognition.

$275—One person participating in a group language-training course.

$475—A language-training CD-ROM, 12 interactive lessons with a teacher over the Internet and homework incorporating Web sites in foreign languages.

$4000—A one-time fee to set up video conferencing equipment ($1,500) and 50 hours of instruction from a language-training teacher ($50 per hour).

$10,000—A two-day cross-cultural program and eight days in a language immersion program for the employee and partner.

As with any other skill training, these investments can pay off only if the trainee is willing to work hard at developing the new skill outside the training sessions. Allowing even 10 days to pass without practicing your target language will result in a sharp decline in your ability to use that language.

Skill-Building Exercise 6-4 presents a low-cost, pleasant method of enhancing your foreign language and cross-cultural skills.

Skill-Building Exercise 6-4

USING THE INTERNET TO HELP DEVELOP FOREIGN LANGUAGE SKILLS

A useful way of developing skills in another language, and learning more about another culture, is to create a "bookmark" or "favorite" written in your target language. In this way, each time you go to the Internet on your own computer, your cover page will contain fresh information in the language you want to develop.

To get started, use a search engine such as Yahoo! or Excite that offers choices in several languages. Enter a search word such as "newspaper" or "current events" in the search probe. After you find a suitable choice, enter the edit function for "Favorites" or "Bookmarks" and insert that newspaper as your cover page. For example, imagine that French is your target language and culture. The Yahoo! France search engine might have brought you to www.france2.fr. This Web site keeps you abreast of French and international news, sports, and cultural events—written in French. Now every time you access the Internet, you can spend five minutes on your second language and becoming multicultural. You can save a lot of travel costs and time using the Internet to help you become multicultural, including developing proficiency in another language.

DIVERSITY TRAINING (TRAINING IN VALUING DIFFERENCES)

The general purpose of cultural training is to help workers understand people from other cultures. Understanding can lead to dealing more effectively with them as work associates or customers. **Diversity training** (or **valuing-differences training**) has a slightly different purpose. It attempts to bring about workplace harmony by teaching people how to get along better with diverse work associates. Quite often the program is aimed at minimizing open expressions of racism and sexism. Valuing-differences training takes a number of forms. Nevertheless, all center around increasing awareness of and empathy for people who are different in some noticeable way from oneself.

Training sessions in valuing differences focus on the ways that men and women or people of different races reflect different values, attitudes, and cultural backgrounds. These sessions can vary from several hours to several days. Training sessions can also be held over a long period of time. Sometimes the program is confrontational, sometimes not. As described by diversity consultant H. Roosevelt Thomas, Jr., the objectives of valuing-differences training include one or more of the following:[15]

➤ Fostering awareness and acceptance of individual differences.

➤ Helping participants understand their own feelings and attitudes about people who are "different."

➤ Exploring how differences might be tapped as assets in the workplace.

➤ Enhancing work relations between people who are different from each other.

An essential part of relating more effectively to diverse groups is to empathize with their points of view. To help training participants develop empathy, representatives of various groups explain their feelings related to workplace issues. A representative segment of a training program designed to enhance empathy took the following format. A minority group member was seated at the middle of a circle. First, the coworkers listened to a Vietnamese woman explain how she felt excluded from the in-group composed of whites and African-Americans in her department. "I feel like you just tolerate me. You do not make me feel that I am somebody important."

The next person to sit in the middle of the circle was a Muslim. He complained about people wishing him Merry Christmas. "I would much prefer that my coworkers stop to think that I do not celebrate Christian holidays. I respect your religion, but it is not my religion."

Skill-Building Exercise 6-5 provides you an opportunity to simulate an empathy-building experience in a valuing-differences training program.

Cautions About Diversity Training

Diversity (or valuing-differences) training has frequently improved cross-cultural relationships in the workplace. Yet such programs can also create ill will and waste time. One problem is that participants are sometimes encouraged to be too confrontational and express too much hostility. Companies have found that when employees are too blunt during these sessions, it may be difficult to patch up interpersonal relations in the work group later on.

Another problem is that revelations made during a diversity training session may backfire against the company. During one session, for example, a manager admitted that the company had intentionally denied a promotion to an African-American sales representative because he was perceived as a troublemaker. Several months later the sales representative initiated a lawsuit against the company.

A negative consequence of diversity training programs is that they sometimes result in perpetuating stereotypes about groups, such as people from Latin America not placing much value on promptness for meetings. A related problem is that a valuing-differences program might focus too much on differences instead of similarities.[16] For example, even if people are raised with different cultural values they must all work harmoniously together to accomplish work. Although a worker believes that relationships are more important than profits, he or she must still produce enough to be a good investment for the company.

SUMMARY

Today's workplace has become more culturally diverse, and business has become increasingly international. As a result, to succeed one must be able to relate effectively to people from different cultural groups from within and outside one's country. The true meaning of valuing diversity is to respect and enjoy a wide range of cultural and individual differences. The diversity umbrella con-

Skill-Building Exercise 6-5

DEVELOPING EMPATHY FOR DIFFERENCES

Class members come up to the front of the room one by one and give a brief presentation (perhaps even three minutes) of any way in which they have been perceived as different, and how they felt about this perception. The difference can be of any kind, relating to characteristics such as ethnicity, race, choice of major, physical appearance, height, weight, hair color, or body piercing. After each member of the class (perhaps even the instructor) has presented, class members discuss what they learned from the exercise. It is also important to discuss how this exercise can improve relationships on the job.

tinues to include more people as the workforce encompasses a greater variety of people.

The groundwork for developing effective cross-cultural relations is to understand cultural differences. Three important goals for understanding cultural differences are (1) cultural sensitivity, (2) respect for all workers and all cultures, and (3) cultural fluency—the ability to conduct business in a diverse, international environment.

Countries differ in their national values, leading to differences in how most people from a given country will react to situations. The values studied here are (a) individualism versus collectivism; (b) high power distance (accepting authority) versus low power distance; (c) low uncertainty avoidance versus high uncertainty avoidance; (d) materialism versus concern for others; (e) long-term orientation versus short-term orientation; (f) formality versus informality; (g) urgent time orientation versus casual time orientation; and (h) high-context versus low-context cultures.

An effective way of being culturally sensitive is to minimize actions that are likely to offend people from another culture based on their values. These cultural bloopers can take place when working in another country or when dealing with foreigners in one's own country. Studying potential cultural bloopers is helpful, but recognize also that individual differences may be of significance.

Communication barriers created by cultural differences can often be overcome by the following: (a) Be sensitive to the fact that these barriers exist; (b) show respect for all workers; (c) use straightforward language and speak slowly and clearly; (d) observe cultural differences in etiquette; (e) be sensitive to differences in nonverbal communication; and (f) do not be diverted by style, accent, grammar, or personal appearance.

Improved cross-cultural understanding can improve profits through attracting and retaining diverse customers. Similarly, establishing good rapport with valuable employees from other cultures can improve employee retention.

Cultural training is a set of learning experiences designed to help employees understand the customs, traditions, and beliefs of another culture. In today's diverse business environment and international marketplace, learning

about individuals raised in different cultural backgrounds has become more important. Learning a foreign language is often part of cultural training, yet it can also be a separate activity.

Diversity training (or valuing-differences training) attempts to bring about workplace harmony by teaching people how to get along better with diverse work associates. Most forms of valuing-differences training center around increasing awareness of and empathy for people who are different in some noticeable way from yourself.

QUESTIONS FOR DISCUSSION AND REVIEW

1. Several well-known companies conduct *awareness weeks* to celebrate certain diverse groups such as Hispanics or homosexuals. What is your opinion of the effectiveness of such activities for bringing about workplace harmony?

2. In recent years many middle-aged white males have emphasized that they want to be included under the diversity umbrella. What is your reaction to their demands?

3. Some companies, such as Singapore Airlines, make a deliberate effort for customer-contact personnel to all be of the same ethnic group (Singapore natives). How justified is this practice in an era of cultural diversity and valuing differences?

4. A major purpose of diversity programs is to help people celebrate differences. Why should people celebrate a difference such as an attention deficit disorder?

5. Provide an example of cultural insensitivity of any kind that you have seen, read about, or could imagine.

6. Classified ads for positions listed in the French newspaper *Le Figaro* often require the applicant to be fluent in two languages in addition to French. What implications might this information have for your career?

7. How could you use the information presented in Table 6-1, comparing U.S. values to those of other countries, to help you succeed in business?

8. If you were a supervisor, how would you deal with a group member who had a very low value for power distance?

9. The cultural bloopers presented in Skill-Building Exercise 6-2 all dealt with errors people make in regard to people who are not American. Give an example of a cultural blooper a person from another country might make in the United States.

10. Many people speak loudly to deaf people, blind people, and those who speak a different language. Based on the information presented in this chapter, what mistakes are these people making?

CONFUSED AND CONCERNED IN SOUTH KOREA

Annie Lee, an American business student with Korean heritage, was given the opportunity several summers ago to work for SKAC, the largest animation company in South Korea. SKAC is known for its advanced technology animation used in such projects as Disney's *The Little Mermaid* and *The Simpsons* television show. To help establish itself as a major player in the animation industry, SKAC launched *Animatoon,* the first animation magazine. The purpose of the magazine was to inform other animation companies about new technology, new faces, and events around the globe in the animation industry. Another division of the company produced animated cartoons.

Lee was hired by the founder, Nelson Shin, to work in the magazine department translating reports and interviews from English into Korean and vice versa. Shin warmly welcomed Lee. He, too, was Korean American, and he acknowledged the differences in working environments between the two countries. At the outset of employment Shin said, "Your day starts at eight and ends at five, Monday through Friday. Saturdays are optional since we don't work on weekends in the States."

The translation department consisted of 60 percent Korean Americans. All business was therefore supposed to be conducted in accordance with Western (non-Asian) business culture. Annie Lee enjoyed working with fellow Korean Americans in a prestigious company and receiving high pay.

SKAC worked with big U. S. entertainment companies such as Warner Brothers and Disney Corporation on a long-term basis. Annie Lee and her coworkers were held accountable to maintain the positive working relationships with the U.S. companies. A major reason for emphasizing the positive relationships is that SKAC could not stay in business if these customers were lost.

From Annie Lee's perspective, her job was going well and she was making a good contribution to the translation department. Then one day her manager, Kim Young, confronted her in these words: "Why don't you come in at six in the morning like the secretaries do? You could clean the office, make coffee, and run small errands."

Surprised by Young's comments, Annie said, "Why should I do those things? To my knowledge, my job title does not include the word 'secretary'."

Young replied, "You Americans have no sense of values and respect. How can you call yourself Korean? You are in Korea, and you must listen to your elders."

Upset and frustrated, Annie left without making further comment. During lunch hour, she expressed her concerns to her coworkers. Her close friend, Jen Sooko, who had been working at the company for six months, told Annie about a similar experience she had with Young. "I was ready to punch him out when he said he needed a pack of cigarettes," she said.

"So what did you do?" asked Annie.

Jen replied, "What was I supposed to do? I went across the street and bought him a pack of cigarettes."

Other employees had similar experiences, but no one had tried to resolve the problem. During a six-month period, six women employees quit, with no one explaining to top management why they quit.

Annie started to feel increasingly uncomfortable working under Young's supervision. She began to see the quality of her work diminish rapidly. She was no longer proud of the translations she was producing.

Jen took Annie aside one day and said, "You've been making a lot of mistakes lately. I'm worried about you."

Case Questions

1. What cross-cultural errors is Kim Young committing?

2. What cross-cultural errors are Annie Lee and her coworkers committing?

3. What can higher management do to restore harmony in the translation department?

Case researched by Annie Lee, Rochester Institute of Technology, 1999.

Chapter 7

Resolving Conflicts with Others

Learning Objectives

After reading and studying this chapter and doing the exercises you should be able to

➤ Specify why so much interpersonal conflict exists in organizations.

➤ Recognize your typical method of resolving conflict.

➤ Identify the five modes of handling conflict.

➤ Develop effective techniques for resolving conflict and negotiating.

➤ Understand how to combat sexual harassment in the workplace.

"Sorry, I can't let you take off three days to attend your friend's wedding in Indianapolis," said Gerry, the accounting supervisor, to Wendy, the accountant. *"This is our busiest season, and I just can't spare you."*

"What do you mean you can't spare me?" asked Wendy. *"My best friend is getting married, and I'm the maid of honor. I have to go."*

"You may think you have to attend the wedding," replied Gerry, *"but we need you here to help us manage our peak workload. If you decide to take three unauthorized days from work, you will face company discipline."*

The unfortunate incident between Gerry and Wendy illustrates several different meanings of **conflict**. A conflict is a situation in which two or more goals, values, or events are incompatible or mutually exclusive. Gerry wants Wendy to be present every day during the busy tax season, and Wendy wants to attend an out-of-town wedding. A conflict is also a strife, quarrel, or battle. Gerry and Wendy are in a quarrel. Finally, conflict is said to occur when one side interferes with, disrupts, or in some way makes the other side less effective. This aspect of conflict will occur only if Wendy is disciplined by a harsh measure such as suspension or termination.

This chapter will help you improve your ability to resolve conflicts with people at work. The same techniques are also useful in personal life. To improve your understanding of how to resolve conflict, we will present specific techniques and also explain why so much conflict exists. To get you started relating the topic of conflict to yourself, take Self-Assessment Quiz 7-1.

SOURCES OF INTERPERSONAL CONFLICT IN ORGANIZATIONS

HURT: Herida, lesion, golpe lastimadura.

Conflict between and among people has many sources, or causes. In this section we describe some of the leading sources. If you understand the cause of a conflict, it can help you resolve the conflict and help prevent a similar recurrence. For example, if you learn that much conflict on the job is caused by a series of little hurts (*pinches*), you can apologize for these hurts. You can also be on guard to avoid such pinches in the future. Although specific sources of conflict can be identified, keep in mind an important fact. All conflict includes the underlying theme of incompatibility between your goals, values, or events and those of another person.

Subyacente

COMPETITION FOR LIMITED RESOURCES

An underlying source of job conflict is that few people can get all the resources they want. These resources include money, material, and human resources (or personnel). Conflicts arise when two or more people squabble over who should get the resources. Even in a prosperous organization, resources have to be divided in such a manner that not everybody gets what he or she wants.

Assume that you believe you need to have a desktop computer immediately accessible the full workday. Yet the company has decided that three people

STYLES OF CONFLICT MANAGEMENT

Directions: Check the alternative that best fits your typical reaction to the situation described.

Part I: The Quiz

1. When someone is overly hostile toward me, I usually:

 _____ A. respond in kind

 _____ B. persuade him or her to cool down

 ✓ C. hear the person out

 _____ D. walk away

2. When I walk in on a heated argument, I'm likely to:

 _____ A. jump in and take sides

 ✓ B. mediate

 _____ C. keep quiet and observe

 _____ D. leave the scene

3. When I suspect that another person is taking advantage of me, I:

 _____ A. try to get the person to stop

 ✓ B. rely on persuasion and facts

 _____ C. change how I relate to the person

 _____ D. accept the situation

4. When I don't see eye to eye with someone, I typically:

 _____ A. try to get him or her to see things my way

 _____ B. consider the problem logically

 ✓ C. search for a workable compromise

 _____ D. let the problem work itself out

5. After a run-in with someone I care about a great deal, I:

 _____ A. try to make him or her see it my way

 ✓ B. try to work out our differences

 _____ C. wait before renewing contact

 _____ D. let it lie

(Continued)

6. When I see conflict developing between two people I care about, I usually:

_____ A. express disappointment

___✓___ B. try to mediate

_____ C. watch to see what develops

_____ D. leave the scene

7. When I see conflict developing between two people who are relatively unimportant to me, I usually:

_____ A. express disappointment

_____ B. try to mediate

___✓___ C. watch to see what develops

_____ D. leave the scene

8. The feedback people give me indicates that I:

_____ A. push hard to get what I want

___✓___ B. try to work out differences

_____ C. take a conciliatory stance

_____ D. sidestep conflict

9. When having serious disagreements, I:

_____ A. talk until I've made my point

___✓___ B. talk a little more than I listen

_____ C. listen and make sure I understand

_____ D. listen passively

10. When someone does something that angers me, I generally:

_____ A. use strong, direct language

_____ B. try to persuade him or her to stop

___✓___ C. go easy, explaining how I feel

_____ D. say and do nothing

(Continued)

Part II: Score Analysis

When you've completed the questions, add all the As, Bs, Cs, and Ds to find where you collected the most responses. Then consider these profiles:

A. *Competitive.* If you picked mostly *A* responses, you feel best when you're able to direct and control others. Taken to extremes, you can be intimidating and judgmental. You are generally contemptuous of people who don't stand up for themselves, and you feel frustrated when you can't get through to someone.

B. *Collaborative.* If you scored high in this category, you may be from the "use your head to win" school of conflict management-strong—willed and ambitious, but not overbearing. You'll use persuasion, not intimidation, and are willing to compromise to end long-running conflicts.

C. *Sharing.* People who score high here don't get fired up. They listen to the opponent's point of view, analyze situations, and make a factual pitch for their case. But in the end, they will defer to opponents in the interest of harmony.

D. *Accommodative.* A high score suggests that you avoid conflict and confrontation at all costs and suppress your feelings—strong as they may be—to keep peace.

Observation: No one style of conflict management is better than another. Most people use all four, depending on the situation. But if you rely too much on one, start shifting your approach.

Source: Adapted with permission from *Executive Strategies*, National Institute of Business Management, February 20, 1990, p. 6.

must share one computer. As a result, you are likely to enter into conflict with the two others sharing the computer. The conflict will be intense if your two coworkers also think they need full-time access to a desktop computer.

ROLE CONFLICT

A major source of conflict (and stress) on the job relates to being placed in a predicament. **Role conflict** is having to choose between two competing demands or expectations. If you comply with one aspect of a role, compliance with the other is difficult or impossible. An important example would be receiving contradictory orders from two people above you in your company. If you comply with the wishes of one person, you will antagonize the other.

A high-performing sales representative received a job offer from a manager in another division in her company. Her present manager told her she was not allowed to transfer and made her a counteroffer. The sales representative found herself in conflict with the two managers. Distraught over the conflict, she found employment with a competitive firm in a comparable position to the internal job offer she had received.

Role conflict can take various forms. You might be asked to accomplish two objectives that are in apparent conflict. If your boss asked you to hurry up and

finish your work but also decrease your mistakes, you would experience this type of conflict (plus perhaps a headache!). Another problem is when two or more people give you incompatible directions. Your immediate supervisor may want you to complete a crash project on time, but company policy temporarily prohibits authorizing overtime payments to clerical help or hiring office temporaries.

Role conflict also results when two different roles that you play are in conflict. Your company may expect you to travel 50 percent of the time, whereas your spouse threatens a divorce if you travel over 25 percent of the time. To complete the picture, a form of role conflict takes place when the role(s) your organization expects you to occupy are in conflict with your basic values. Your company may ask you to fire substandard performers, but this could be in conflict with your humanistic values.

BUILDING STONE WALLS

The slow and steady growth of a conflict situation has been likened by Richard J. Mayer to the building of a stone wall. The seed of the conflict is a minor incident that is not dealt with openly, called a *pinch*. Next, the person pinched unconsciously gathers data to support his or her view of the situation because of a need to be right. Much of the data are subject to perceptual distortion (seeing things in a way that fits our needs). As a result, a wall of minor incidents is built. The incidents eventually become an insurmountable obstacle (or stone wall), preventing honest and candid interaction with the *pincher*.[1]

A typical pinch occurs when an employee fails to share credit for a good idea he or she received from a coworker. The coworker feels slighted and then looks for other incidents of the first person being dishonest. Communication breaks down between the two, and they are involved in frequent arguments. The employee who failed to share credit may be unaware of how or why the conflict began. If the pinched worker had confronted the issue early on, the conflict might not have festered. Have you ever been pinched psychologically and said nothing about it?

PERSONALITY CLASHES

Many workplace disagreements arise because people simply dislike each other. A **personality clash** is thus an antagonistic relationship between two people based on differences in personal attributes, preferences, interests, values, and styles. A personality clash reflects negative chemistry between two people, while personal differences are based more specifically on a value clash. People involved in a personality clash often have difficulty specifying why they dislike each other. The end result, however, is that they cannot maintain an amiable work relationship. A peculiarity about personality clashes is that people who get along well may begin to clash after working together for a number of years. A contributing factor is that as both people change and as the situation changes, the two people may no longer be compatible.

AGGRESSIVE PERSONALITIES, INCLUDING BULLIES

Coworkers naturally disagree about topics, issues, and ideas. Yet some people convert disagreement into an attack that puts down other people and damages their self-esteem. As a result, conflict surfaces. **Aggressive personalities** are people who verbally, and sometimes physically, attack others frequently. Verbal aggression takes the form of insults, teasing, ridicule, and profanity. The aggression may also be expressed as attacks on the victim's character, competence, background, and physical appearance.[2]

Aggressive personalities are also referred to as *workplace bullies*. Among their typical behaviors are interrupting others, ranting in a loud voice, and making threats. One bullying manager would frequently ask people, "Are you going to be stupid the rest of your life?" Bullied workers complain of a range of psychological and physical ailments such as the following: anxiety, sleeplessness, headache, irritable bowel syndrome, skin problems, panic attacks, and low self-esteem.[3]

Aggressiveness can also take the extreme form of the shooting or knifing of a former boss or colleague by a mentally unstable worker recently dismissed from the company. Violence has become so widespread that homicide is a leading cause of workplace deaths. Most of these deaths result from a robbery or commercial crime. Many of these killings, however, are perpetrated by a disgruntled worker or former employee harboring an unresolved conflict. As companies have continued to reduce their workforce despite being profitable, these incidents have increased in frequency.[4]

CONFLICT-MANAGEMENT STYLES

The information presented so far is designed to help you understand the nature of conflict. Such background information is useful for resolving conflict because it helps you understand what is happening in a conflict situation. The next two sections offer more specific information about managing and resolving conflict. Before describing specific methods of resolving conflict, it is useful to present more details about five general styles, or modes, of handling conflict. You received preliminary information on four of these five styles when you completed Self-Assessment Quiz 7-1.

As shown in Figure 7-1, Kenneth Thomas identified five major styles of conflict management. Each style is based on a combination of satisfying one's own concerns (assertiveness) and satisfying the concerns of others (cooperativeness).[5]

Competitive Style
The competitive style is a desire to win one's own concerns at the expense of the other party, or to dominate. A person with a competitive orientation is likely to engage in power struggles in which one side wins and the other loses (an approach referred to as *win-lose*).

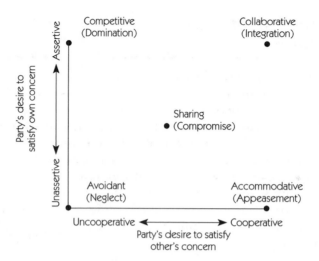

Figure 7-1 Conflict-Handling Styles According to Degree of Cooperation and Assertiveness

Source: Kenneth W. Thomas, "Organizational Conflict," in Steven Kerr, ed., *Organization Behavior* (Columbus, Ohio: Grid Publishing, 1979), p. 156.

Accommodative Style

The accommodative style favors appeasement, or satisfying the other's concerns without taking care of one's own. People with this orientation may be generous or self-sacrificing just to maintain a relationship. An irate customer might be accommodated with a full refund, just to calm down the person. The intent of such accommodation might also be to retain the customer's loyalty.

Accommodation sounds harmless, but, according to Sidney Simon, when it runs unchecked at the expense of what somebody really wants it can lead to debilitating resentment, sickness, or even violence.[6] The problem is that the suppressed feelings create inner conflict and stress.

Sharing Style

The sharing style is halfway between domination and appeasement. Sharers prefer moderate but incomplete satisfaction for both parties, which results in a compromise. The term *splitting the difference* reflects this orientation and is commonly used in such activities as purchasing a house or car.

Collaborative Style

In contrast to the other styles, the collaborative style reflects a desire to fully satisfy the desires of both parties. It is based on an underlying philosophy of **win-win**, the belief that after conflict has been resolved, both sides should gain something of value. The use of a win-win approach is genuinely aimed at arriving at a settlement that meets the needs of both parties, or at least does not badly damage the welfare of the other side. The option chosen results in a *mutual gain*. When collaborative approaches to resolving conflict are used, the relationships among the parties are built on and improved. The following example uses a win-win approach to resolve conflict.

Skill-Building Exercise 7-1

WIN-WIN CONFLICT RESOLUTION

The class organizes into small problem-solving groups. Each group spends about 10 minutes finding a win-win solution to one of the following conflict situations:

1. Two coworkers want you to go to lunch with them more regularly, but you believe that you are too busy to go out to lunch regularly.
2. Deborah, a computer operator, wants workmates to call her "Deborah." Yet several people in the office persist in calling her "Deb" or "Debbie." *"Call her Deborah"*
3. You are offered a transfer within your company to an exciting job that you want strongly. Your manager says he cannot let you go because you are too valuable. *Raise*

Bruce is an office assistant in a company that supplies food to restaurants, hospitals, and nursing homes. According to his budget analysis, Bruce needed a 5 percent salary increase to meet his monthly expenses. The company owner explained that there was no money in the budget for a salary increase. A cordial discussion about the issue led to an option for mutual gain. Bruce would receive the 5 percent salary increase as long as he increased his productivity enough to cover the increase. His target was to increase his productivity to the point that the company could decrease the hours worked by an office temporary. The amount of the decrease covered the 5 percent salary increase.

Finding win-win solutions to problems (or options for mutual gain) is one of the most important conflict-resolution skills. To obtain practice in this skill, do Skill-Building Exercise 7-1.

Avoidant Style

The avoider is a combination of uncooperative and unassertive. He or she is indifferent to the concerns of either party. The person may actually be withdrawing from the conflict to rely upon fate.

In the following description of specific techniques for resolving conflict, attempt to relate most of them to these five key styles. For example, you will observe that the confrontation and problem-solving technique reflects the collaborative style.

GUIDELINES AND TECHNIQUES FOR RESOLVING CONFLICTS

Interpersonal conflict in organizations is inevitable. A career-minded person must therefore learn effective ways of resolving conflict. In this section we describe methods of conflict resolution that you can use on your own. All are

based somewhat on the underlying model of win-win, or integrating the interests of both parties. Integrating the interests focuses on resolving the underlying concerns of the parties in conflict. By dealing with these concerns, it is more worthwhile for both sides to resolve the conflict than it is to have no agreement.[7]

> Suppose a man named Bill Budweiser wanted to open a beer brewery and name his beer Budweiser. The company lawyers from Anheuser-Busch who own the rights to the brand name Budweiser would attempt to block him from using the same brand name—even if his family name is Budweiser. Bill Budweiser would hire his own lawyer to fight back. Two key concerns must be addressed. Mr. Budweiser's underlying concern is that he feels his civil liberties have been violated because he cannot name a business after himself. And Bill Budweiser must deal with Anheuser-Busch's concern about a smaller company capitalizing on its well-known name (brand equity).

Later in the chapter you will be asked to resolve the beer company conflict. For now, the five methods are as follows:

1. Confrontation and problem solving.

2. Constructive handling of criticism.

3. Image exchanging.

4. Cognitive restructuring.

5. Negotiating and bargaining.

CONFRONTATION AND PROBLEM SOLVING

The ideal approach to resolving any conflict is to confront the real issue and then solve the problem. Confrontation means taking a problem-solving approach to differences and identifying the underlying facts, logic, or emotions that account for them. When conflicts are resolved through confronting and understanding their causes, people feel responsible for finding the soundest answer.[8]

Confrontation can proceed gently, in a way that preserves a good working relationship, as shown by this example. Assume that Mary, the person working at the desk next to you, loudly cracks chewing gum while she works. You find the gum chewing both distracting and nauseating. If you don't bring the problem to Mary's attention, it will probably grow in proportion with time. Yet you are hesitant to enter into an argument about something that a person might regard as a civil liberty (the right to chew gum in public places).

A psychologically sound alternative is for you to approach her directly in this manner:

You: Mary, there is something bothering me that I would like to discuss with you.

She: Go ahead, I don't mind listening to other people's problems.

You: My problem concerns something you are doing that makes it difficult for me to concentrate on my work. When you chew gum you make loud cracking noises that grate on my nerves. It may be my problem, but the noise does bother me.

She: I guess I could stop chewing gum when you're working next to me. It's probably just a nervous habit.

CONSTRUCTIVE HANDLING OF CRITICISM

Learning to profit from criticism is an effective way of benefitting from conflict. People who benefit from criticism are able to stand outside themselves while being criticized. It is as if they are watching the criticism from a distance and looking for its possible merits. People who take criticism personally anguish when receiving negative feedback. Following are several specific suggestions for dealing with criticism, including two methods that will often get the other party on your side.[9]

1. *See yourself at a distance.* Place an imaginary Plexiglas shield between you and the person giving the criticism. Attempt to be a detached observer looking for useful information.

2. *Ask for clarification and specifics.* Ask politely for more details about the negative behavior in question so you can change if change is warranted. If your boss is criticizing you for being rude to customers, you might respond: "I certainly do not want to be rude. Can you give me a couple of examples of how I was rude? I need your help in working on this problem." After asking questions, you can better determine whether the criticism is valid.

3. *Decide on a response.* An important part of learning from criticism is to respond appropriately to the critic. Let the criticizer know what you agree with. Apologize for the undesirable behavior, such as saying, "I apologize for being rude to customers. I know what I can do differently now. I'll be more patient so as not to appear rude."

4. *Disarm the opposition.* As an extension of the point just made, you will often decide to agree with the criticizer because the person has a legitimate complaint about you. If you deny the reality of that person's complaint, he or she will continue to harp on that point and the issue will remain unresolved. By agreeing with the criticism of you, you may set the stage for a true resolution of the problem.

Agreeing with criticism made by a person with formal authority over you is effective, because by doing so you are then in a position to ask for his or her help in improving the situation. Rational managers realize that it is their responsibility to help subordinates overcome problems, not merely to criticize them. Imagine that you have been chronically late with reports during the last six months. It is time for a performance review, and you know that you will be reprimanded for your tardiness. You also hope that your manager will not

Skill-Building Exercise 7-2

DISARMING THE OPPOSITION

In each of these two scenarios, one person plays the role of the person with more power in the situation. The other person plays the role of the individual attempting to disarm the criticizer.

1. A representative from a credit organization telephones you at work to inform you that you are 60 days behind schedule on your car payment. The agent wants a settlement as soon as possible. Unfortunately, the credit agent is correct. Run this happy scenario for about five minutes.

2. Your manager calls you into the office to discuss the 10-page report you just submitted. The boss says in a harsh tone, "Your report is a piece of trash. I counted 25 word-use mistakes such as writing *whether* for *weather* and *seen* for *scene.* (Your spell checker couldn't catch these errors.) Besides that I can't follow many of your sentences, and you left out the table of statistics. I'm wondering if you are qualified for this job."

downgrade all other aspects of your performance because of your tardy reports. Here is how disarming the opposition would work in this situation:

Your manager: Have a seat. It's time for your performance review, and we have a lot to talk about. I'm concerned about some things.

You: So am I. It appears that I'm having a difficult time getting my reports in on time. I wonder if I'm being a perfectionist. Do you have any suggestions?

Your manager: Well, I like your attitude. Maybe you are trying to make your reports too perfect before you turn them in. I think you can improve in getting your reports in on time. Try not to figure everything out to five decimal places. We need thoroughness around here, but we can't overdo it.

Disarming is effective because it takes the wind out of the other person's sails and has a calming effect. The other person is often waiting to clobber you if you deny guilt. If you admit guilt, you are more difficult to clobber. Skill-Building Exercise 7-2 gives you an opportunity to practice disarming the opposition.

IMAGE EXCHANGING

The essential point of **image exchanging** is that you and your antagonist make it clear that you understand each other's point of view. Empathy of this kind may then lead to a useful and productive compromise. A convenient application of this method is for you to list on a sheet of paper (a) your side of the argument and (b) what you think is the other person's side of the argument. Next, the other person does the same for you. Figure 7-2 is an example of how images might be exchanged. Each person makes up an image sheet without

You: My side of the story	What I think is your side of the story
1. I'm usually on time for work.	1. I'm not very dependable.
2. I live on the other side of town.	2. I live too far from the office.
3. Public transportation is unreliable in this city.	3. I take the last possible bus.
Your boss: My side of the story	What I think is your side of the story
1. You are late too often.	1. I'm as punctual as most people in the office.
2. If you cared more about your job you would consider moving closer to the office.	2. I think you don't take my transportation problems seriously.
3. If you got out of bed earlier, you could take an earlier bus.	3. I try hard to get here on time. It's not my fault that I'm late sometimes.

Figure 7-2 An Image-Exchanging List Between You and Your Team Leader, Based on a Conflict About Punctuality

consulting the other person. After the images are exchanged, discussion (and sometimes fireworks) begins.

COGNITIVE RESTRUCTURING

An indirect way of resolving interpersonal conflict is to lessen the conflicting elements in a situation by viewing them more positively. According to the technique of **cognitive restructuring**, you mentally convert negative aspects into positive ones by looking for the positive elements in a situation.[10] How you frame or choose your thoughts can determine the outcome of a conflict situation. Your thoughts influence your actions. If you search for the beneficial elements in the situation, there will be less area for dispute. Although this technique might sound like a *mind game* to you, it can work effectively.

Imagine that a coworker of yours, Jeff, has been asking you repeated questions about how to carry out a work procedure. You are about ready to tell Jeff, "Go bother somebody else; I'm not paid to be a trainer." Instead, you look for the positive elements in the situation. You say to yourself, "Jeff has been asking me a lot of questions. This does take time, but answering these questions is valuable experience. If I want to become a manager, I will have to help group members with problems."

After having completed this cognitive restructuring, you can then deal with the conflict situation more positively. You might say to Jeff, "I welcome the opportunity to help you, but we need to find a mutually convenient time. In that way, I can better concentrate on my own work." To get started with cognitive restructuring, do Skill-Building Exercise 7-3.

NEGOTIATING AND BARGAINING

Conflicts can be considered situations calling for **negotiating**, or conferring, with another person to resolve a problem. When you are negotiating a fair salary for yourself, you are trying to resolve a conflict. At first the demands of

Skill-Building Exercise 7-3

COGNITIVE RESTRUCTURING

The following are examples of negative statements about coworkers. In the space provided, cognitively restructure (reframe) each comment in a positive way.

Negative: Nancy is getting on my nerves. It takes her two weeks longer than anyone else on the team to complete her input.

Positive: _At least I'll have more time to do the previous input._

Negative: My boss is driving me crazy. He is forever telling me what I did wrong and making suggestions for improvement. He makes me feel like I'm in elementary school.

Positive: _He wants to train or he is training me to become a manager and wants me to be as good a manager as he is._

the two parties may seem incompatible, but through negotiation, a salary figure may emerge that satisfies both.

Managers and staff specialists must negotiate both internally (e.g., with subordinates, managers, and team leaders) and externally (e.g., with suppliers and government agencies). Considerable negotiation also takes place among coworkers. Team members, for example, sometimes negotiate among themselves about work assignments. One might say to the other, "I'm willing to be notetaker this year if there is some way I can cut back on the amount of plant visits I make this year." Five leading negotiating tactics are presented here. Before studying them, do Self-Assessment Quiz 7-2.

Focus on Interests, Not Positions

Rather than clinging to specific negotiating points, keep your overall interests in mind and try to satisfy them. Remember that the true object of negotiation is to satisfy the underlying interests on both sides, as in the case of Bill Budweiser. Here is how this strategy works:

You are considering accepting a job offer that will enable you to work on the type of problems you prefer and also develop your professional skills. You have a starting salary in mind that would make you very happy—15

Self-Assessment Quiz 7-2

THE NEGOTIATOR QUIZ

Directions: The following quiz is designed to give you tentative insight into your tendencies toward being an effective negotiator. Answer each statement "Mostly true" or "Mostly false" as it applies to you.

	Mostly true	Mostly false
1. Settling differences of opinion is a lot of fun.		✓
2. I try to avoid conflict and confrontation with others as much as possible.		✓
3. I am self-conscious asking people for favors they have not offered me spontaneously.		✓
4. I am generally unwilling to compromise.		✓
5. How the other side feels about the results of our negotiation is of little consequence to me.	✓	✓
6. I think very well under pressure.		✓
7. People say that I am tactful and diplomatic.		✓
8. I'm known for my ability to express my viewpoint clearly.		✓
9. Very few things in life are not negotiable.		✓
10. I always (or would always) accept whatever salary increase is offered to me.		✓
11. A person's facial expression often reveals as much as what the person actually says.		✓
12. I wouldn't mind taking a few short-range losses to win a long-range battle.		✓
13. I'm willing to work long and hard to win a small advantage.	✓	
14. I'm usually too busy talking to do much listening.	✓	
15. It's fun to haggle over price when buying a car.		✓
16. I almost always prepare in advance for a negotiating session.		✓
17. When there is something I need from another person I usually get it.	✓	
18. It would make me feel cheap if I offered somebody only two-thirds of his or her asking price.	✓	
19. People are usually paid what they are worth, so there's no use haggling over starting salaries.	✓	
20. I rarely take what people say at face value.	✓	

(Continued)

	Mostly true	Mostly false
21. It's easy for me to smile when involved in a serious discussion.	_____	✓
22. For one side to win in negotiation, the other side has to lose.	_____	✓
23. Once you start making concessions, the other side is bound to get more than you.	_____	✓
24. A good negotiating session gets my competitive urges flowing.	_____	✓
25. When negotiations are completed, both sides should walk away with something valuable.	✓	_____

Total Score _____

Scoring and Interpretation: Score yourself +1 for each of your answers that agrees with the scoring key. The higher your score, the more likely it is that you currently have good negotiating skills, *providing your self-assessment is accurate.* It might prove useful to also have somebody who has observed you negotiate on several occasions to answer the Negotiator Quiz for you. Scores of 7 or lower and 20 or higher are probably the most indicative of weak or strong negotiating potential. Here is the scoring key:

1. Mostly true	8. Mostly true	15. Mostly true	22. Mostly false
2. Mostly false	9. Mostly true	16. Mostly true	23. Mostly false
3. Mostly false	10. Mostly false	17. Mostly true	24. Mostly true
4. Mostly false	11. Mostly true	18. Mostly false	25. Mostly true
5. Mostly false	12. Mostly true	19. Mostly false	
6. Mostly true	13. Mostly true	20. Mostly true	
7. Mostly true	14. Mostly false	21. Mostly true	

percent higher than you are currently making. Your negotiating position is thus your present salary plus 15 percent. However, your true interests are probably to have more discretionary income than at present. (You want to make more purchases and invest more.) You will therefore be better off negotiating for a work situation that spreads your money further. You can now accept the offer by negotiating other points in addition to a 15 percent higher salary, including (a) working in a geographic area with a lower cost of living, (b) a better opportunity for earning a bonus, or (c) a generous expense account.

Compromise

The most widely used negotiating tactic is **compromise**, settlement of differences by mutual concessions. One party agrees to do something if the other party agrees to do something else. Compromise is a realistic approach to resolving conflict. Most labor-management disputes are settled by compromise. For instance, labor may agree to accept a smaller salary increase if management will subcontract less work to other countries.

Some people argue that compromise is not a win-win tactic. The problem is that the two parties may wind up with a solution that pacifies both but does not solve the problem. One example would be purchasing for two department heads half the new equipment each one needs. As a result, neither department really shows a productivity gain. Nevertheless, compromise is both inevitable and useful.

Begin with a Plausible Demand or Offer, Yet Allow Room for Negotiation

The commonsense approach to negotiation suggests that you begin with an extreme, almost fanciful demand or offer. The final compromise will therefore be closer to your true demand or offer than if you opened the negotiations more realistically. However, a plausible demand is useful because it shows you are bargaining in good faith. Also, if a third party has to resolve a conflict, a plausible demand or offer will receive more sympathy than an implausible one will.

> A judge listened to the cases of two people who claimed they were the victims of age discrimination by the same employer. The lawyer for the first alleged victim asked for $10 million in damages; the lawyer for the second victim asked for $200,000. The first person was awarded $50,000 in damages, and the second person $150,000. An inside source reported that the judge was so incensed by the first lawyer's demands that she decided to teach him a lesson.

Although it is advisable to begin with a plausible demand, one must still allow room for negotiation. A basic strategy of negotiation is to begin with a demand that allows room for compromise and concession. If you think you need $5,000 in new software for your department, you might begin negotiations by asking for a $7,000 package. Your boss offers you $4,000 as a starting point. After negotiation, you may wind up with the $5,000 you need.

Make Small Concessions Gradually

Making steady concessions leads to more mutually satisfactory agreements in most situations. Gradually, you concede little things to the other side. The hard-line approach to bargaining is to make your concession early in the negotiation and then grant no further concession. The tactic of making small concessions is well suited to purchasing a new car. In order to reach a price you consider acceptable, you might grant concessions such as agreeing to finance the car through the dealer or purchasing a service contract.

Know Your Best Alternative to a Negotiated Agreement (BATNA)

The reason you would probably negotiate would be to produce something better than the result obtainable without negotiating. The goal of negotiating is thus not just to agree, but to obtain more valuable results than would otherwise have occurred. When you are aware of your best alternative to a negotiated agreement (BATNA), it sets a floor to the agreement you are willing to accept. Your BATNA becomes the standard that can protect both parties from accept-

ing terms that are too unfavorable. It also keeps you from walking away from terms that would be beneficial for you to accept.

What might a BATNA look like in practice? Suppose you are negotiating a starting salary for a full-time, professional position. The figure you have in mind is $35,000 per year. Your BATNA is $29,500 because this is the salary your future in-laws will pay you to enter the family business. You will therefore walk away from any offer of less than $30,000—just taking salary into account.

Knowing the other side's BATNA is also important because it helps define the other participant's bargaining zone. Understanding each other's bargaining zones makes it possible to arrive at mutually profitable trade-offs. In the preceding salary negotiations, the company's BATNA might be to hire a less well educated job candidate at $25,000 and then upgrade his or her knowledge on the job.

Effective negotiation, as with any other form of conflict resolution, requires extensive practice and knowledge of basic principles and techniques. As a starting point you might take one of the negotiating tactics just described and practice it where the stakes are not so high. You might attempt to negotiate the price of a consumer electronics device, or negotiate for getting a particular Friday afternoon off from work.

COMBATTING SEXUAL HARASSMENT: A SPECIAL TYPE OF CONFLICT

Many employees face conflict because they are sexually harassed by a supervisor, coworker, or customer. **Sexual harassment** is generally defined as unwanted sexually oriented behavior in the workplace that results in discomfort and/or interference with the job. It can include an action as violent as rape or as subtle as a sexually oriented comment about a person's body or appearance. Here we will focus on the types and frequency of sexual harassment, recent legal rulings on the nature of harassment, the effects of harassment, and guidelines for dealing with the problem.

TYPES AND FREQUENCY OF HARASSMENT

Two types of sexual harassment are recognized by the courts. In quid pro quo sexual harassment, the individual suffers job loss, or threatened loss of a job benefit, as a result of his or her responses to a request for sexual favors. The demands of a harasser can be explicit or implied. An example of quid pro quo harassment would be a manager promising an employee a promotion in exchange for sexual favors and then not promoting the employee because the employee refused.

The other form of sexual harassment is hostile environment harassment. It occurs when someone in the workplace creates an intimidating, hostile, or offensive working environment. No tangible loss has to be suffered in this form of sexual harassment. An employee who is subjected to sexually suggestive comments, lewd jokes, or advances is a victim of hostile environment harassment.

Sexual harassment through creating an intimidating environment received worldwide attention starting in 1991. The occasion was Congressional hearings to determine whether Judge Clarence Thomas, a Supreme Court justice nominee, had sexually harassed a former employee, Professor Anita F. Hill. Although Congress subsequently approved Thomas as a Supreme Court justice, employers became more sensitive to the problem of sexual harassment. A long series of sexual harassment charges against U.S. Senator Robert Packwood two years later brought further attention to the problem. Still later, President Bill Clinton was charged with sexual harassment for an incident that allegedly took place when he was governor of Arkansas. A higher court judge later ruled the complaint did not merit a trial, and the woman making the complaint received an out-of-court settlement.

Sexual harassment is also regarded as an expression of power by one individual over another, because the harasser has more formal power than the harassed. The harasser, following this logic, is a power abuser as well as a legal offender.

Sexual harassment is widespread in the U. S. workplace and in other countries as well. According to one compilation of figures, at least one-half of all women have been harassed at some point in their career. Furthermore, at least 10 percent have quit a job because of sexual harassment. Women in nontraditional jobs (such as welder or pressroom supervisor) are especially likely to be harassed. In a study of women business firm employees, 68 percent indicated that they had experienced at least one sexually harassing behavior on the job during the previous 24 months. Also, the number of sexual harassment claims reported to the Equal Employment Opportunity Commission keeps rising.[11]

RECENT SUPREME COURT RULINGS ON SEXUAL HARASSMENT

An important fact to understand about sexual harassment is that the definition of what constitutes harassment continues to evolve. Many courts at all levels continue to create new rules about liability for sexual harassment and what specific act can be considered a form of sexual harassment. To illustrate the complexity of the problem, we will look at the essence of three U. S. Supreme Court rulings made in 1998.[12]

1. *Can the behavior be considered sexual harassment when the misconduct is between members of the same sex?* In *Oncale vs. Sundowner Offshore Services Inc.,* the Supreme Court ruled unanimously that sexual harassment is actionable even when the people involved are of the same sex. The case involved a male deckhand whose supervisors and coworkers forcibly subjected him on numerous occasions to humiliating, sex-related actions in front of the rest of the crew. What matters is the conduct at issue, not the sex of the people involved. Also of importance, the presence or absence of sexual desire, same sex or opposite sex, is not a determining factor for behavior to be considered sexual harassment.

2. *Can the behavior be considered sexual harassment where there is no tangible adverse effect to the job?* In *Burlington Industries Inc. vs. Ellerth*, the Court ruled 7 to 2 that an employer can be liable for sexual harassment whether or not a supervisor's threats to job status are carried out. However, the employer can be relieved of liability if it exercised reasonable care to prohibit and remedy harassment. An equally important factor is whether the employee took advantage of the corrective opportunities offered by the employer. The case involved a marketing assistant whose manager, a regional vice president, made repeated passes at her. Despite rebuffing his advances, the woman did not suffer any job detriment. Also, the woman never informed the company about the manager's misconduct.

3. *Is an organization liable for sexual harassment when the organization is unaware of a supervisor's misconduct?* In *Farager vs. City of Boca Raton, Florida*, the Court ruled 7 to 2 that an employer is liable for a pervasive, hostile atmosphere of harassment. At the same time, an employer is potentially liable for its supervisors' misconduct, whether the company was aware of the harassment or not. The case involved a woman lifeguard who claimed she endured repeated sexual harassment from two male supervisors during the five years she worked on the Boca Raton beaches. The city had failed to disseminate its anti-sexual-harassment policy to its lifeguard employees and supervisors.

THE ADVERSE EFFECTS OF SEXUAL HARASSMENT

Aside from being unethical, immoral, and illegal, sexual harassment is widely thought to have adverse consequences. The harassed person may experience job stress, lowered morale, severe conflict, and lowered productivity. A study with business and university workers documents some of the problems associated with sexual harassment. It was found that even at low levels of frequency, harassment exerts a significant impact on women's psychological well-being, job attitudes, and work behaviors. For both business and university workers, women who had experienced high levels of harassment reported the worst job-related and psychological effects. The study also found that women who had experienced only a moderate level of harassment suffered from negative outcomes.[13]

A related study of the long-term effects of sexual harassment indicated that the negative effects remained two years after the incident. For example, 24 months after an incident of sexual harassment many women still experienced stress, a decrease in job satisfaction, and lowered productivity.[14]

GUIDELINES FOR PREVENTING AND DEALING WITH SEXUAL HARASSMENT

A starting point in dealing with sexual harassment is to develop an awareness of the types of behaviors that are considered sexual harassment. Often the difference is subtle. Suppose, for example, you placed copies of two nudes painted by Renoir, the French painter, on a coworker's desk. Your coworker might

call that harassment. Yet if you took that coworker to a museum to see the originals of the same nude prints, your behavior usually would not be classified as harassment. Following is a sampling of behaviors that will often be interpreted as environmental harassment:[15] If people refrain from doing them, many instances of sexual harassment will be avoided.

➤ *Inappropriate remarks and sexual implications.* Coworkers, subordinates, customers, and suppliers should not be referred to as sexual beings, and their appearance should not be referred to in a sexual manner. Telling a coworker she has gorgeous feet, or he has fabulous biceps, is out of place at work.

➤ *Terms of endearment.* Refrain from calling others in the workplace by names such as "cutie," "sweetie pie," "honey," "dear," or "hunk." One might argue that these terms are simply *sexist* (different roles for men and women) and not sexual harassment. However, this argument is losing ground, because any behavior that puts people down based on their gender can be interpreted as harassment from a legal perspective. Keep in mind also that some people find terms of endearment to have a sexual connotation. If you felt no physical attraction toward another adult would you call that person "cutie" or "hunk"?

➤ *Suggestive compliments.* It is acceptable to tell another person he or she looks nice, but avoid sexually tinged comments such as mentioning that the person's clothing shows off his or her body to advantage.

➤ *Physical touching.* To avoid any appearance of sexual harassment it is best to restrict physical touching to handshakes and an occasional sideways hug. Hugging a long-term work associate is much more acceptable than hugging a new hire. Minimize such behaviors as adjusting a coworker's earring, touching hair, and tweaking a person's chin.

➤ *Work-related kissing.* It is best to avoid all kissing in a work context—except, perhaps, a light kiss at an office party. It is much more professional to greet a work associate with a warm, sincere handshake.

Company management also plays a major role in preventing and dealing with sexual harassment. Based on the observations of dozens of human resource specialists and employment law attorneys, several actions by management are critical.[16] The cornerstone of control of sexual harassment is creating and widely disseminating a policy about harassment. Dissemination includes stuffing copies of the sexual harassment policy in pay envelopes, distributing the policy to all employees by e-mail, and discussing the policy in department meetings.

The policy should carefully define harassment and state that the company has zero tolerance for such behavior. Company officials designated for hearing complaints should be specified. In addition, the company should have an *open door policy* about harassment. Such a policy means that any employee with a con-

The potential or actual victim of sexual harassment is advised to use the following methods and tactics to deal with the problem.

Formal Complaint Procedure. Whenever an employee believes that he or she has encountered sexual harassment, or if an employee is suspected to be the perpetrator of sexual harassment, the complainant should report the incident to his or her immediate supervisor (if that person is not the harasser) or to the next higher level of management if the supervisor *is* the harasser. The supervisor contacted is responsible for contacting a designated company official immediately regarding each complaint. The officer will explain the investigative procedures to the complainant and any supervisor involved. All matters will be kept strictly confidential, including private conversations with all parties.

Dealing with the Problem on Your Own. The easiest way to deal with sexual harassment is to speak up before it becomes serious. The first time it happens, respond with a statement such as: "I won't tolerate this kind of talk." "I dislike sexually oriented jokes." "Keep your hands off me."

Write the harasser a stern letter shortly after the first incident. Being confronted in writing dramatizes your seriousness of purpose in not wanting to be sexually harassed. Tell the actual or potential harasser: "You're practicing sexual harassment. If you don't stop, I'm going to exercise my right to report you to management." Or: "I think I heard you right. Would you like to accompany me to the boss's office and repeat what you said to me?"

Figure 7-3 How to Deal with Sexual Harassment

cern about being harassed is able to go directly to a senior manager without worrying about his or her supervisor's taking revenge.

Brief company training programs covering the type of information presented in this chapter are also part of a serious program to prevent and deal with sexual harassment. However, a one-time presentation of a 15-minute videotape about sexual harassment is not sufficient. Periodic discussion about the topic is recommended.

After sexual harassment has taken place, the victim will usually want to resolve the conflict. Two key strategies are either to use a formal complaint procedure or to resolve the conflict on your own. If you choose the latter course you will save yourself the time of going through a lengthy investigation procedure. Figure 7-3 presents details about the two key strategies for dealing with sexual harassment. Skill-Building Exercise 7-4 offers you an opportunity to simulate the control of sexual harassment.

SUMMARY

A conflict is a situation in which two or more goals, values, or events are incompatible or mutually exclusive. Interpersonal conflicts have many sources or causes. An underlying source of job conflict is that people compete for limited resources. Another leading cause of incompatibility is role conflict,

Skill-Building Exercise 7-4

COMBATTING SEXUAL HARASSMENT

The two role plays in this exercise provide practice in applying the recommended techniques for combatting sexual harassment. The activities have an implied sexual content, and they are for educational purposes only. Any students offended by these role plays should exclude themselves from participating.

Scenario 1: The Offensive Jester. One student plays the role of Max, a man who delights in telling sexually oriented jokes and anecdotes in the office. He often brings a tabloid newspaper to the office to read sexually oriented passages to coworkers, both male and female. Another student assumes the role of Maxine, a woman in the office who takes offense to Max's humor. She wants to convince Max that he is committing sexual harassment with his sexually oriented humor. Max does not see himself as committing sexual harassment.

Scenario 2: The Flirtatious Office Manager. One student assumes the role of Bertha, an office manager who is single. Another student plays the role of Bert, a married man who recently joined the company as an office assistant. Bert reports to Bertha, and she finds him physically attractive. Bertha visits Bert at his desk and makes such comments as "It looks like you have great quadriceps. I wonder what you look like in running shorts?" Bert wants to be on good terms with Bertha, but he feels uncomfortable with her advances. He also wants to behave professionally in the office.

Run both role plays in front of the class for about eight minutes. Other students in the class will observe the role plays and then provide feedback about how well Maxine and Bert were able to prevent or stop sexual harassment.

having to choose between two competing demands or expectations. Other key sources of conflict are as follows: building of stone walls (the accumulation of minor hurtful incidents); personality clashes; and aggressive personalities, including bullies.

Five major styles of conflict management have been identified: competitive, accommodative, sharing, collaborative (win-win), and avoidant. Each style is based on a combination of satisfying one's own concerns (assertiveness) and satisfying the concerns of others (cooperativeness).

Confrontation and problem solving is the ideal method for resolving conflict. Learning to benefit from criticism is an effective way of benefitting from conflict. People who benefit from criticism are able to stand outside themselves while being criticized. Another way to deal with criticism is to disarm the opposition by agreeing with his or her criticism. Image exchanging deals with conflict by enabling each party to understand the other's viewpoint. Cognitive restructuring lessens conflict by the person looking for the positive elements in a situation.

An Interpersonal Relations Case Problem

SMOKERS' RIGHTS

Child-Decor, a manufacturer of children's furniture, recently placed a total smoking ban on employees. The official policy stated that company employees were not allowed to smoke on company premises, but they were allowed to smoke outside the building. If caught smoking inside the factory or office they would be subject to discipline, such as written documentation in their personnel files, suspension, or demotion. Repeated violators would be subject to dismissal.

Company president Bill Garrison, himself a former two-pack-a-day smoker, was proud of Child-Decor's new policy. In a speech to employees, he stated: "Our company has taken a giant step forward in creating a safe work environment. We are helping hundreds of our employees avoid the biggest job hazard they will ever face—passive smoking. It is much more dangerous than anything else you will inhale in a furniture factory. Every Child-Decor employee has a right to breathe air unpolluted with carcinogens. I am certain that the few remaining smokers among you will agree that the health and safety of the majority must take precedence over the addictions of the minority.

"My door is always open to discuss our new policy. And please keep your supervisors informed of any difficulties encountered in creating a smoke-free environment."

Thirty days after the new policy began, Garrison asked his administrative assistant, Kathy Chang, to investigate how well the policy was working. While wandering around the office and the factory, Chang spoke to a number of Child-Decor employees to obtain a clear perspective on how well the smoking ban was being received.

"To be truthful," commented Bruce Garcia, a production scheduler, "this new policy is making me physically sick. And I intend to fight back. These smokers are revolting. They gather outside every doorway to smoke throughout the day. When you walk in on a still day you hit this wall of putrid smoke. It's as bad as the rest rooms used to be when smoking was only allowed there. Smokers should not be allowed to smoke within 50 feet of a building entrance."

Inge Goldfarb, an office assistant, offered these observations with anger in her voice: "Never in my 15 years of working for this company have I been treated so shabbily. Forcing me to go outside my building to engage in a perfectly legal activity smacks of totalitarianism. What right do nonsmokers have to make smoking a crime? Show me the scientific evidence that smoking in a ventilated area is harming people who do not smoke. If you ask me, Mr. Garrison has gone overboard."

Terry McWorth, an industrial engineer, said to Chang: "It's too early to provide hard data, but I think the smoking ban is lowering productivity. I've heard a lot of complaints that the smokers are spending too much time outside the building smoking. They are missing time from work, and people have to be shifted around to cover for them. It's a tough sell to convince a nonsmoking worker to cover for a smoker who is outside the building puffing away.

"Another problem the smoking ban has created is that I see evidence of hard feelings between some smokers and nonsmokers. The smoking ban has been divisive. It shows up in little ways, like a smoker not cooperating with a nonsmoker. The reason seems to be that the smoker now feels like a second-class citizen."

Melody Lewis, a purchasing assistant, informed Chang: "I and a few other smokers are willing to put up with this policy for now. So far the weather has been cooperating. But can you imagine being forced to smoke outside the building when it's snowing, raining, sleeting, or freezing cold? Smoking outside in 100-degree weather wouldn't be too comfortable either. It's ludicrous. Give us back our smoking lounge,

(Continued)

QUESTIONS FOR REVIEW AND DISCUSSION ➤ 151

and treat us like human beings. This is a furniture factory, not a prison. I'm getting ticked off at these smug nonsmokers who have made life so uncomfortable for us."

Gil McAlister, a customer service representative, told Chang: "I like the policy. I was smoking a pack a day on the job. I'm now down to 10 cigarettes, and I enjoy the breaks outside. Since it's company policy to smoke outside, I don't have to feel guilty. I wish those other smokers would stop complaining. They may be killing off a good thing."

Chang reported back to Garrison that the ban on smoking inside the building was creating problems, and she wondered whether something should be done about the situation. "There are more animosities being created than is good for the company," said Chang.

Case Questions

1. What actions, if any, should the company take to resolve conflict between smokers and nonsmokers?

2. What methods of conflict resolution should smokers and nonsmokers use to resolve conflict among themselves?

3. What is your opinion about whether the rights of smokers are being violated?

Negotiating is a major approach to resolving conflict. It includes focusing on interests rather than positions, compromise, beginning with a plausible demand or offer yet allowing room for negotiation, and making small concessions gradually. It is also important to know your BATNA (best alternative to a negotiated agreement).

Sexual harassment is a form of interpersonal conflict with legal implications. The two forms of sexual harassment are (1) demanding sex in exchange for favors and (2) creating a hostile environment. Sexual harassment is widespread in the workplace, and the U. S. Supreme Court has reached three recent decisions to help interpret the meaning of sexual harassment. Research has pinpointed adverse mental and physical consequences of sexual harassment.

A starting point in dealing with sexual harassment is to develop an awareness of the types of behaviors it encompasses. Company policies and complaint procedures about harassment are a major part of dealing with the problem. To deal directly with harassment, the harassed person can file a formal complaint or confront the harasser when the behavior first begins.

QUESTIONS FOR DISCUSSION AND REVIEW

1. How might conflict among students to obtain high grades be seen as competition for limited resources?

2. What good does it do for you to know a work associate's conflict style?

3. What are the disadvantages of having an accommodative style of handling conflict?

4. Remember the hypothetical conflict between Bill Budweiser and the Anheuser-Busch Company? What solution do you propose to satisfy the underlying interests of both parties?

An Interpersonal Relations Role Play

IMAGE EXCHANGING

Assume that the company decides to resolve some of the conflict between smokers and non-smokers using image exchanging. Several students play the role of representatives of the smokers, and another group plays the role of representatives of the nonsmokers. Play out the image exchange, going through the steps outlined in Figure 7-2. The four key elements are as follows: (1) the nonsmokers' side of the story, (2) the nonsmokers' perception of the smokers' side of the story, (3) the smokers' side of the story, and (4) the smokers' perception of the nonsmokers' side of the story.

5. Experts have observed that it is difficult for most people to confront others. Why is confrontation so difficult for so many people?

6. Have you ever attempted to disarm the opposition? How effective was the tactic?

7. How might a student use cognitive restructuring to get over the anger of having received a low grade in a course?

8. Visualize yourself buying a new car of your choice. Which negotiating technique (or techniques) would you be the most likely to use?

9. What would be an appropriate punishment or reprimand for a company president or CEO who was found guilty of quid pro quo sexual harassment with 10 different women during one year?

10. Is inviting a coworker to dinner a second time a form of sexual harassment if the coworker refused the first invitation?

Chapter 8

Becoming an Effective Leader

Learning Objectives

After reading and studying this chapter and doing the exercises you should be able to

➤ Identify key leadership traits for personal development.

➤ Develop several attitudes and behaviors that will help you appear charismatic.

➤ Develop your team leadership skills.

➤ Understand how you can develop your leadership potential.

> *The director of e-commerce of an infant's and juvenile's furniture company invited Melissa Antonelli to her office. "Melissa, we're asking you to be the Web site team leader," said the director. "It's been obvious to us that you have good leadership potential, so we're giving you the opportunity."*
>
> *Pleased, Melissa responded that she was flattered. Yet Melissa asked what she had done that suggested leadership potential. The manager answered, "You have a great work ethic, and you have expert knowledge of maintaining a Web site. Besides that, you get along fabulously with people. For those reasons, we know you will be an outstanding team leader."*

Melissa's invitation to become a team leader illustrates two key points about developing leadership capability. You need the *right stuff* (effective personal characteristics) for leadership. You also need to carry out the *right actions* (such as getting along well with people). Leadership in the workplace deals with influencing and persuading people to achieve worthwhile goals. It also involves helping to bring about constructive change, such as increasing sales or streamlining work.

In working toward improving your leadership ability, the following definition is a goal to strive for. **Leadership** is the ability to inspire support and confidence among the people who are needed to achieve company goals. A company president might have to inspire thousands of people, while a team leader such as Melissa is concerned with inspiring about six people. Both of these leaders play an important role.

Leadership has also been defined in many other ways. Bill Bradley, former U. S. Senator and professional basketball player, uses a definition of leadership that points to what a leader actually accomplishes. Bradley sees leadership as getting people to think, believe, see, and do what they might not have without your presence.[1] In other words, the leader makes a difference.

Becoming a leader does not necessarily mean that the company has to put you in charge of others (or assign you a formal leadership position). You can also rise to leadership when people come to respect your opinion and personal characteristics and are thus influenced by you. Your greatest opportunity for exerting leadership will come about from a combination of holding a formal position and exerting personal influence. An individual with appealing personal characteristics and expertise who is placed in a position of authority will find it relatively easy to exert leadership.

The purpose of this chapter is twofold. One is to make you aware of the basic concepts you will need to become a leader. The other purpose is to point you toward developing skills necessary for leadership effectiveness. As a starting point in thinking about your leadership skills, do Self-Assessment Quiz 8-1.

KEY LEADERSHIP TRAITS TO DEVELOP

An important part of being an effective leader is to have the *right stuff*. In this section and the following one about charisma, we describe personal attributes

Self-Assessment Quiz 8-1

TEST YOUR LEADERSHIP SKILLS

Rate yourself on basic leadership characteristics:

	Always	Sometimes	Rarely
1. I'm a good listener.	☐	☑	☐
2. I'm accessible.	☑	☐	☐
3. I'm decisive.	☑	☐	☐
4. I'm gracious.	☑	☐	☐
5. I keep it simple.	☐	☑	☐
6. I'm optimistic.	☑	☐	☐
7. I give credit where due.	☐	☐	☐
8. I confront problems.	☑	☐	☐
9. I speak directly.	☑	☐	☐
10. I acknowledge mistakes.	☑	☐	☐
11. I have a can-do attitude.	☑	☐	☐
12. I'm enthusiastic.	☑	☐	☐
13. I seek strong subordinates.	☑	☐	☐
14. I have a positive attitude.	☑	☐	☐

To Score:

Number of responses in Always column × 5 = _____ 60

Number of responses in Sometimes column × 3 = _____ 6

Number of responses in Rarely column × 1 = _____ 0

Total Score (add the three totals): _____ 66

Analyze Your Score:

More than 50: You have a great deal of natural leadership ability.
30–50: You have a good base of leadership characteristics.
Less than 30: Underdeveloped leadership skills may be hampering your ability to manage and supervise successfully. It will be helpful for you to study leadership and attend a leadership development course.

Source: Pryor Resources Inc., P.O. Box 2951, Shawnee Mission, KS 66201. Reprinted with permission.

People who possess the traits listed below are usually well suited to being an effective leader. However, many other traits and behaviors are also important contributors to effective leadership.

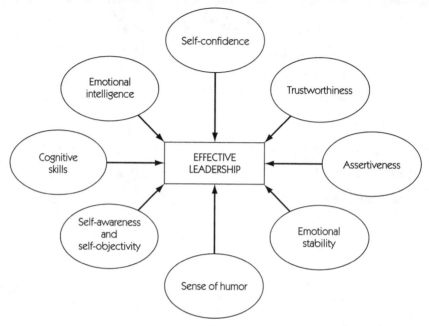

Figure 8-1 Eight Key Leadership Traits

that help a person lead others in many situations. Recognize, however, that radically different situations require a different set of leadership characteristics. For example, a leader might have to be more assertive with group members performing distasteful work than with those whose work is enjoyable.

Each of the eight leadership traits described next, and shown in Figure 8-1, can be developed. For such development to take place, you need to be aware of the importance of the personal characteristic, and then monitor your own behavior to make progress. To assist you with such development, the description of each trait is accompanied by a suggestion for improvement.

SELF-CONFIDENCE

In virtually every leadership setting, it is important for the leader to be realistically self-confident. A leader who is self-assured without being bombastic or overbearing instills confidence in group members. Self-confidence was among the first leadership traits researchers identified. Current research with leaders in many situations has continued to underscore the importance of this trait. In addition to being self-confident, the leader must project that self-confidence to the group.[2]

Self-confidence is not only a personality trait. It also refers to the behavior a person exhibits in a number of situations. It is similar to being cool under pressure. We can conclude that a person is a self-confident leader when he or

she retains composure during a crisis, such as flood damage during a busy season.

You can appear more self-confident to the group by using definitive wording, maintaining good posture, and making appropriate gestures such as pointing an index finger outward. Developing self-confidence is a lifelong process of performing well in a variety of situations. You need a series of easy victories to establish self-confidence. Further development of your self-confidence requires performing well in challenging circumstances. Taking risks, such as volunteering to work on an unfamiliar project, contributes to self-confidence when the risk proves to be worthwhile.

TRUSTWORTHINESS

Group members consistently believe that leaders must display honesty, integrity, and credibility—and therefore be trustworthy. Leaders themselves believe that honesty makes a difference in their effectiveness. Being honest with team members helps to build trust, which in turn leads to good cooperation and team spirit. Management authority Dale Zand regards trust, along with knowledge and power, as one of the three foundations of leadership.[3] To trust group members, the leader has to be willing to give up some control over them, such as letting group members make more decisions and not challenging their expense accounts. The following anecdote told by Fred Smith, the founder of FedEx, illustrates what trust can mean in an organization:

> A blizzard shut down a radio relay located on top of a mountain, cutting phone service to several FedEx offices. The phone company said it would take five days to repair the problem. On his own, a FedEx telecommunications expert named Hal chartered a helicopter to get to the site. The pilot was unable to land, but he got close enough to the ground for Hal to jump safely. Hal slogged through the deep snow and fixed the problem.

According to Smith, Hal went to such great lengths to keep the organization going because there was mutual trust between employer and employee. Hal knew he would not be reprimanded for going to such expense to fix the telephone problem.[4]

Chapter 13, about ethical behavior, provides details about honesty on the job. Being honest is an effective way of getting others to trust you. A starting point in developing a strong sense of honesty is to follow a variation of the Golden Rule: Be as honest with others as you want them to be with you.

ASSERTIVENESS

A widely recognized leadership trait is **assertiveness**, being forthright in expressing demands, opinions, feelings, and attitudes. If you are self-confident, it is easier to be assertive with people. Remember Ursula Burns, the manufacturing executive at Xerox Corp. mentioned in Chapter 7? When discussing the prospects of cutting worldwide manufacturing costs by 15 to 20 percent, she said, "It's totally doable, easily."[5] This statement reflects self-confidence in her leadership capabilities and assertiveness in expressing exactly what she thinks.

Assertiveness helps leaders perform many tasks and achieve goals. Among them are confronting group members about their mistakes, demanding higher performance, and setting high expectations. An assertive leader will also make legitimate demands on higher management, such as asking for equipment needed by the group.

To be assertive differs significantly from being aggressive or passive (or nonassertive). Aggressive people express their demands in an overly pushy, obnoxious, and abrasive manner. Passive people suppress their own ideas, attitudes, feelings, and thoughts as if they were likely to be perceived as controversial. Nonassertive people are also too accommodating.

Developing assertiveness is much like attempting to become less shy. You must force yourself to take the opportunity to express your feelings and demands. For example, if something a teammate does annoys you, make the statement, "I enjoy working with you in general, but what you are doing now annoys me." You can also practice expressing positive emotion, such as telling a coworker, "I'm happy that you and I are working on this project together, because I like your approach to work."

Expressing demands is easier for most people to practice than expressing feelings. People who do start expressing their demands are often surprised at the result. For example, if you are contemplating the purchase of an item that is beyond your budget, try this statement: "I like this product very much. Yet all I have to spend is $45 below your asking price. Can we do business?"

For a reading on your own level of assertiveness, do Self-Assessment Quiz 8-2.

EMOTIONAL STABILITY

Anyone who has ever worked for an unstable supervisor will attest to the importance of emotional stability as a leadership trait. (As described in Chapter 2, emotional stability is one of the Big Five personality traits.) Emotional stability is important for a leader because group members expect and need consistency in the way they are treated.

Kenneth Chenault, the chief executive officer of American Express—and the first African American man to be the top executive of a Fortune 500 company—is known for his even temperament. Although an assertive and tough executive, he is calm and in control. A survey of Chenault's former and present colleagues found that his personality is free of the rough edges that usually accompany fierce ambition. Nobody questioned could recall Chenault losing his temper or even raising his voice.[6]

Emotional stability is difficult to develop, but people can learn to control many of their emotional outbursts. People who cannot control their emotions, yet still want to become leaders, should seek assistance from a mental health professional.

SENSE OF HUMOR

A sense of humor is borderline between being a trait or a behavior. However you classify it, the effective use of humor is considered an important part of a

THE ASSERTIVENESS SCALE

Directions: Indicate whether each of the following statements is mostly true or mostly false as it applies to you. If in doubt about your reaction to a particular statement, think of how you would generally respond.

	Mostly true	Mostly false
1. It is extremely difficult for me to turn down a sales representative when that individual is a nice person.	_____	_____
2. I express criticism freely.	_____	_____
3. If another person were being very unfair, I would bring it to his or her attention.	_____	_____
4. Work is no place to let your feelings show.	_____	_____
5. No use asking for favors; people get what they deserve.	_____	_____
6. Business is not the place for tact; say what you think.	_____	_____
7. If a person looked as if he or she were in a hurry, I would let that person in front of me in a supermarket line.	_____	_____
8. A weakness of mine is that I'm too nice a person.	_____	_____
9. I usually give other people what they want rather than do what I think is best, just to avoid an argument.	_____	_____
10. If the mood strikes me, I will laugh out loud in public.	_____	_____
11. People would describe me as too outspoken.	_____	_____
12. I am quite willing to return merchandise that I find has a minor blemish.	_____	_____
13. I dread having to express anger toward a coworker.	_____	_____
14. People often say that I'm too reserved and emotionally controlled.	_____	_____
15. Nice guys and gals finish last in business.	_____	_____
16. I fight for my rights down to the last detail.	_____	_____
17. I have no misgivings about returning an overcoat to the store if it doesn't fit me right.	_____	_____
18. After I have an argument with a person, I try to avoid him or her.	_____	_____
19. I insist on my spouse (or roommate or partner) doing his or her fair share of undesirable chores.	_____	_____

(Continued)

	Mostly true	Mostly false
20. It is difficult for me to look directly at another person when the two of us are in disagreement.	_____	_____
21. I have cried among friends more than once.	_____	_____
22. If someone near me at a movie kept up a conversation with another person, I would ask him or her to stop.	_____	_____
23. I am able to turn down social engagements with people I do not particularly care for.	_____	_____
24. It is in poor taste to express what you really feel about another individual.	_____	_____
25. I sometimes show my anger by swearing at or belittling another person.	_____	_____
26. I am reluctant to speak up at a meeting.	_____	_____
27. I find it relatively easy to ask friends for small favors such as giving me a ride to work while my car is being repaired.	_____	_____
28. If another person were talking very loudly in a restaurant and it bothered me, I would inform that person.	_____	_____
29. I often finish other people's sentences for them.	_____	_____
30. It is relatively easy for me to express love and affection toward another person.	_____	_____

Scoring Key

1. Mostly false	11. Mostly true	21. Mostly true
2. Mostly true	12. Mostly true	22. Mostly true
3. Mostly true	13. Mostly false	23. Mostly true
4. Mostly false	14. Mostly false	24. Mostly false
5. Mostly false	15. Mostly true	25. Mostly true
6. Mostly true	16. Mostly true	26. Mostly false
7. Mostly false	17. Mostly true	27. Mostly true
8. Mostly false	18. Mostly false	28. Mostly true
9. Mostly false	19. Mostly true	29. Mostly true
10. Mostly true	20. Mostly false	30. Mostly true

Interpretation: Score yourself a plus one (+1) for each of your answers that agrees with the scoring key. If your score is 15 or less it is probable that you are currently nonassertive. A score of 16 through 24 suggests that you are assertive. A score of 25 or higher suggests that you are aggressive. Retake this quiz about 30 days from now to give yourself some indication of the stability of your answers. You might also discuss your answers with a close friend to determine whether that person has a similar perception of your assertiveness.

Skill-Building Exercise 8-1

THE WITTY LEADER

Groups of about five students gather in problem-solving groups to invent humorous comments a leader might make in the following scenarios. After the problem-solving groups have formulated their witty comments, the comments can be shared and compared. Groups also have the option of deciding that a particular scenario is too grim for humor.

Scenario 1: A store manager wants to communicate to employees how bad business has been lately. Sales have declined about 20 percent for three consecutive weeks.

Scenario 2: A leader has to communicate to the group that salaries have been frozen for another year due to limited business. The leader knows that group members have been eagerly awaiting news about the salary increase.

Scenario 3: Due to an unprecedented surge in orders, all salaried personnel will be required to work about 65 hours per week for the next 10 weeks. Furthermore, the office and factory must be staffed on Saturdays and Sundays.

Scenario 4: A consulting firm that specializes in helping companies downsize their work force has seen the demand for their services decline substantially in recent months. The company must therefore downsize itself. The company founder has to announce the layoff decision to the company.

leader's role. Humor serves such functions in the workplace as relieving tension and boredom and defusing hostility. Because humor helps the leader dissolve tension and defuse conflict, it helps him or her exert power over the group. A study conducted in a large Canadian financial institution indicated that leaders who made frequent use of humor had higher-performing units. (Another interpretation is that it's easier to laugh when the group is performing well!) Among the forms of humor used by the managers were "[using] humor to take the edge off during stressful periods" and "[making] us laugh at ourselves when we are too serious."[7]

Self-effacing humor is the choice of comedians and organizational leaders alike. When you are self-effacing, nobody else is insulted or slighted, yet a point can be made. A vice president of marketing at Sun Microsystems once said, "I want you people to design a workstation so uncomplicated that even managers at my level could learn how to use it."

Creativity is required for humor. Just as creativity can be enhanced with practice, so can a sense of humor. To gather some experience in making humorous comments in the workplace, do Skill-Building Exercise 8-1.

SELF-AWARENESS AND SELF-OBJECTIVITY

Effective leaders are aware of their strengths and limitations. This awareness enables them to capitalize upon their strengths and overcome their weaknesses. A leader, for example, might realize that he or she is naturally distrustful of others. Awareness of this problem cautions the leader to not distrust people without good evidence. Another leader might realize that he or she is adept at counseling team members. This leader might then emphasize that activity in an effort to improve performance. Self-objectivity refers to being detached or nonsubjective about your perceived strengths and limitations.

You can enhance your self-awareness and self-objectivity by regularly asking for feedback from others. You then compare the feedback to your self-perception of your standing on the same factor. You might, for example, think that you communicate in colorful, interesting terms. In speaking to others about your communication style, you might discover that others agree. You can then conclude that your self-awareness about your communication skills is accurate.

Another technique for improving self-awareness and self-objectivity is to take a good number of the type of self-examination exercises found in this text. Even if they do not describe you exactly, they stimulate you to reflect on your characteristics and behaviors.

COGNITIVE SKILLS

Mental ability, as well as personality, is important for leadership success. To inspire people, bring about constructive changes, and solve problems creatively, leaders need to be mentally sharp. Problem-solving and intellectual skills are referred to collectively as **cognitive factors**. The term *cognition* refers to the mental process or faculty by which knowledge is gathered.

A major reason that cognitive skills have increased in importance for leadership is that they enable the leader to acquire knowledge. And the processing of knowledge is now considered to be the *core competence* (key ability) of organizations. The leader's role is to both originate useful ideas and collect them from smart people throughout the organization.[8]

Two cognitive skills were discussed in Chapter 2: mental ability and the personal factor of openness to experience. Another cognitive skill of major importance is *knowledge of the business,* or technical skill. An effective leader has to be technically or professionally competent in some discipline, particularly when leading a group of specialists. It is difficult for the leader to establish rapport with group members when he or she does not know what they are doing. A related damper on leadership effectiveness is when the group does not respect the leader's technical skill.

The importance of knowledge of the business as a leadership trait was reflected in the appointment of Cynthia Mary Trudell as the head of the Saturn Division of General Motors. At the time of the appointment, Trudell was truly a *car guy,* having spent 19 years in transmission and engine factories and a foundry. Her experience reflected some of the grittiest, dirtiest, most dangerous, and most macho workplaces in the auto industry. One of her jobs involved

supervising 150 workers who were machining transmission gears—a job she chose because she wanted to learn manufacturing from the ground up.[9]

Increasing one's mental ability, or raw intelligence, may not be easy to accomplish. Yet people can develop their cognitive skills by continuous study and by working on challenging problems. The mere act of keeping up with developments in your field can keep you mentally sharp.

EMOTIONAL INTELLIGENCE

Emotional intelligence, as described in Chapter 2, refers to the ability to recognize your emotions and those of people around you. Emotional intelligence also refers to being able to work effectively with the emotions of others to resolve problems, including listening and empathizing. Research conducted by Daniel Goleman in many different firms suggests that superb leaders all have one trait in common: superb emotional intelligence.[10] A specific example is that an effective manager/leader can often recognize the motives behind an employee's actions.

> Visualize yourself as a team leader. Vanessa, one of the team members, says to you, "I'm worried about Rick. I think he needs help. He looks like he has a drinking problem." If you have good emotional intelligence, you might think to yourself, "I wonder why Vanessa is telling me this. Is she simply being helpful? Or is she out to backstab Rick?" So you would seek some tangible evidence about Rick's alleged problem before acting. You would also seek to spend more time with Vanessa so you can better understand her motives.
>
> With much less emotional intelligence, you would immediately get in touch with Rick, accuse him of having a drinking problem, and tell him to get help or get fired.

Emotional intelligence can be developed through working on some of its components, as described in Chapter 2. It is also important to develop the habit of looking to understand the feelings and emotions of people around you. Also, ask yourself, "How do I feel about what's going on here?" When you have a hunch about people's motives, look for feedback in the future to see if you were right. For example, a little investigation might indicate that indeed Vanessa and Rick are rivals and have a personality clash.

SUGGESTIONS FOR DEVELOPING CHARISMA

The study of leadership in recent years has emphasized the importance of inspirational leaders who guide others toward great heights of achievement. Such leaders are said to possess **charisma**, a special quality of leaders whose purposes, powers, and extraordinary determination differentiate them from others.[11] An important fact about charisma is that it reflects a subjective perception on the part of the person being influenced. A leader such as Bill Gates of Microsoft Corp. is regarded as powerful and inspirational by many. Yet he is

Skill-Building Exercise 8-2

CREATING A VISION

The class organizes into small problem-solving groups. Each group constructs a vision for a unit of an organization or for a total organization of its choosing. Students can choose an organization with which they are familiar or a well-known business firm or government agency. The vision should be approximately 25 words long and depict a glorious future. A vision is not simply a straightforward goal, such as "In 2005 our firm will gross $10 million in sales." Remember, the vision statement you draw should inspire people throughout the organization.

also disliked by many people and is the subject of derogatory cartoons in newspapers and a large number of Web sites devoted to downgrading him.

The term *charisma* is most frequently used in association with nationally and internationally known leaders. Yet first-level supervisors, team leaders, and minor sports coaches can also be charismatic. Possessing a naturally dynamic personality is a major contributor to charisma, but a person can engage in many tangible actions that also contribute to charisma. Following are a number of suggestions for behaving charismatically, all based on characteristics and behaviors often found among charismatic leaders. If you are not currently a leader, remember that being perceived as charismatic will help you become one.

1. *Communicate a vision.* A charismatic leader offers an exciting image of where the organization is headed and how to get there. A vision is more than a forecast because it describes an ideal version of the future of an entire organization or an organizational unit such as a department. Richard Branson, the colorful British entrepreneur, has inspired hundreds of employees with his vision of the Virgin brand being a leader in dozens of fields. Among his accomplishments to reach this vision have been the Virgin Atlantic airline, Virgin Megastores, and Virgin Cinema. The supervisor of paralegal services might communicate a vision such as "Our paralegal group will become known as the most professional and helpful paralegal group in Arizona." Skill-Building Exercise 8-2 will give you a chance to develop visioning skills (a new buzzword in business).

2. *Make frequent use of metaphors and analogies.* To inspire people, the charismatic leader uses colorful language and exciting metaphors and analogies. Develop metaphors to inspire people around you. A commonly used one after a group has suffered a setback is, "Like the phoenix, we will rise from the ashes of defeat." To pick up the spirits of her maintenance group, a maintenance supervisor told the group, "We're a lot like the heating and cooling system in a house. A lot of people don't give us much thought, but without us their lives would be very uncomfortable."

3. *Inspire trust and confidence.* Make your deeds consistent with your promises. As mentioned earlier in this chapter, being trustworthy is a key leadership trait. Get people to believe in your competence by making your accomplishments known in a polite, tactful way.

4. *Be highly energetic and goal oriented.* Impress others with your energy and resourcefulness. To increase your energy supply, exercise frequently, eat well, and get ample rest. Closely related to being goal oriented is being optimistic about what you and the group can accomplish. People also associate optimism with energy. Being grumpy is often associated with being low on energy. You can also add to an image of energy by raising and lowering your voice frequently, and avoiding a slow pace.

5. *Be emotionally expressive and warm.* A key characteristic of charismatic leaders is the ability to express feelings openly. Assertiveness is therefore an important component of charisma. In dealing with team members, refer to your feelings at the time, such as "I'm excited because I know we are going to hit our year-end target by mid-October." Nonverbal emotional expressiveness, such as warm gestures and frequent touching (nonsexual) of group members, also exhibits charisma.

6. *Make ample use of true stories.* An excellent way of building rapport is to tell stories that deliver a message.[12] People like to hear stories about how a department or company went through hard times when it started, such as how Dell Computer began in a dormitory room at the University of Texas. Telling positive stories has become a widely accepted technique for building relationships with employees. Storytelling adds a touch of warmth to the teller and helps build connections among people who become familiar with the same story.

7. *Smile frequently, even if you are not in a happy mood.* A warm smile seems to indicate a confident, caring person, which contributes to a perception of charisma.[13]

8. *Be candid.* Practice saying what you want directly, rather than being indirect and evasive. If you want someone to help you, don't ask, "Are you busy?" Instead, ask, "Can you help me with a problem I'm having right now?"

9. *Make everybody you meet feel that he or she is important.* For example, at a company social gathering, shake the hand of every person you meet. Also, thank people frequently both orally and by written notes.

10. *Multiply the effectiveness of your handshake.* Shake firmly without creating pain, and make enough eye contact to notice the color of the other person's eyes. When you take that much trouble, you project care and concern.

11. *Stand up straight and use other nonverbal signals of self-confidence.* Practice having good posture. Minimize fidgeting, scratching, foot tapping, and speaking in a monotone. Walk at a rapid pace without

appearing to be panicked. Dress fashionably without going to the extreme that people notice your clothes more than they notice you.

12. *Be willing to take personal risks.* Charismatic leaders are typically risk takers, and risk taking adds to their charisma. Risks you might take would include extending additional credit to a start-up business, suggesting a bright but costly idea, and recommending that a former felon be given a chance in your firm.

13. *Be self-promotional.* Charismatic leaders are not shy. Instead, they toot their own horns and allow others to know how important they are. Without appearing self-absorbed, you, too, might let others know of your tangible accomplishments. Explain to others the key role that you played on your team or how you achieved a few tough goals.

DEVELOPING TEAM LEADERSHIP SKILLS

As organizations continue to increase the use of teams, some of the best opportunities for practicing leadership occur as a team leader. A team leader typically reports to a higher-level manager. The team leader is not a boss in the old-fashioned sense, but a facilitator or coach who shares decision making with team members. (A facilitator is a person who helps make things happen without taking control.) A team leader practices **participative leadership**, or sharing authority with the group. Self-Assessment Quiz 8-3 gives you an opportunity to gauge your attitudes toward being a participative leader. Here we describe six techniques that would contribute to your effectiveness as a team leader, as outlined in Figure 8-2.

BUILD A MISSION STATEMENT

A starting point in developing teamwork is to specify the team's mission. The mission should contain a specific goal and purpose, and it should be optimistic and uplifting. Here is an example from a service team at a Cadillac dealership:

> To plan and implement a level of automobile service and repair of the highest quality, at a competitive price, that will delight customers and retain their loyalty.

The leader can help develop the mission statement when the team is first formed or at any other time. Developing a mission statement for a long-standing team breathes new life into its activities. Being committed to a mission improves teamwork, as does the process of formulating a mission statement. Skill-Building Exercise 8-3 gives you practice in developing a mission statement for a team.

ESTABLISH A SENSE OF URGENCY AND HIGH PERFORMANCE STANDARDS

To build teamwork, members need to believe that the team has urgent, constructive purposes. A demanding performance challenge helps create and sus-

Self-Assessment Quiz 8-3

HOW PARTICIPATIVE IS YOUR LEADERSHIP STYLE?

Directions: The purposes of this quiz are to (a) specify what kind of behaviors are represented by an ideal participative leader and (b) give you an opportunity to compare your behavior (or potential behavior) to that ideal. Be more concerned about giving yourself the gift of candid self-appraisal than attempting to give the "right" answer. Grade your leadership style by rating the frequency with which you use (or *would* use if placed in the situation) the behaviors listed: 3 = Almost always; 2 = Sometimes; 1 = Never.

	Almost always	Sometimes	Never
1. I believe that employee involvement is critical to my work group's success.	3	2	1
2. I hardly ever review our corporate mission statement with our group.	3	2	1
3. My work group develops their own measurable goals.	3	2	1
4. I communicate how my work group contributes to the success of the entire organization.	3	2	1
5. I allow my group to establish its own performance measures.	3	2	1
6. I provide informal performance feedback to my group.	3	2	1
7. My group members play an active role in determining their own recognition and rewards.	3	2	1
8. I appropriately delegate my responsibilities to my work group.	3	2	1
9. I support my work group by providing the resources they need.	3	2	1
10. I emphasize the importance of work.	3	2	1

Scoring and Interpretation: Subtract your answers to questions 2, 3, 5, and 7 from the sum of your remaining questions.

11–14 You are already a participative leader (or already think and act like one).
7–10 You are well on your way to becoming a participative leader.
4–6 You have begun the shift to participative leadership (or you are beginning to think in that direction).
0–3 You are still leading in a traditional manner (or are thinking like one who does).

Source: Adapted from a quiz from Suzanne W. Zoglio, *The Participative Leader* (Doylestown, Pa.: Tower Hill Press, 1994).

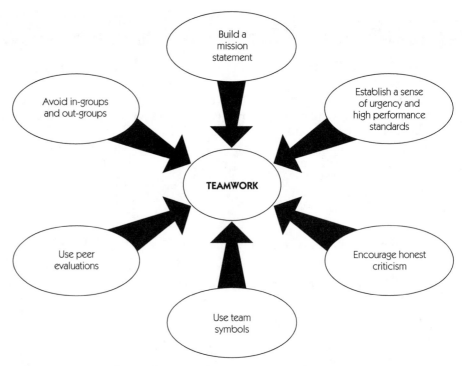

FIGURE 8-2 Developing Teamwork

tain the team. Team members also want to know exactly what is expected of them. The more urgent and relevant the rationale, the more likely it is that the team will perform well.[14] Based on this information, as a team leader you might project a sense of urgency and encourage setting high goals.

ENCOURAGE HONEST CRITICISM

A superficial type of camaraderie develops when team members avoid honestly criticizing each other for the sake of group harmony. Avoiding criticism can result in groupthink. As a team leader you should therefore explain that being a good team player includes offering honest feedback on mistakes and flawed ideas. The team benefits from mutual criticism. A stronger team spirit will develop because team members realize they are helping each other through honest feedback. An example of honest criticism took place in the shipping department of a manufacturer of small kitchen appliances:

> One member of a quality-improvement team had designed a satisfaction survey to mail to customers. The purpose of the survey was to investigate whether the packing materials were of satisfactory quality. Another member said, "Are you sure you want to do this? Would we just annoy our customers by asking about packing ingredients? Why waste more paper? We've never had a complaint about packing materials."

> The person whose idea was challenged was miffed at first, but then expressed appreciation. She said, "I guess I went a little overboard on trying to

Skill-Building Exercise 8-3

DEVELOPING A TEAM MISSION STATEMENT

The class organizes into teams of about six people and appoints a team leader. Each team plays the role of a specific team within a company, government agency, or hospital. An example would be the customer service team at a gas and electric company. The task is to develop a mission statement approximating the type described in the text. The team leader might also take notes for the group.

Remember that a mission statement contains a goal and a purpose, and it is uplifting and optimistic. Allow about 20 minutes for preparing the mission statements. The groups then compare mission statements. One representative from each group presents the mission statements to the rest of the class.

measure customer satisfaction. Maybe we should save our survey dollars for a more important issue."

USE TEAM SYMBOLS

Teamwork on the athletic field is enhanced by team symbols such as uniforms and nicknames. The term "Fighting Irish," for example, deserves some credit for contributing to the mystique of the Notre Dame football team. Symbols can also be an effective team builder in business. Trademarks, logos, mottoes, and other indicators of products both advertise the company and signify a joint effort. Company jackets, caps, T-shirts, mugs, ballpoint pens, and business cards can be modified to symbolize a work unit. As a team leader, you might therefore invest part of your team's budget in an appropriate symbol. Use the opportunity to practice participative leadership. Conduct a group problem-solving session to develop a team logo to place on a T-shirt or cap.

Caution: Screen team logo suggestions carefully. A member of a production team at a Harley-Davidson plant suggested that each team member tatoo his or her arm with a drawing of an armadillo!

USE PEER EVALUATIONS

In the traditional performance-evaluation system, the manager evaluates group members at regular intervals. With peer-evaluation systems, the team members contribute to the evaluation by submitting evaluations of each other. The evaluations might consist of filling out rating forms about each other's performance. Sometimes brief essays are written about each other and then synthesized by the team leader.

Peer evaluations contribute to teamwork because team members realize that helping each other becomes as important as helping the boss. Similarly,

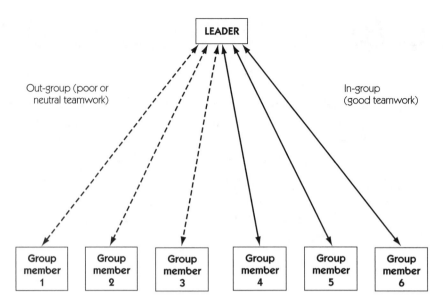

Figure 8-3 The Leader-Member Exchange Model

team members recognize that pleasing each other counts as much as pleasing the boss.

As a team leader, you might not have the authority to initiate a peer-evaluation system without first checking with your manager. Making a recommendation for peer input into evaluations might demonstrate that you are committed to participative leadership.

MINIMIZE FORMATION OF IN-GROUPS AND OUT-GROUPS

An established leadership theory, the **leader-exchange model**, provides useful information for the aspiring team leader. According to this theory, leaders establish unique working relationships with group members. By so doing, they create in-groups and out-groups. The in-groups become part of a smoothly functioning team headed by the leader. Out-group members are less likely to experience good teamwork.[15] Figure 8-3 depicts the major concept of the leader-exchange model.

The in-group may come about because the leader prefers certain group members and therefore is motivated to form good working relationships with them. Conversely, the leader may neglect to form good relationships with people with whom he or she has limited rapport. First impressions count heavily when the leader decides on who is "in" and who is "out." Team leaders should therefore guard against the formation of out-groups just because they are not fond of a few team members, or because a given team member gives a poor first impression.

The leader-exchange model does not mean that the team leader should avoid forming unique relationships with team members. What should be avoided is forming an out-group. A study investigated the relationships a group of female sales managers established with both men and women members of their sales groups. Treating members differently based on their needs contributed to leadership effectiveness, such as producing good results.[16] An example of a unique relationship would be to give more recognition to a sales representative who craved recognition.

DEVELOPING YOUR LEADERSHIP POTENTIAL

Much of this book deals directly and indirectly with information that could improve your leadership effectiveness. Chapter 3, on communications, is a case in point. Improving your communications effectiveness would be one way to enhance your ability to lead people. Formal education and leadership development programs also contribute to enhancing leadership potential. (Many such programs include some of the activities found in this chapter.) Here we describe five strategies for developing your leadership potential, in addition to studying and participating in formal programs.

1. *Acquire broad experience.* Because leadership varies somewhat with the situation, a sound approach to improving leadership effectiveness is to attempt to gain supervisory experience in different settings. A person who wants to become an executive is well advised to gain supervisory experience in at least two different organizational functions, such as marketing and operations.

First-level supervisory jobs are an invaluable starting point for developing your leadership potential. It takes considerable skill to manage a fast-food restaurant or direct a public playground during the summer. First-level supervisors frequently face situations in which group members are poorly trained, poorly paid, and not well motivated to achieve company objectives. Motivating and inspiring entry-level workers is one of the major challenges facing organizations. One of the lessons from the U. S. Marines is that if you want to fire up the front line, you must use discipline to develop pride. The point is that entry-level workers often take pride in being able to abide by tough rules.[17]

2. *Model effective leaders.* Another strategy for leadership development is to observe capable leaders in action and then model some of their approaches. You may not want to copy a particular leader entirely, but you can incorporate a few of the behavior patterns into your own leadership style. For instance, most inexperienced leaders have difficulty confronting others. Observe how a skilled confronter handles the situation, and try that person's approach the next time you have unfavorable news to communicate to another person.

TABLE 8-1 360-Degree Feedback Chart

Manager Evaluated: Holly Partridge

Behavior or Attitude (10 is highest)	Self-Rating	Average Group Rating	Gap
1. Gives right amount of structure.	9	7.5	–1.5
2. Is considerate of people.	10	6.2	–3.8
3. Sets a direction.	9	3.9	–5.1
4. Sets high standards.	7	9.0	+2.0
5. Gives frequent feedback.	10	6.3	–3.7
6. Gets people pulling together.	9	5.1	–3.9
7. Inspires people.	10	2.8	–7.2
8. Gives emotional support.	8	3.7	–4.3
9. Is a helpful coach.	10	4.5	–5.5
10. Encourages people to be self-reliant.	6	9.4	+3.4

Note: A negative gap means you rate yourself higher on the behavior or attitude than does your group. A positive gap means the group rates you higher than you rate yourself.

3. *Self-develop leadership traits and behaviors.* Study the leadership traits and behaviors described earlier in this chapter. As a starting point, identify several attributes you think you could strengthen within yourself, given some determination and perhaps combined with the right training program. For example, you might decide that with some effort you could improve your sense of humor. You might also believe that you could remember to encourage honest criticism within the team. It is also helpful to obtain feedback from valid sources (such as a trusted manager) about which traits and behaviors you particularly need to develop.

A formal method for obtaining feedback about your leadership effectiveness is the *360-degree survey,* in which a variety of work associates evaluate your leadership behavior and traits. Many companies use this method to provide managers with feedback about their leadership effectiveness. The feedback is communicated to the leader (as well as to others being evaluated by the same technique) with the assistance of a company human resources professional or an outside psychologist. The feedback is supposed to help the leader overcome problem areas. Manager/leaders also rate themselves and then compare self-evaluations with evaluations by others.

Table 8-1 is a representative example of the behaviors evaluated. Assume that a manager rates himself a 10 on "Is considerate of people." If others rate him a 1 on this behavior, the manager might be counseled on how to be more considerate of others.

4. *Become an integrated human being.* A philosophical approach to leadership suggests that the model leader is first and foremost a fully functioning person. According to William D. Hitt, mastering the art of leadership comes with self-mastery. Leadership development is the process of self-development. As a result, the process of becoming a leader is similar to the process of becoming an integrated human being. For example, you need

to develop values that guide your behavior before you can adequately guide the behavior of others.

The model (or ideal) leader, according to Hitt, must possess six character traits: identity (know thyself), independence, authenticity, responsibility, courage, and integrity.[18] All of these traits have everyday meanings, but they can also have personal meanings. Part of becoming an integrated person is to answer such questions as "What do I mean when I say I have integrity?"

5. *Practice a little leadership.* An effective way to develop your leadership skills is to look for opportunities to exert a small amount of helpful leadership in contrast to waiting for opportunities to accomplish extraordinary deeds. The "little leadership" might involve such behaviors as mentoring a struggling team member, coaching somebody about how to use a new high tech-device, or making a suggestion about improving a product. In the words of Michael E. McGill and John W. Slocum, Jr., "For those who want to stand atop the dugout, dance with the elephants, fly with the buffaloes, soar with eagles, or perform other mystical and heroic acts of large leadership, our little leadership may seem all too managerial, too modest, and too mundane.[19]

SUMMARY

Effective leadership depends on having the right personal characteristics and taking the appropriate actions. Leadership is the ability to inspire support and confidence among the people who are needed to achieve company goals. People can exercise leadership whether or not they occupy a formal leadership position.

Certain traits contribute heavily to leadership effectiveness. Among them are self-confidence, trustworthiness, assertiveness, emotional stability, sense of humor, self-awareness and self-objectivity, cognitive skills (including intelligence), and emotional intelligence.

Although charisma depends heavily on personal characteristics, people can work toward being charismatic. Suggestions for behaving charismatically include the following:

1. Communicate a vision.

2. Make frequent use of metaphors and analogies.

3. Inspire trust and confidence.

4. Be highly energetic and action goal oriented.

5. Be emotionally expressive and warm.

6. Make ample use of true stories.

7. Smile frequently.

An Interpersonal Relations Case Problem

BIG CHANGES AT STATE BANK OF INDIA, CALIFORNIA

State Bank of India (SBI) is the oldest and largest bank in India, and it also has offices throughout the world. Brejein Kumar, a manager who had been with the bank for 31 years, had developed a reputation as a troubleshooter who could turn around problem situations. In 1992, he was sent on a four-year assignment as manager of SBI Washington. Two years later, however, he was appointed as the president and CEO of SBI California, located in Los Angeles. The change in assignment came about because the California division was experiencing numerous problems.

SBI California is composed of the downtown Los Angeles branch, the Los Angeles agency, and the Artesia branch. When Kumar arrived in Los Angeles, he was shocked to discover the poor visibility and reputation of SBI California. The bank was virtually unknown to the large Indian community in California. Many new customers closed their accounts after a short time because of what they perceived to be poor service and lack of caring for customer welfare. Regulatory agencies had given the bank a poor rating because of its sloppy policies and procedures.

Kumar said, "SBI California was the greatest challenge of my life. I needed to change the bank by improving its performance and build good relations with customers and regulators. It was also necessary to make the Indian community aware of the bank."

Kumar focused first on improving relations with the regulators, with the hope of improving SBI California's ratings. He dug into paperwork, reviewing as many details as possible of the previous years to understand why the bank was not performing well. After three weeks of analysis, Kumar devised a strategy for improving the bank's performance. He personally interviewed 25 employees to obtain their suggestions for improving the bank's reputation and performance. He added policies and procedures, all of which complied with government regulations. As a result, SBI California received an above-average rating by the regulators.

Next, Kumar focused on strengthening customer relations. He arranged for customer-contact workers to take training courses in management and customer relations. Employees deficient in computer skills were given appropriate training. Soon the entire work environment was computerized, allowing for faster customer service. Unlike previous bank managers, Kumar met personally with customers. He organized several meetings to which he invited prominent Indian businesspersons to see the improved SBI California.

Another Kumar initiative was to sponsor programs such as Youth Awards, events for India's Independence and Republic Days, and Indian classical music concerts. He redesigned many of SBI's brochures and promoted the bank through advertisements that were telecast on the International Channel during Indian programming. Another change Kumar implemented was to assemble an impressive panel of the board of directors comprised of corporate executives and industrialists, as well as the former ambassador to India.

SBI made front-page news in the Indian newspapers distributed in California. New business started pouring into the bank, and profits increased substantially. In the summer of 1996, SBI's chairman came from India to visit the California operation and was greatly impressed by the bank's outstanding performance. The regulators, along with the board of directors, persuaded the chairman to extend Kumar's stay in California one more year.

Company officers requested that Kumar open a branch in San José based on both the booming Silicon Valley and the substantial Indian population in the area. Kumar played a

(Continued)

major role in all aspects of launching the San José branch, from choosing the site, overseeing the setup, hiring employees, and developing an information technology environment. He also developed a branch slogan that caught on quickly: "An American Bank with an Indian Heritage." The branch became an immediate success.

Kumar's U.S. assignment ended in September 1997. He received several awards for his enormous efforts and for his contribution to the Indian community as a whole. Upon his departure several bank employees said there would never be another leader as dynamic as Brejein Kumar.

Case Questions

1. Identify three leadership traits displayed by Kumar, and cite the evidence for your conclusion.

2. What suggestions do you have for improving Kumar's approach to leadership and management?

3. To what extent does Kumar qualify as a charismatic leader?

Source: Case researched by Kamini Kumar, Rochester Institute of Technology.

8. Be candid.

9. Make others feel important.

10. Shake hands effectively.

11. Appear self-confident through nonverbal signals.

12. Take personal risks.

13. Be self-promotional.

A team leader acts as a facilitator or coach who shares decision making with team members, thus practicing participative leadership. The following are some techniques for effective team leadership:

1. Build a mission statement.

2. Establish a sense of urgency and high performance standards.

3. Encourage honest criticism.

4. Use team symbols.

5. Use peer evaluations.

6. Minimize forming in-groups and out-groups.

In addition to participating in formal leadership development programs, five strategies for developing leadership potential are to (1) acquire broad experience; (2) model effective leaders; (3) self-develop leadership traits and behaviors; (4) become an integrated human being (a fully functioning person); and (5) practice small leadership acts.

QUESTIONS FOR DISCUSSION AND REVIEW

1. Visualize a work associate or fellow student who you think has good leadership potential. On what basis did you conclude that this person would be effective as a leader?

2. How do you explain the fact that a person can be a leader even though he or she lacks a job that includes responsibility for others?

3. What does it mean to say that a person has the "right stuff" for being a leader?

4. Assume that you worked for a manager who was dishonest with customers and suppliers, yet honest with employees. How would that affect your perception of the manager's leadership effectiveness?

5. Assertiveness is said to be important for leadership effectiveness. Yet can you give an example of an effective leader who is downright aggressive and obnoxious? (If necessary, give an example from sports leadership.)

6. A sense of humor is important for leadership effectiveness, yet telling rehearsed jokes is not considered effective. How do you account for this discrepancy?

7. What does the term *self-objectivity* mean to you, and why is it important for leadership?

8. In what ways do the concepts of charismatic leadership and participative leadership differ substantially from each other?

9. Give an example of somebody you have worked for, or have read about, practicing a *little leadership*.

10. Assume that a student obtains a part-time job as an assistant store manager. What can this person do to capitalize on this position for leadership experience?

Chapter 9

Motivating
Others

> *"I'm having a technical problem that I need your help with," said Derek to Priscilla. "As Francisco [their boss] requested," continued Derek, "I traveled down to the warehouse to take a video of the flood damage. I'm scheduled to show my videotape to Francisco at four this afternoon. Normally, I would run the camcorder through the VCR. The video would then appear on the TV monitor. But I'm stuck. The VCR is broken, and I don't know how to run the camcorder directly through the TV monitor.*
>
> *"Priscilla, I know you're pretty good at playing around with camcorders and TV monitors. Could you show me how to run the camcorder directly through the monitor so I can play my video this afternoon?"*
>
> *"Gosh, that would take a lot of work," said Priscilla. "Maybe you can read the TV manual to figure out what to do. Or maybe somebody else might help you. I'm pretty busy now."*

The preceding scenario could illustrate that Priscilla is being a poor team player or is lazy. Another possible analysis is that Derek is doing a poor job of motivating Priscilla to help him with his problem. He is not using a systematic approach to getting a coworker to put effort into accomplishing a goal he thinks is important (aligning the camcorder and TV monitor). From this perspective, Derek needs to know more about **motivation**. Motivation has two meanings: (1) an internal state that leads to effort expended toward objectives and (2) an activity performed by one person to get another to accomplish work.

We often think of a manager or leader attempting to motivate group members. Yet many people in the workplace have a need to motivate others. To accomplish their work, people must motivate individuals who report to them, coworkers, supervisors, or customers. Developing motivational skills will therefore help you accomplish more work than you would if you relied strictly on the good nature and team spirit of others.

This chapter describes how to develop motivational skills based on four related explanations of motivation. We progress from the simplest to the most complex explanation. As a starting point in thinking through how to motivate others, do Self-Assessment Quiz 9-1.

MOTIVATION SKILL BASED ON THE PRINCIPLE OF "WHAT'S IN IT FOR ME?"

The most fundamental principle of human motivation is that people are motivated by self-interest. This principle is referred to as "What's in it for me?" or WIIFM (pronounced *wiff'em*). Reflect on your own experience. Before working hard to accomplish a task, you probably want to know how you will benefit. If your manager asks you to work extra hours to take care of an emergency, you will most likely oblige. Yet underneath you might be thinking, "If I work these extra hours, my boss will think highly of me. As a result, I will probably receive a good performance evaluation and maybe a better-than-average salary increase."

MY APPROACH TO MOTIVATING OTHERS

Instructions: Describe how often you act or think in the way indicated by the following statements when you are attempting to motivate another person. Circle the appropriate number for each statement. Scale: Very infrequently (VI); Infrequently (I); Sometimes (S); Frequently (F); Very frequently (VF).

	VI	I	S	F	VF
1. I ask the other person what he or she is hoping to achieve in the situation.	(1)	2	3	4	5
2. I attempt to figure out whether the person has the ability to do what I need done.	1	2	3	4	(5)
3. When another person is heel-dragging, it usually means he or she is lazy.	5	4	(3)	2	1
4. I explain exactly what I want to the person I'm trying to motivate.	1	2	3	4	(5)
5. I like to give the other person a reward up front so he or she will be motivated.	5	4	(3)	2	1
6. I give lots of feedback when another person is performing a task for me.	1	2	(3)	4	5
7. I like to belittle another person enough so that he or she will be intimidated into doing what I need done.	(5)	4	3	2	1
8. I make sure that the other person feels treated fairly.	1	2	3	4	(5)
9. I figure that if I smile nicely I can get the other person to work as hard as I need.	5	(4)	3	2	1
10. I attempt to get what I need done by instilling fear in the other person.	(5)	4	3	2	1
11. I specify exactly what needs to be accomplished.	1	2	3	4	(5)
12. I generously praise people who help me get my work accomplished.	1	2	3	4	(5)
13. A job well done is its own reward. I therefore keep praise to a minimum.	(5)	4	3	2	1
14. I make sure I let people know how well they have done in meeting my expectations on a task.	1	2	3	4	(5)
15. To be fair, I attempt to reward people similarly no matter how well they have performed.	5	4	3	(2)	1
16. When somebody doing work for me performs well, I recognize his or her accomplishments promptly.	1	2	3	4	(5)
17. Before giving somebody a reward, I attempt to find out what would appeal to that person.	1	2	3	(4)	5
18. I make it a policy not to thank somebody for doing a job he or she is paid to do.	(5)	4	3	2	(1)

(Continued)

	VI	I	S	F	VF
19. If people do not know how to perform a task, motivation will suffer.	1	2	3	4	(5)
20. If properly laid out, many jobs can be self-rewarding.	1	2	3	4	(5)

Total Score _____

Scoring and Interpretation: Add the circled numbers to obtain your total score.

90–100 You have advanced knowledge and skill with respect to motivating others in a work environment. Continue to build on the solid base you have established.

50–89 You have average knowledge and skill with respect to motivating others. With additional study and experience you will probably develop advanced motivational skills.

20–49 To effectively motivate others in a work environment you will need to greatly expand your knowledge of motivation theory and techniques.

Source: The idea for this quiz, and a few items, are from David A. Whetton and Kim S. Cameron, *Developing Management Skills,* 2d ed. (New York: HarperCollins, 1991), pp. 336–337.

If your instructor asks you to prepare a lengthy research paper, you might be motivated to work up to the best of your ability. But before getting down to the task, it is likely that questions have raced through your mind, such as "Will this paper elevate my grade?" or "Will I pick up information that will help me in my career?"

A perplexing issue is how the WIIFM principle explains why people are motivated to help others. Why would a company president donate gift baskets of food to the homeless? Why hire a virtually unemployable person for a non-productive job in the mail room? People who perform acts of social good receive the reward of feeling better about themselves. In psychological terms, they satisfy their needs to nurture (take care of) others. More cynically, helping the unfortunate leads to recognition for being a good Samaritan.

According to Gerald Kushel, to use the WIIFM principle in motivating others you have to be aware of the intensity of the person's desire.[1] A person can be highly motivated, mildly motivated, or only slightly motivated, depending on the intensity of his or her WIIFM principle. A company might offer outstanding performers the opportunity to work at home one day per week. Employees who are intensely motivated to work at home will work virtually up to capacity to achieve a rating of outstanding performer.

To use the WIIFM principle in motivating others you must find out what needs, desires, or motives a person is attempting to satisfy. In general language, responding to the needs of people is referred to as *touching their hot buttons*. You find out what these needs are by asking people what they want or by observing what interests them. For instance, the way a manager might motivate a recognition-hungry group member is to tell that person, "If you perform 10 percent above quota for six consecutive months, we will get you a plaque signifying your achievement to hang on the wall."

Employee needs have been classified in many ways, yet most of these lists overlap. According to a representative classification, 99 percent of employees are motivated by one or more of the following seven needs:

1. *The need for achievement.* Employees with strong achievement needs seek the satisfaction of completing projects successfully. They want to apply their talents to attain success, and they find joy in accomplishment for its own sake.

2. *The need for power.* Employees with a strong power need derive satisfaction from influencing and controlling others, and they aspire to becoming executives. These employees like to lead and persuade and be in charge of resources such as budgets.

3. *The need for affiliation.* Employees with a strong need for affiliation derive satisfaction from interacting with others, being part of a work group, and forming friendships. The same employees are motivated to avoid working alone for long periods of time.

4. *The need for autonomy.* Employees with a strong need for autonomy seek freedom and independence, such as having almost complete responsibility for a project. The same employees are motivated to avoid working in a team effort for long periods of time. Many industrial sales representatives (those who sell to companies) have a strong need for autonomy.

5. *The need for esteem.* Employees with a strong need for esteem want to feel good about themselves, and they judge their worth to a large extent based on how much recognition and praise they receive.

6. *The need for safety and security.* Employees with strong needs for safety and security seek job security, steady income, ample medical and dental insurance, and a hazard-free work environment.

7. *The need for equity.* Employees with a strong need for equity seek fair treatment. They often compare working hours, job responsibilities, salary, and privileges to those of coworkers, and they will become discouraged if coworkers are receiving better treatment.[2]

Recognizing such needs, as well as other needs and interests, helps you apply the WIIFM principle. Skill-Building Exercise 9-1 gives you the opportunity to do the preliminary work needed for applying the WIIFM principle.

USING BEHAVIOR MODIFICATION TO MOTIVATE OTHERS

The most widely used formal method of motivating people in the workplace is **behavior modification**, an attempt to change behavior by manipulating rewards and punishments. Behavior modification is based on a fundamental principle of human behavior: the law of effect. According to the **law of effect**,

Skill-Building Exercise 9-1

BACKGROUND WORK FOR THE WIIFM

The class divides into pairs of students. In each pair, one student plays the role of a team leader who is developing a plan to highly motivate the team member being interviewed. The other student plays the role of the team member being interviewed. The twist to this role play, however, is that the team member reflects on his or her actual motivators.

The team leader might ask several or all of these questions while conducting an interview for approximately 15 minutes. In addition, when the team member reveals an important piece of information, the team leader will dig for more details. The team leader should use effective listening skills, as described in Chapter 3. Suggested interview questions are as follows:

1. Why are you working on this team?
2. What can the company do to make you really happy?
3. What would be a fair reward for performing up to your capacity? On a 1-to-10 scale, how badly do you want this reward?
4. What would be an outstanding reward for you for performing up to your capacity? On a 1-to-10 scale, how badly do you want this reward?
5. What would be a fantasy reward for you for performing up to your capacity? On a 1-to-10 scale, how badly do you want this reward?
6. What do you hope to get out of this job?

A brief class discussion might follow the completion of the interviews. A key issue to address in the discussion is the extent to which the interview would be helpful in motivating the team member.

behavior that leads to a positive consequence for the individual tends to be repeated, whereas behavior that leads to a negative consequence tends not to be repeated.

The focus of behavior modification on the job is to reward employees for behaving in ways that support what the organization is attempting to accomplish. A survey of how companies are using rewards indicated that a growing number of firms are giving specific rewards to workers who reach targeted business results.[3] An example is that a Web specialist might be rewarded for developing a new corporate Web site that (a) attracted more visitors who stayed longer, and (b) led to achieving or exceeding a specified sales volume.

Our approach to skill development in behavior modification is to summarize its key strategies and present rules for its application.

BEHAVIOR MODIFICATION STRATEGIES

Behavior modification is an entire field of study in itself. Nevertheless, the techniques of behavior modification can be divided into four strategies: positive reinforcement, negative reinforcement, punishment, and extinction.

Positive reinforcement means increasing the probability that behavior will be repeated by rewarding people for making the desired response. The phrase *increasing the probability* means that positive reinforcement improves learning and motivation but is not 100 percent effective. The phrase *making the desired response* is also noteworthy. To use positive reinforcement properly, a reward must be contingent upon doing something right. Simply paying somebody a compliment or giving the person something of value is not positive reinforcement. Behavior modification involves linking consequences to what the person has or has not accomplished.

Give something good

Positive reinforcement is easy to visualize with well-structured jobs such as data entry or producing parts. Yet positive reinforcement is also used to encourage desired behavior in highly paid, complex jobs. Scientific laboratories often reward scientists, engineers, and technicians for producing profitable products. John D. McMillan, who has investigated motivational techniques in scientific settings, reached this conclusion:[4]

> One of the big problems in research, engineering, and software development is the fact that these employees want to be very professional and create the most perfect product or system technically possible, whether or not that is what the market wants. But by basing the incentive not on an invention's technical elegance, but on its commercial acceptance, you get the developer to focus on what the customer really wants.

Negative reinforcement *(avoidance motivation)* means rewarding people by taking away an uncomfortable consequence of their behavior. It is the withdrawal or avoidance of a disliked consequence. You are subject to negative reinforcement when you are told, "Your insurance rate will go down if you receive no traffic violations for 12 months." The uncomfortable consequence removed is a high insurance premium. Removing the undesirable consequence is contingent upon your making the right response—driving within the law.

Take something bad

Be careful not to make the common mistake of confusing negative reinforcement with punishment. Negative reinforcement is the opposite of punishment. It involves rewarding someone by removing a punishment or uncomfortable situation.

Punishment is the presentation of an undesirable consequence or the removal of a desirable consequence because of unacceptable behavior. A supervisor can punish an employee by suspending the employee for violating an important safety rule. Or the employee can be punished by taking away his or her chance to earn overtime pay because of violating the rule. Punishment on the job is often referred to as *discipline*.

Extinction is decreasing the frequency of undesirable behavior by removing the desirable consequence of such behavior. A company might use extinction by ceasing to pay employees for making frivolous cost-saving suggestions. Extinction is sometimes used to eliminate annoying behavior. Assume that a team member persists in telling gross jokes. The joke telling can often be extinguished by the group's agreeing not to laugh at the jokes.

Positive reinforcement is usually the most effective of the four behavior modification strategies. The vast majority of people respond better to rewards

than to punishments. When dealing with coworkers, supervisors, and customers, positive reinforcement is the most feasible strategy. Punishing a superior or customer for doing something you do not like usually is not feasible.

RULES FOR THE USE OF BEHAVIOR MODIFICATION

To use behavior modification effectively, certain rules and procedures must be followed. Although using rewards and punishments to motivate people seems straightforward, behavior modification requires a systematic approach. The following rules emphasize rewards, but they also incorporate the judicious use of punishment. The rules are specified from the standpoint of the person trying to motivate another individual, such as a group member, coworker, supervisor, or customer.

Rule 1: State Clearly What Behavior Will Lead to a Reward or Punishment

The nature of good performance, or the goals, must be agreed upon by the manager and group member. Clarification might take this form: "We need to decrease by 40 percent the number of new credit card customers who have delinquent accounts of 60 days or more." Workers also need to know specifically which types of behavior will lead to punishment, such as being late for work three or more times in one month. Unless workers know precisely what they are trying to accomplish or avoid, it will be difficult for them to earn a reward or avoid being punished.

Rule 2: Choose an Appropriate Reward or Punishment

An appropriate reward or punishment is (a) effective in motivating a given person and (b) feasible from the standpoint of the individual or the company. If one reward does not motivate the person, try another. The importance of choosing the right reward underscores the fact that not all rewards are reinforcers. A reward is something of perceived value by the person giving the reward. However, if the reward does not lead to strengthening a desired response (such as wearing safety goggles), it is not a true reinforcer.[5]

When rewards do not work, punishment may be necessary. It is generally best to use the mildest form of punishment that will motivate the person, such as simply giving the person negative feedback.

Lists of potential rewards and forms of punishment to use on the job are presented in Figures 9-1 and 9-2. These can be kept in mind in the quest for appropriate rewards and punishments.

Rule 3: Supply Ample Feedback

Behavior modification cannot work without frequent feedback to individuals. Feedback can take the form of simply telling people they have done something right or wrong. Brief e-mail messages or handwritten notes are other forms of feedback. Many effective motivators, including Jack Welch, the long-time CEO of General Electric, make extensive use of handwritten thank-you notes. Negative feedback by e-mail should be written tactfully to avoid resentment.

Monetary	Recognition and Pride Related
Salary increases or bonuses	Compliments
Company-paid vacation trip	Encouragement
Discount coupons	Comradeship with boss
Company stock	Access to confidential information
Extra paid vacation days	Pat on back or handshake
Bonus or profit sharing	Public expression of appreciation
Paid personal holiday (such as birthday)	Meeting of appreciation with executive
Movie, concert, or athletic event tickets	Flattering letter from customer distributed over e-mail
Free or discount airline tickets	Note of thanks to individual
Discounts on company products or services	Open note of thanks distributed over e-mail
Gift selection from catalog	Employee-of-the-month award
Race-car driving camp	Wall plaque indicating accomplishment
	Special commendation
Job and Career Related	Company recognition program
Challenging work assignment	Team uniforms, hats, tee shirts, or mugs
Empowerment of employee	
Change of job status from temporary to permanent	**Status Symbols**
Promise of job security	Bigger desk
Assignment to high-prestige team or project	Bigger office or cubicle
Favorable performance appraisal	Exclusive use of fax machine or copier
Freedom to choose own work activity	Freedom to personalize work area
Promotion	Private office
Having fun built into work	Cellular phone privileges
More of preferred task	On-line privileges
Role as supervisor's stand-in when he or she is away	
Opportunity to contribute to presentations to top management	**Time Off**
Job rotation	Three-day weekend
Encouragement of learning and continuous improvement	Company time bank with deposits made for unusual effort or success
Ample encouragement	Personal leave days for events chosen by employee
Privilege of setting	
Food and Dining	
Business luncheon paid by company	
Company picnics	
Department parties or special banquet	
Holiday turkeys and fruit baskets	

Figure 9-1 Rewards Suitable for Use in Positive Reinforcement

A large number of potential rewards can by used to motivate individuals and teams, and many of them are low cost or no cost. An important condition for something being rewarding is that the person being motivated thinks it is valuable. The viewpoint of the reward giver alone about the value of a reward is not sufficient.

Source: A few of the rewards listed here are suggested by Dot Yandle, "Rewarding Good Work: What Do Your Employees Want?" *Success Workshop* (a supplement to *Managers Edge*) May 1999, pp. 1–4; Bob Nelson, "Does One Reward Fit All?" *Workforce*, February 1997, p. 70; and Jennifer J. Laabs, "Targeted Rewards Jump-start Motivation," *Workforce*, February 1998, pp. 88–93.

Rule 4: Schedule Rewards Intermittently

Rewards should not be given on every occasion of good performance. **Intermittent rewards** sustain desired behaviors longer and also slow down the process of behaviors fading away when they are not rewarded. If each correct performance results in a reward, the behavior will stop shortly after a per-

Feedback on undesired behavior
Documentation of poor performance
Criticism
Withdrawal of privileges
Undesirable assignment, including being assigned the worst equipment in the office
Refusing to cooperate with coworker
Excluding person from group social activities such as being invited to lunch
Reporting on coworker to management
Threat of sanctions
Fining
Withholding of any valued reward
Probation
Suspension
Firing
Charging customer top price

Figure 9-2 Punishments of Potential Use on the Job

formance in which the reward is not received. Another problem is that a reward given continuously may lose its impact. A practical value of intermittent reinforcement is that it saves time. Few managers or team leaders have enough time to dispense rewards for every correct action by group members.

Rule 5: Make Sure the Rewards and Punishments Follow the Observed Behavior Closely in Time

For maximum effectiveness, people should be rewarded soon after doing something right and punished soon after doing something wrong. A built-in, or intrinsic, feedback system, such as a computer program's working or not working, capitalizes on this principle. If you are administering rewards and punishments, strive to administer them the same day they are earned.

Rule 6: Make the Reward or Punishment Fit the Behavior

People who are inexperienced in applying positive reinforcement often overdo the intensity of spoken rewards. When an employee does something of an ordinary nature correctly, a simple word of praise such as "Good job" is preferable to something like "Fantastic performance." A related idea is that the magnitude of the reward should vary with the magnitude of the accomplishment. Likewise, punishment should fit the crime. An employee should not be fired for one small expense account irregularity; and an executive guilty of quid pro quo sexual harassment should not receive only an oral warning.

Rule 7: Make the Rewards Visible and the Punishments Known

Another important characteristic of an effective reward is the extent to which it is visible, or noticeable, to other employees. When other workers notice the

Skill-Building Exercise 9-2

BEHAVIOR MODIFICATION

In both of the following scenarios, one student plays the role of the person attempting to modify the behavior of (motivate) the other individual. Another student plays the role of the person who is the recipient of these attempts at motivation.

Scenario 1: Rewarding a Customer Service Representative. The customer service manager carefully reviews customer service reports to discover that one service rep has resolved the most complaints for four weeks in a row. Since this rep has been on the job only six months, the manager wants to make sure the rep feels amply rewarded and appreciated. The manager calls the rep into the office to discuss this outstanding performance and give an appropriate reward.

Scenario 2: Punishing a Customer Service Representative. The customer service manager carefully reviews customer service reports to discover that one service rep has resolved the fewest complaints for four weeks in a row. Furthermore, three customers have written the company complaining of rude treatment by this same representative. Since this rep has been on the job only six months, the manager wants to make sure the rep begins to make substantial improvements. The manager calls the rep into the office to discuss this poor performance and administer an appropriate punishment.

Others in the class observe the two scenarios so they can provide feedback on how well behavior modification principles were applied.

reward, its impact multiplies because other people observe what kind of behavior is rewarded.[6] Assume that you are being informed about a coworker's having received an exciting assignment because of high performance. You might strive to accomplish the same level of performance.

Most people are aware that public punishments are poor human relations. Yet when coworkers become aware of what behaviors are punished, they receive an important message. A good example took place in a security systems office when a new member of the team distributed a series of sexually offensive jokes by e-mail to coworkers. The man was immediately put on probation, and coworkers received a message about what constitutes unacceptable behavior.

Rule 8: Change the Reward Periodically

Rewards do not retain their effectiveness indefinitely. Employees and customers lose interest in striving for a reward they have received many times in the past. This is particularly true of a repetitive statement such as "Nice job" or "Congratulations." It is helpful for the person giving out the rewards to study the list of potential rewards and try different ones from time to time.

Now do Skill-Building Exercise 9-2 to practice several of these rules for using behavior modification.

USING RECOGNITION TO MOTIVATE OTHERS

Motivating others by giving them recognition and praise can be considered a direct application of positive reinforcement. Nevertheless, recognition is such a potentially powerful motivator that it merits separate attention. Also, recognition programs to reward and motivate employees are a standard practice in business and nonprofit firms. Examples would be rewarding high-performing employees with a crystal vase (company logo inscribed) or designating them "employee of the month." In keeping with the theme of this book, our emphasis is on individual, rather than organizational, use of recognition to motivate.

Recognition is a strong motivator because it is a normal human need to crave recognition. At the same time, recognition is effective because most workers feel they do not receive enough. Several studies conducted over a 50-year time span have indicated that employees welcome praise for a job well done as much as a regular paycheck. This finding should not be interpreted to mean that praise is an adequate substitute for salary. Employees tend to regard compensation as an entitlement, whereas recognition is perceived as a gift.[7] Workers, including your coworkers, want to know that their output is useful to somebody.

To appeal to the recognition need of others, identify a meritorious behavior and then recognize that behavior with an oral, written, or material reward. The rules for the use of behavior modification are directly applicable. You will notice that many of the rewards listed in Figure 9-1 are recognition related. The category *status symbols* might also be interpreted as a form of recognition. Some specific examples of using recognition to sustain desired behavior (a key aspect of motivation) follow:

➤ A coworker shows you how to do an important routine with the Internet you were struggling with. Three days later, you send her an e-mail message with a copy to the boss: "Hi Jessica, Your suggestion about copying company logos was dynamite. I've used it five times with success since you showed me what to do." (You are reinforcing Jessica's helpful and cooperative behavior.)

➤ As the team leader, you receive a glowing letter from a customer about how Kent, one of your team members, solved their problem. You have the letter laminated and present it as a gift to Kent. (The behavior you are reinforcing is good customer service.)

➤ One member of your department, Jason, is a mechanical engineer. While at a department lunch taking place during National Engineers Week, you stand up and say, "I want to toast Jason in celebration of National Engineers Week. I certainly wouldn't want to be sitting in this office building today if a mechanical engineer hadn't assisted in its construction." (Here the only behavior you are reinforcing is the good will of Jason, so your motivational approach is general rather than specific.)

An outstanding advantage of recognition, including praise, as a motivator is that it is no cost or low cost, yet powerful. Recognition thus provides an enormous return on investment in comparison to a cash bonus. A challenge in using recognition effectively is that not everyone responds well to the same form of recognition. A good example is that highly technical people tend not to like general praise such as "Great job" or "Awesome." Instead, they prefer a laid-back, factual statement of how their output made a contribution.

USING EXPECTANCY THEORY TO MOTIVATE OTHERS

So far we have described motivating others through applying the principle of "What's in it for me?" (WIIFM) and behavior modification, including recognition. We now shift to expectancy theory, a more comprehensive explanation of motivation that includes elements of the two other approaches. Expectancy theory is given special attention here for these reasons. First, the theory is comprehensive because it incorporates many different aspects of motivating others. Second, expectancy theory can help you diagnose motivational problems. Third, it gives the person attempting to motivate others many guidelines for triggering and sustaining constructive effort from group members.

CAPSULE OVERVIEW OF EXPECTANCY THEORY

The **expectancy theory** of motivation is based on the premise that how much effort people expend depends on the reward they expect to receive in return. (Notice the similarity to WIIFM?) Expectancy theory assumes that people are rational and logical. In any given situation, they want to maximize gain and minimize loss. The theory assumes that people choose among alternatives by selecting the one they think they have the best chance of attaining. Furthermore, they choose the alternative that appears to have the biggest personal payoff. How intensely they want that alternative is also an important consideration. Given a choice, people select an assignment they think they can handle and that will benefit them the most.

An example will help clarify the central thesis of expectancy theory. Hector, a 27-year-old credit analyst at a machine tool company, recognizes that he needs to increase his income by about $400 per month to cover his expenses. After carefully reviewing his options, Hector narrows his alternatives to the following three choices:

1. Work as a dining-room server one night a week and on most weekends, with a variable income of somewhere between $350 and $600 per month.

2. Work for an income tax preparation service about four months per year for 20 hours per week, yielding an annual income of about $4,200.

3. Work extra hard at his regular job, including taking a course in corporate finance, to improve his chances of receiving a promotion and a salary increase of $400 per month.

Hector rejects the first choice. Although he knows he can do the work, he anticipates several negative outcomes. He would much prefer to engage in extra work related to his field of expertise. The unpredictable income associated with being a dining-room server is also a concern. Hector sees merit in the second alternative because income tax preparation work relates to his accounting background. Furthermore, the outcome (amount of pay) is relatively certain. But Hector also has some concerns that working so many extra hours for four months a year could hurt his performance on his day job.

Hector decides to take a chance with the third alternative of going all out to position himself for promotion. He is confident he can elevate his performance, but he is much less certain that hard work will lead to promotion. Yet Hector attaches such high value to being promoted and upgrading his professional credentials that he is willing to gamble.

BASIC COMPONENTS OF EXPECTANCY THEORY

All versions of expectancy theory have the following three major components: effort-to-performance expectancy, performance-to-outcome expectancy, and valence.[8] Figure 9-3 presents a glimpse of expectancy theory.

Effort-to-Performance Expectancy

Effort-to-performance expectancy is the probability assigned by the individual that effort will lead to performing the task correctly. An important question rational people ask themselves before putting forth effort to accomplish a task is this: "If I put in all this work, will I really get the job done properly?" Each behavior is associated in the individual's mind with a certain expectancy, or subjective hunch of the probability of success.

Expectancies range from 0 to 1.0. The expectancy would be 0 if the person thought that there was no chance of performing the task correctly. An expectancy of 1.0 would signify absolute faith in being able to perform the task properly. Expectancies thus influence whether you will even strive to earn a reward. Self-confident people have higher expectancies than do those with low

Person will be motivated under these conditions	
	A. Effort-to-performance expectancy is high: Person believes he or she can perform the task.
	B. Performance-to-outcome expectancy is high: Person believes that performance will lead to certain outcomes.
	C. Valence is high: Person highly values the outcomes.

Figure 9-3 A Basic Version of Expectancy Theory

self-confidence. Being well trained will also increase your subjective hunch that you can perform the task.

The importance of having high expectancies for motivation meshes well with a new thrust in work motivation that emphasizes the contribution of self-efficacy, the confidence in your ability to carry out a specific task. If you have high self-efficacy about the task, your motivation will be high. Low self-efficacy leads to low motivation. Some people are poorly motivated to sky dive because they doubt they will be able to pull the rip cord while free-falling at 120 mph. A more technical definition and explanation will help you appreciate self-efficacy's contribution to motivation.[9]

> Self-efficacy refers to an individual's convictions (or confidence) about his or her abilities to mobilize the motivation, cognitive resources, and course of action needed to successfully execute a specific task within a given context.

In short, if you are confident about your task-related skills, you will get your act together to do the task. This is one reason you have to give people the skills and confidence they need for them to put forth effort.

Performance-to-Outcome Expectancy

Performance-to-outcome expectancy is the probability assigned by the individual that performance will lead to certain outcomes or rewards. When people engage in a particular behavior, they do so with the intention of achieving a desired outcome or reward. Performance-to-outcome expectancies also range from 0 to 1.0. If you believe there is no chance of receiving the desired reward, the assigned probability is 0. If you believe the reward is certain to follow from performing correctly, the assigned probability is 1.0. For example: "I know for sure that if I show up for work every day this month, I will receive my paycheck."

Valence

A **valence** is the value, worth, or attractiveness of an outcome. It signifies how intensely you want something (as described in WIIFM). In each work situation there are multiple outcomes, each with a valence of its own. Remember Hector, the credit analyst? The potential outcomes of working part time as an income tax preparer would include extra income, new experience, and interference with his day job.

In the version of expectancy theory presented here, valences range from −100 to +100. A valence of +100 means that you desire an outcome strongly. A valence of −100 means that you are strongly motivated to avoid an outcome, such as being fired. A valence of 0 means that you are indifferent toward an outcome, and it is therefore no use as a motivator. An outcome with a probable valence of 0 would be as follows: To gain the cooperation of coworkers, you promise them gold stars as a reward (or outcome).

Skill-Building Exercise 9-3 will help sensitize you to the importance of estimating valences when attempting to motivate others. A major problem faced by managers and others who attempt to motivate others is that they have limited knowledge about the valences of their motivators (or rewards).

Skill-Building Exercise 9-3

ESTIMATING VALENCES FOR APPLYING EXPECTANCY THEORY

Proveniento — Derivados - NA vide s

Directions: Listed here are rewards and punishments (outcomes) stemming from the information in Figures 9-1 and 9-2. Also included is a space for rating the reward or punishment on a scale of −100 to +100. Work with about six teammates, with each person rating all the rewards and punishments. Compute the mean (average) rating for each reward and punishment.

Potential Outcome	Rating (−100 to +100)
1. A 20 percent salary increase	+100
2. Profit-sharing plan in successful company	+50
3. Stock ownership in company	+50
4. Fully paid three-day leave	+50
5. $5,000 performance bonus	+50
6. $100 gift certificate	+25
7. Outstanding performance review	+25
8. Above-average performance review	0
9. One-step promotion	+25
10. Two-step promotion	+25
11. Flexible working hours	+100
12. Chance to work at home one day per week	+100
13. Chance to do more of preferred task	+50
14. Take over for supervisor when supervisor is away	0
15. Fancy job title without change in pay	0
16. Bigger work area	0
17. Private office	0
18. Company-paid cellular telephone	−100
19. Wall plaque indicating accomplishment	−100
20. Employee-of-the-month designation	−100
21. Warm smile and word of appreciation	−100
22. Compliment in front of others	−50
23. Threat of being suspended for one month	−100
24. One-month suspension without pay	−100
25. Demotion to undesirable job	−100
26. Being fired	−100
27. Being fired combined with promise of negative references	−100
28. Being placed on probation	−50

(Continued)

29. Being ridiculed in front of others −100

30. A 30 percent pay reduction −100

After completing the ratings, discuss the following topics:

1. Which outcomes received the most variable ratings?
2. Which outcomes received the most similar ratings?
3. Which are the three most desirable rewards?
4. Which are the three most undesirable punishments?

Another analytical approach would be to compute the class mean for all 30 outcomes. Each student could then compare his or her rating with the class average.

To apply this technique to the job, modify the preceding outcomes to fit the outcomes available in your work situation. Explain to team members that you are attempting to do a better job of rewarding and disciplining and that you need their input. The ratings made by team members will give strong clues to which rewards and punishments would be the most effective in motivating them.

DIAGNOSING MOTIVATION WITH EXPECTANCY THEORY

An important potential contribution of expectancy theory to interpersonal relations is that it helps a person diagnose whether motivation is present and the intensity of the motivation. In performing your diagnosis, seek answers to the following questions:

1. Does the person I am attempting to motivate have the skills and self-efficacy to do the job? If the person feels ill-equipped to perform, he or she will be discouraged and show very little motivation.

2. What assurance does the person have that if he or she performs the work the promised reward will be forthcoming? Does the company have a decent reputation for following through on promises? What about me? Have I established my credibility as a person who follows through on promises? (If you and/or the company are not trusted, motivation could be reduced to zero.)

3. How badly does the person want the reward being offered in the situation? Am I offering a reward that will make it worthwhile for the person to do what I need done? If the sum of the valences of the outcomes in the situation is close to 0 (some positive, some negative), motivation will be absent.

4. Are there any 0s in response to the first three questions? If there are, motivation will be absent, because the expectancy theory equation is Motivation = (effort-to-performance expectancies) × (performance-to-

outcome expectancies) \times (the sum of the valences for all the outcomes). Remember what happens when you multiply by 0 in an equation.

Guidelines for Applying Expectancy Theory

The information about expectancy theory presented so far provides ideas for motivating others. Here we present several additional specific guidelines to improve your skill in motivating others.

1. *Train and encourage people.* If you are a manager you should give employees the necessary training and encouragement to be confident that they can perform the required task. Some employees who appear to be poorly motivated simply lack the right skills and self-efficacy. *The Confidence in Your Ability To Carry out A specific Task.*

2. *Make explicit the link between rewards and performance.* Employees should be reassured that if they perform the job up to standard, they will receive the promised reward. It is sometimes helpful for employees to speak to coworkers about whether they received promised rewards.

3. *Make sure the rewards are large enough.* Some rewards fail to motivate people because, although they are the right kind, they are not in the right amount. The promise of a large salary increase might be motivational, but a 1 percent increase will probably have little motivational thrust for most workers. *Empush*

4. *Understand individual differences in valences.* To motivate others in the workplace effectively, you must discover individual differences in preferences for rewards. An attempt should be made to offer a worker rewards to which he or she attaches a high valence. For instance, one employee might value a high-adventure assignment; another might attach a high valence to a routine, tranquil assignment. Also keep individual differences in mind when attempting to motivate customers. One customer might attach a high valence to a volume discount, while another might favor follow-up service.

5. *Use the Pygmalion effect to increase effort-to-performance expectancies.* The **Pygmalion effect** refers to the phenomenon that people will rise (or fall) to the expectations another person has of them. Even if these *Pigmalion →* expectations are not communicated explicitly, the other person will catch on to the nonverbal language. As the levels of expectation increase, so will performance. The high expectations thus become a self-fulfilling prophecy.

It is difficult to keep all the points made about expectancy theory in your head at the same time. Nevertheless, with practice and by referring to this book and your notes, you can apply many of the ideas. Skill-Building Exercise 9-4 will help you get started applying expectancy theory.

Skill-Building Exercise 9-4

APPLYING EXPECTANCY THEORY

One student plays the role of the manager of telemarketing (selling over the telephone). Another student plays the role of Terry, a telemarketing specialist who has been with the company for three months. Terry is 40 percent below target in selling magazine renewals. The manager calls Terry into the office for a discussion of the problem.

Terry goes on at length to explain how confusing the job has become. Terry makes comments such as "I don't even know if I have the right kind of voice for this job. People I reach on the phone think I'm just a kid." Terry also wonders what kind of money he can make in this job and whether it is a dead-end job. (The student who plays the role of Terry can improvise about more of these kinds of problems.)

The manager will apply expectancy theory to motivate Terry to achieve satisfactory performance. Other class members should jot down statements the manager makes that indicate the use of expectancy theory. Also, observe whether it appears that Terry is being helped.

APUNTAR, ANOTAR

SUMMARY

GASTADO

Motivation refers to an internal state that leads to effort expended toward objectives and to an activity performed by one person to get another person to work. Managers, as well as people working by themselves, often need to motivate others.

The most fundamental principle of human motivation is that people are motivated by self-interest, referred to as "What's in it for me?" (WIIFM). Even those who help others are simultaneously helping themselves by feeling good. In using the WIIFM principle, be aware of the intensity of a person's desire for a reward.

Behavior modification is an attempt to change behavior by manipulating rewards and punishments. Its key principle is the law of effect—behavior that leads to a positive effect tends to be repeated, while the opposite is also true. The basic behavior modification strategies are positive reinforcement, negative reinforcement, punishment, and extinction.

Rules for the effective use of behavior modification include the following:

1. State clearly what behavior will lead to a reward or punishment.
2. Choose an appropriate reward or punishment.
3. Supply ample feedback.
4. Schedule rewards intermittently.
5. Give rewards and punishments close in time to the event.

6. Make the reward or punishment fit the behavior.

7. Make the rewards visible and the punishments known.

8. Change the reward periodically.

Motivating others by giving them recognition and praise is a direct application of positive reinforcement. Recognition is a strong motivator because it is a normal human need to crave recognition, and most workers feel they do not get enough recognition.

The expectancy theory of motivation assumes that people are decision makers who choose among alternatives by selecting the one that appears to have the biggest personal payoff at the time. Expectancy theory has three major components: expectancies about being able to perform, expectancies about performance leading to certain outcomes, and valence (the value attached to the reward).

Expectancy theory is useful in diagnosing whether motivation is present by examining the strength of the expectancies and the valences of the rewards. If any element is 0, motivation will not be present. Expectancy theory provides important ideas for motivating others, including the following:

1. Train and encourage people.

2. Show the link between rewards and performance.

3. Make the rewards large enough.

4. Observe individual differences.

5. Use the Pygmalion effect to increase effort-to-performance expectancies.

QUESTIONS FOR DISCUSSION AND REVIEW

1. For what purpose would someone need to motivate his or her supervisor?

2. Provide an example of (a) how a person who is highly motivated at work is also highly motivated in other situations and (b) how a person who is poorly motivated at work is highly motivated in other situations.

3. If people really live by the WIIFM principle, how can a leader still achieve teamwork?

4. What evidence can you suggest that people who do exciting and interesting work still expect exceptional financial rewards?

5. How might an instructor use negative reinforcement (avoidance motivation) to improve a student's performance?

6. Identify several rewards in Figure 9-1 that you think would be particularly effective in motivating managers and professionals. Explain your reasoning.

An Interpersonal Relations Case Problem

MOTIVATING THE KITCHEN STAFF AT THE BLUE GARDENIA

Jimmy Gomez aspires to someday be the manager of a large hotel. To help work toward that goal he is working part time on a degree in food and hotel administration. He attends classes at various times to fit his demanding full-time position as the kitchen staff supervisor at the Blue Gardenia, a well-established downtown hotel. Gomez supervises a staff of about 45 kitchen workers, including food preparers, butchers, bakers, and cooks. The highly-paid chefs report to the restaurant manager, Sonya Rosato, who is also Gomez's manager.

The average wage is $8.00 per hour for the kitchen staff reporting to Gomez. Half of these workers work part time and receive almost no benefits. The full-time staff receive a few modest benefits, such as vacation, a $20,000 life insurance policy, and medical insurance. Blue Gardenia management believe strongly that they pay competitive wages for kitchen staff and that paying them much more would eat into profits too much.

FIJAR METAS

During a goal-setting conference with Rosato, Gomez agreed that an important area for improvement in his operation would be to reduce turnover and increase productivity among the kitchen staff. Rosato pointed out that although the turnover rate for Jimmy's employees was about average for kitchen staff in the geographic area (75 percent per year), it was still too high. If the turnover rate could be trimmed down to about 45 percent, it would save the hotel thousands of dollars in hiring and training costs. Also, less food would be wasted because trainees make so many mistakes in food preparation. Skilled workers also drop fewer dishes and glasses.

Rosato and Gomez also agreed that lower turnover would mean more kitchen staff would have good job skills and would therefore be able to produce more. For example, a skilled salad-maker can make twice as many salads as a beginner. Another concern Rosato expressed was that many of the kitchen staff seemed lazy.

During the week following the meeting with his boss, Gomez kept thinking about the problem. He decided tentatively that he was really dealing with a motivational issue. Jimmy reasoned that if the staff were better motivated, they would stay with the job longer and obviously should not appear lazy. As a starting point in attempting to better motivate the kitchen staff, he conducted a few informal interviews with them during breaks and toward the end of the workday. Jimmy asked 12 of the kitchen workers what Blue Gardenia management could do to keep kitchen staff on the job longer and working harder. A few of the comments Jimmy collected were as follows:

> "What do you expect for $8.00 an hour? Some kind of superman? I work as hard as a factory worker, but I don't get paid like a factory worker."

> "This is like a dead-end job. If I could find a job with a better future, I'd be out of here in no time."

> "I like this job fine. But just like a few of the other guys here, I've got a problem. My wife and I are expecting a child. If I stay in this job, I won't be able to support my child. My wife wants to drop out of work for a year to care for the baby."

> "Not me, but I think some of the workers here think management doesn't care much about them. So if they can find another job that pays even 25 cents more per hour, they're gone."

> "I like this kind of work. I mean, we're really doing some good. People like nice

(Continued)

entertainment, and eating good food is a form of entertainment. Also, we're keeping people healthy and helping them live longer. Our food is made with the best ingredients. Even the beef we prepare is lean and healthy.

FASTIDIAR - MOLESTAR

"My gripe is not with the work, but that we don't get enough respect. The chef gets the glory, but we do a lot of the real work. I think I'm doing important work, but nobody tells me I am. Sometimes I think I'm treated like just another piece of kitchen equipment. A few of the other guys and gals feel the same way about how they're treated."

After the interviews were completed, Jimmy thought to himself that he had a lot of information. Yet he wondered how he could translate all

this information into an action plan that would reduce turnover and keep the kitchen staff working harder.

Case Questions

1. How effective do you think it was for Jimmy Gomez to interview members of the kitchen staff to investigate possible motivational problems?

2. What does the information revealed by the kitchen staff tell you about their valences?

3. Which needs among the people interviewed are not being satisfied?

4. What recommendations can you make to Blue Gardenia management about decreasing the turnover and increasing the productivity of the kitchen staff?

7. Answer question 6 for entry-level service workers, such as supermarket cashiers.

8. How do individual differences show themselves in attempting to motivate others?

9. How might you use expectancy theory to improve your own level of work motivation?

10. How might cultural differences affect the valence ratings in Skill-Building Exercise 9-3?

Chapter 10

Helping Others Develop and Grow

Learning Objectives

After reading and studying this chapter and doing the exercises you should be able to

➤ Recognize your responsibility for helping others in your work environment grow and develop.

➤ Understand how being a nurturing, positive person can influence the development of coworkers.

➤ Specify the behaviors and skills helpful for being a mentor and role model.

➤ Acquire beginning skills in coaching and training.

➤ Deal with difficult people on the job.

Three months after joining the company, Keith was sent on his first on-site visit to a customer to help install a new system for recycling waste paper. Back at the office his task was to fill out his first travel and expense report for the company. Keith had spent two hours the night before wrestling with the project. Ten o'clock the next morning, Keith approached Gloria, a coworker, to discuss his concerns:

"Gloria, you've been traveling for the company for several years. I wonder if you could help me prepare my travel and expense report. It's all so confusing. I don't know what I should and shouldn't include as a legitimate expense. I've heard so many different stories of what to do."

Gloria asked, "What do you mean different stories?"

"Well," said Keith, "Some people tell me it's only fair to eat at a fast food restaurant and collect the per diem. That should net me about $8.00, which I can apply toward some of the hidden expenses from traveling. One of these hidden expenses was putting my dog in a kennel during the trip. Also, do I charge the company for dry cleaning? I started the trip with a freshly dry-cleaned suit. By the time I returned, the suit was all wrinkled, so it had to be cleaned again. Yet there is no space on the expense report for dry cleaning."

Gloria replied, "You're right Keith. Filling out the expense report is complicated. It requires a lot of judgment calls. You don't want to look like a cheat, yet you don't want to short yourself. I'm too busy to help you now. Yet tomorrow, I'll be filling out my report right after work. You can watch me and ask questions. Can you meet me at my cubicle at 5:30 tomorrow?"

"Thanks Gloria," said Keith. "I can sure use your help. See you tomorrow at 5:30."

This chapter describes the major ways in which employees help each other and lays the groundwork for skill development in these vital activities. Among the key helping roles are nurturing others, mentoring, coaching and training, and helping difficult people become more cooperative. Do Self-Assessment Quiz 10-1 to gain preliminary insight into your attitudes toward helping others in the workplace.

BEING A NURTURING, POSITIVE PERSON

A major strategy for helping others grow and develop is to be a nourishing, positive person. A **nurturing person** promotes the growth of others. Nurturing people are positive and supportive and typically look for the good qualities in others. A **toxic person** stands in contrast to a nourishing person, because he or she dwells on the negative.[1] Visualize the following scenario to appreciate the difference between a nurturing person and a toxic one:

Randy, a purchasing specialist, enters the office where two coworkers are talking. One is a nurturing person, the other is toxic. With a look of panic, Randy says, "I'm sorry to barge in like this, but can anybody help me? I've been working for three hours preparing a file on the computer, and it seems to have vanished. Maybe one of you can help me retrieve it."

Self-Assessment Quiz 10-1

ATTITUDES TOWARD HELPING OTHERS

Directions: Describe how well you agree with the following statements by circling the appropriate letter after each statement: Disagree (D); Neutral (N); Agree (A).

1. If I see a coworker make a mistake, I do not inform him or her of the mistake. D N A

2. It should be part of everybody's job to share skills and ideas with coworkers. D N A

3. The manager should have exclusive responsibility for coaching people within the work unit. D N A

4. I can think of many instances in my life when somebody thanked me for showing him or her how to do something. D N A

5. I have very little patience with coworkers who do not give me their full cooperation. D N A

6. To save time, I will do a task for another person rather than invest the time needed to show him or her how to do it. D N A

7. I would take the initiative to put an inexperienced worker under my wing. D N A

8. As a child, I often took the time to show younger children how to do things. D N A

9. Rather than ask a coworker for help, I will wait until the manager is available to help me. D N A

10. It is best not to share key information with a coworker, because that person could then perform as well as or better than me. D N A

Total Score: _____

Scoring and Interpretation: Use the following score key to obtain your score for each answer, and then calculate your total score.

1. D = 3, N = 2, A = 1
2. D = 1, N = 2, A = 3
3. D = 3, N = 2, A = 1
4. D = 1, N = 2, A = 3
5. D = 3, N = 2, A = 1
6. D = 3, N = 2, A = 1
7. D = 1, N = 2, A = 3
8. D = 1, N = 2, A = 3
9. D = 3, N = 2, A = 1
10. D = 3, N = 2, A = 1

25–30 Very positive attitudes toward helping, developing, and training others in the workplace. Such attitudes reflect strong teamwork and a compassion for the growth needs of others.

16–24 Mixed positive and negative attitudes toward helping, developing, and training others in the workplace. You may need to develop more sensitivity to the growth needs of others to be considered a strong team player.

10–15 Negative attitudes toward helping, developing, and training others in the workplace. Guard against being so self-centered that it will be held against you.

Margot, the nourishing person, says, "I'm no computer expert, but since I'm not the one who lost the file, I can be calm enough to help. Let's go right now." Ralph, the toxic person, whispers to Margot: "Tell Randy to use his computer manual. If you help him now, you'll only find him on your doorstep every time he needs help."

If you listen to toxic people long enough, you are likely to feel listless, depressed, and drained. Toxic people have been described as *energy vampires* because they suck all the positive energy out of you.[2] Nurturing people, in contrast, are positive, enthusiastic, and supportive.

The guideline for skill development here is to engage in thoughts and actions every day that will be interpreted by others as nourishing. Three actions and attitudes that support being a nourishing person are as follows:

1. *Recognize that most people have growth needs.* Almost everybody has a need or self-fulfillment, although people vary widely in the extent of this need. If you recognize this need, it may propel you toward helping people satisfy the need. You might engage in interactions with coworkers such as sharing new skills with them, clipping relevant news articles, or telling them about an important new Web site you have discovered. You might also tell them about an exciting course you have taken that has enhanced your self-confidence.

2. *Team up with a coworker in your department or another one so the two of you can form a buddy system.* The buddy system is used during war combat and with children in a swimming program. The same system can be used by you and a friend to keep each other informed of decisions and events that could affect your careers. You might nurture your buddy by telling about growth opportunities in the company he or she might not have heard about. Your buddy would reciprocate. One person told her buddy about expanding opportunities for company employees who were fluent in both English and Spanish. The two buddies, who already knew some Spanish, worked together to become fluent.

3. *Be a role model for others.* An indirect way of being a nurturing, positive person is to conduct yourself in such a way that others will model your behavior. By serving as a role model, you help another person develop. How to become a role model for coworkers is as comprehensive a topic as learning to be successful. Among the many factors that make you role-model material are a strong work ethic, job expertise, personal warmth, good speaking ability, a professional appearance, and great ethics. Do you qualify yet, or do you need some more work?

Being a nurturing, positive person is a lifelong process rather than a tactic that can be used at will. Nevertheless, making a conscious attempt to be nurturing and positive can help you develop the right mind-set. Skill-Building Exercise 10-1 provides an opportunity to practice being a positive person.

Skill-Building Exercise 10-1

THE NURTURING, POSITIVE PERSON

One student plays the role of Pat, a worker who is experiencing difficulty on the job and in her personal life. Pat approaches a coworker during lunch in the company cafeteria and says, "What a day. I just received a rotten performance appraisal. If my work doesn't improve within a month, the company may let me go. To add to my woes, my fiancé has threatened to break off the engagement if I don't get a big raise or a promotion. I feel like my whole world is collapsing." The other person plays the role of Leslie, who attempts to be nurturing and positive in order to help get Pat out of the doldrums. Run the role play for about 10 minutes.

The rest of the class provides feedback on Leslie's skill in being nurturing and helpful. Jot down specific behaviors you think are nurturing and helpful.

BEING A MENTOR TO COWORKERS

In Homer's tale *The Odyssey*, Mentor was a wise and trusted friend as well as a counselor and adviser. The term *mentor* has become a buzzword in the workplace. A **mentor** is generally defined as an individual with advanced experience and knowledge who is committed to giving support and career advice to a less experienced person. The less experienced person is the **protégé** (from the French word for *protected*).

A mentor usually outranks the protégé and is much older. For the present purpose, however, be aware that one coworker can be a mentor to another. As long as you are more experienced and wiser than a coworker in some important aspect of the job, you can be a mentor. A person who is not a manager can also be a mentor in another important way. He or she can select an entry-level person in the firm and serve as the inexperienced person's coach and adviser.

Mentoring is more important than ever because it supports the modern, team-based organization. More people work together as equals, and they are expected to train and develop each other. Mentoring facilitates such learning and also supports the current emphasis on continuous learning.[3]

Serving as a mentor is an excellent way of helping others on the job. Mentoring is also gaining acceptance off the job. Many communities have developed programs whereby working adults volunteer to serve as mentors to youths. Mentoring in these programs is designed to help the adolescents and teenagers succeed at school and avoid a life of crime and substance abuse.

To be a mentor, a person engages in a wide range of helping behaviors, all related to being a trusted friend, coach, and teacher. To prepare you for mentoring a less experienced person, a list of specific mentoring behaviors follows:[4]

➤ *Sponsoring.* A mentor actively nominates somebody else for promotions and desirable positions. In some situations, one person is asked to nominate a coworker for a promotion to supervisor or team leader or for a special assignment.

➤ *Coaching.* A mentor gives on-the-spot advice to the protégé to help her or him improve skills. Coaching is such an important part of helping others that it receives separate mention in this chapter.

➤ *Protecting.* A mentor might shield a junior person from potentially harmful situations or from the boss. For example, the mentor might tell her protégé, "In your meeting today with the boss, make sure you are well prepared and have all your facts at hand. He is in an ugly mood and will attack any weakness."

➤ *Sharing challenging assignments.* One member of the team does not ordinarily give assignments to another, yet in some situations you can request that your protégé help you with a difficult task. You would then offer feedback on your protégé's performance. The purpose of these high demands is to help the protégé develop more quickly than if he or she were brought along too slowly.

➤ *Acting as a referral agent.* The mentor sometimes refers the protégé to resources inside and outside the company to help with a particular problem. For example, the protégé might want to know how one goes about getting the employee benefits package modified.

➤ *Role modeling.* An important part of being a mentor is to give the protégé a pattern of values and behaviors to emulate. Several of the specific behaviors included under being a role model were described earlier in connection with being a positive, nurturing person.

➤ *Accepting.* A mentor can be helpful just by giving support and encouragement. In turn, the protégé is supposed to support the mentor by offering compliments and defending the mentor's ideas. In a team meeting, for example, the protégé might make a statement such as "I think John's ideas will work wonders. We should give them a try."

➤ *Counseling.* A mentor listens to the protégé's problems and offers advice. Given that counseling plays such a central role in helping others, it, too, receives separate mention in this chapter.

➤ *Providing friendship.* A mentor is, above all, a trusted friend, and the friendship extends two ways. Trusted means that the mentor will not pass on confidential information or stab you in the back.

➤ *Encouraging problem solving.* Mentors help their protégés solve problems by themselves and make their own discoveries. A comment frequently made to mentors is "I'm glad you make me think through the problem myself. You jogged my mind."

➤ *Explaining the ropes.* A general-purpose function of the mentor is to help the protégé learn the ropes, which translates into explaining the values and do's and don'ts of the organization.

➤ *Teaching the right skills.* The original role of the mentor in teaching skills (such as a master teaching an apprentice) are highly relevant today. Among the many skills a mentor can help the protégé develop are those dealing with information technology, customer service, corporate finance, and achieving high quality.

As implied by the preceding list, mentoring is a complex activity that involves a variety of helping behaviors. To develop mentoring skills, you need to offer help to several people for at least six months.

Mentoring, as conducted by senior managers and coworkers, has become recognized as an important vehicle for the advancement of minorities in the workplace. A survey of successful minority executives indicated that 48 percent of the respondents said they had a role model who guided them toward early career goals. The role model/mentors were primarily the same ethnic, racial, or cultural origin. A specific finding was that successful minorities with supportive managers and coworkers have faster compensation growth and progress more rapidly in their firms.

A sponsor of the survey said, "Minority executives believe that mentors are very helpful in advocating for upward mobility and teaching them how to navigate through the corporation."[5]

In preparation for becoming a mentor, it is helpful to think of the type of person you would prefer as a protégé. Skill-Building Exercise 10-2 is designed to help you think through this issue.

COACHING AND TRAINING OTHERS

Two direct approaches to helping others in the workplace are coaching and training. In the traditional organization, managers have most of the responsibility for coaching and training, with some assistance from the human resources department. In the new workplace, team members share responsibility for coaching and training. An example is the Leaders in Learning program at Rosenbluth International, a global travel firm. Frontline workers volunteer to be *leaders in learning.* Those selected for the position attend training for three days on how to coach and share information with coworkers to solve problems immediately. Workers post learning needs on a conference room flip chart. The leaders in learning put notes next to the needs they can address, such as "Sit with me as I work with international clients, and I'll show you how to monitor those accounts."[6]

Here we describe coaching and training separately, but recognize that the two processes are closely related.

Skill-Building Exercise 10-2

SELECTING A PROTÉGÉ

To be a successful mentor it is necessary to select protégés who will respond well to your advice and coaching. Since the mentor–protégé relationship is personal, much like any friendship, one must choose protégés carefully. In about 50 words (in the space provided), describe the type of person you would like for a protégé. Include cognitive, personality, and demographic factors in your description (refer to Chapter 2 for ideas). Indicate why you think the characteristics you chose are important.

My Ideal Protégé

As many class members as time allows can present their descriptions to the rest of the class. Look for agreement on characteristics of an ideal protégé.

COACHING SKILLS AND TECHNIQUES

Most readers probably have some experience in coaching whether or not the activity was given a formal label. If you have helped somebody else improve his or her performance on the job, on the athletic field, in a musical band, or on the dance floor, you have some coaching experience. In the workplace, **coaching** is a method of helping workers grow and improve their job competence by providing suggestions and encouragement. The suggestions for coaching presented next are generally easier to implement if you have formal authority over the person being coached. Nevertheless, with a positive, helpful attitude on your part, coworkers are likely to accept your coaching.

Coaching other employees requires skill. One way of acquiring this skill is to study basic principles and then practice them on the job. Another way is to coach under simulated conditions such as role playing and modeling an effective coach. Here we describe eight suggestions for effective coaching. For the best results, combine them with the suggestions for effective listening presented in Chapter 3.

1. *Provide specific feedback.* Instead of making generalities about an improvement area for another person, pinpoint areas of concern. A generality might be, "You just don't seem as if you're into this job." A specific on the same problem might be, "You neglect to call in on days that you are going to be out ill. In this way, you are letting down the team." Sometimes it can be effective to make a generalization (such as not being "into the job") after you first produce several concrete examples. Closely related to minimizing generalizations is to avoid exaggerating, for example, by saying such things as "You are always letting down the team." Specific feedback is sometimes referred to as *behavioral feedback* because it pinpoints behavior rather than personal characteristics or attitudes. "Neglecting to call in" pinpoints behavior, whereas "not into the job" focuses more on an attitude.

2. *Encourage the person you are coaching to talk.* Part of being a good listener is encouraging the person being coached to talk. Ask the person you are coaching open-ended questions. Closed questions do not provide the same opportunity for self-expression, and they often elicit short, uninformative answers. Assume you are coaching a coworker on how to use the e-mail system properly. An effective open-ended question might be, "Where are you having the biggest problems using e-mail?" A closed question covering the same topic might be, "Do you understand how to use e-mail?" The latter question would not provide good clues to specific problem areas faced by your coworker.

3. *Give emotional support.* By being helpful and constructive, you provide much-needed emotional support to the person who needs help in improving job performance. A coaching session should not be an interrogation. An effective way of providing emotional support is to use positive rather than negative motivators. For example, as a team leader you might say to a team member, "If you learn how to analyze manufacturing costs, you will be eligible for an outstanding performance review." A negative motivator on the same topic might be, "If you don't learn how to analyze manufacturing costs, you're going to get zapped on your performance appraisal."

4. *Give some constructive advice.* Too much advice giving interferes with two-way communication, yet some advice can lead to improved performance. Assist the person being coached to answer the question "What can I do about this problem?" Advice in the form of a question or suppositional statement is often effective. One example is, "Could the root of your problem be that you have not studied the user manual?"

5. *Coach with "could," not "should."* When instructing somebody else to improve, tell the person he or she *could* do something rather than *should* do it. *Should* implies the person is doing something morally wrong, such as "You should recycle the used-up laser cartridges." *Could* leaves the person with a choice to make: to accept or reject your input and weigh the consequences.[7]

6. *Interpret what is happening.* An interpretation given by the person doing the coaching is an explanation of why the person being coached is acting in a particular manner. The interpretation is designed to give the person being coached insight into the nature of the problem. For instance, a food service manager might be listening to the problems of a cafeteria manager with regard to cafeteria cleanliness. After a while the food service manager might say, "You're angry and upset with your employees because they don't keep a careful eye on cleanliness. So you avoid dealing with them, and it only makes problems worse." If the manager's diagnosis is correct, an interpretation can be extremely helpful.

7. *Help remove barriers to good performance.* Many problems of poor work performance are caused by factors beyond a worker's control. By showing a willingness to intervene in such problems the supervisor or team leader displays a helpful and constructive attitude and gives emotional support. One manager helped her advertising and sales promotional manager improve performance through a simple remedy:

Marketing manager: The main job objective that you missed in this review period was having the Web site updated on time to introduce our new line of information devices. What happened?

Advertising and sales promotion manager: As I've hinted several times in the past, our budget for support help is too tight. It was virtually impossible to get the Web page out on time without more help for my dozens of other urgent responsibilities.

Marketing manager: Then I'll get you more help, even if I have to lend you my own assistant one day a week.

8. *Allow for modeling of desired performance and behavior.* An effective coaching technique is to show the person being coached an example of what constitutes the desired behavior. A customer service manager was harsh with customers when facing heavy pressure. One way the supervisor coached the service manager was by taking over the manager's desk during a busy period. The service manager then watched the supervisor deal tactfully with demanding customers.

One implication of the coaching suggestions just presented is that some people are more adept at coaching than others. Self-Assessment Quiz 10-2 provides insight into the *right stuff* for being an effective coach. After doing that exercise and reading the suggestions, you will be prepared for Skill-Building Exercise 10-3, about coaching.

FALLACIES ABOUT COACHING

Another approach to understanding how to be an effective coach is to overcome certain common misperceptions about coaching. Several of these false stereotypes, as explained by Ian Cunningham and Linda Honold, are presented next.[8] One false belief is that *coaching only applies in one-to-one work.* In reali-

CHARACTERISTICS OF AN EFFECTIVE COACH

Directions: Following is a list of traits, attitudes, and behaviors of effective coaches. Indicate next to each trait, attitude, or behavior whether you need to improve (for example, "need to become more patient"). Prepare an action plan for improving each trait, attitude, or behavior that you need to develop.

Trait, attitude, or behavior	*Action plan for improvement*
Empathy	*Sample:* Will listen until I understand person's point of view.
	Your own: _____

Listening skill	*Sample:* Will concentrate extra hard to listen.
	Your own: _____

Ability to size up people	*Sample:* Will jot down observations about people upon first meeting; then verify in the future.
	Your own: _____

Diplomacy and tact	*Sample:* Will study book of etiquette.
	Your own: _____

Patience toward people	*Sample:* Will practice staying calm when someone makes mistake.
	Your own: _____

Concern for welfare of others	*Sample:* When interacting with another person will ask self, "How can this person's interests best be served?"
	Your own: _____

Self-confidence	*Sample:* Will attempt to have at least one personal success each week.
	Your own: _____

Noncompetitiveness with team members	*Sample:* Will keep reminding myself that all boats rise with the same tide.
	Your own: _____

Enthusiasm for people	*Sample:* Will search for the good in each person.
	Your own: _____

Skill-Building Exercise 10-3

COACHING A GOOD PERFORMER

Visualize a team of five people working at a Sir Speedy print shop. The shop provides such services as photocopying, desktop publishing, and printing. One student plays the role of the team leader and owner of this Sir Speedy franchise. Another student plays the role of Chris, a team member who is a standout performer. A problem, however, is the impatience Chris displays toward teammates when taking care of a good customer. When Chris is taking care of a large job, he expects others on the team to drop everything to help with that customer. "When I'm serving a customer, that customer's needs come first," says Chris.

The team leader and Chris get together for a coaching session initiated by the team leader. Chris is convinced that he is right to place customer needs over those of team members. Students not actively participating in this role play will observe the two role players. Be alert for indicators of both good and poor coaching by the team leader.

ty, the team or another group can also be coached. As a team member, or team leader, you might make a suggestion to the group, such as "Why are we rushing through such an important issue?"

A major misperception is that *coaching is mostly about providing new knowledge and skills*. The truth is that people often need more help with underlying habits than knowledge and skills. A good example is coaching another person about work habits and time management. You can provide the individual with loads of useful knowledge and techniques. However, if the person is a procrastinator, he or she must reduce procrastination before time management skills will help. (See Chapter 14.)

Another stereotype deals with an important ethical issue: *If coaches go beyond giving instruction in knowledge and skills, they are in danger of getting into psychotherapy*. The counterargument is that coaches should simply follow the model of effective parents. This involves listening to the other person, attempting to understand his or her real concerns, and offering support and encouragement. Another stereotype that is particularly resistant to extinction is that *coaches need to be expert in something to coach*. To use a sports analogy, a good coach doesn't have to be or have been an outstanding athlete. An important role for the coach is to ask pertinent questions and listen. Questioning and listening can help the other person set realistic learning goals.

An understandable stereotype is that *coaching has to be done face to face*. The face-to-face approach facilitates coaching. Nevertheless, telephone and e-mail are useful alternatives when time and distance create barriers. A worker on a field trip, for example, might send his coworker/coach an e-mail message asking, "The customer says that if I make a mistake with this installation, he'll never do business with us again. Any suggestions?"

TRAINING OTHERS

A direct way of helping others in the workplace is to train them. **Training** is the process of helping others acquire a job-related skill. Supervisors and trainers are responsible for much of the training in organizations. Yet as organizations operate with fewer managers, coworkers have more responsibility to train each other. An effective example of peer training took place at Eastern Lutheran Brotherhood, a giant financial services firm. Several years ago the company used peer training to teach its 1,500-member sales force to use new laptop computers in just five weeks.

While training others, keep in mind certain time-tested principles that facilitate learning—and therefore training. Applying these principles consistently will increase the chances that the people you are training will acquire new skills.

1. *Encourage concentration.* Not much learning takes place unless the trainee concentrates carefully on what is being learned. Concentration improves the ability to do both mental and physical tasks. In short, encourage the person you are training to concentrate.

2. *Motivate interest.* People learn best when they are interested in the problem facing them. Explain to the trainee how the skill being taught will enhance his or her value as an employee, or relate the skill to the person's professional goals. Trainees can be encouraged to look for some relationship between the information at hand and their personal welfare. With this relationship in mind, the person will have a stronger intention to learn.

3. *Distribute practice.* An effective way of learning something is a little bit at a time. Most people retain more, and thus make better use of training, when they break up learning with frequent rest periods. Suppose you were training a coworker in the full details of preparing customer invoices. It would probably be best to work on these complicated procedures 30 minutes at a time than to spend five-hour blocks on training.

4. *Ensure the meaningfulness of material.* The material to be learned should be organized in a meaningful manner. Each successive experience should build on the other. In training another person how to process a customer order, you might teach the skill in terms of the flow of activities from customer inquiry to product delivery.

5. *Give feedback on progress.* As a person's training progresses, motivation may be maintained and enhanced by providing knowledge on progress. To measure progress it may be necessary to ask the trainee questions or ask for a job sample. For example, you might ask the person being trained on invoices to prepare a sample invoice.

6. *Deal with trainee defensiveness.* Training is sometimes retarded because the person being trained is defensive about information or skills that

Skill-Building Exercise 10-4

DESIGNING A TRAINING PROGRAM

The class organizes into training-design teams of approximately six people. Each team sketches the design of a training program to teach an interpersonal skill to employees, such as being polite to customers or interviewing job candidates. The teams are not responsible for selecting the exact content of the training program they choose. Instead, they are responsible for designing a training program based on the principles of learning.

The activity should take about 15 minutes and can therefore be done inside or outside of class. After the teams have designed their programs, they can compare the various versions.

clash with his or her beliefs and practices. The person might have so much emotional energy invested in the status quo that he or she resists the training. For example, a sales representative might resist learning how to use e-commerce because she believes that her warm smile and interpersonal skills have made her an excellent communicator. She is concerned that if she communicates with customers exclusively through e-mail, her human touch will be lost. Sensing this defensiveness, the trainer is advised to talk about e-commerce as being a supplement to, but not a substitute for, in-person communication. (However, the sales rep might also be worried that her position will be eliminated.)

7. *Rely on the magic number seven.* The immediate memory span of an adult seems fixed at about seven items. Most people can remember up to about seven categories of most things. It is probably not coincidental that we have seven days of the week, seven primary colors, seven deadly sins, and seven notes on the musical scale. When you are trying to teach people new information, arrange it into seven large chunks. New bits of information can be added to one of these seven chunks.

To start applying these principles of learning to training, do Skill-Building Exercise 10-4.

HELPING DIFFICULT PEOPLE

A challenge we all face from time to time is dealing constructively with workers who appear intent on creating problems. For a variety of reasons, these difficult or counterproductive people perform poorly themselves or interfere with

the job performance of others. A **difficult person** is an individual who creates problems for others, yet has the skill and mental ability to do otherwise. Here we will describe briefly various types of difficult people, and then emphasize methods for helping them behave more productively. To pretest your skill in dealing with and helping difficult people, do Self-Assessment Quiz 10-3.

TYPES OF DIFFICULT PEOPLE

Dozens of types of difficult people have been identified, with considerable overlap among the types. For example, one method of classifying difficult people might identify the *dictator*, while another method might identify the *bully*. Our purposes will be served by listing a sampling of the many types of difficult people found in the workplace and as customers. As you read the following list, look for familiar types:[9]

➤ *Know-it-alls* believe they are experts on everything. They have opinions on any issue, yet when they are wrong they pass the buck or become defensive.

➤ *Blamers* are workers who never solve their own problems. When faced with a challenge or a hitch, they think the problem belongs to the supervisor or a group member.

➤ *Gossips* spread negative rumors about others and attempt to set people against each other.

➤ *Dictators* bully, cajole, and intimidate others. They are blunt to the point of being insulting. Dictators constantly make demands on workmates.

➤ *Repulsives* are people whose poor personal hygiene, eating habits, appearance, or foul language disrupt the tranquility of others.

➤ *Yes-people* agree to any commitment, promise any deadline, yet rarely deliver. Although sorry about being late, they cannot be trusted to deliver as promised.

➤ *No-people* are negative and pessimistic and quick to point out why something will not work. They are also inflexible, resist change, and complain frequently.

➤ *Jekyll and Hydes* have a split personality. When dealing with supervisors, customers, or clients, they are pleasant, engaging people; yet when carrying out the role of supervisors they become tyrannical.

➤ *Backstabbers* pretend to befriend you and encourage you to talk freely about problems or personality clashes you face. Later, the backstabber reports the information—often in exaggerated form—to the person you mentioned in a negative light. Or the backstabber simply says negative things about you behind your back to discredit you to others.

Self-Assessment Quiz 10-3

HELPING DIFFICULT PEOPLE

Directions: For each of the following scenarios, choose the method of handling the situation you think would be the most effective. Make a choice, even though more than one method of handling the situation seems plausible.

1. A coworker in the cubicle next to you is talking loudly on the telephone about the fabulous weekend she and a few friends enjoyed. You are attempting to deal with a challenging work problem. To deal with this situation, you

 a. Get up from your chair, stand close to her, and say loudly, "Shut up, you jerk. I'm trying to do my work."

 b. Slip her a handwritten note that says, "I'm happy that you had a great weekend, but I have problems concentrating on my work when you are talking so loudly. Thanks for your help."

 c. Get the boss on the phone and ask that she please do something about the problem.

 d. Wait until lunch and then say to her, "I'm happy that you had a great weekend, but I have problems concentrating on my work when you are talking so loudly. Thanks for your help."

2. One of your coworkers, Olaf, rarely carries his fair load of the work. He forever has a good reason for not having the time to do an assignment. This morning he has approached you to load some new software onto his personal computer. You deal with this situation by

 a. Carefully explaining that you will help him, providing he will take over a certain specified task for you.

 b. Telling him that you absolutely refuse to help a person as lazy as he is.

 c. Counseling him about fair play and reciprocity.

 d. Reviewing with him a list of five times at which he has asked other people to help him out. You then ask if he thinks this is a good way to treat coworkers.

3. In your role as supervisor, you have noticed that Diane, one of the group members, spends far too much work time laughing and joking. You schedule a meeting with her. As the meeting opens, you

 a. Joke and laugh with her to establish rapport.

 b. Explain to Diane that you have called this meeting to discuss her too-frequent laughing and joking.

 c. Talk for a few moments about the good things Diane has done for the department, then confront the real issue.

 d. Explain to Diane that she is on the verge of losing her job if she doesn't act more maturely.

(Continued)

4. As a team member, you have become increasingly annoyed with Jerry's ethnic, racist, and sexist jokes. One day during a team meeting, he tells a joke you believe is particularly offensive. To deal with the situation, you

 a. Meet privately with the team leader to discuss Jerry's offensive behavior.

 b. Catch up with Jerry later when he is alone, and tell him how uncomfortable his joke made you feel.

 c. Confront Jerry on the spot and say, "Hold on Jerry. I find your joke offensive."

 d. Tell the group an even more offensive joke to illustrate how Jerry's behavior can get out of hand.

5. You have been placed on a task force to look for ways to save the company money, including making recommendations for eliminating jobs. You interview a supervisor about the efficiency of her department. She suddenly becomes rude and defensive. In response, you

 a. Politely point out how her behavior is coming across to you.

 b. Get your revenge by recommending that three jobs be eliminated from her department.

 c. Explain that you have used up enough of her time for today and ask for another meeting later in the week.

 d. Tell her that unless she becomes more cooperative this interview cannot continue.

Scoring and Interpretation: Use the following key to obtain your score:

1. a. 1	2. a. ④	3. a. 1	4. a. 2	5. a. 4
b. ④	b. 1	b. 4	b. ④	b. 1
c. 2	c. 3	c. ③	c. 3	c. ②
d. 3	d. 2	d. 2	d. 1	d. 3

18–20 You have good intuition about helping difficult people.
10–17 You have average intuition about helping difficult people.
5–9 You need to improve your sensitivity about helping difficult people.

TACTICS FOR DEALING WITH DIFFICULT PEOPLE

How one deals most effectively with a difficult person depends to some extent on the person's type. For example, you might need more time to get through to a passive person than to a bully. Figure 10-1 presents specific ideas for dealing with a bully. (You will recall that bullying was described in Chapter 7 as a source of workplace conflict.) The following techniques have wide applicability for helping difficult people change to a more constructive behavior pattern. This general approach should prove more helpful than being concerned with specific tactics for each type of difficult person you encounter.

Give Ample Feedback

The primary technique for dealing with counterproductive behavior is to feed back to the difficult person how his or her behavior affects you. Focus on the person's behavior rather than on characteristics or values. If a *repulsive type* is

Christine Pearson, a management professor at the University of North Carolina at Chapel Hill, says there are steps employees can take to keep uncivil behavior out of the workplace.[10]

➤ The first step is to admit to yourself that you are being bullied and that the bullying is unfair and unjustified.

➤ If the bully is affecting you physically, see your doctor.

➤ Stand up for yourself and be confident.

➤ Check out your body language. If you stoop, hang your head, or hunch over, you may give giving off *victim signals.*

➤ Try not to show that the bully has upset you; the bully may get bored and leave you alone.

➤ Don't suffer in silence; tell someone you trust.

➤ Find out about your rights, consider using any complaints procedure available in your company, and if necessary, consult a lawyer.

Figure 10-1 How to Be a Bully Buster

annoying you by constantly eating when you are working together, say something to this effect: "I have difficulty concentrating on the work when you are eating." Such a statement will engender less resentment than saying, "I find you repulsive, and it annoys me."

Criticize Constructively

Feedback sets the stage for criticism. It is best to criticize in private and to begin with mild criticism. Base your criticism on objective facts rather than subjective impressions. Point out, for example, that the *yes-person's* lack of follow-through resulted in $10,000 in lost sales. Express your criticism in terms of a common goal. For example, "*We* can get the report done quickly if *you'll* firm up the statistical data while I edit the text." When you criticize a coworker, avoid acting as if you have formal authority over the person.

Use Tact and Diplomacy

Tactful actions on your part can sometimes take care of annoying behavior by coworkers without having to confront the problem. Close your door, for example, if noisy coworkers are gathered outside. When subtlety does not work, it may be necessary to proceed to a confronting type of feedback.

Tact and diplomacy can still be incorporated into confrontation. In addition to confronting the person, you might also point out a strength of the individual. In dealing with a know-it-all you might say, "I realize you are creative and filled with good ideas. However, I wish you would give me an opportunity to express my opinion."

Use Humor

Nonhostile humor can often be used to help a difficult person understand how his or her behavior is blocking others. Also, the humor will help you defuse the conflict between you and that person. The humor should point to the person's unacceptable behavior, yet not belittle him or her. Assume that you and a

coworker are working jointly on a report. For each idea that you submit, your coworker gets into the know-it-all mode and informs you of important facts you neglected. An example of nonhostile humor that might jolt the coworker into realizing that his or her approach is annoying is as follows:

> If there is ever a contest to choose the human being with a brain that can compete against a CD-ROM, I will nominate you. But even though my brain is limited to human capacity, I still think I can supply a few facts for our report.

Your humor may help the other person recognize that he or she is attempting to overwhelm you with facts at his or her disposal. You are being self-effacing and thereby drawing criticism away from your coworker. Self-effacement is a proven humor tactic.

Work Out a Deal

A direct approach to dealing with problems created by a difficult person is to work out a deal or a negotiated solution. Workers who do not carry their load are successful in getting others to do their work. The next time such a worker wants you to carry out a task, agree to it if he or she will reciprocate by performing a task that will benefit you. For working out a deal to be effective, you must be specific about the terms of the deal. The worker may at first complain about your demands for reciprocity, so it is important to be firm.

Reinforce Civil Behavior and Good Moods

In the spirit of positive reinforcement, when a generally difficult person is behaving acceptably, recognize the behavior in some way. Reinforcing statements would include, "It's fun working with you today" and "I appreciate your professional attitude."

The tactics for dealing with difficult people just described require practice to be effective. When you next encounter a difficult person, try one of the tactics that seems to fit the occasion. Role plays, such as those presented in Skill-Building Exercise 10-5, are a good starting point for implementing tactics in dealing with difficult people.

SUMMARY

Workers have a responsibility to help each other learn, grow, and develop. A major strategy for helping others grow and develop is to be a nurturing, positive person. A toxic person stands in contrast to a nurturing person because he or she dwells on the negative. Nurturing people are positive, enthusiastic, and supportive. Three actions and attitudes that support being a nuturing person are to (1) recognize growth needs in others, (2) use the buddy system, (3) be a role model.

Being a mentor is another way to help others. To be a mentor, a person engages in a wide range of helping behaviors. Among them are sponsoring, coaching, protecting, sharing challenging assignments, and being a referral agent. Mentors also help protégés solve problems and learn the ropes of an

Skill-Building Exercise 10-5

DEALING WITH DIFFICULT PEOPLE

In both of the following scenarios, one person plays the role of a group member whose work and morale suffer because of a difficult person. The other person plays the role of the difficult person who may lack insight into what he or she is doing wrong. It is important for the suffering person to put emotion into the role.

Scenario 1: The Dictator. A dictator is present at a meeting called to plan a company morale-boosting event. Several students play the roles of the group members. One student plays the role of a group member who suggests that the event center around doing a social good such as refurbishing a poor family's house or conducting a neighborhood cleanup. Another student plays the role of a dictator who thinks the idea is a bummer. The group member being intimidated decides to deal effectively with the dictator.

Scenario 2: A No-Person. One student plays the role of a worker with a lot of creative energy whose manager is a no-person. The energetic worker has what he or she thinks is a wonderful way for the company to generate additional revenue—conduct a garage sale of surplus equipment and furnishings. The worker presents this idea to the no-person manager, played by another student. If the manager acts true to form, the worker will attempt to overcome his or her objections.

organization. Mentoring has become recognized as an important vehicle for the advancement of minorities in the workplace.

Coaching and training are direct helping roles. Coaching is a method of helping workers grow and develop by providing suggestions and encouragement. Suggestions for effective coaching include the following:

1. Provide specific feedback.

2. Encourage the person you are coaching to talk.

3. Give emotional support.

4. Give some constructive advice.

5. Coach with "could," not "should."

6. Interpret what is happening.

7. Help remove barriers to good performance.

8. Allow for modeling of desired performance and behavior.

Effective coaching also takes into account certain common misperceptions about coaching, including the following: (a) coaching only applies to one-to-one work; (b) coaching is mostly about providing new knowledge and skills; and, (c) coaching has to be done face to face.

Complacer—hacer un favor.

An Interpersonal Relations Case Problem

THE DEMANDING PROTÉGÉ

Dawn Albright is a sales representative for an office-supply company. She has five years of successful experience selling furnishings and interior designs to business firms in her area. Dawn worked her way up from taking telephone orders for small supplies such as computer paper, print cartridges, pencils, ballpoint pens, and pencils. By the fifth year of her employment, Dawn became the highest producer in the office.

One day Dawn's manager, Jim Bastian, requested a favor: "Dawn, would you be willing to take Marilyn Lake under your wing? Marilyn is the newest member of the sales staff. I think she could benefit from the guidance of a real pro like yourself." Dawn enthusiastically agreed to assume responsibility for becoming Marilyn's mentor. She told Jim, "I sure could have used help myself when I was getting started."

Jim explained to Dawn that Marilyn might need a lot of help. He pointed out that the company was taking a chance on placing Marilyn in a sales position. Jim's reasoning was that although Marilyn made a professional appearance, she didn't appear to have much self-confidence. When Dawn asked Jim to give her a few specifics, he commented: "A lot of little things have given me the impression that Marilyn needs more self-confidence. When I interviewed her, Marilyn could not give me any example of how she had ever been a leader in anything. Also, when I ask her opinion about almost anything, she says, 'I'm really not sure' or 'I don't have an informed opinion.'"

Dawn later met with Marilyn to explain that although she was not her boss she had volunteered to spend time showing her the ropes. Marilyn expressed appreciation and acknowledged that she had a lot to learn about the business.

Dawn began working with Marilyn by taking her along on visits to a few of her best accounts. Dawn even allowed Marilyn to receive credit for the sale of a few desks, chairs, and coffee tables because she assisted in the sales. Over the next several months, Dawn would discuss Marilyn's sales progress with her from time to time. The two would discuss Marilyn's tactics and the plans she formulated to develop each account. Marilyn listened attentively and followed Dawn's advice carefully.

Toward the end of the sixth month of their working relationship, Dawn received a telephone call from Marilyn late one night. Marilyn pleaded with Dawn to accompany her on a sales call to a potentially big account. "I know that if you are present at this meeting, between the two of us we will close the sale," said Marilyn.

Dawn's first thought was that Marilyn needed the experience of closing a big sale herself, yet she obliged. "Marilyn has a point," thought Dawn to herself. "Experience is a big factor in closing such a large account. And our firm could sure use the business."

As the months rolled by Marilyn made an increasing number of requests for Dawn's advice on sales tactics. Twice more she pressured Dawn into helping her close big sales. Dawn hinted that Marilyn should close the sale herself, but Marilyn insisted that she needed help just one more time.

Soon Marilyn began to seek Dawn's advice on matters outside work. One day Dawn asked if Marilyn would help her choose a dress for an engagement shower. Another time Marilyn sought Dawn's advice on how she should handle her parents' negative reaction to her latest boyfriend. Soon Marilyn was telephoning Dawn at least twice a weekend, asking to discuss questions about both work and her personal life.

One day Dawn thought to herself, "My being a mentor to Dawn has gone too far. I'm her confidante, her big sister, and her sales consultant. At times I also feel I'm her mother. This relationship is draining me."

(Continued)

Case Questions

1. How effective is Dawn as Marilyn's mentor?

2. In what way might Dawn be hindering her protégée's development?

3. What should Dawn do about her relationship with Marilyn?

4. What underlying issue might Dawn be neglecting in dealing with Marilyn?

Training involves helping people acquire job skills. To facilitate training, apply principles of learning such as the following: (a) encourage concentration; (b) motivate interest; (c) distribute practice; (d) ensure the meaningfulness of material; (e) give feedback; (f) deal with trainee defensiveness; and (g) rely on the magic number seven.

Dealing with difficult people is a major challenge in helping others. The many types of difficult people include know-it-alls, blamers, gossips, dictators, repulsives, yes-people, no-people, Jekyll and Hydes, and backstabbers. Among the tactics for dealing with them are the following: (a) give ample feedback; (b) criticize constructively; (c) use tact and diplomacy; (d) use humor; (e) work out a deal; and (f) reinforce civil behavior and good moods.

QUESTIONS FOR DISCUSSION AND REVIEW

1. Explain your position on whether workers have a responsibility to help each other grow and develop.

2. Why is there more emphasis today than in the past on workers helping each other grow and develop?

3. What is your opinion of the potential effectiveness of the buddy system in your career?

4. If you were to have a mentor (or do have one), what roles would you want (or do you want) that person to play?

5. If you were choosing a mentor or protégé, to what extent would the person's gender be an influential factor?

6. In what way does a coach in the workplace function much like an athletic coach?

7. Describe any barrier to good performance you have encountered. How might your supervisor have helped?

8. Do you think trainee defensiveness is a bigger problem in teaching technical or interpersonal skills? Explain.

9. What do you think are the motives of a person who acts like Jekyll and Hyde?

10. How might humor help you deal with the repulsive type of difficult person? Supply an example of a witty comment you might use.

Chapter 11

Positive
Political
Skills

Four office mates were seated around a table in the employee lounge during a rest break. The conversation shifted from weather and sports to how Jeremy, one of their former coworkers, was promoted to supervisor. "I don't see why Jeremy was chosen for a supervisory position and one of us wasn't," commented Kristine. "His qualifications aren't better than ours."

"I think I know the answer," said Sue. "We laughed when Jeremy wrote progress reports to upper management. We poked fun at him when he explained how his day-by-day work helped the company reach its major goals. We said he was kissing up. Jeremy disagreed. He thought that staying in touch with the right people and looking at the big picture are effective ways of getting noticed. I guess he knew what he was doing."

An implication of Sue's comments is that the proper use of positive political tactics helps build good interpersonal relationships. In turn, these good relationships can facilitate achieving career goals. Recognize, however, that being competent in your job is still the most effective method of achieving career success. After skill come hard work and luck as important success factors. A fourth ingredient is also important for success—positive political skills.

Few people can achieve success for themselves or their group without having some awareness of the political forces around them and how to use them to advantage. It may be necessary for the career-minded person to take the offensive in using positive and ethical political tactics.

As used here, **organizational politics** refers to gaining power through any means other than merit or luck. (Luck, of course, is what happens when preparation meets opportunity.) Politics are played to achieve power, either directly or indirectly. **Power** refers to the ability or potential to control anything of value and to influence decisions. The results of such power may take such diverse forms as being promoted, being transferred, receiving a salary increase, or avoiding an uncomfortable assignment. Figure 11-1 depicts the relationship among politics, power, and control and influence.

In this chapter we approach skill development in organizational (or office) politics from several standpoints. Information is presented about such topics as managing your impression, using political tactics to improve interpersonal relationships, and avoiding hazardous political mistakes. In addition, you will have the opportunity to take two quizzes about political tactics and engage in skill-building exercises. To measure your current tendencies toward playing politics, do Self-Assessment Quiz 11-1.

Figure 11-1 Relationship Among Politics, Power, and Influence
Political tactics, such as developing contacts with key people, lead to power, which enables one to control and influence others.

ORGANIZATIONAL POLITICS QUESTIONNAIRE

Directions: Answer each question Mostly agree or Mostly disagree, even if it is difficult for you to decide which alternative best describes your opinion.

	Mostly agree	Mostly disagree
1. The boss or team leader is always right.		✓
2. It is wise to flatter important people.	✓	
3. If you do somebody a favor, remember to cash in on it.	✓	
4. Given the opportunity, I would cultivate friendships with powerful people.	✓	
5. I would be willing to say nice things about a rival in order to get that person transferred from my department.		✓
6. If it would help me get ahead, I would take credit for someone else's work.		✓
7. Given the chance, I would offer to help my boss build some shelves for his or her den.		✓
8. I laugh heartily at my boss's humor, even if I do not think it is funny.		✓
9. Dressing for success is silly. At work, wear clothing that you find to be the most comfortable.	✓	✓
10. Never waste lunchtime by eating with somebody who can't help you solve a problem or gain advantage.		✓
11. I think using e-mail to zap somebody for his or her mistakes, and sending copies to key people, is a good idea.		✓
12. If somebody higher up in the organization offends you, look for ways to get even with him or her.		✓
13. Honesty is the best policy even if it means insulting somebody.	✓	
14. Power for its own sake is one of life's most precious commodities.		✓
15. If I had a legitimate gripe against my employer, I would air my views publicly (such as distributing my comments over the Internet).		✓
16. I would invite my boss or team leader to a party at my home even if I didn't like him or her.		✓
17. An effective way to impress people is to tell them what them they want to hear.	✓	
18. Having a high school or skyscraper named after me would be an incredible thrill.	✓	

(Continued)

	Mostly agree	Mostly disagree
19. Hard work and good performance are usually sufficient for career success.		✓
20. Even if I made only a minor contribution to a project, would get my name listed as being associated with it.		✓
21. I would never publicly correct mistakes made by my boss or team leader	✓	✓
22. I would never use my personal contacts in order to gain a promotion.	✓	
23. If you happen to dislike a person who receives a big promotion in your firm, don't bother sending that person a congratulatory note.		✓
24. I would never openly criticize a powerful executive in my organization.	✓	
25. I would stay late in the office just to impress my boss or team leader.	✓	

Scoring and Interpretation: Give yourself a +1 for each answer you gave in agreement with the keyed answer. Note that we did not use the term *correct* answer. Whether or not an answer is correct is a question of personal values and ethics. Each question that receives a score of +1 shows a tendency toward playing organizational politics. The scoring key is as follows:

1. Mostly agree	10. Mostly agree	18. Mostly agree
2. Mostly agree	11. Mostly agree	19. Mostly disagree
3. Mostly agree	12. Mostly disagree	20. Mostly agree
4. Mostly agree	13. Mostly disagree	21. Mostly agree
5. Mostly agree	14. Mostly agree	22. Mostly disagree
6. Mostly agree	15. Mostly disagree	23. Mostly disagree
7. Mostly agree	16. Mostly agree	24. Mostly agree
8. Mostly agree	17. Mostly agree	25. Mostly agree
9. Mostly disagree		

For an earlier version of this test, based on a sample of 750 men and women managers, professionals, administrators, sales representatives, and business owners,* the mean score is 10. Scores of 1 through 7 suggest a below-average tendency to play politics. Scores between 8 and 12 suggest an average tendency to play office politics. Scores of 13 and above suggest an above-average tendency to play office politics and a strong need for power.

*Andrew J. DuBrin, "Career Maturity, Organizational Rank, and Political Behavior Tendencies: A Correlational Analysis of Organizational Politics and Career Experience," *Psychological Reports*, vol. 63, 1988, pp. 531–37; DuBrin, "Sex Differences in Endorsement of Influence Tactics and Political Behavior Tendencies," *Journal of Business and Psychology*, Fall 1989, pp. 3–14.

IMPRESSION MANAGEMENT AND ETIQUETTE

Being an effective, responsible contributor is not always sufficient to gain you the attention you deserve. It may also be necessary to make others aware of your capability. **Impression management** is a set of behaviors directed at enhancing one's image by drawing attention to oneself. Often the attention is directed toward superficial aspects of the self, such as clothing and appearance. Impression management also includes telling people about your accomplishments and appearing self-confident. Our presentation of impression management includes a listing of specific tactics and a discussion of business etiquette.

TACTICS OF IMPRESSION MANAGEMENT

Managing the impression you create encompasses dozens of specific tactics, limited only by your imagination of what will impress others. A study of 178 men and 124 women in higher-level positions specified 28 different tactics designed to impress work associates.[1] As you work through Self-Assessment Quiz 11-2, you will become familiar with these tactics. The numbered items constitute a representative list of what higher-level workers can do to impress others—including doing an outstanding job.

When managing the impression you create, be mindful of the advice offered by William L. Gardner III. He urges that you be yourself. When selecting an image, do not attempt to be somebody you are not, because people will see through this facade. Gardner concludes, "Make every effort to put your best foot forward—but never at the cost of your identity or integrity!"[2] Gardner's comment helps emphasize the fact that impression management is geared toward looking good, but not creating a false impression.

BUSINESS ETIQUETTE

A major component of managing your impression is practicing good etiquette. **Business etiquette** is a special code of behavior required in work situations. The term *manners* has an equivalent meaning. Both manners and etiquette generally refer to behaving in a refined and acceptable manner. Studying etiquette is important because knowing and using proper business etiquette contributes to individual and business success.[3] People who are considerate of the feelings of others, and companies who are courteous toward customers, are more likely to succeed than their rude counterparts.

What is considered proper etiquette and manners in the workplace changes over time and may vary with the situation. At one time, addressing one's superior by his or her first name was considered brash. Today it is commonplace behavior.

Business etiquette includes many aspects of interpersonal relations in organizations, as described in the following discussion.[4] A sampling of etiquette guidelines is helpful. Nevertheless, a general principle of being considerate of the feelings of work associates is more important than any one act of etiquette or courtesy. Keep in mind also, that you will find a few contradictory statements

Self-Assessment Quiz 11-2

THE POSITIVE-IMPRESSION SURVEY

Directions: Please indicate how often you use the following ways of impressing work associates, including customers. Use the following ratings: 1 = Very infrequently (VI); 2 = Infrequently (I); 3 = Sometimes (S); 4 = Frequently (F); and 5 = Very frequently (VF). Circle the most accurate answer.

Tactic or Method	*VI*	*I*	*S*	*F*	*VF*
1. Dressing well	1	2	3	4	(5)
2. Making a favorable appearance other than through dress	1	2	3	4	(5)
3. Using colorful speech	1	2	(3)	4	5
4. Being cheerful	1	2	3	4	(5)
5. Appearing self-confident	1	2	3	(4)	5
6. Being neat and orderly	1	2	3	4	(5)
7. Pretending to others that I am in demand	(1)	2	3	4	5
8. Talking about quality as it relates to the job	1	2	3	4	(5)
➤ 9. Talking about own accomplishments	(1)	2	3	4	5
✝10. Being knowledgeable about the topic at hand	1	2	3	(4)	5
✝11. Achieving high job performance	1	2	3	(4)	5
12. Creating a problem and then solving it to look good	(1)	2	3	4	5
13. Talking about team play	1	2	3	(4)	5
14. Being diplomatic	1	2	3	4	(5)
15. Sharing expertise with others	1	2	3	4	(5)
16. Sharing credit with others	1	2	3	4	(5)
17. Giving warmth and support	1	2	3	4	(5)
18. Following through with promises	1	2	3	(4)	5
➤19. Exaggerating my accomplishments	(1)	2	3	4	5
20. Saying what other person wants to hear	1	2	3	(4)	5
21. Listening carefully	1	2	3	(4)	5
22. Making small talk	1	2	3	(4)	5
23. Talking about work	1	2	3	4	(5)
24. Showing good ethics	1	2	3	4	(5)
25. Sending greeting cards to work associates	1	2	(3)	4	5
26. Avoiding a direct "No" in dealing with others	1	2	3	4	(5)
✝ 27. Being calm under pressure	1	2	3	4	(5)
➤ 28. Flattering others	(1)	2	3	4	5

(Continued)

Interpretation: This questionnaire is not designed to provide a score. Instead, compare your frequency ratings to a group of 300 men and women holding a variety of managerial, sales, and professional jobs. The following mean scores refer to ratings on the 1-to-5 scale.

1. Dressing well, 4.1
2. Favorable appearance, 4.3
3. Colorful speech, 3.6
4. Cheerfulness, 4.3
5. Self-confident appearance, 4.5
6. Neatness, 4.2
7. Pretending to be in demand, 2.0
8. Talk of quality, 4.2
9. Talk of accomplishments, 2.6
10. Knowledge of topic, 4.2
11. High performance, 4.7
12. Creating problems, 1.8
13. Team player talk, 3.6
14. Diplomacy, 4.0
15. Share expertise, 4.2
16. Share credit, 3.9
17. Warmth and support, 4.1
18. Following through, 4.4
19. Exaggeration, 2.0
20. Saying what people want to hear, 2.7
21. Listening, 4.1
22. Small talk, 3.0
23. Work talk, 3.3
24. Ethics display, 4.4
25. Greeting cards, 2.6
26. Avoid direct "No," 3.1
27. Pressure handling, 4.1
28. Flattery, 0.9

Your rating of the impression-management tactics may provide useful clues to skill development. If you use a given tactic much less frequently than others, you might consider evaluating whether you are using this tactic enough. For example, if you make very infrequent use of warmth and support to impress others, you might increase the frequency of such behavior to the norm (4.1 = frequently). In other instances, you might decide that you are overusing a tactic (such as exaggerating).

Note: In the comparison groups, only one statistically significant difference was found between men and women in the use of these impression tactics. Women gave a mean frequency rating of 2.9 for the use of greeting cards, while men gave a frequency rating of 2.3.

Source: Andrew J. DuBrin, "Sex Differences in the Use and Effectiveness of Tactics of Impression Management," *Psychological Reports,* vol. 74, 1994, pp. 531–544.

in writings about etiquette. Before reading ahead, you are invited to take the Self-Assessment Quiz 11-3.

Etiquette for Work Behavior and Clothing

General work etiquette includes all aspects of performing in the work environment, such as completing work on time, punctuality, being a good team player, listening to others, and following through. For instance, having the courtesy to complete a project when it is due demonstrates good manners and respect for the work of others.

Clothing might be considered part of general work behavior. The casual standards in the information technology field, along with dress-down days, has created confusion about proper office attire. A general rule is that *casual* should not be interpreted as sloppy, such as torn jeans or a stained sweatshirt.

Self-Assessment Quiz 11-3

BUSINESS ETIQUETTE

1. How would you introduce a sales representative to your supervisor?
 a. Ms. Mint, this is Joe Majors, a sales rep from Power Office Machines.
 b. Joe Majors, I would like you to meet my boss, Ms. Alice Mint.
 c. Joe, this is the boss.
 d. Ms. Alice Mint, meet Joe.

2. Who should exit first on an elevator?
 a. all women
 b. the woman closest to the door
 c. the closest man or woman to the door
 d. the largest person on the elevator, male or female

3. When a woman conducts business in a foreign country, she should always
 a. explain clearly that she will not serve coffee or run errands.
 b. play a subjugated (inferior) role to male business companions.
 c. be sensitive to differences in culture.
 d. enjoy complete freedom.

4. At a business dinner, how should you signal a server that you are ready to order?
 a. In a loud, but nonthreatening voice, call the server.
 b. Close the menu.
 c. Speak in a low, but audible voice, "Where's our server?" when another server or bus person is nearby.
 d. Stand up and make the hand gesture that signals "Come over here."

5. In a restaurant, when is it proper to unfold a napkin and place it in your lap?
 a. as soon as you sit down
 b. when the first course arrives
 c. immediately after beverages have been ordered
 d. whenever you feel so inclined

6. When is it appropriate to put elbows on the table?
 a. only between courses
 b. always
 c. never
 d. whenever you are drinking a beverage

(Continued)

7. How much should the host tip a wine steward?
 - a. $3 to $4 per bottle
 - b. 15% of the price of the meal plus the wine
 - c. 10% of the price of the wine
 - d. nothing, because tipping is not necessary

8. At a cocktail party, even if no alcohol is consumed, which hand holds the drink glass?
 - a. right
 - b. left
 - c. right for right handers, left for left handers
 - d. left for right handers, right for left handers

9. If, by oversight, you are left out of the introduction in a group at the office, what is the best way to correct the error?
 - a. ignore the oversight
 - b. make a joke about how the other group members are jealous of you
 - c. introduce yourself
 - d. point out the oversight in a strong manner

10. Jennifer (age 26), a sales rep, invites Max (age 49), a vice president of purchasing, to lunch. What should take place after the server brings the check?
 - a. Jennifer should pay because Max is the customer and she invited him.
 - b. The person closest to where the check was placed by the server should pay.
 - c. Jennifer and Max should each pay one-half the bill.
 - d. Max should pay because he is male and older.

Answers: 1. a; 2. c; 3. c; 4. b; 5. a; 6. a; 7. a; 8. b; 9. c; 10. a.

The higher you scored, the more you know about business etiquette. A low score most likely means you need to study and observe more about business etiquette.

Source: Adapted and expanded from "A Business Etiquette Quiz," *Keying In,* January 1996, p. 7.

Etiquette for Meeting People

Displaying proper etiquette in meeting others includes receiving guests, making their visit pleasant and constructive, introducing people, shaking hands, and remembering names. One guideline is that visitors should be informed of accommodations, such as restroom facilities and coat closets. Another guideline is that the person of highest rank is introduced first (named first). An example: "Mr. CEO, this is our new information technology specialist." If rank is equal, then the older person is named first. When introducing a new employ-

ee (or visitor) to a group of people, name the new employee first, then each member of the group. Use first and last names when introducing people.

Telephone Etiquette

Despite the prominence of voice mail and answering machines, most business communication over the phone requires live interaction between people. Guidelines for proper telephone usage include the following:

➤ Answer the phone by the third ring.

➤ Identify your company, your department, and yourself.

➤ Say good morning, good afternoon, or good evening.

➤ Always end the call on a pleasant note and say goodbye. Never say bye-bye (except for social calls).

➤ If possible, avoid call waiting and other forms of putting people on hold. Putting people on hold after the conversation has begun is a low point in rudeness.

Etiquette for Dining

Etiquette surrounding meals involves planning for the meeting, making seating arrangements, bill paying, tipping, using proper table manners, and appropriate drinking of alcoholic beverages. We all know not to slurp spaghetti one strand at a time, pour ketchup over sauce, or leave a 50¢ tip. Less obvious are the following guidelines:

➤ Arrange seating for meal meetings in advance.

➤ Establish with the server who will be paying the check.

➤ You will be served from the right, so be prepared to lean slightly to the left to allow the server to place the food and beverages.

➤ Place your napkin on your lap immediately after being seated.

➤ Bread should not be used to push food on to a fork or spoon.

➤ Attempt to pace your eating to those of others at the table.

➤ The wait staff, not the diners, should be responsible for moving plates around the table.

Etiquette for Hard Copy and E-Mail Correspondence

Etiquette for letter writing is better established than for e-mail or internal hard-copy memos. Guidelines for writing letters include using a courtesy title in the inside address, typing the name and address correctly, and using the correct closing lines. Many people believe that formality and careful use of language can be neglected when sending messages by e-mail. Remember, however, that the way in which any message is sent tells something about the sender. E-mail messages should be proofread, should be sent only when necessary, and should generally be not longer than one screen—not including attachments.

Using Electronic Devices in Addition to E-Mail

Electronic devices such as Internet access devices, copying machines, and cellular telephones create opportunities for good and poor etiquette. Violations of etiquette surrounding the Internet including receiving non-work-related material on your monitor in the presence of others and surfing the Internet on company time. Key violations of copy-machine etiquette include hogging the machine, jumping in ahead of others, and leaving the machine at a setting only you require. A generally accepted guideline is that if you are using the photocopying machine for a large job and somebody approaches with a small job, let that person go first.

A major etiquette problem with cellular telephones in the workplace is similar to that in personal life. Cell phone users often speak loudly in an open area, interrupting the concentration and tranquillity of others. It is particularly rude to sit in a public waiting room and conduct a prolonged conversation with a work associate.

Etiquette for Other Cultures

What constitutes proper etiquette may differ from culture to culture. Be alert to differences in etiquette in areas such as gift giving, dining, drinking alcoholic beverages, and when and where to discuss business. Many of these differences in customs were described in Chapter 6 about cross-cultural relations. Violating these customs is poor etiquette. For example, using the index finger to point is considered rude in most Asian and Middle Eastern countries. Also, people in Middle Eastern countries tend to stand as close as two or three inches from the person with whom they are talking. To back away is interpreted as an insult.

Suppose you are in doubt about the proper etiquette for any situation, and you do not have a handbook of etiquette readily available. As a substitute, observe how your host or a successful person in the group behaves.

Skill-Building Exercise 11-1 gives you an opportunity to practice appropriate etiquette in several situations.

BUILDING RELATIONSHIPS WITH MANAGERS

The political purpose of building good relationships with managers is to gain power through such means as being recommended for promotion and key assignments. Building these good relationships is also important because it helps create a positive, supportive work environment for yourself. Good relationships can also be established with managers for the nonpolitical purpose of trying to get the job accomplished. The strategies and tactics described next are outlined in Figure 11-2.

Network with Influential People

A basic success strategy is developing contacts, or **networking**, with influential people. In addition to making contacts, networking involves gaining the trust and confidence of the influential people.[5] Networking also takes place with peo-

Skill-Building Exercise 11-1

BUSINESS ETIQUETTE

An effective way of improving business etiquette is by using self-discipline to use one's best manners and courtesy in real-life situations. Role-playing etiquette scenarios can also contribute to helping you develop the right mental set for using good etiquette.

Scenario 1: Dining Etiquette. A small group of students plan to conduct a high-etiquette meal at a local fast-food restaurant during nonpeak hours. Pretend the plastic eating utensils are fine silver and that the Styrofoam cups are crystal. Assume that your Big Mac is beef Wellington or that your submarine sandwich is a delicately prepared capon. Each class member uses his or her best etiquette. At the same time, each group member carefully observes the etiquette displayed by the other members.

At the conclusion of the meal, critique each other's etiquette. If you were courteous enough to invite your instructor to your high-etiquette meal, get his or her feedback.

Scenario 2: Telephone Etiquette. Bring two telephone receivers into class, with the two people on the phones being separated by about six feet. Several pairs of students might conduct telephone conversations covering such matters as customer complaints, inquiring about a job, or asking about product availability. Students not making the calls will carefully observe the callers. Look for examples of good and poor telephone etiquette. Feedback will be provided after the phone conversations are completed.

ple inside and outside the organization who are not your managers. Developing contacts with influential people is likely to pay big career dividends.

A standard procedure is to create a card or computer file of the people in your network and update it frequently. To keep your network effective, it is necessary to contact people on your list periodically. Sending greeting cards, as noted in Self-Assessment Quiz 11-2, is one small way of maintaining your network.

Developing a network of influential people requires alertness and planning. You have to identify influential people and then think of a sensible reason to contact them. Here are a few possibilities.

1. Network with influential people.
2. Help your manager succeed.
3. Volunteer for assignments.
4. Flatter influential people sensibly.
5. Use information power.
6. Appear cool under pressure.
7. Laugh at your manager's humor.

Figure 11-2 Strategies and Tactics for Building Relationships with Managers

➤ Send an e-mail message to a high-ranking manager, offering a money-saving or revenue-producing suggestion. A related tactic is to inform the person of something of significance you did that might lie directly in his or her area of interest.

➤ Do a standout job as a member of a task force or committee that includes a high-ranking official.

➤ Discuss your career plans with a neighbor who has an outstanding position.

➤ Take the initiative to develop a friendship with an influential person who is a member of your athletic club, YMCA, YWCA, or place of worship.

Help Your Manager Succeed

The primary reason you are hired is to help your manager achieve the results necessary to succeed. Avoid an adversarial relationship with your manager. Also figure out both obvious and subtle ways of ensuring the manager's success. One subtle way of increasing your manager's chances for success is to help that person out when he or she is under attack from another department. One example would be to supply information to support your manager's position on a controversial issue. Also keep in mind the cornerstone tactic of performing your job superbly. Your manager will then share in your success.

Volunteer for Assignments

An easily implemented method of winning the approval of superiors is to become a "hand raiser." By volunteering to take on assignments that do not fit neatly into your job description, you display the kind of initiative valued by employers. Among the many possible activities to volunteer for are fundraising campaigns assigned to your company, project membership, and working over-time when most people prefer not to (for example, on a Saturday in July). As noted under the discussion of networking, task force assignments are also useful for being noticed by key people in the organization. As a team member, volunteer to assume any leadership responsibility you think you can handle. If your team offers rotating leadership assignments, express interest in taking your turn.

Flatter Influential People

One of the most effective relationship builders is to flatter people sensibly and credibly. Despite the risk of being called obsequious or a cheap office politician, the flatterer wins. A study on how to advance in big business pointed out that a company's top employees tend to be equal in performance. So advancing was based on image (30 percent) and contact time with the manager (50 percent). Flattery can play a big role in both.[6] Psychology professor Ronald Deluga conducted a study of 152 pairs of supervisors and employees in which the employees admitting to trying to make the supervisor feel important. The flattering techniques served to (a) note that the supervisor had brains, talent, and experience; (b) show respect; (c) express values similar to those of the

Skill-Building Exercise 11-2

FLATTERING AN INFLUENTIAL PERSON

A perceptive, intelligent reader like yourself has probably already guessed the nature of this role play. One student plays the role of a newcomer to the organization who is seeking to advance, or at least to secure, his or her position in the organization. Another person plays the role of a vice president who is visiting the newcomer's department.

The newcomer is asked to escort the vice president to another part of the building. The walk should take about five minutes, giving the newcomer an opportunity to work in some flattery. Although the vice president is not naive, he or she is proud of his or her accomplishments. The two role players conduct the five-minute walk, perhaps circling the classroom.

supervisor; and (d) make the employees appear humble. Deluga concluded that the flatterers gain a 5 percent edge over nonflatterers in receiving positive evaluations and high marks for future promise.[7]

An effective, general-purpose piece of flattery is to tell another person that you are impressed by something he or she accomplished. The following anecdote illustrates this approach:

> A management trainee told the purchasing manager that she was impressed with his modern operation. "It's very similar to the ideal material management system described in my production and operations management course," said the trainee. Her flattery appeared to be instrumental in her being asked to become a permanent member of the purchasing department after her training period ended.

During the next two weeks, try out the flattery tactic with an influential person. In the interim, do Skill-Building Exercise 11-2.

Use Information Power

Power accrues to those who control vital information. At the same time, being a source of useful information will help you build constructive working relationships with managers. You will be relied on as an important contributor. Controlling vital information includes knowing how to gain access to useful information that others do not know how to retrieve. Many workers are aware of the mechanics of using the Internet, but many fewer have the skills to use the Net to retrieve commercially useful information. During a tight labor market, for example, human resource specialists can acquire power if they know how to use the Internet to find talented people who might want to join the company.

Information power is closely related to *expert power,* which refers to having valuable expertise. If your expertise or skill is in high demand at the moment, power will flow in your direction. Currently, an important type of expert power

is knowing how to operate enterprise software that links together several parts of an organization.

Appear Cool Under Pressure

Showing signs of panic generally hurts your reputation with influential people. In contrast, appearing to be in emotional control when things around you are falling apart helps convey the impression that you are worthy of additional responsibility. Being cool under pressure is part of emotional stability, and it is a key leadership characteristic. An example of coolness under pressure follows.

> A snow-making machine technician was rushed to a Vermont ski resort three days before the start of the holiday season. The problem was that the equipment wasn't spraying water with enough pressure for the water to convert to snow. When the technician arrived at the ski resort, a snarling owner said that if the equipment was not working within 24 hours his company would be sued for $5 million. Despite all the mental pressure, the technician fixed the water pressure problem within four hours. Several weeks later he was promoted to field maintenance supervisor.

Laugh at Your Manager's Humor

When you indicate by your laughter that you appreciate your manager's sense of humor, it helps establish rapport between the two of you. An indicator of good two-way communication between people is that the two parties comprehend each other's subtle points. Most humor in the workplace deals with subtle meanings about work-related topics. To implement the tactic of laughing at your manager's jokes, do not worry excessively about having heard the joke before.

BUILDING RELATIONSHIPS WITH COWORKERS AND OTHER WORK ASSOCIATES

Another strategy for increasing your power is to form alliances with coworkers and other work associates. You need the support of these people to get your work accomplished. Also, when you are being considered for promotion, coworkers and other work associates may be asked their opinion of you. Under a peer-evaluation system, the opinion of coworkers about your performance counts heavily. Here we describe nine representative strategies and techniques for developing good interpersonal relationships at or below your level (see Figure 11-3). The information about developing teamwork skills presented in Chapter 4 is also relevant here.

Maintain Honest and Open Relationships

Although being honest may appear to contradict organizational politics, it is representative of the nature of positive politics. Giving coworkers frank but tactful answers to their requests for your opinion is one useful way of developing open relationships. Assume that a coworker asks your opinion of an e-mail he intends to send to his supervisor. As you read it, you find it somewhat incoherent and filled with spelling and grammatical errors. An honest response to

1. Maintain honest and open relationships.
2. Develop allies.
3. Express an interest in their work.
4. Be diplomatic.
5. Exchange favors.
6. Ask advice.
7. Share constructive gossip.
8. Buddy up to the tech fixers.
9. Follow group standards of conduct.

Figure 11-3 Strategies and Tactics for Developing Relationships with Coworkers and Other Work Associates

this message might be: "I think your idea is a good one. But I think your e-mail needs more work before that idea comes across clearly."

Accurately expressing your feelings, whether positive or negative, also leads to constructive relationships. If you have been singled out for good performance, let other team members know that you are happy and proud. If you arrive at work upset over a personal problem and appearing obviously fatigued, you can expect some reaction. A coworker might say, "What seems to be the problem? Is everything all right?" A dishonest reply would be "Everything is fine." In addition to making an obviously untrue statement, you would also be perceived as rejecting the person who asked the question. If you prefer not to discuss your problem, an honest response would be, "Thanks for your interest. I am facing some problems today. But I think things will work out."

Develop Allies

A key strategy for developing good relationships with coworkers and other work associates is to create allies rather than enemies. Your allies can support you when you need help. The printing and photocopying specialist you befriended may alert you to an upcoming opening within the company for which you qualify (at a higher job level than yours). Equally important, a network of allies establishes you as a leader, which increases your chances for promotion.

Express an Interest in Their Work

How to develop allies is an important issue. A simple yet valuable technique for cultivating sideways and downward relationships is to express genuine interest in the work of others. A basic way to accomplish this end is to ask other employees questions such as the following:

How is your work going?

How does the company use output from your department?

How did you establish all the contacts you did to be so successful in sales?

How did you develop the skills to do your job?

Expressing an interest in the work of others is an effective tactic because so many people are self-centered. They are eager to talk about their own work,

but rarely pause to express a genuine interest in others. Expressing an interest in the work of others is also effective because it is a form of recognition.

Be Diplomatic

Despite all that has been said about the importance of openness and honesty in building relationships, most people fail to be convinced. Their egos are too tender to accept the raw truth when faced with disapproval of their thoughts or actions. Diplomacy is still an essential part of governmental and office politics. Translated into action, diplomacy often means finding the right phrase to convey disapproval, disagreement, or discontent. Here is an example of a delicate situation and the diplomatic phrase used to handle it.

> During a staff meeting, a coworker suggests that the entire group schedule a weekend retreat to formulate a five-year plan for the department. The boss looks around the room to gauge the reactions of others to the proposal. You want to say: "What a stupid idea. Who needs to ruin an entire weekend to do something we could easily accomplish on a workday afternoon?" The diplomatic response is: "I've heard that retreats sometimes work. But would spending that much time on the five-year plan be cost effective? Maybe we could work on the plan during one long meeting. If we don't get the planning accomplished in that time frame, we could then consider the retreat."

Exchange Favors

An important part of human interaction on and off the job is to reciprocate with others. Exchanging favors with others can make it easier for people to accomplish their work because they are able to call on assistance when needed. The adept political player performs a favor for another employee without asking a favor in return. The favor is then cashed in when a favor is needed. Several examples of workaday exchanges are as follows:

➤ A paralegal agrees to help another overburdened paralegal in the same law office, knowing that the other paralegal will reciprocate if needed in the future.

➤ A credit manager agrees to expedite a credit application for a sales representative. In reciprocation, the sales rep agrees to not commit the company to a delivery date on the next sale until the customer's credit has been evaluated.

➤ An assistant restaurant manager agrees to substitute for another assistant manager on New Year's Eve. A month later the first person asks the second to take over her shift so she can get away for the weekend.

Ask Advice

Asking advice on technical and professional topics is a good way of building relationships with other employees. Asking for advice from another person—someone whose job does not require giving it—will usually be perceived as a compliment. Asking advice transmits the message "I trust your judgment

enough to ask your opinion on something important to me." You are also saying, "I trust you enough to think that the advice you give me will be in my best interest."

To avoid hard feelings, inform the person whose advice you are seeking that his or her opinion will not necessarily be binding. A request for advice might be prefaced with a comment such as, "I would like your opinion on a problem facing me. But I can't guarantee that I'll be in a position to act on it."

Share Constructive Gossip

An effective way of building workplace relationships is to share constructive gossip with others. Gossip serves as a socializing force because it is a mode of intimate relationships for many employees. Workers get close to each other through the vehicle of gossip. It also serves as the lifeblood of personal relationships on the job. If you are the person supplying the gossip, people will develop positive attitudes toward you. **Positive gossip** is unofficial information that does not attack others, is based on truth, and does not leak confidential information. Given these restrictions, here are two examples of positive gossip:

➤ "I heard that business is really picking up. If this week is any example, the company's profits for the quarter will far exceed expectations."

➤ "I heard yesterday that the director of public relations just got engaged to a cool guy she met on a cruise."

Buddy Up to the Tech Fixers

An indirect way of acquiring power is to be able to get information technology help when you need it in a hurry. A tech fixer is a person whose formal or informal role is to lend expert assistance in solving information technology problems. Many tech fixers feel they are treated more like pieces of machinery than total human beings. If you can befriend a tech fixer or two before you have an urgent computer problem, you might receive quicker and better service when stuck. Mark Durrant, a director of technical services, explains that there is an emerging etiquette in dealing with tech fixers. It is important to make an appointment, even with internal technical staff, and to avoid emotional outbursts over such matters as corrupted files.[8]

Follow Group Standards of Conduct

A summary principle to follow in getting along with other employees is to heed **group norms**, the unwritten set of expectations for group members. If you do not deviate too far from these norms, much of your behavior will be accepted by the group. If you deviate too far, you will be subject to much rejection and therefore lose some of your power base. Yet if you conform too closely to group norms, higher-level management may perceive you as unable to identify with management. Employees are sometimes blocked from moving up the ladder because they are regarded as "one of the gang."

Skill-Building Exercise 11-3 provides an opportunity to practice several of the techniques for building interpersonal relationships with coworkers and other work associates.

Skill-Building Exercise 11-3

GETTING ALONG WITH COWORKERS

An inventory auditor in a department store chain decides to take action aimed at getting along better with coworkers. In each of the following two scenarios, one person plays the role of the inventory auditor. Another person plays the role of an employee whom the auditor is attempting to cultivate.

Scenario 1: Exchanging Favors. The auditor decides to strike a bargain with a store associate. (The role player decides what this exchange of favors should be.) Unknown to the auditor, the store associate is concerned about an inventory audit because he is worried about being accused of stealing merchandise.

Scenario 2: Express an Interest in Their Work. The auditor decides to express an interest in a tech fixer because he can be a valuable ally when conducting an inventory audit. The inventory audit is computerized, and the appropriate software is confusing and crashes frequently. The tech fixer has a heavy workload and is not much prone toward small talk, but he does get excited talking about information technology.

AVOIDING POLITICAL BLUNDERS

DISPARATES - EQUIVOCACIONES

A strategy for not losing whatever power you have accumulated is to refrain from making power-eroding blunders. Committing these politically insensitive acts can also prevent you from attaining power. Self-Assessment Quiz 11-4 will get you started thinking about blunders. Several leading blunders are described in the following list.

1. *Criticizing your manager in a public forum.* The oldest saw in human relations is to "praise in public and criticize in private." Yet in the passion of the moment, you may still surrender to the irresistible impulse to criticize your manager publicly. As a result, the manager will harbor resentment toward you and perhaps block your chances for advancement.

2. *Bypassing the manager.* Many people believe that because most organizations are more democratic today, it is not important to respect the layers of authority (the chain of command). In reality, following etiquette is highly valued in most firms. Going around the manager to resolve a problem is therefore hazardous. You might be able to accomplish the bypass, but your career could be damaged and your recourses limited. It is much better to work out differences with your manager using standard methods of resolving conflict.

Self-Assessment Quiz 11-4

THE BLUNDER QUIZ

Indicate whether you agree or disagree with the following statements.

	Agree	Disagree
1. It's fine to criticize your manager in a meeting as long as the criticism is valid.		✓
2. Dressing for success is a sham. You should wear whatever clothing you find the most comfortable.		✓
3. I am willing to insult any coworker if the insult is deserved.		✓
4. I see no problem in using competitors' products or services and letting my superiors know about it.		✓
5. If I thought the CEO of my company were way overpaid, I would send him or her an e-mail making my opinion known.		✓
6. Never bother with company-sponsored social events, such as holiday parties, unless you are really interested.	✓	
7. If I disagreed with something my employer did, I would voice my opinion in a letter to the editor of a local newspaper or over the Internet.		✓
8. I'm very open about passing along confidential information.		✓
9. I openly criticize most new ventures my company or department is contemplating.		✓
10. I avoid office politics of any kind.		✓

Scoring and Interpretation: The greater the number of statements you agree with, the more prone you are to political blunders that can damage your interpersonal relationships and your career. You need to raise your awareness level of blunders on the job.

Abierto, Publico

3. *Overt displays of disloyalty.* Being disloyal to your organization is a basic political blunder. Making it known that you are looking for a position elsewhere is the best-known form of disloyalty. Criticizing your company in public settings, praising the high quality of competitors' products, and writing angry internal e-mail messages about your company are others. You may not get fired, but overt signs of disloyalty may place you in permanent disfavor.

4. *Being a pest.* Common wisdom suggests that diligently pressing for one's demands is the path to success. This may be true up to a point, but when assertiveness is used too often it becomes annoying to many people. The overpersistent person comes to be perceived as a pest, and

this constitutes a serious political blunder. An example of being a pest would be asking your manager every month when you are going to receive the raise you deserve.

5. *Burning your bridges.* A potent political blunder is to create ill will among former employers or people who have helped you in the past. The most common form of bridge burning occurs when a person departs from an organization. A person who leaves involuntarily is especially apt to express anger toward those responsible for the dismissal. Venting your anger may give a temporary boost to your mental health, but it can be detrimental in the long run.

If you want to overcome having committed a blunder, avoid defensiveness. Demonstrate that you are more interested in recovering from the blunder than in trying to share the blame for what happened. Focus on solutions to the problem rather than faultfinding. Suppose you have been too critical of your team leader in a recent team meeting. Explain that your attempts to be constructively critical backfired and that you will choose your words more carefully in the future.

APLOMO-SERENO

Another way to patch up a blunder is to stay poised. Admit that you made the mistake and apologize, but don't act or feel inferior. Mistakes are inevitable in a competitive work environment. Avoid looking sad and distraught. Instead, maintain eye contact with people when you describe your blunder.

DISTRACTED

SUMMARY

Positive political tactics help build good interpersonal relationships. Organizational politics refers to gaining power through any means other than merit or luck. Power refers to the ability or potential to control anything of value and influence decisions. Impression management is one aspect of organizational politics. Managing the impression you create encompasses a wide range of behaviors designed to create a positive influence on work associates, as indicated by Self-Assessment Quiz 11-1.

A major component of managing the impression you create is business etiquette. The general principle of etiquette is to be considerate of the feelings of work associates. Areas of business etiquette include work behavior and clothing, meeting people, telephone use, dining, hard copy and e-mail correspondence, using other electronic devices, and dealing with other cultures.

Political strategies and tactics for building relationships with managers include the following: network with influential people; help your manager succeed; volunteer for assignments; flatter influential people sensibly; use information power; appear cool under pressure; and laugh at your manager's humor.

Political strategies and tactics for developing relationships with coworkers and other work associates include the following: maintain honest and open relationships; develop allies; express an interest in their work; be diplomatic;

exchange favors; ask advice; share constructive gossip; buddy up to the tech fixers; and follow group standards of conduct.

A strategy for not losing whatever power you have accumulated is to refrain from making political blunders. Political blunders can also prevent you from attaining power. Representative blunders include criticizing your manager publicly, bypassing your manager, overt disloyalty, being a pest, and burning your bridges. If you want to make up for a blunder, avoid defensiveness and stay poised.

QUESTIONS FOR DISCUSSION AND REVIEW

1. How important do you think political tactics are for getting ahead in business?

2. Would you want to work for a person who achieved a maximum score on the Organizational Politics Questionnaire (Self-Assessment Quiz 11-1)? Explain.

3. Identify three impression-management tactics presented in Self-Assessment Quiz 11-2 that would be acceptable to you. Explain your reasoning.

4. Identify three impression-management tactics presented in Self-Assessment Quiz 11-2 that would be unacceptable to you. Explain your reasoning.

5. Identify three jobs in which you think practicing good business etiquette would be extremely important.

6. Identify three jobs in which you think practicing good business etiquette would be less important.

7. A candidate for an information systems analyst position was well on his way to receiving a job offer. As part of the final screening process, he was taken to lunch by the team leader and two team members. During lunch the candidate left a spoon in his coffee cup and sucked in a few stands of spaghetti. Based on these table manners, the team declined to extend the candidate a job offer. What is your reaction to this scenario?

8. It has been said that although most business people can see through flattery, the technique still works. How would you explain this observation?

9. How ethical is it to ask a person for advice with a problem even if you already know which solution you will use?

10. Give an example you have observed of a person being a pest on the job. What was the outcome?

An Interpersonal Relations Case Interview Analysis

WHY "GOOD" GIRLS (WOMEN) DON'T GET PROMOTED

Kate White, the editor of *Redbook* magazine, was interviewed by the National Institute of Business Management (NIMB) about her views on women advancing in their careers. White is also the author of *Why Good Girls Don't Get Ahead, But Gutsy Girls Do* (New York: Warner Books, 1995).

NIMB: Why are some women "good girls"?

White: You think it's going to pay off to be nice. You get these messages to "be a team player" and "don't rock the boat." These things worked for you in high school, so you buy in. But I think a lot of women are gutsy by nature. Being gutsy isn't really about changing, it's about finding that six-year-old inside of you that had the guts to climb trees and beat the boys at their own game.

I remember winning a race against this boy and being so thrilled that I had won. Then my uncle pulled me over and whispered, "A tip: Never beat your future husband in a race." I felt such shame that I was not only wrong for winning, but that I was wrong for feeling so good afterward. That's how it starts. You're born gutsy, then it's pushed down with messages like that.

NIMB: You advise women to ask for things in such a way that the company wins, too. How does that work?

White: When people ask me for things, they often ask in a way that's not very smart. It's only about their needs. I hear people say, "I really deserve it," or "It's my turn." The boss wants to know what's in it for her. You have to explain that.

It's also important to let your boss know that you enjoy working with her. Share your ideas. Say, "I like being part of your team, and I want to contribute more." That's not kissing [expletive deleted] if it's the truth.

NIMB: What do you do if the answer is no?

White: The most important thing is to get more information. Paraphrase what the boss just told you: "It sounds like you're saying you don't feel I'm ready for this yet." Once you have the information, walk away with it and analyze it. Don't do anything yet. Take the time to think through every possibility.

If you don't agree, make your case. If the boss is right, I would say, "It's clear that you are unhappy with my performance. Let's set up a time to talk more about what I need to do to change that perception." If the boss feels she's been heard, she's going to deal with you in a more positive way.

NIMB: How do you handle the boss who can't handle your "gutsiness"?

White: Start looking for another job. But ask yourself if you could be doing something to improve the situation. Maybe you're being a loose cannon—you need to keep her better informed.

Remember, you have to manage your boss. My brother once had a boss who gave him a middle-of-the-road review despite his excellent performance. He said my brother didn't come back to him enough on things. My brother hated people who told him every move they made, so he deliberately didn't do it. But that's all his boss wanted. He didn't have to change anything except to make his boss feel a part of things.

(Continued)

NIMB: Your book warns women not to become "Barney bosses." What are they, and why are they bad?

White: The "Barney boss" likes being the Earth mother. She's nurturing. She thinks, "We're all one big family." I tend to be one myself. But I found that if you're too nice, if you solve everybody's problems, they'll ultimately like you and they'll like the work environment, but you're not really challenging them.

People like a tough boss because it helps them grow. I don't mean you should throw fits—that seems out of control to me. But stick to your ground and demand the best from your staff. They may get defensive, but often when people are prickly, it's because they know you're right.

NIMB: How do you draw the line between gutsy and bitchy?

White: A lot of bitchiness is a sign of a good *girl*. You're overcompensating for not getting what you want. People who act bitchy have bought into that assertiveness-training talk of the '80s—make

demands, go in with both guns blazing. Women sometimes feel that's the way to get what they want, but I think being diplomatic, even a little manipulative, is the better way.

The goal is not to show how mad or strong you are, but to get what you want. You have to ask yourself what's the best way to get what you want. Screaming at people doesn't work. When people get scared of you, they stop communicating.

Case Questions

1. Which tactics of organizational politics are mentioned in White's comments?

2. Which tactics of impression management, including etiquette, are mentioned in White's comments?

3. Why might a "Barney boss" not be an effective mentor?

4. What style of conflict resolution does White recommend?

5. What communication barriers might White be creating with her choice of terms?

Source: Reprinted from interview with Kate White, "Why 'Good' Girls Don't Get Promoted," *In Their Own Words*, National Institute of Business Management Special Report 250, McLean, VA, 1997.

Chapter 12

Customer Satisfaction Skills

Learning Objectives

After reading and studying this chapter and doing the exercises you should be able to

➤ Enhance your ability to satisfy customers by using general principles of customer satisfaction.

➤ Create bonds with present or future customers.

➤ Have a plan for dealing effectively with customer dissatisfaction.

➤ Understand the contribution of customer service training.

Purchasing agent Hal said to Cynthia, a sales representative calling on his firm, "Our company has decided to take advantage of your volume discount. We want to order one gross of laser cartridges, model number 7PL89. You said we would receive a 25 percent discount by buying in bulk."

"That's exactly what I said last week, Hal. Our company would like to sell you 144 cartridges in one shot. But I have some new information that suggests you should limit your purchase to two dozen for now. Those two dozen are the older cartridges. The manufacturer recently shifted to a new components supplier. Some quality problems have been found with the latest cartridges. Let's hold off on that big order until we can be sure you will receive the quality that your company needs and deserves."

"It's a pleasure doing business with you, Cynthia," said Hal. "My company and I are happy to know that you are looking out for our best interests."

The conversation between Hal and Cynthia may sound idealistic, but it represents an important new thrust in relationships between buyers and sellers. Many companies today emphasize total customer satisfaction over short-range profits. An important reason is that excellent customer service leads to goodwill, repeat business, and referrals. This chapter presents information and exercises that can enhance your ability to satisfy both external and internal customers at a high level.

External customers fit the traditional definition of customers that includes clients, guests, and patients. External customers can be classified as retail or industrial. The latter represents one company buying from another, such as purchasing steel or a gross of printer cartridges. *Internal customers* are the people you serve within the organization or those who use the output from your job. Also, everyone you depend upon is an internal customer. The emphasis in this chapter is on satisfying external customers. Much of the rest of the book deals with better serving internal customers, because improved interpersonal relationships enhance the satisfaction of work associates.

Customer satisfaction skills are required by all workers in contact with customers, including sales representatives, customer service representatives (those who back up sales and take care of customer problems), and store associates. Various aspects of developing customer satisfaction skills are divided into three parts in this chapter: general principles, bonding with customers, and dealing with customer dissatisfaction. To reflect on your attitudes toward satisfying customers, do Self-Assessment Quiz 12-1.

GENERAL PRINCIPLES OF CUSTOMER SATISFACTION

Knowing how to satisfy customers is a subset of effective interpersonal relations in organizations. Nevertheless, there are certain general principles that will sharpen your ability to satisfy customers and thereby improve customer retention. This section presents seven key principles for satisfying customers.

WOULD YOU BUY FROM YOU?

One of the most effective ways to assess your effectiveness in handling customers is by asking the question "If you were the customer, would you buy from yourself?" You would if you scored well on the following quiz. Answer each question by checking the appropriate Yes or No blank. If you do not deal with external customers, take this quiz in relation to your handling of internal customers. If you are not currently working, just imagine how you would handle the situations described.

	Yes	*No*
1. Is your image one of honest and straightforward sincerity?	_____	_____
2. Based on your experience with customers over the past year or so, *from the buyer's point of view,* would you be classified as reliable?	_____	_____
3. Could you say your customers obtained special benefits dealing with you they wouldn't have obtained from others?	_____	_____
4. Do you think you come off as an expert in the eyes of your customers?	_____	_____
5. Have you been effective in helping to solve customer problems?	_____	_____
6. Wherever possible, would you say you handled customer complaints to the buyer's satisfaction?	_____	_____
7. Is *integrity* one of the most important words in your vocabulary?	_____	_____
8. Do you think customers believe you have their personal welfare and well-being at heart with respect to business?	_____	_____
9. Can you honestly say most of your company's customers believe you have their personal welfare and well-being at heart even outside of business?	_____	_____
10. Do customers look upon you as a good, reliable source of product and industry information?	_____	_____
11. Has doing business with you contributed positively to most of your customers' profit performance?	_____	_____
12. Would most of your company's customers continue dealing with you even if a competitor approached them with a price that's a little bit lower?	_____	_____

Total Number of Yes Answers _____

Scoring and Interpretation: Multiply the sum of your Yes answers by 5. If you achieved a score of 55 or higher, it's a privilege to do business with you. A score of 50 is well above average; 40 to 45 is mediocre to fair.

Source: Adapted from *Making . . . Serving . . . Keeping . . . Customers* (Chicago: Dartnell Corporation, 1995).

Figure 12-1 Levels of Customer Satisfaction

Remember, however, that *satisfaction* is considered a minimum expectation. If you do an outstanding job of satisfying customers, they will experience *delight*, as shown in Figure 12-1.

Customer satisfaction is important for several reasons. Satisfied customers are likely to tell friends and acquaintances about their satisfactory experiences, helping a firm grow its business. In contrast, dissatisfied customers—especially those with an unresolved problem—are likely to tell many people about their dissatisfaction, thus dissuading a large number of people from becoming new customers. Customer satisfaction is also highly valued because it breeds customer loyalty, which in turn is very profitable, as demonstrated in Table 12-1.

Another reason for satisfying customers is the humanitarian aspect. Satisfying people enhances their physical and mental health, whereas dissatisfaction creates negative stress. Have you ever been so angry with poor service that you experienced stress?

SATISFIED EMPLOYEES PROVIDE BETTER CUSTOMER SERVICE

Researchers have observed frequently that employees who are happy with their jobs are the most likely to satisfy customers. Treating employees well puts them in a better frame of mind to treat their customers well. One example of this

TABLE 12-1 The Value of Customer Retention

Customer loyalty goes directly to the bottom line. Here are the financial consequences of increases in customer retention for various industries:

Industry	Increase in Retention	Profit Increase
Employer services such as payroll	4%	21%
Banking	5%	40%
Insurance	5%	60%
Laundry	5%	60%

Source: Adapted from Theodore Garrison III, "The Value of Customer Service," in Rick Crandall, ed., *Celebrate Customer Service* (Corte Madera, CA: Select Press, 1999), p. 7.

Responses to the 10 questions below from an employee attitude survey had a high impact on employee behavior and therefore on customer satisfaction.

1. I like the kind of work I do.
2. My work gives me a sense of accomplishment.
3. I am proud to say I work at Sears.
4. How does the amount of work you are expected to do influence your *overall attitude* about your job?
5. How do your physical working conditions influence your *overall attitude* about your job?
6. How does the way you are treated by those who supervise you influence your *overall attitude* about your job?
7. I feel good about the future of the company.
8. Sears is making the changes necessary to compete effectively.
9. I understand our business strategy.
10. Do you see a connection between the work you do and the company's strategic objective?

Figure 12-2 Key Aspects of Employee Satisfaction for Sears Employees

Source: Adapted from Anthony J. Rucci, Steven P. Kim, and Richard T. Quinn, "The Employee–Customer–Profit Chain at Sears," *Harvard Business Review,* January–February 1998, p. 90. One-time permission to reproduce granted by Harvard Business School Publishing.

relationship was found at the Metropolitan Property and Casualty Insurance Company.[1] The company recognized that the difference between success and failure in the property and casualty insurance field is often the quality of service and speed of handling transactions.

Human resources specialists at Metropolitan observed that customer service and employee satisfaction were closely related to each other. Customers, for example, expect outstanding customer service. Employees want recognition and compensation that relates to the achievement of customer service goals. Customers want to deal with knowledgeable customer-contact personnel who can make decisions. Employees want to be led, inspired, and recognized.

An extensive case history analysis of Sears also found a strong relationship between employee and customer satisfaction. Employees who were satisfied influenced customers to be satisfied, resulting in more purchases and profits.[2] Figure 12-2 presents a list of the 10 aspects of the job and company that had the biggest impact on the satisfaction of Sears employees. Question 1 can be used to illustrate the basics of the process:

> Employee feels, "I like the kind of work I do." → Smiles at customer and is courteous. → Customer feels positive about Sears → buys a new lawnmower and two pairs of jeans → improves profits for Sears.

Acting alone, you cannot improve company conditions that contribute to job satisfaction. What you can control to some extent, however, is your own attitudes that are related to job satisfaction. A checklist of attitudes and beliefs related to job satisfaction, and over which you can exert some control, follows:

➤ *Interest in the work itself.* Job satisfaction stems directly from being interested in what you are doing. People who love their work experience high job satisfaction and are therefore in the right frame of mind to satisfy customers.

➤ *A feeling of self-esteem.* If you have high self-esteem you are more likely to experience high job satisfaction. High-status occupations contribute more to self-esteem than do those of low status. Feelings of self-esteem also stem from doing work the individual sees as worthwhile. This perception is less influenced by external standards than is the status associated with a particular job or occupation.

➤ *Optimism and flexibility.* An optimistic and flexible person is predisposed to be a satisfied employee. A pessimistic and rigid person will most likely be a dissatisfied employee. Every company has its share of "pills" who always find something to complain about. Some evidence suggests that a tendency toward optimism versus pessimism is inherited.[3] If you have a predisposition toward pessimism it does not mean that you cannot become more optimistic with self-discipline. You can, for example, look for the positive aspects of a generally unpleasant situation.

➤ *Positive self-image.* People possessing a positive self-image are generally more satisfied with their jobs than are those possessing a negative self-image. One explanation is that the people who view themselves negatively tend to view most things negatively. You have to like yourself before you can like your job.

➤ *Positive expectations about the job.* People with positive expectations about their jobs are frequently more satisfied than are those with low expectations. These expectations illustrate a self-fulfilling prophecy. If you expect to like your job, you will behave in such a way that those expectations will be met. Similarly, if you expect your job not to satisfy your needs, you will do things to make your expectations come true. Assume that a worker expects to earn low commissions in a sales job. The person's negativism may come through to customers and prospective customers, thereby ensuring low customer satisfaction and low commissions.

UNDERSTAND CUSTOMER NEEDS AND PUT THEM FIRST

The most basic principle of selling is to identify and satisfy customer needs. One challenge is that many customers may not be able to express their needs clearly. To help identify customer needs, you may have to probe for information. For example, the associate in a camera and video store might ask, "What uses do you have in mind for a video camera?" Knowing such information will help the associate identify which camcorder will satisfy the customer's needs.

The basic idea of satisfying customer needs continues to be expressed in different ways. Recent thinking suggests that highly competitive markets and

abundant information (such as searching the Internet for prices) have caused a shift in power from suppliers to customers. Instead of being product centered, successful companies have become customer centered. The idea is to identify profitable customers and then anticipate their priorities.[4] If you satisfy customer needs, you are *adding value* for them. A person might be willing to pay $10 more per ticket to watch an athletic event if the extra $10 brought a better view and a chair instead of a backless bench. (The better view and more comfortable back add value for the spectator.) Part of the rebirth of Sears was management's emphasis on understanding its women customers better—"The Softer Side of Sears."

After customer needs have been identified, the focus must be on satisfying those needs rather than the needs of oneself or the company. Assume that the customer says, "The only convenient time for me to receive delivery this week would be Thursday or Friday afternoon." The sales associate should not respond, "On Thursday and Friday our truckers prefer to make morning deliveries." Instead, the associate should respond, "I'll do whatever is possible to accommodate your request."

FOCUS ON SOLVING PROBLEMS, NOT JUST TAKING ORDERS

Effective selling uses sales representatives to solve problems rather than merely taking orders. An example is the approach taken by sales representatives for Xerox Corp. Instead of focusing of the sale of photocopiers and related equipment, the sales reps look to help customers solve their information flow problems. The solution could involve selling machines, but it might also involve selling consulting services.

The focus on problem solving enables sales representatives to become partners in the success of their customers' businesses. By helping the customer solve problems, the sales representative enhances the value of the supplier–customer relationship to the customer. The customer is receiving consulting services in addition to the merchandise or service being offered. In some situations, a store associate can capitalize on the same principle. If the customer appears unsure about a purchase, ask him or her what problem is being faced that the product will solve. The following scenario in a computer store illustrates this point:

Customer: I think I would like to buy this computer. I'm pretty sure it's the one I want. But I don't know too much about computers.

Store Associate: I am happy you would like to purchase a computer. But could you tell me what problems you are facing that you want a computer to help you solve?

Customer: Right now I feel I'm not capitalizing on the Internet revolution. I want to get on line so I can communicate with people of similar interests all over the world and shop from my home.

Store Associate: To solve your problem you will need a more powerful computer than the one you are looking at. I would like you to consider anoth-

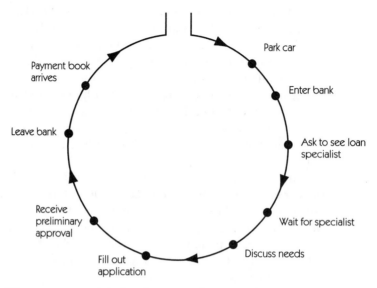

Figure 12-3 A Cycle-of-Service Chart for Obtaining a Car Loan at a Bank

er model that is about the same price as the one you have chosen. The difference is that it has just the memory you need to make communicating with people and shopping from home easy.

RESPOND POSITIVELY TO MOMENTS OF TRUTH

An effective customer contact person performs well during situations in which a customer comes in contact with the company and forms an impression of its service. Such situations are referred to as **moments of truth**. If the customer experiences satisfaction or delight during a moment of truth, the customer is likely to return when the need for service arises again. A person who is frustrated or angered during a moment of truth will often not be a repeat customer.

You can probably visualize many moments of truth in your experiences with service. Reflect on how you were treated by a store associate when you asked for assistance; the instructions you received when an airplane flight was canceled; or how you were treated when you inquired about financial aid. Each business transaction has its own moment of truth. Yet they all follow the theme of a key interaction between a customer and a company employee.

One way you can track moments of truth is to prepare a cycle-of-service chart, as shown in Figure 12-3. The **cycle-of-service chart** summarizes the moments of truth encountered by a customer during the delivery of a service.[5] To gain insight into these charts, do Skill-Building Exercise 12-1.

BE READY TO ACCEPT EMPOWERMENT

A major strategy for improving customer service is to empower customer-contact employees to resolve problems. **Empowerment** refers to managers transferring, or sharing, power with lower-ranking employees. In terms of customer

Skill-Building Exercise 12-1

MOMENTS OF TRUTH

The class organizes into small groups to discuss what can go right versus what can go wrong during customer moments of truth. First refer to the cycle-of-service chart shown in Figure 12-3. Discuss what can go right or wrong at each moment of truth. Second, the team develops its own cycle-of-service chart for another service, using its own experiences and imagination.

After making the two analyses, discuss the usefulness of a cycle-of-service chart for improving customer satisfaction.

relations it means pushing decision making and complaint resolution downward to employees who are in direct contact with customers. The traditional method of dealing with all but the most routine customer problems is for the customer-contact worker to refer them to the manager. Many manufacturing firms and service firms now authorize customer contact workers to take care of customer problems within limits. Employees at Ritz-Carlton hotels have the authority to spend up to $2,000 to solve a customer problem. At less luxurious hotels, such as the Hampton Inn, any worker can offer a guest a free night of lodging to compensate for a service problem.

Empowerment is not giving away the store, especially because limits are established to the customer contact worker's authority. Empowerment does involve taking a reasonable risk based on company principles to provide meaningful customer service. For empowerment to work, the company must grant decision-making latitude to employees. The employees, in turn, must be willing to accept empowerment (or decision-making authority).[6] Imagine yourself in a customer-contact position. For empowerment to work effectively, you should be able to answer affirmatively to the following statements:

- ➤ I am willing to arrive at a quick decision as to whether the company or the customer is right.

- ➤ I would be willing to admit to a customer that the company has made a mistake.

- ➤ I would be willing to take the risk that at times I will lose money for the company on a given transaction.

- ➤ I would be comfortable making an out-of-the-ordinary decision about a customer problem without consulting a manager.

ENHANCE CUSTOMER SERVICE THROUGH INFORMATION TECHNOLOGY

Much has been said and written about how information technology has depersonalized customer service, such as having customers select from a long menu

of choices on a touch-tone telephone. Information technology, however, also plays an important role in recording customer preferences and individualizing service. A major application of information technology that enhances customer service is to use databases to have information at hand about customer preferences. When sending an e-mail message, or making a telephone call to rent a car, the agent might make a statement such as, "The last time you rented a vehicle from us, you wanted a high-performance coupe with front-wheel drive. Is that still your preference? And will you want to take advantage of additional liability insurance again?"

Another example of enhancing customer service using information technology comes from Monsanto, the manufacturer of the artificial sweeteners NutraSweet and Equal. A major customer segment for artificial sweeteners is diabetics. Several years ago the customer service department identified people with diabetes in its customer database. These people were sent a newsletter that contained recipes and health information. The newsletter now has a circulation of over 1 million copies, and it has contributed to cultivating customer loyalty.[7]

AVOID RUDENESS

We have reserved the most frequently violated principle of good customer service for last: Avoid being rude to customers. Although rudeness to customers is obviously a poor business practice, the problem is widespread. Rudeness by customer contact personnel is a major problem from the employer's standpoint. Rude treatment creates more lost business than does poor product quality or high prices.

A representative example of the importance of not being rude to customers took place at Alamo Rent A Car. To overcome customer complaints (and to improve coworker relationships) the company initiated a Best Friends program, explained as follows:

> Make your customers your best friends; treat them that way all the time, and they will always be your customers. And they will always be your best friends. Extend this concept to your fellow Alamo family members. Make each one with whom you come in contact your best friend.
>
> What happens then? Our work environment becomes a happy place with a caring, family atmosphere. It becomes a pleasure to come to work every day. Moreover, because you have a caring attitude, because you have created a family atmosphere, the customer senses it and responds accordingly.

The idea of actually making your customers your best friends may seem far-fetched; nevertheless, the Best Friends program did show good results. After one year, business transactions increased 30 percent, and the number of repeat customers rose 70 percent. Complaints about sales and service both decreased about 15 percent.[8]

To elevate your awareness level about rudeness among customer-contact personnel, do Self-Assessment Quiz 12-2.

Self-Assessment Quiz 12-2

AM I BEING RUDE?

Directions: Following is a list of behaviors of customer contact workers that would be interpreted as rude by many customers. Indicate whether you have engaged in such behavior in your dealings with customers, or whether you would be likely to do so if your job did involve customer contact.

	Yes	No
1. I talk to a coworker while serving a customer.	___	___
2. I conduct a telephone conversation with someone else while serving a customer.	___	___
3. I address customers by their first names without having their permission.	___	___
4. I address customers as "You guys."	___	___
5. I chew gum or eat candy while dealing with a customer.	___	___
6. I laugh when customers describe an agonizing problem they are having with one of our company's products or services.	___	___
7. I minimize eye contact with customers.	___	___
8. I say the same thing to every customer, such as "Have a nice day," in a monotone.	___	___
9. I accuse customers of attempting to cheat the company before carefully investigating the situation.	___	___
10. I hurry customers when my break time approaches.	___	___
11. I comment on a customer's appearance in a flirtatious, sexually oriented way.	___	___
12. I sometimes complain about or make fun of other customers when I am serving another customer.	___	___

Interpretation: The more of these behaviors you have engaged in, the ruder you are and the more likely that you are losing potential business for your company. If you have not engaged in any of these behaviors, even when faced with a rude customer, you are an asset to your employer. You are also tolerant.

> ➤ A Customer is the most important person ever in this office . . . in person or by mail.
>
> ➤ A Customer is not dependent on us . . . we are dependent on him.
>
> ➤ A Customer is not an interruption of our work . . . he is the purpose of it. We are not doing a favor by serving him . . . he is doing us a favor by giving us the opportunity to do so.
>
> ➤ A Customer is not someone to argue or match wits with. Nobody ever won an argument with a customer.
>
> ➤ A Customer is a person who brings to us his wants. It is our job to handle them profitably to him and ourselves.

Figure 12-4 What Is a Customer?

Source: L.L. Bean, Freeport, Maine.

CREATING A BOND WITH YOUR CUSTOMER

Another key perspective on achieving customer satisfaction and delight is to create a bond—or emotional relationship—with customers. The rationale is that if you form warm, constructive relationships with your customers, they will keep buying. Staying focused on the importance of customers will help provide the motivation for forming such a bond. Figure 12-4 explains how employees at a famous consumer-products company are requested to regard customers.

Creating a bond is aimed at increasing sales, but it also enhances service. If the customer relies on and trusts the sales representative, the customer will perceive the service to be of high quality. Similarly, people perceive medical and legal services to be of high quality if they trust the physician or lawyer.

Virtually all of the principles and techniques presented in this chapter will help form a bond with customers. However, six key principles are as follows:

1. Create a welcoming attitude.
2. Provide exceptional service.
3. Show care and concern.
4. Make the buyer feel good.
5. Build a personal relationship.
6. Invite the customer back.

Create a Welcoming Attitude, Including a Smile

An effective starting point in creating a customer bond is to use enthusiastic expressions, including a smile, when greeting customers. Attempt to show a sincere, positive attitude that conveys to customers and prospects, "I'm here to make you happy."[9] In addition to being an effective greeting, smiling is also a natural relationship builder and can help you bond with your customer. Smile several times at each customer meeting, even if your customer is angry with your product or service. A camcorder is a useful device for getting feedback on

the quality of your smile. Practicing your smile in a mirror might feel a little less natural, but it is still helpful.

Smiling at customers has a potential disadvantage, despite its general effectiveness. Twelve Safeway employees filed grievances over the supermarket chain's smile-and-make-eye-contact rule. The women complained that they were being propositioned by shoppers who mistake the friendliness for flirting. A produce clerk complained that she is hit on every day by men who think she is "coming on" to them.[10] It would appear that some customer-contact workers need training in how to smile in a way that will be interpreted professionally, not personally. What is your opinion on this issue?

Provide Exceptional Service

The best-accepted axiom about keeping customers is to provide exceptional service. Many successful companies contend that their competitive advantage is good service. An excellent example is USAA, the fourth largest insurer and financial services firm in the United States. The company has a much lower than industry average percentage of customer defectors, and its business grows primarily through referrals. USAA has no external salespeople and does not use insurance agents. Most customer concerns and inquiries are settled within minutes by calling an 800 number. The mission of the firm is expressed in one word: *service.*

Exceptional service includes dozens of customer transactions, including prompt delivery, a fair-returns policy, accurate billing, and prompt attention to a customer's presence. Exceptional service also includes giving customers good advice about using the product or service.

Show Care and Concern

During contacts with the customer, the sales representative should show concern for the customer's welfare. The representative should ask questions such as: "How have you enjoyed the optical scanner you bought a while back?" "How are you feeling today?" After asking the question, the sales representative should project a genuine interest in the answer.

Make the Buyer Feel Good

A fundamental way of keeping a relationship going is to make the buyer feel good about himself or herself. Also, the customer should be made to feel good because of having bought from the representative. Offer compliments about the customer's appearance or about a report that specified vendor requirements clearly. An effective feel-good line is: "I enjoy doing business with you."

Build a Personal Relationship

Building a good working relationship with a customer often leads to a positive personal relationship. A bold approach is to do the reverse—build a working relationship based on an authentic personal relationship. You gather personal facts about the interests of your customers and then appeal to those interests. A case history of a bank manager, Jack Foxboro, shows the potential effectiveness of this technique:

Several years ago Foxboro was a commercial loan officer. He acquired a base of existing accounts from the previous officer and gradually increased his base. Jack invested considerable time telephoning and sending e-mails to existing loan holders. He collected facts about them, such as birthdays, the names of family members, golf handicaps, hobbies, and favorite sports teams. Jack entered all this information into a database.

Jack would send cards to customers in recognition of their birthdays and special accomplishments. When a customer visited the bank to talk about an existing loan or to apply for a new one, he would retrieve relevant personal facts from the database. Jack's clients were so impressed that he enlarged existing accounts and received substantial referral business.

Invite the Customer Back

The southern U. S. expression "Y'all come back, now!" is well suited for bonding with customers. Specific invitations to return may help increase repeat business. The more focused and individualized the invitation, the more likely it will be to have an impact on customer behavior. ("Y'all come back, now!" is sometimes used too indiscriminately to be effective.) Pointing out why you enjoyed doing business with the customer, and what future problems you could help with, is an effective technique. An industrial cleaning company supervisor might say, "Our crew enjoyed cleaning such a fancy office. Keep us in mind when you would like your windows to sparkle."

Skill-Building Exercise 12-2 gives you an opportunity to practice techniques for bonding with customers.

DEALING WITH CUSTOMER DISSATISFACTION

Most companies put honest effort into preventing customer dissatisfaction. In addition to employing many of the principles and techniques already cited, many companies routinely survey customers to detect problem areas that could lead to dissatisfaction. A representative survey is shown in Figure 12-5. Despite all these efforts to achieve total customer satisfaction, some customer dissatisfaction is inevitable. One reason is that mistakes in serving customers are almost inevitable; for example, a piece of equipment may have a faulty component unknown to the seller. A second reason is that some customers have a predisposition to complain. They will find something to complain about with respect to any product or service.

Dealing openly with dissatisfaction and complaints can improve both customer retention and sales. One study found that 63 percent of dissatisfied customers who do not complain will not buy from the company again. Given a chance to complain and have their problem resolved, 90 percent will remain loyal customers.[11]

Here we describe approaches to handling customer dissatisfaction from three aspects: dealing with complaints and anger, involving the customer in resolving a problem, and handling unreasonable requests.

Skill-Building Exercise 12-2

BONDING WITH CUSTOMERS

Role players in this exercise will demonstrate two related techniques for bonding with customers: Show care and concern and make the buyer feel good.

Scenario 1: Show Care and Concern. A sales representative meets with two company representatives to talk about installing a new information system for employee benefits. One of the company representatives is from the human resources department and the other from the telecommunications department. The sales representative will attempt to show care and concern for both company representatives during the same meeting.

Scenario 2: Make the Buyer Feel Good. A couple, played by two role players, enters a new-car showroom to examine a model they have seen advertised on television. Although they are not in urgent need of a new car, they are strongly interested. The sales representative is behind quota for the month and would like to close a sale today. The rep decides to use the tactic "make the buyer feel good" to help form a bond.

DEAL CONSTRUCTIVELY WITH CUSTOMER COMPLAINTS AND ANGER

In an era when customer satisfaction is so highly valued, both retail and industrial customers are likely to be vocal in their demands. When faced with an angry customer, use one or more of the following techniques recommended by customer satisfaction specialists.[12]

1. *Acknowledge the customer's point of view.* Make statements such as "I understand," "I agree," and "I'm sorry." Assume, for example, a customer says: "The accounts payable department made a $1,000 overcharge on my account last month. I want this fixed right away." You might respond, "I understand how annoying this must be for you. I'll work on the problem right away."

2. *Avoid placing blame.* Suggesting that the customer is responsible for the problem intensifies the conflict. With the customer who claims to have been overcharged, refrain from saying: "Customers who keep careful accounts of their orders never have this problem."

3. *Use six magic words to defuse anger.* The magic words are *I understand* [that this is a problem], *I agree* [that it needs to be solved], and *I'm sorry* [that this happened to you].

4. *Apologize for the problems created by you or your company.* To recover from a breakdown in customer service, it is best to acknowledge an error immediately. Apologies are most effective when stated in the first person (such as "I created the problem"). The corporate "we're sorry"

HOW ARE WE DOING?

DICK'S CLOTHING & SPORTING GOODS

NAME (OPTIONAL)

ADDRESS

PHONE NUMBER

CITY

DATE AND TIME OF VISIT

NAME OF ASSOCIATE WHO HELPED YOU

	EXCELLENT	GOOD	AVERAGE	NEEDS IMPROVEMENT	POOR
PROMPT AND COURTEOUS GREETING	☐	☐	☐	☐	☐
KNOWLEDGEABLE SALESPEOPLE	☐	☐	☐	☐	☐
STORE CLEANLINESS	☐	☐	☐	☐	☐
STORE DISPLAYS	☐	☐	☐	☐	☐
PRICES	☐	☐	☐	☐	☐
SPEEDY CHECKOUTS	☐	☐	☐	☐	☐
HOW DO YOU RATE US OVERALL?	☐	☐	☐	☐	☐

	NEWSPAPER	TV	RADIO	OTHER
WHAT BROUGHT YOU TO DICK'S?	☐	☐	☐	☐

DID YOU MAKE A PURCHASE? _____

ITEMS YOU WANTED THAT WE DID NOT HAVE? _____

GENERAL COMMENTS: _____

Figure 12-5 A Retail Store Customer Satisfaction Survey

Source: Dick's Clothing & Sporting Goods, Corporate Park Drive, P.O. Box 206, Conklin, NY 13748-9984.

sounds less sincere than when one specific person accepts responsibility for what went wrong.

5. *Follow up on the resolution of the problem.* Following up to see whether the resolution to the problem is satisfactory brings closure to the incident. The follow-up also helps the service deliverer know that he or she can rebound from an episode of customer dissatisfaction. One useful form

of follow-up is to telephone the customer whose problem was solved. For example, a representative from the service department of an automobile dealership might telephone a customer whose new car required substantial warranty repairs. "Hello, this is Jill Gordon from Oak Automotive. We replaced your original transmission last month. How is the new transmission working?"

A less personal, and usually less effective, form of follow-up is to send a customer satisfaction questionnaire to the person with the problem. The questionnaire will often be interpreted as a company procedure that does not reflect specific concern about the individual's problem.

INVOLVE THE CUSTOMER IN WORKING OUT THE PROBLEM

Mistakes and problems in serving customers are inevitable, however hard the customer contact worker strives for perfection. To minimize the perception of poor service, the customer should be involved in deciding what should be done about the problem. By being involved in the solution to the problem, the customer is more likely to accept a deviation from the service promised originally. The ideal condition is for the customer service representative and dissatisfied customer to work as partners in resolving the problem. The following case history illustrates the technique of customer involvement and partnering.

Seth Bradbury is a sales promotion specialist at an advertising agency. A furniture store hired the agency to prepare and mail 3,000 post cards advertising a new line of furniture. One side of the post card contained a photograph of the furniture, and the other side contained product details and space for addressing and stamping the card. After the cards were mailed, Seth received an urgent call from the client. "The photograph of the furniture is printed vertically. It looks horrible. We agreed on a horizontal shot. This means 3,000 cards have been mailed with a mistake."

After allowing the client to finish his complaint, Seth responded, "You're right, it is a vertical shot. Perhaps we misinterpreted your directions. However, I think your furniture still looks beautiful. The extra white space the vertical shot provides creates an interesting effect. "It's unfortunate that the cards have already been mailed. What would you like us to do? It's important that you are satisfied."

The client responded, "I guess there is nothing we can do to change the photograph. Would you be willing to give us a discount off the price we agreed on?"

Seth checked with his manager, and the agency agreed to a 15 percent discount on the job. The client accepted these terms and was doubly pleased because the mailer achieved his targeted response rate. Seth had impressed his client because he listened fully to the complaint and involved the client in achieving a workable compromise to settle the problem.

ANTICIPATE HOW TO HANDLE AN UNREASONABLE REQUEST

No matter how hard the customer contact worker attempts to provide outstanding customer service, at some point a customer comes along with an unreasonable request. Or the customer may raise an unfair objection. Speak to any experienced store associate to obtain a case history of a "customer from Hell." For example, a small-business owner demanded that a store associate grant him exchange credit for six printer ribbons. The ribbons were purchased four years previously and were now obsolete.

Recognize that the customer who makes an unreasonable demand is usually aware of the unreasonableness. The customer may not expect to be fully granted the request. Instead the customer is bargaining by beginning with an unreasonable demand. The small-business owner who brought in the printer ribbons was probably looking to salvage whatever he could.

Sales representatives and other customer contact workers who stand their ground with dignity and courtesy generally will not lose customers with unreasonable requests. The suggestions presented next will help you deal with unreasonable demands while retaining the customer's business.[13]

> ➤ Let your customers retain their dignity by stating your position politely and reasonably.

> ➤ Avoid arguing with an upset customer. As the adage says, "You never win an argument with a customer."

> ➤ Appeal to your customer's sense of fair play and integrity. Explain that your intention is to do what is right and fair.

> ➤ Be firm by repeating the facts of the situation, but keep your temper under control.

> ➤ Accept responsibility for your decision rather than blaming company policy or your manager. Making somebody else the villain may intensify the problem.

> ➤ Be willing to say no to a customer when it is justifiable. Saying yes to an outrageous demand opens the door for a series of outrageous demands.

Dealing diplomatically and effectively with difficult customers requires an awareness of the types of tactics described in the previous several pages. Practice on the firing line is indispensable. The type of experience provided by Skill-Building Exercise 12-3 is helpful.

CUSTOMER SERVICE TRAINING AT A LUXURY HOTEL CHAIN

The information and exercises already presented in this chapter have provided you with an appreciation of the nature of customer service training. (Such

Skill-Building Exercise 12-3

DEALING WITH DIFFICULT CUSTOMERS

The following scenarios require one person to play the role of the customer contact worker and another person to play the difficult customer. As usual, the role players project their feelings into the role play by imagining how they would behave in the situation.

Scenario 1: One person is a store associate in a high-fashion women's clothing store. A woman who bought a $1,000 gown the previous week brings the gown back today. She claims that she is returning the gown because it doesn't fit comfortably. The store associate strongly suspects the woman bought the gown originally with the intent of wearing it for a special occasion and then returning it.

Scenario 2: One person plays the role of a customer service representative in a consumer-electronics store. Another person plays the role of a customer who purchased a $3,500 giant-screen television receiver three months ago. He comes up to the service rep's counter ranting about the store's ineptitude. The customer claims that the TV has broken down three times.

After the first repair, the TV worked for two weeks and then broke down again. The second repair lasted two weeks, only for the TV to break down during a Super Bowl party at his house. The customer is red in the face and shouting loudly. The service rep wants to resolve the customer's problem and prevent him from bad-mouthing the store.

training should result in the development of customer satisfaction skills.) To help reinforce this information, we present portions of an interview with Leonardo Inghilleri, the senior vice president of human resources for the Ritz-Carlton Hotel Company.[14] The company attributes much of the success of its 35 hotels to rigorous customer service training. Observe also how the Ritz Carlton takes into account individual and cultural differences in achieving excellent customer service.

Why does Ritz-Carlton feel it's important that every one of its nearly 16,000 employees undergo rigorous customer service training?

Customers who come to our hotel pay a premium for perfection. We have the tremendous challenge to meet and exceed customer expectations. That's why we discuss customer service every single day of our lives. It starts with how we select our employees. We use scientific interviews to understand if an individual has the necessary behavioral traits to make him or her successful in our company. Only one of every 10 applicants is hired.

What sort of traits? And how do you "scientifically" determine if a prospective employee has these traits?

A person who works for us has to be hospitable, quality-oriented, attentive to details, and so on. We've identified the top performers by job (waiters,

chefs, housekeepers, etc.), and with the help of a psychological test we're able to determine the ideal profile for each specific job. If you want to be a successful housekeeper, for example, you have to have certain talents; and if you don't have these traits, you're not going to be hired. There also has to be the desire to use your talents, which a lot of people don't have. We interview each one of our employees in a scientific way to understand if that person possesses specific talents.

How are the 120 hours of customer service training actually divvied up?

It depends. Our entire training system is a combination of two key elements: technical skills and the Ritz-Carlton customer service philosophy.

By technical training I mean how to serve in a fine-dining restaurant or how to make a bed according to standards. There may be 19 steps to making a bed. Until you make those beds perfectly, you're not going to earn a certification.

Customer service training is a little more complicated. We train our people how to resolve guest challenges. After all, it's an imperfect business we're in, and a lot of things that can go wrong will go wrong. A television at a certain point might break down. You have to train your people to instantly pacify our guests.

What sort of financial and time commitments are we talking about here?

It's a huge investment on our side. Think about it: Every employee spends 15 minutes every day in a meeting. Some might see this as a 15-minute loss of productivity, but we believe these are the most valuable 15 minutes of the day. We use this time to recognize and celebrate people, and create a sense of belonging.

What exactly do your employees come away with after 120 or more hours of customer service training?

From the training, they become professionals in the hospitality industry. In this industry, you're either a professional or you're a servant. Making beds and cleaning toilets and serving meals are professions if they are done with pride. We create professional employees who have the desire to provide exceptional customer service, and who want to be part of our company.

Does the fact that you have 35 hotels all over the world cause any sort of cultural problems when hiring and training employees in a customer service industry?

We had to focus a lot on the cultural aspects. Every single culture has it own sense of hospitality. In Bali, we will not ask our ladies and gentlemen to say good morning and good afternoon. Instead, they'll greet in the traditional way by joining hands and bowing. We try to identify what makes that specific country special from a hospitality point of view. And then we adapt to its citizens' way of being hospitable.

The type of customer service training just described is a vehicle for achieving customer satisfaction. Customer service training in other industries, such as retailing or telecommunications, might have different content, but the principles are similar.

SUMMARY

Many companies today emphasize total customer satisfaction because it leads to goodwill, repeat business, and referrals. Customer satisfaction skills are required by all workers in contact with customers. Seven key principles for satisfying and delighting customers are as follows:

1. Satisfied employees provide better customer service. (Some of your own attitudes, such as optimism and flexibility, influence your job satisfaction.)

2. Understand customer needs and put them first.

3. Focus on solving problems, not just taking orders.

4. Respond positively to moments of truth (points at which the customer forms an impression of company service).

5. Be ready to accept empowerment. (Being empowered enables you to solve customer problems.)

6. Enhance customer service through information technology.

7. Avoid rudeness. (Rude treatment of customers creates lost business.)

Another key perspective on achieving customer satisfaction and delight is to create a bond—or emotional relationship—with customers. Almost any act of good customer service helps create a bond, but the following six principles are highlighted here:

1. Create a welcoming attitude.

2. Provide exceptional service.

3. Show care and concern.

4. Make the buyer feel good.

5. Build a personal relationship.

6. Invite the customer back.

Despite the best efforts on the company's part, some customer dissatisfaction is inevitable. One approach to dealing with customer dissatisfaction is to deal constructively with customer complaints and anger. Tactics for achieving this end include the following:

1. Acknowledge the customer's point of view.

2. Avoid placing blame.

3. Defuse anger.

4. Apologize for the problem created.

5. Follow up on the problem resolution.

Another approach to dealing with customer dissatisfaction is to involve the customer in working out the problem. The customer contact worker must sometimes deal with an unreasonable request. Remember that the customer probably recognizes that he or she is being unreasonable. Do not argue with an unreasonable customer, but at times you must say no.

Customer service training encompasses many of the ideas in this chapter. Providing a high level of customer service can be a competitive advantage for a company.

QUESTIONS FOR DISCUSSION AND REVIEW

1. Visualize Billy, whose job it is to prepare French fries at a McDonald's. Who are Billy's internal customers?

2. For what reason is a satisfied employee more likely to provide better customer service?

3. Describe a situation in your life when you experienced customer delight. What made the experience delightful?

4. Imagine any sales situation involving a major purchase. Describe how you might identify customer needs.

5. Describe several customer moments of truth you have experienced this week. What made you classify them as moments of truth?

6. Visualize yourself as an executive at Wal-Mart. Develop a policy to empower customer service desk associates to resolve customer problems, including the limits to their empowerment.

7. Identify several typical ways in which customers are rude to customer contact workers.

8. What do you think of the ethics of forming a bond with customers?

9. Can you identify any ways in which a customer contact worker has made you feel good? If so, please provide the details.

10. How effective is the principle "the customer is always right" when dealing with dissatisfied customers?

An Interpersonal Relations Case Problem

THE TROUBLESOME BIG SCREEN

The Chavez nuclear family consists of Maria, an office manager at a hospital; Tony, an ambulance medic; and their daughter Jennifer, an eighth-grade student. A happy family, they share many activities. Among their joint activities is watching MTV (music television). The family regularly scrunch down to watch their favorite music shows on a 10-year-old, 13-inch color television.

One Thursday evening, Jennifer sighed, "Mom and Dad, I have a great idea. Let's do something exciting with some of your money. Let's buy a giant TV so we can have more fun watching the rock channel."

Maria and Tony thought that Jennifer's idea had merit. However, they both agreed that a giant-screen TV was a luxury item they could ill afford right now. Just before they fell asleep, the issue surfaced again. Maria said to Tony, "Deep down, we both agree with Jennifer. For less than $1,000 we could bring much joy into our home."

Friday night the Chavez family visited Appliance City to look at television sets. Maria spotted a 29-inch TV that seemed ideal. A store associate, however, convinced them that the model they were inspecting was of mediocre quality. Instead, he recommended a domestic brand with a 32-inch screen that he claimed was the highest-quality model in its class. Spearheaded by Jennifer's exuberance, the Chavez family was convinced. The cost, including a three-year complete service warranty, was $1,157.

The television set was delivered Monday evening as scheduled. For several days the Chavez family enjoyed watching MTV and other favorite programs on their new big-screen set. Friday evening, however, Maria, Tony, and Jennifer were mystified by an image that appeared on their screen. Shortly after Jennifer punched the menu button, an advertisement appeared on the screen touting the features of the set. Among the messages was one indicating that if the owner of this set were in a noisy room, he or she could mute the audio and watch the video.

Tony laughed as he explained that the demonstration mode was somehow triggered, and that the solution would be to just punch a few buttons. Next, Maria and he punched every button on the receiver and the TV remote control. The demonstration mode remained. Tony then pulled the plug and reinserted it, only for the demonstration mode to reappear.

Maria, Tony, and Jennifer then searched the owner's manual, but they found no information about the problem. Maria telephoned the dealer and got through to the service department after six minutes of being placed on hold. The service department said they knew nothing about the problem, but that she should speak to the sales department. After Maria explained her problem to a sales associate, she was told to speak to the service department.

Maria called back the service department and explained the problem again. A customer service specialist said that the store relied on an outside TV-appliance-repair firm to handle such problems. She said she would call the repair firm on Monday and that the firm would contact the Chavez family. By Tuesday morning the Chavez family still had not heard from the repair firm.

In desperation, Tony scanned a customer information booklet that came with the TV receiver. He found a list of 10 authorized service centers throughout the United States and Canada that repaired his brand of television. Tony telephoned a service center in California. A cheerful woman answered the phone and listened to Tony's problem. With a sympathetic laugh, she said, "We get lots of calls like this. No problem. Just push the volume-up and volume-down buttons at the same time. The demo mode will disappear. The mode was activated when somebody pressed the menu up and down buttons at the same time." Tony raced into the living room, and triumphantly restored the TV set to normal functioning.

(Continued)

Friday, a representative from the local television repair shop called. She said, "This is Modern TV and Appliance. Do you still need service on your set?" With anger in her voice, Maria explained how the problem was finally resolved.

Later that night, as the family gathered to watch MTV, Maria said, "I guess we all love our new giant-screen TV, but I wouldn't go back to Appliance City to buy even an electric can opener."

Case Questions

1. What mistakes in customer satisfaction principles did Appliance City personnel make?

2. What mistakes in customer satisfaction principles did Modern TV and Appliance make?

3. What would you have done if you experienced a similar problem with an expensive TV receiver?

4. Should the manufacturer of the giant-screen TV set have any responsibility for the problem faced by the Chavez family?

Chapter 13

Enhancing Ethical Behavior

Learning Objectives

After reading and studying this chapter and doing the exercises you should be able to

➤ Recognize the importance of ethical behavior for establishing good interpersonal relationships in organizations.

➤ Identify several character traits associated with being an ethical person.

➤ Identify job situations that often present ethical dilemmas.

➤ Use a systematic method for making ethical decisions and behaving ethically.

"I like this sedan quite a lot," said Malcolm to the new-car sales representative. "We agree on the price, and I'm ready to buy today, with one exception. I would like a sunroof. How much extra would that cost?" Paula, the sales representative, said she would return shortly with the information.

After checking in the office, Paula said that the sunroof would cost $525. She told Malcolm, "We are adding the sunroof at cost as a service to you. Auto Works will install it. They do a great job."

Later that day Malcolm was speaking to a friend about his new purchase. His friend said, "You'll love a sunroof. My neighbor just had one installed at Auto Works. I remember it cost him $425." Puzzled by this price discrepancy, Malcolm telephoned Auto Works to inquire about the price of his sunroof. The company representative said, "We charged $425. I can show you the invoice."

Infuriated by the price markup, Malcolm went back to the dealer and confronted Paula. She explained that the dealership typically charges a handling fee when an outside shop installs an option. The fee is part of the cost. Enraged, Malcolm spoke to the manager of the dealership. The manager agreed to refund the handling fee. Malcolm was satisfied with the refund but felt mistreated by Paula and the dealership.

The situation at the auto dealership illustrates ethical issues in the workplace. By being deceptive about the cost of the sunroof, Paula added to the deal a little profit for the firm and a small commission for herself. Some would say Paula was using a clever business tactic, while others might question her ethics. **Ethics** refers to what is good and bad, right and wrong, just and unjust, and what people should do.

We study ethics here because a person's ethical code has a significant impact on his or her interpersonal relationships. Our approach will emphasize the importance of ethics, common ethical problems, and guidelines for behaving ethically. Self-Assessment Quiz 13-1 gives you the opportunity to examine your ethical beliefs and attitudes.

WHY BE CONCERNED ABOUT BUSINESS ETHICS?

When asked why ethics is important, most people would respond something to the effect that, "ethics is important because it's the right thing to do. You behave decently in the workplace because your family and religious values have taught you what is right and wrong." All true so far, but the justification for behaving ethically is more complex, as described next.[1]

A major justification for behaving ethically on the job is to recognize that people are motivated by both self-interest and moral commitments. Most people want to maximize gain for themselves (remember the expectancy theory of motivation?). At the same time, most people are motivated to do something morally right. As one of many examples, vast numbers of people donate money to charity, although keeping that amount of money for themselves would provide more personal gain.

THE ETHICAL REASONING INVENTORY

Directions: Describe how well you agree with each of the following statements. Use the following scale: Disagree strongly (DS); Disagree (D); Neutral (N); Agree (A); Agree strongly (AS).

	DS	D	N	A	AS
1. When applying for a job, I would cover up the fact that I had been fired from my most recent job.	5	(4)	3	2	1
2. Cheating just a few dollars in one's favor on an expense account is OK if a person needs the money.	(5)	4	3	2	1
3. Employees should inform on each other for wrongdoing.	1	(2)	3	4	5
4. It is acceptable to give approximate figures for expense account items when one does not have all the receipts.	5	4	3	(2)	1
5. I see no problem with conducting a little personal business on company time.	5	(4)	3	2	1
6. Just to make a sale, I would stretch the truth about a delivery date.	5	(4)	3	2	1
7. I would fix up a purchasing agent with a date just to close a sale.	5	(4)	3	2	1
8. I would flirt with my boss just to get a bigger salary increase.	5	(4)	3	2	1
9. If I received $200 for doing some odd jobs, I would report it on my income tax return.	1	2	3	4	(5)
10. I see no harm in taking home a few office supplies.	5	4	3	2	(1)
11. It is acceptable to read the e-mail messages and faxes of other workers, even when not invited to do so.	(5)	4	3	2	1
12. It is unacceptable to call in sick in order to take a day off, even if only done once or twice a year.	1	2	3	4	(5)
13. I would accept a permanent, full-time job even if I knew I wanted the job for only six months.	5	4	3	(2)	1
14. I would first check company policy before accepting an expensive gift from a supplier.	1	2	3	4	(5)
15. To be successful in business, a person usually has to ignore ethics.	5	(4)	3	2	1
16. If I felt physically attracted toward a job candidate I would hire that person over a more qualified candidate.	5	(4)	3	2	1
17. On the job, I tell the truth all the time.	1	2	3	4	(5)
18. If a student were very pressed for time, it would be acceptable to either have a friend write the paper or purchase one.	(5)	4	3	2	1
19. I would authorize accepting an office machine on a 30-day trial period, even if I knew we had no intention of buying it.	5	4	(3)	2	1
20. I would never accept credit for a coworker's ideas.	1	2	3	4	(5)

(Continued)

Scoring and Interpretation: Add the numbers you have circled to obtain your total score.

90–100 You are a strongly ethical person who may take a little ribbing from coworkers for being too strait-laced.

60–89 You show an average degree of ethical awareness, and therefore should become more sensitive to ethical issues.

41–59 Your ethics are underdeveloped, but you at least have some awareness of ethical issues. You need to raise your level of awareness of ethical issues.

20–40 Your ethical values are far below contemporary standards in business. Begin a serious study of business ethics.

Many business executives want employees to behave ethically because a good reputation can enhance business. A favorable corporate reputation may enable firms to charge premium prices and attract better job applicants. A favorable reputation also helps attract investors, such as mutual fund managers who purchase stock in companies. Certain mutual funds, for example, invest only in companies that are environmentally friendly. Managers want employees to behave ethically because unethical behavior is costly—for example, employee theft, lost production time, lawsuits.

Behaving ethically is also important because many unethical acts are also illegal, which can lead to financial loss and imprisonment. A company that knowingly allows workers to engage in unsafe practices might be fined and the executives held personally liable. Furthermore, unsafe practices can kill people. In recent history, two employees burned to death in a fire they could not escape in a chicken processing plant. Management had blocked the back doors to prevent employees from sneaking chicken parts out of the plant.

A subtle reason for behaving ethically is that high ethics increases the quality of work life. Ethics provides a set of guidelines that specify what makes for acceptable behavior. Being ethical will point you toward actions that make life more satisfying for work associates. A company code of ethics specifies what constitutes ethical versus unethical behavior. When employees follow this code, the quality of work life improves. Several sample clauses from ethical codes are as follows:

➤ Demonstrate courtesy, respect, honesty, and fairness.

➤ Do not use abusive language.

➤ Do not bring firearms or knives to work.

➤ Do not offer bribes.

➤ Maintain confidentiality of records.

➤ Do not harass (sexually, racially, ethnically, or physically) subordinates, superiors, coworkers, customers, or suppliers.

To the extent that all members of the organization abide by this ethical code, the quality of work life will improve. At the same time, interpersonal relations in organizations will be strengthened.

COMMON ETHICAL PROBLEMS

To become more skilled at behaving ethically, it is important to familiarize yourself with common ethical problems in organizations. Whether or not a given situation presents an ethical problem for a person depends to some extent on its **moral intensity**, or how deeply others might be affected.[2] A worker might face a strong ethical conflict about dumping mercury into a water supply but would be less concerned about dumping cleaning fluid. Yet both acts would be considered unethical and illegal. Here we look at some data about the frequency of ethical problems and an analysis of predictable ethical temptations. We also examine the subtle ethical dilemma of choosing between rights.

A SURVEY OF THE EXTENT OF ETHICAL PROBLEMS

A substantial number of managers and employees engage in unethical behavior, often because they feel pressured into making a quick profit. Feeling under pressure, in general, or not taking the time to think through the ethics of an issue, can lead to unethical behavior in order to save time. A study of 1,324 workers conducted by the American Society of Chartered Life Underwriters & Chartered Financial Consultants and the Ethics Officer Association provides some illuminating facts. Highlights of the study are that:[3]

➤ 60 percent of workers feel a substantial amount of pressure on the job.

➤ 56 percent of workers feel some pressure to act unethically or illegally on the job.

➤ 48 percent of workers admitted they had engaged in one or more unethical and/or illegal actions during the last year, such as: cutting corners on quality; abusing or lying about sick days; lying to or deceiving customers; lying to or deceiving a manager about a serious matter; and taking credit for a coworker's ideas.

➤ 52 percent of workers feel more pressure from balancing work and family.

➤ 60 percent of workers believe that ethics and business practices can indeed mix.

The 60 percent of respondents just mentioned believed that ethical dilemmas could be reduced if more communication about ethical problems took place. Also, top-level managers must show a stronger commitment to ethical behavior.

FREQUENT ETHICAL DILEMMAS

According to Linda K. Treviño and Katherine A. Nelson, mishandling an ethical issue can severely damage your career. Although this observation may be disturbing, there is also comforting news. Many ethical dilemmas in business are predictable. Here we list a number of common ethical problems faced by business executives as well as workers at lower job levels.[4]

The Temptation to Illegally Copy Software

A rampant ethical problem is whether or not to illegally copy software. Figure 13-1 offers details about and insight into this widespread ethical dilemma.

Treating People Unfairly

Being fair to people means equity, reciprocity, and impartiality. Fairness revolves around the issue of giving people equal rewards for accomplishing equal amounts of work. The goal of human resource legislation is to make decisions about people based on their qualifications and performance—not on the basis of demographic factors such as sex, race, or age. A fair working environment is where performance is the only factor that counts (*equity*). Employer–employee expectations must be understood and met (*reciprocity*). Prejudice and bias must be eliminated (*impartiality*).

To treat people fairly—and therefore ethically—an overemphasis on political factors would be unethical. Yet this ethical doctrine is not always easy to implement. It is human nature to want to give bigger rewards (such as fatter raises or bigger orders) to people we like.

Job Discrimination

A major aspect of unfairness is **job discrimination**, or an unfavorable action brought against a person because of a characteristic unrelated to job performance. Discriminating against others is illegal as well as unethical. Many federal, state, and local laws prohibit discrimination in all phases of employment. A case in point is the Americans with Disabilities Act (ADA) of 1991. The act is designed to protect people with disabilities from discrimination in employment, public accommodations, transportation, and telecommunications. The ADA defines **disability** as a physical or mental condition that substantially limits an individual's major life activities. In recent years many workers have made unethical interpretations of the ADA to protect themselves from job loss. An example is an employee who physically attacked another employee and was therefore dismissed. He claimed he was suffering from job stress and should not have been fired because job stress is a disability! At first he won his case, but a higher court overruled.

The obvious situations in which to guard against discrimination are in hiring and promoting people. It is also important to guard against discrimination when choosing coworkers as team members and luncheon companions. A highly ethical person reaches out to diverse people, including young and old, able-bodied and disabled, white and people of color.

A flagrant unethical *and illegal* job behavior is unauthorized copying of software. When confronted with software pirating, people are quick to rationalize their actions. Here are the top ten defenses of software pirates. (None of them are likely to hold up if you are caught.)

1. *I'm allowed to make a backup disk in case something happens to the original, so it must be okay to use it on another machine.* A backup is strictly a backup to be used on the same computer. The original should be safely locked away, and the copy should be stored away only.

2. *I didn't copy it—a friend gave it to me.* Technically you are right. You would not be guilty of illegally copying software in this case, although your friend would. However, since illegally copied software is regarded as stolen property, you are just as guilty as you would be for stealing it in the first place.

3. *My boss (or department head, or instructor) told me to. It's that person's problem.* The defense "I was just following orders" is a weak one. Complying with your boss's demands to commit an illegal act does not get you off the hook. You could be fired for obeying an order to commit a crime.

4. *I bought the software; shouldn't I be able to do what I want with it?* Software is seldom ever sold to individuals. What is sold is a license to use the software, not full rights to do what you want. When you break open the package, the law assumes that you have agreed to abide by those terms.

5. *It's not like I'm robbing somebody.* Software is intellectual property just like a song, a book, an article, or a trademark. You are taking bread from the table of software engineers when you copy their work.

6. *It's OK if you're using the software for educational purposes.* If education were a justification for theft, driving instructors would be able to steal cars with impunity. There is a doctrine of *fair use* that allows some limited use of written materials in classrooms without permission from the copyright holder.

7. *I needed it, but the price was unreasonably high. If I had to actually pay for it, there is no way I could ever afford it.* Software prices are high for the same reason the price of houses is high: both require a lot of highly skilled labor to create. You cannot steal a VCR just because you cannot afford one.

8. *I didn't know it was illegal.* Unauthorized duplication of software is a felony in many states and provinces. State and federal laws provide for civil and criminal penalties if you are convicted. It would be difficult to convince a judge or jury that you had no idea that unauthorized copying was illegal.

9. *It's only illegal if you get caught.* Criminal behavior is illegal whether or not you are caught. If you do get caught illegally copying software, you could face fines, imprisonment, and/or civil penalties. Some educational institutions take disciplinary action against software pirates, including suspension.

10. *Oh, come on, everyone is doing it.* This excuse has been used to justify everything from speeding to lynching. The popularity of a criminal act does not make it legal.

Figure 13-1　The Top Ten Reasons for Illegally Copying Software (and Why None of Them Are Good Enough)

Source: Adapted with permission from Vince Incardona, "The Top Ten Reasons for Illegally Copying Software (and Why None of Them Are Good Enough)," *ITS News* (Rochester Institute of Technology), October 1998, p. 3.

Sexual Harassment

In Chapter 7 we looked at sexual harassment as a source of conflict and an illegal act. Sexual harassment is also an ethical issue, because it is morally wrong and unfair. All acts of sexual harassment flunk an ethics test. Before sexually harassing another person, the potential harasser should ask, "Would I want a loved one to be treated this way?"

Conflict of Interest

Part of being ethical is making business judgments only on the basis of the merits or facts in a situation. Imagine that you are a supervisor who is romantically involved with a worker within the group. When it comes time to assign raises, it will be difficult for you to be objective. A **conflict of interest** occurs when your judgment or objectivity is compromised. Conflicts of interest often take place in the sales end of business. If a company representative accepts a large gift from a sales representative, it may be difficult to make objective judgments about buying from the representative. Yet being taken to dinner by a vendor would not ordinarily cloud one's judgment. Another common example of a conflict of interest is making a hiring decision about a friend who badly needs a job, but is not well qualified for the position.

Dealing with Confidential Information

An ethical person can be trusted by others not to divulge confidential information unless the welfare of others is at stake. Suppose a coworker tells you in confidence that she is upset with the company and is therefore looking for another job. Behaving ethically, you do not pass this information along to your supervisor even though it would help your supervisor plan for a replacement. Now suppose the scenario changes slightly. Your coworker tells you she is looking for another job because she is upset. She tells you she is so upset that she plans to destroy company computer files on her last day. If your friend does find another job, you might warn the company about her contemplated activities.

The challenge of dealing with confidential information arises in many areas of business, many of which affect interpersonal relations. If you learned that a coworker was indicted for a crime, charged with sexual harassment, or facing bankruptcy, there would be a temptation to gossip about the person. A highly ethical person would not pass along information about the personal difficulties of another person.

Use of Corporate Resources

A corporate resource is anything the company owns, including its name and reputation. If Jake Petro worked for Ford Motor Company, for example, it would be unethical for him to establish a body shop and put on his letterhead "Jake Petro, Manufacturing Technician, Ford Motor Company." Other uses of corporate resources fall more into the gray area. It might be quite ethical to borrow a laptop computer for the weekend from your employer to conduct work at home. But it would be less ethical to borrow the laptop computer to prepare income taxes. In the latter case you might be accused of using corporate resources for personal purposes.

1. Do not use a computer to harm other people. (This includes not taking precautions against others' developing repetitive motion disorders.)
2. Do not interfere with other people's computer work. (This includes intentionally spreading computer viruses.)
3. Do not snoop around in other people's files.
4. Do not use a computer to steal.
5. Do not use a computer to bear false witness.
6. Do not use or copy software for which you have not paid (see Figure 13-1).
7. Do not use other people's resources without authorization.
8. Do not appropriate other people's intellectual output.
9. Do think about the social consequences of the program you write.
10. Do use a computer in ways that show consideration and respect.

Figure 13-2 The Ten Commandants for Computer Ethics

Source: Adapted and updated from Arlene H. Rinaldi and Florida Atlantic University, rinaldi @acc.fau.edu.

Possible Ethical Violations with Computers and Information Technology

As computers dominate the workplace, many ethical issues have arisen in addition to pirating software. One ethical dilemma that surfaces frequently is the fairness of tracking the Web sites a person visits and those he or she buys from. Should this information be sold, like a mailing list? Another issue is the fairness of having an employee work at a keyboard for 60 hours in one week when such behavior frequently leads to repetitive motion disorder. Figure 13-2 lists some major ethical issues involved in computer use.

You may have observed that these common ethical problems are not always clear cut. Aside from obvious matters such as prohibitions against stealing, lying, cheating, and intimidating, subjectivity enters into ethical decision making. Skill-Building Exercise 13-1 provides an opportunity to try out your ethical reasoning.

CHOOSING BETWEEN TWO RIGHTS: DEALING WITH DEFINING MOMENTS

Ethical decision making usually involves choosing between two options: one we perceive to be right and one we perceive to be wrong. A challenging twist to ethical decision making is to sort through your values when you have to choose between two *rights*, or two morally sound choices. Joseph L. Badaracco, Jr., uses the term **defining moment** to describe choosing between two or more ideals in which we deeply believe.[6] If you can learn to work through defining moments, your ethical skills will be enhanced. Let's first take a nonwork example to illustrate a defining moment.

Imagine yourself as a basketball referee in a league for boys 10 years old and younger. Luis, the smallest boy on the team has a self-confidence problem in general, and he has not scored a goal yet this season. This is the final game of the season. The other team is ahead by 10 points with one

Skill-Building Exercise 13-1

THE ETHICS GAME

Citicorp (now part of Citigroup) has developed an ethics game, *The Work Ethic*.[5] The game teaches ethics by asking small teams of employees to confront difficult scenarios such as those that follow. Discuss these ethical problems in teams. As you discuss the scenarios, identify the ethical issues involved.

Scenario 1: One of your assignments is to find a contractor to conduct building maintenance for your company headquarters. You invite bids for the job. High-Performance Cleaners, a firm staffed largely by teenagers from troubled families who have criminal records, bids on the job. Many of these teenagers also have severe learning disabilities and cannot readily find employment. High-Performance Cleaners proves to be the second-highest bidder. You:

a. Advise High-Performance Cleaners that its bid is too high for consideration and that your company is not a social agency.

b. Award the bid to High-Performance Cleaners and justify your actions with a letter to top management talking about social responsibility.

c. Falsify the other bids in your report to management, making High-Performance Cleaners the low bidder—and thus the contract winner.

d. Explain to High-Performance Cleaners that it lost the bid, but you will award the company a piece of the contract because of its sterling work with needy teenagers.

Scenario 2: You live in Texas and your company sends you on a three-day trip to New York City. Your business dealings in the Big Apple will keep you there Wednesday, Thursday, and Friday morning. You have several friends and relatives in New York, so you decide to stay there until Sunday afternoon. Besides, you want to engage in tourist activities such as taking a boat tour around Manhattan and visiting Radio City Music Hall. When preparing your expense report for your trip, you request payment for all your business-related costs up through Friday afternoon, *plus*

a. Your return trip on Sunday.

b. The return trip and the room cost for Friday and Saturday nights.

c. The return trip and one-half of your weekend food expenses and two extra nights in the hotel.

d. The return trip and your food costs for the weekend (which you justify because you ate at fast-food restaurants on Wednesday, Thursday, and Friday).

Scenario 3: You are the leader of a self-managing work team in a financial services company. The work of your team has expanded to the point where you are authorized to hire another team member. The team busily interviews a number of candidates from inside and outside the company. The other team members agree that one of the candidates (Pat) has truly outstanding credentials. You agree that Pat is a strong candidate. Yet you don't want Pat on the team because you and Pat were emotionally involved with each other for about one year in the past. You think that working with Pat would disrupt your concentration and bring back hurtful memories. You decide to

(Continued)

a. Tell the group that you have some negative information about Pat's past that would disqualify Pat for the job.

b. Telephone Pat and beg that Pat find employment elsewhere.

15 c. Tell the group that you agree Pat is qualified, but explain your concerns about the disruption in concentration and emotional hurt.

d. Tell the group that you agree Pat is right for the position, and mention nothing about the past relationship.

Scoring and Observation:

Scenario 1, about High-Performance Cleaners, raises dozens of ethical questions, including whether humanitarian considerations can outweigh profit concerns. Teams that chose *a* receive 0 points; *b*, 20 points; *c*, –10 points; *d*, 10 points.

Scenario 2 raises ethical issues about using company resources. Teams that chose *a* receive 20 points; *b*, –10 points; *c*, –15 points; *d*, 0 points.

Scenario 3 raises issues about fairness in making selection decisions. Teams that choose *a* receive –20 points; *b*, –10 points; *c*, 15 points; *d*, 0 points.

minute to go. Luis lets fly with a shot that goes into the basket, but his right heel is on the line. If the goal is allowed, Luis will experience one of the happiest moments in his life, and his self-confidence might increase. You strongly believe in helping people grow and develop. Yet you also strongly believe in following the rules of sports. What to do?

You may have recognized that a defining moment is a role conflict in which you have to choose between competing values. A CEO might deeply believe that she has an obligation to the stockholders to make a profit, and also believe in being generous and fair toward employees. However, to make a profit this year she will be forced to lay off several good employees with long seniority. The CEO now faces a moment of truth. Badaracco suggests that the individual can work through a defining moment by discovering "Who am I?" You discover who you are by soul searching answers to three questions:

1. What feelings and intuitions are coming into conflict in this situation?

2. Which of the values that are in conflict are the most deeply rooted in my life?

3. What combinations of expediency and shrewdness, coupled with imagination and boldness, will help me implement my personal understanding of what is right?

Skill-Buildling Exercise 13-2 gives you an opportunity to deal with defining moments. The three questions just asked could help you find answers, but do not be constrained by these questions.

Skill-Building Exercise 13-2

DEALING WITH DEFINING MOMENTS

The toughest ethical choices for many people occur when they have to choose between two *rights*. The result is a defining moment, because we are challenged to think in a deeper way by choosing between two or more ideals. Working individually or in teams, deal with the two following defining moments. Explain why these scenarios could require choosing between two rights, and explain the reasoning behind your decisions.

Scenario 1: You are the manager of a department in a business firm that assigns each department a fixed amount of money for salary increases each year. An average-performing member of the department asks you in advance for an above-average increase. He explains that his mother has developed multiple sclerosis and requires the services of a paid helper from time to time. You are concerned that if you give this man an above-average increase, somebody else in the department will have to receive a below-average increase.

Scenario 2: You are the team leader of an e-tailing (retail selling over the Internet) group. In recent months each team member has been working about 60 hours per week, with little prospect of the workload decreasing in the future. Since the e-tailing project is still losing money, higher management insists that one person be dropped from the team. One member of the team, Mildred, is willing to work only about 45 hours per week because she spends considerable time volunteering her time to work with autistic children. Mildred's work is satisfactory, but her output is the lowest in the group because of her shorter number of working hours. You must make a decision about whether to recommend that Mildred be dismissed.

GUIDELINES FOR BEHAVING ETHICALLY

Following guidelines for ethical behavior is the heart of being ethical. Although many people behave ethically without studying ethical guidelines, they are usually following guidelines programmed into their minds early in life. The Golden Rule exemplifies a guideline taught by parents, grandparents, and kindergarten teachers. In this section we approach ethical guidelines from four perspectives: (1) developing the right character traits, (2) using corporate programs for ethics, (3) following a guide for ethical decision making, and (4) developing close relationships with work associates.

DEVELOPING THE RIGHT CHARACTER TRAITS

Character traits develop early in life, yet with determination and self-discipline many people can modify old traits or develop new ones. A **character trait** is an enduring characteristic of a person that is related to moral and ethical behavior that shows up consistently. For example, if a person has the character trait

of untruthfulness, he or she will lie in many situations. Conversely, the character trait of honesty leads to behaving honestly in most situations.

The Character Counts Coalition is an organization formed to encourage young people to develop fairness, respect, trustworthiness, responsibility, caring, and good citizenship. The Coalition has developed a list of 10 key guidelines as a foundation for character development.[7] If you develop, or already have, these traits, it will be easy for you to behave ethically in business. As you read the following list, evaluate your own standing on each character trait. Remember, however, that extra effort is required to evaluate one's character traits, because most people have an inflated view of their honesty and integrity.

1. *Be honest.* Tell the truth; be sincere; do not mislead or withhold information in relationships of trust; do not steal.

2. *Demonstrate integrity.* Stand up for your beliefs about right and wrong; be your best self; resist social pressure to do wrong.

3. *Keep promises.* Keep your word and honor your commitments; pay your debts and return what you borrow.

4. *Be loyal.* Stand by family, friends, employers, community, and country; do not talk about people behind their backs.

5. *Be responsible.* Think before you act; consider consequences; be accountable and "take your medicine."

6. *Pursue excellence.* Do your best with what you have; do not give up easily.

7. *Be kind and caring.* Show you care through generosity and compassion; do not be selfish or mean.

8. *Treat all people with respect.* Be courteous and polite; judge all people on their merits; be tolerant, appreciative, and accepting of individual differences.

9. *Be fair.* Treat all people fairly; be open-minded; listen to others and try to understand what they are saying and feeling.

10. *Be a good citizen.* Obey the law and respect authority; vote; volunteer your efforts; protect the environment.

If you score high on all of the preceding character traits and behaviors, you are an outstanding member of your company, community, and school. Your ethical behavior is superior.

USING CORPORATE ETHICS PROGRAMS

Many organizations have various programs and procedures for promoting ethical behavior. Among them are committees that monitor ethical behavior, training programs in ethics, and vehicles for reporting ethical violations. The

presence of these programs is designed to create an atmosphere in which unethical behavior is discouraged and reporting on unethical behavior is encouraged.

Ethics hot lines are one of the best-established programs to help individuals avoid unethical behavior. Should a person be faced with an ethical dilemma, the person calls a toll-free line to speak to a counselor about the dilemma. Sometimes employees ask questions to help interpret a policy, such as "Is it okay to ask my boss for a date?" or "Are we supposed to give senior citizen discounts to customers who qualify but do not ask for one?" At other times, a more pressing ethical issue might be addressed, such as "Is it ethical to lay off a worker just five months short of his qualifying for a full pension?"

Sears, Roebuck and Co., has an ethics hot line the company refers to as an "Assist Line" because very few of the 15,000 calls it receives per year represent crises. Often the ethics specialists who handle the calls just listen; at other times they intervene to help resolve the problem. The Ethics Assist Line is designed to help with these kinds of calls: guidance about company policy; company Code of Conduct issues; workplace harassment/discrimination; selling practices; theft; and human resource issues. At times an ethical problem of such high moral intensity is presented that employee confidentiality cannot be maintained. However, the Ethics Office handles the inquiries in as confidential a manner as practical and assigns them case identification numbers for follow up.[8]

Despite the help of the Ethics Office, Sears has faced well-publicized ethical problems in its auto service centers, such as being accused of charging customers for tire balancing that was not performed. Quite often the individual must resist pressures from managers to carry out acts of questionable ethics.

FOLLOWING A GUIDE TO ETHICAL DECISION MAKING

A powerful strategy for behaving ethically is to follow a guide for ethical decision making. Such a guide for making contemplated decisions includes testing their ethics. **Ethical screening** refers to running a contemplated decision or action through an ethics test. Such screening makes the most sense when the contemplated action or decision is not clearly ethical or unethical. If a sales representative were to take a favorite customer to McDonald's for lunch, an ethical screen would not be necessary. Nobody would interpret a Big Mac to be a serious bribe. Assume, instead, that the sales rep offered to give the customer an under-the-table gift of $400 for placing a large offer with the rep's firm. The sales representative's behavior would be so blatantly unethical that conducting an ethical screen would be unnecessary.

Several useful ethical screens, or guides to ethical decision making, have been developed. A guide developed by Treviño and Nelson is presented here because it is current and incorporates the basic ideas in other ethical tests.[9] After studying this guide, you will be asked to ethically screen two different scenarios. The eight steps to sound ethical decision making follow.

1. *Gather the facts.* When making an important decision in business it is necessary to gather relevant facts. Ask yourself the following questions: "Are there any legal issues involved here?" "Is there precedent in our firm with respect to this type of decision?" "Do I have the authority to make this decision?" "Are there company rules and regulations governing such a decisions?"

The manager of a child-care center needed to hire an additional child-care specialist. One of the applicants was a 55-year-old male with experience as a father and grandfather. The manager judged him to be qualified, yet she knew that many parents would not want their preschool children to be cared for by a middle-aged male. Many people perceive that a younger woman is better qualified for child care than an older man. The manager therefore had to gather considerable facts about the situation, including facts about job discrimination and precedents in hiring males as child-care specialists.

2. *Define the ethical issues.* The ethical issues in a given decision are often more complicated than a first glance suggests. When faced with a complex decision, it may be helpful to talk over the ethical issues with another person. The ethical issues might involve character traits such as being kind and caring and treating others with respect. Or the ethical issues might relate to some of the common ethical problems described earlier in the chapter. Among them are conflict of interest, dealing with confidential information, and use of corporate resources.

The manager of the child-care center is facing such ethical issues as fairness, job discrimination, and meeting the demands of customers at the expense of job applicants. The manager is also facing a diversity issue: Should the workforce in a child-care center be culturally diverse, or do we hire only young women?

3. *Identify the affected parties.* When faced with a complex ethical decision it is important to identify all the affected parties. Major corporate decisions can affect thousands of people. If a company decides to shut down a plant and move the manufacturing to a low-wage country, thousands of individuals and many different parties are affected. Workers lose their jobs, suppliers lose their customers, the local governments loses out on tax revenues, and local merchants lose many of their customers. You may need to brainstorm with a few others to think of all the parties affected by a given decision.

The parties affected by the decision about hiring or not hiring the 55-year-old male include the applicant himself, the children, the parents, and the board of directors of the child-care center. The government might also be involved if the man were rejected and filed charges of age and sex discrimination.

4. *Identify the consequences.* After you have identified the parties affected by a decision, the next step is to predict the consequences for each party. It may not be necessary to identify every consequence, yet it is impor-

tant to identify the consequences with the highest probability of occurring and those with the most negative outcomes. The problem is that many people can be harmed by an unethical decision, such as not fully describing the possible side effects of a diet program.

Both short-term and long-term consequences should be specified. The company's closing a plant might create considerable short-term turmoil, but in the long term the company might be healthier. People participating in a diet program might achieve their short-term objective of losing weight. Yet in the long term, their health might be adversely affected because the diet is not nutritionally balanced.

The *symbolic* consequences of an action are important. Every action and decision sends a message (the decision is a symbol of something). If a company moves manufacturing out of a community to save on labor costs, it means that the short-term welfare of domestic employees is less important than profit.

Let's return to the day-care manager and the job applicant. If the applicant does not get the job, his welfare will be adversely affected. He has been laid off by a large employer and cannot find work in his regular field. His family will also suffer because he will not be able to make a financial contribution to the family. Yet if the man is hired, the day-care center may suffer. Many traditionally minded parents will say, "Absolutely not. I do not want my child cared for by a middle-aged man. He could be a child molester." (It may be unethical for people to have vicious stereotypes, yet they still exist.) If the child-care center does hire the man, the act will symbolize the fact that the owners of the center value diversity.

5. *Identify the obligations.* Identify the obligations and the reasons for each obligation when making a complex decision. The manufacturer of automotive brakes has an obligation to produce and sell only brakes that meet high safety standards. The obligation is to the auto manufacturer who purchases the brakes and, more important, to the ultimate consumer whose safety depends on effective brakes. The reason for the obligation to make safe brakes is that lives are at stake.

The child-care owner has an obligation to provide for the safety and health of the children at the center. She must also provide for the peace of mind of the parents and be a good citizen of the community in which the center is located. The decision about hiring the candidate in question must be balanced against all these obligations.

6. *Consider your character and integrity.* A core consideration when faced with an ethical dilemma is to consider how relevant people would judge your character and integrity. What would your family, friends, significant others, teachers, and coworkers think of your actions? To refine this thinking even further, how would you feel if your actions were publicly disclosed in the local newspaper or over e-mail? Would you want the world to know that you gave an under-the-table kickback or that you sexually harassed a frightened teenager working for you? If you would be proud for others to

know what decision you made when you faced an ethical dilemma, you are probably making the right decision.

The child-care center manager might ponder how she would feel if the following information were released in the local newspaper:

> The manager of Good Times Child Care recently rejected the application of a 55-year-old man for a child-care specialist position. She said that although Mr. _____ was well qualified from an experience and personality standpoint, she couldn't hire him. She said that Good Times would lose too much business because many parents would fear that Mr. _____ was a child molester.

7. *Think creatively about potential actions.* When faced with an ethical dilemma, put yourself in a creative-thinking mode. Stretch your imagination to invent several options rather than thinking you have only two choices—to do or not to do something. Creative thinking may point toward a third, and even fourth, alternative. Imagine this ethical dilemma: A purchasing agent is told that if her firm awards a contract to the sales representative's firm, she will find a leather jacket of her choice delivered to her door. The purchasing agent says to herself, "I think we should award the contract to the firm, but I cannot accept the gift. Yet if I turn down the gift, I will be forfeiting a valuable possession that the company simply regards as a cost of doing business."

The purchasing agent can search for another alternative. She can say to the sales rep, "We will give the contract to your firm because your product fits our requirements. I thank you for the offer of the leather jacket. But instead, I would like you to give that jacket to the Salvation Army instead of to me."

A creative alternative for the child-care manager might be to offer the applicant the next position that opened for an office manager or maintenance person in the center. In this way she would be offering a qualified applicant a job, but placing him in a position more acceptable to parents. Or do you feel this is a cop-out?

8. *Check your intuition.* So far we have emphasized the rational side of ethical decision making. Another effective way of conducting an ethical screen is to rely on your intuition. How does the contemplated decision feel? Would you be proud of yourself or would you hate yourself if you made the decision? Imagine how you would feel if you took money from the handbag of a woman sleeping in the park. Would you feel the same way if you went ahead and took a kickback, sold somebody a defective product, or sold an 80-year-old man an insurance policy he didn't need? How will the manager of the child-care center feel if she turns down the man for the child-care specialist position?

You are encouraged to use the guide for ethical decision making when you next face an ethical dilemma of consequence. Skill-Building Exercise 13-3 gives you an opportunity to practice using the eight steps for ethical decision making.

Skill-Building Exercise 13-3

ETHICAL DECISION MAKING

Working in small groups, take one or more of the following ethical dilemmas through the eight steps for screening contemplated decisions. If more than one group chooses the same scenario, compare your answers for the various steps.

Scenario 1: To Recycle or Not. Your group is the top management team at a large insurance company. Despite the movement toward computerization, your firm still generates tons of paper each month. Customer payments alone account for truckloads of envelopes each year. The paper recyclers in your area claim they can hardly find a market any longer for used paper, so they will be charging you just to accept your paper for recycling. Your group is wondering whether to recycle.

Scenario 2: The Job Applicants with a Past. A state (or provincial) government official approaches your bank asking you to hire three people who are soon to be released from prison. All were found guilty of fraudulently altering computer records in a bank for personal gain. The official says the men have paid their debt to society, and they need jobs. Your company has three openings for computer specialists; all three men obviously have good computer skills. Your group is wondering whether to hire these people.

Scenario 3: The High-Profit Toys. You are a toy company executive starting to plan your holiday season line. You anticipate that the season's hottest item will be Robo-Woman, a battery-operated crime fighter and superheroine. Robo-Woman should wholesale for $18.50 and retail for $38.00. Your company figures to earn $10 per unit. You receive a sales call from a manufacturing broker who says he can produce any toy you want for one-third of your present manufacturing cost. He admits that the manufacturer he represents uses prison labor in China, but insists that his business arrangement violates no law. You estimate you can earn $14 per unit if you do business with the manufacturing broker. Your decision is whether to do business with him.

DEVELOPING CLOSER RELATIONSHIPS WITH WORK ASSOCIATES

A recent explanation of the causes of unethical behavior emphasizes the strength of relationships among people.[10] Assume that two people have close ties to each other, such as having worked together for a long time or knowing each other both on and off the job. As a consequence they are likely to behave ethically toward one another on the job. In contrast, if a weak relationship exists between two people, either party is more likely to engage in an unethical relationship. The owner of an auto service center is more likely to behave unethically toward a stranger passing through town than toward a long-time customer. The opportunity for unethical behavior between strangers is often minimized because individuals typically do not trust strangers with sensitive information or valuables.

The ethical skill-building consequences of information about personal relationships is that building closer relationships with people is likely to enhance ethical behavior. If you build close relationships with work associates, you are likely to behave more ethically toward them. Similarly, your work associates are likely to behave more ethically toward you. The work associates we refer to are all your contacts, or internal and external customers.

SUMMARY

Ethics refers to what is good and bad, right and wrong, just and unjust, and what people should do. A person's ethical code has a significant impact on his or her interpersonal relationships.

Understanding ethics is important for a variety of reasons. First, people are motivated by self-interest and a desire to be morally right. Second, good ethics can enhance business and avoid illegal acts. Third, high ethics improves the quality of work life.

A substantial number of managers and employees engage in unethical behavior, often because they feel pressured into making a quick profit. Commonly faced ethical problems include the following: the temptation to illegally copy software; treating people unfairly; job discrimination; sexual harassment; conflict of interest; mistreating confidential information; misuse of corporate resources; and misuse of computers and information technology.

A challenging twist to ethical decision making is to sort through your values when you have to choose between two morally sound choices. A defining moment is when you have to choose between two or more ideals in which you deeply believe.

One strategy for behaving ethically is to develop the right character traits, as specified by the Character Counts Coalition. Among these traits are honesty, integrity, promise keeping, loyalty, responsibility, kindness, respect for others, fairness, and good citizenship. At times using a corporate program such as an ethics hot line can help a person resolve ethical dilemmas.

Another strategy for behaving ethically is to follow eight steps in making a contemplated decision:

1. Gather the facts.

2. Define the ethical issues.

3. Identify the affected parties.

4. Identify the consequences.

5. Identify the obligations (such as to customers and society).

6. Consider your character and integrity.

7. Think creatively about potential actions.

8. Check your intuition.

Another way to raise the level of ethical behavior is to form close relationships with work associates. This is true because people tend to behave more ethically toward people who are close to them.

QUESTIONS FOR DISCUSSION AND REVIEW

1. How can behaving ethically improve a person's interpersonal relationships on the job?

2. What would most likely be some of the specific behaviors of a manager who scored 20 points on the ethical reasoning inventory?

3. Professions such as medicine, law, accounting, and psychology have their own ethical codes. Why do professional people need an ethical code?

4. Give an example from your own experiences or the media in which a business executive did something of significance that was morally right.

5. Provide an example of an action in business that might be unethical but not illegal.

6. If pirating software is illegal and unethical, why is it practiced so frequently?

7. What "commandment" about computer use would you like to add to the list in Figure 13-2?

8. Is it unethical for a company owner to buy products for the company from a relative even if the products are not the best buy in terms of price and quality?

9. What decision of ethical consequence have you made in the last year that you would not mind having publicly disclosed?

10. Why is using your intuition an effective guide to ethical decision making?

THE OFFICE CHAMELEON

Tom Chatworth joined Ace Industrial Products four years ago as a trainee in the sales order department. His job was to process repeat business from established customers. The inside sales position fit into Tom's career plan. He wanted to become an outside sales representative and also learn the business thoroughly. He aspired to someday become a sales manager in an industrial company.

After three years of good performance as an order specialist, Tom was promoted to outside sales representative. He now had a territory of his own, selling various small pumps and motors to other manufacturers. Tom thought to himself that he was on the right path toward reaching his goals. Tom was achieving his sales quota, yet his sales manager had some concerns about his sales tactics.

During one coaching session, Karen Deauville, his manager, explained to Tom, "I get the impression that you are not telling our customers a consistent story. I can tell from some of the comments they have made to our customer service department. Here's a specific example: You told Albany Machine Works that the reason our pump cost a little more than average is that it meets incredibly high quality standards.

"The next week you told Three Rivers Machining that the reason you could offer the pump to them at such a low price is that it was not built to last 50 years." With a puzzled look on his face, Tom responded: "Hold on, Karen, that's just good salesmanship. If a customer is concerned about quality, you emphasize quality. If the customer is concerned about price, you tell him the price is low. But you need a sensible explanation as to why the price is low."

"I disagree," said Karen. "A professional sales representative sticks with a consistent story about a product. If you tell the truth, you don't have to switch stories."

Tom said, "OK, I get the message. But I don't agree 100 percent. You sometimes have to manipulate the facts just a little to keep a customer happy."

Karen received no further feedback on inconsistencies in Tom's sales presentations, so she dropped her concern that Tom was not creating the best image for the company. Several months later, Karen and Tom were attending the company sales meeting. As she approached the bar for a drink, she heard Tom talking to the vice president of marketing, Grant Edgewood. He commented to Edgewood, "Grant, I can't help admiring that bow tie. It adds a little class to the meeting." Edgewood thanked him for the compliment and went on to explain how he had mastered tying a bow tie.

Later that evening, Karen encountered Tom at the buffet table for desserts. Tom stood right behind Karen as they shuffled along among the choice of desserts. With a smile on his face, Tom said, "Did you see Grant tonight? He's actually wearing a bow tie. The guy thinks he's a Harvard Business School professor or a senator. He makes me laugh."

"Tom, I think you and I must have a little chat again next week," said Karen. "I'll be in touch."

Tom thought to himself, "I wonder what I said to upset Karen? What's wrong with not liking bow ties?"

Case Questions

1. What ethical problems, if any, does Tom display?

2. Does Karen have a right to be concerned about Tom's behavior? Or is she being naive?

3. Should Karen be using information she gathered at a sales meeting as a basis for coaching?

4. Assuming Tom does need help, how should Karen help him?

5. How would you rate Tom on the personality trait of self-monitoring?

Chapter 14

Personal Productivity and Stress Management

Learning Objectives

After reading and studying this chapter and doing the exercises you should be able to

➤ Reduce any tendencies you might have toward procrastination.

➤ Identify attitudes and values that will enhance your productivity.

➤ Identify skills and techniques that will enhance your productivity.

➤ Pinpoint potential time wasters that drain your productivity.

➤ Explain many of the symptoms and consequences of stress, including burnout.

➤ Describe personality factors and job factors that contribute to stress.

➤ Be prepared to manage your own stress effectively.

Forty-one year-old Randolph Blatt of Raleigh, North Carolina, decided to oper-
ate a recruiting firm for computer professionals out of his home. Part of his rea-
soning was that his productivity would increase if he saved commuting time and
had fewer distractions than in a conventional office. Saving on office rent was
also an attraction to setting up shop in his house. After four years of his home-
based business, Blatt knew he would have to modify his work life. As he explains
his problem, "I would get phone calls and I had screaming babies in the back-
ground. I would duck into my laundry room to hide. It never worked."

The solution to his problem was to affiliate with Your Office, a self-described
superstore for the home-based entrepreneur. Your Office functions like a home
away from home for home-based offices that lack certain equipment and for the
owners who are lonely. Among the services offered are temporary office space for
meeting with clients and customers, temporary meeting rooms, secretarial help,
mailboxes, and videoconference equipment. Clients can rent office space by the
hour, day, week, or month.

Blatt says, "At Your Office I regularly run into people, and I feel like I'm
part of the world." He likes the opportunity to chit-chat with people that is lack-
ing in his office at home.[1]

The story just presented about the man with a home-based business finding a
solution to his job stress illustrates two major workplace themes. Workers strive
to be more productive (for example, by working out of the home), and at the
same time they must find ways to manage stress and avoid burnout (for exam-
ple, by dropping by Your Office for some social interaction). Although this
book is primarily about interpersonal skills, information about enhancing per-
sonal productivity and managing stress is relevant. Being more productive and
having stress under control enhances relationships with others. Having your
work under control and not being stressed out enables you to focus better on
interpersonal relationships.

The first half of this chapter describes various approaches to improving
personal productivity, whereas the second half deals with the nature of stress
and how it can be managed. The two topics are as closely related as nutrition
and health. When your work is under control, you avoid the heavy stress of feel-
ing overwhelmed. And when you effectively manage stress, you can be more
productive.

IMPROVING PERSONAL PRODUCTIVITY

Achieving personal productivity is more in vogue than ever. Companies strive
to operate with smaller staffs than in the past by pushing workers to achieve
higher productivity. At the same time, there is a movement toward simplifying
personal life by reducing clutter and cutting back on tasks that do not add
much to the quality of work life. **Personal productivity** refers to the amount of
resources, including time, you consume to achieve a certain level of output.
Assuming that two paralegals receive the same compensation and require the
same amount of supervision. The paralegal who provides the finishing touch-

es on 100 house closings in one month is more productive than the one who completes 50 comparable closings per month.

We approach productivity improvement from four perspectives: (1) dealing with procrastination, (2) attitudes and values that enhance personal productivity, (3) work habits and skills that enhance personal productivity, and (4) overcoming time wasters.

DEALING WITH PROCRASTINATION

The person who **procrastinates** delays action for no good reason. Procrastination lowers productivity because it wastes time and many important tasks never get done. Even productive people sometimes procrastinate. If these people did not procrastinate, they would be even more productive.

Many people regard procrastination as a laughable weakness, particularly because procrastinators themselves joke about the problem. Yet procrastination has been evaluated as a profound, debilitating problem.[2] The enormity of the problem makes it worthwhile to examine methods for bringing it under control. What will work for overcoming procrastination depends somewhat on a person's reason for procrastination. In the extreme case, a person might be procrastinating because he or wants to mess up as a form of self-punishment. Straightforward cognitive suggestions such as "Do it now" may not work for that individual. Do Self-Assessment Quiz 14-1 to think through your own tendencies toward procrastination—and don't wait until tomorrow.

Choose from among the following suggestions for controlling procrastination, based on those that appear to best fit your type of procrastination. A combination of techniques is likely to be the most effective.

1. *Calculate the cost of procrastination.* You can reduce procrastination by calculating its cost. You might lose out on obtaining a high-paying job you really want by not having your résumé and cover letter ready on time. Your cost of procrastination would include the difference in compensation between the job you do find and the one you really wanted. Another cost would be the loss of potential job satisfaction.

2. *Follow the WIFO principle, which stands for "worst in, first out."*[3] If you tackle the worst task on your list first, doing the other tasks may function like a small reward. You get to do what you dislike the least by doing first what you dislike the most. WIFO is particularly effective when faced with a number of tasks simultaneously.

3. *Break the task into manageable chunks.* To reduce procrastination, cut down a task that seems overwhelming into smaller projects that seem less formidable. If your job calls for preparing an enormous database, begin by assembling some readily available information. Then take the next step by assembling another small segment of the database—perhaps all customers whose last names begin with Z. Think of your task as pulling together a series of small databases that will fit into a master database.

Self-Assessment Quiz 14-1

PROCRASTINATION TENDENCIES

Directions: Circle yes or no for each item:

1.	I usually do my best work under the pressure of deadlines.	Yes	No
2.	Before starting a project I go through such rituals as sharpening every pencil, straightening up my desk more than once, and discarding bent paper clips.	Yes	No
3.	I crave the excitement of the "last-minute rush."	Yes	No
4.	I often think that if I delay something, it will go away, or the person who asked for it will forget about it.	Yes	No
5.	I extensively research something before taking action, such as obtaining three different estimates before getting the brakes repaired on my car.	Yes	No
6.	I have a great deal of difficulty getting started on most projects, even those I enjoy.	Yes	No
7.	I keep waiting for the right time to do something, such as getting started on an important report.	Yes	No
8.	I often underestimate the time needed to do a project, and say to myself, "I can do this quickly, so I'll wait until next week."	Yes	No
9.	It is difficult for me to finish most projects or activities.	Yes	No
10.	I have several favorite diversions or distractions that I use to keep me from doing something unpleasant.	Yes	No

Total Yes Responses _____

Scoring and Interpretation: The greater the number of yes responses, the more likely it is that you have a serious procrastination problem. A score of 8, 9, or 10 strongly suggests that your procrastination is lowering your productivity.

4. *Make a commitment to other people.* Try to make it imperative that you get something done on time by making it a commitment to one or more other people. You might announce to coworkers that you are going to get something accomplished by a certain date. If you fail to meet this date, you are likely to feel embarrassed.

5. *Remove some clutter from your mind.* Procrastination escalates when people have many unfinished projects in the back of their mind, draining their concentration. Too much to do can freeze us into inaction. Just eliminating a few trivial items from your to-do list can give you enough mental energy to overcome procrastination on a few major tasks.

Notice carefully that this approach to overcoming procrastination requires that you apply enough self-discipline to take the first step.

6. *Satisfy your stimulation quota in constructive ways.* If you procrastinate because you enjoy the rush of scrambling to make deadlines, find a more constructive way of using busyness to keep you humming. If you need a high level of stimulation, enrich your life with extra projects and learning new skills. The fullness of your schedule will provide you the stimulation you had been receiving from squeezing yourself to make deadlines and reach appointments on time.[4]

ATTITUDES AND VALUES THAT ENHANCE PERSONAL PRODUCTIVITY

Developing good work habits and time-management practices is often a matter of developing the right attitudes toward your work and toward time. If, for example, you think that your schoolwork or job is important and that time is a precious resource, you will be on your way toward developing good work habits. In this section, we describe a group of attitudes, values, and beliefs that can help a person become more productive through better use of time and improved work habits.

Begin with a Mission and Goals

A mission, or general purpose, propels you toward being productive. Assume that a person says, "My mission is to be an outstanding professional in my field and a loving, constructive spouse and parent." The mission serves as a compass to direct your activities, such as being well organized in order to accomplish more work and be highly valued by your employer. Goals are more specific than mission statements; they support the mission statement, but the effect is the same. Being committed to a goal also propels you toward good use of time. If you know that you can obtain the position in international business that you really want by mastering a second language, you are likely to work diligently on learning that language. Skill-Building Exercise 14-1 gives you the opportunity to establish a mission statement and supporting goals.

Work Smarter, Not Harder

People caught up in trying to accomplish a job often wind up working hard, but not in an imaginative way that leads to good results. Much time and energy are therefore wasted. A working-smart approach also requires that you spend a few minutes carefully planning how to implement your task. Searching information on the Internet provides many examples of the importance of working smarter rather than harder. One example will place you on the right mental track.

Suppose you are searching for information about a mutual fund that invests in Internet-related stocks. A *working hard* approach would be to load your search engine with general phrases that would take you to hundreds of Web sites that do not provide the information you are seeking. Among

Skill-Building Exercise 14-1

USING A MISSION STATEMENT AND GOALS TO POWER WORK HABITS

People with a well-defined mission statement and supporting goals tend to have better work habits and time management than those who do not. The following exercise is designed to help you establish a mission statement and goals so you will be energized to be more productive.

A. Mission Statement: To help develop your mission statement, or general purpose in life, ask yourself, "What are my five biggest wishes in life?" These wishes give you a hint to your purpose because they point toward an ideal purpose in life. Feel free to think big, because mission statements tend toward being idealistic.

B. Long-Range Goals to Support Mission Statement: Now write down what long-range goals would support your mission statement. Suppose your mission statement related to "creating a better life for disadvantaged people." Your long-range goals might include establishing a foundation that would fund your efforts. You would also need to be successful enough in your career to get the foundation started.

C. Intermediate-Range Goals to Support Long-Range Goals: Write down the intermediate-range goals needed to support the long-range goals. You will probably need to complete your education, obtain broad experience, and identify a lucrative form of self-employment.

D. Weekly Goals to Support Intermediate-Range Goals: Write down what you have to do this week to help you complete your education, such as researching and writing a paper for a particular course, registering for courses for next term, and inquiring about career opportunities in your field.

E. Today's Goals to Support Weekly Goals (My To-Do List): Here's where your lofty purpose in life gets translated into reality. What do you have to do today to get that paper written? Do you need to get your car battery replaced so you can get to the library so you can write your paper, so you can graduate, so you can become rich, so you can ultimately help all those disadvantaged people? Get going.

these general phrases would be "mutual funds," "Internet investments," and "Internet mutual funds." You might spend hours surfing these sites. The working-smart approach would be to start your search in a highly focused manner, and then branch out if you did not find the information you sought. Why not work very smart and attempt to skip the search engines all together? Take a chance finding your information directly by prefacing your key word with www and following the word with .com. The designation www.Internetfund.com provides exactly the information you were seeking, with a total search time of about three minutes.

Value Orderliness and Cleanliness

An orderly desk, work area, attaché case, or hard drive does not inevitably indicate an orderly mind. Yet it does help most people become more productive because they can better focus their mind. Also, less time is wasted and less energy is expended if you do not have to hunt for information that you thought you had on hand. Knowing where information is and what information you have available is a way of being in control of your job. When your job gets out of control, you are probably working at less than peak efficiency. Valuing cleanliness improves productivity in several ways. According to the Japanese system, cleanliness is the bedrock of quality. Also, after you have thoroughly cleaned your work area, you will usually attain a fresh outlook.

The core attitude here is to perceive clutter negatively. One reason that clutter is counterproductive is that managers spend an estimated five weeks per year hunting for things they have lost. Other workers spend about 10 weeks per year searching for information and things (Internet searches not included). Having less clutter reduces the time spent searching for misplaced items.[5]

Value Good Attendance and Punctuality

Good attendance and punctuality are expected of both experienced and inexperienced employees. You cannot be productive if you are not physically present in your work area. The same principle applies whether you work on company premises or at home. One exception is that some people can work through solutions to job problems while engaged in recreation. Keep in mind, too, that being late for or absent from meetings sends the silent message that you do not regard the meeting as being important.

The relationship of lateness to absenteeism and work performance has been researched. Based on 30 studies and over 9,000 workers it was found that employees who were late also tended to have high absenteeism records. In addition, employees who were late tended to have poorer work performance than workers who were prompt, but the relationship was not strong.[6] Despite this weak association, being late must still be regarded as a productivity drain.

Attain a Balance in Life and Avoid Being a Workaholic

A productive attitude to maintain is that overwork can lead to negative stress and burnout. Proper physical rest and relaxation can contribute to mental alertness and improved ability to cope with frustration. A strategy for preventing overwork is to strive for a balance in which you derive satisfaction from various spheres of life. Major spheres in addition to work include family life, romance, sports, the arts and music, faith, and intellectual growth.

Neglecting the normal need for rest and relaxation can lead to **workaholism**, an addiction to work in which not working is an uncomfortable experience. Some types of workaholics are perfectionists who are never satisfied with their work and therefore find it difficult to leave work behind. In addition, the perfectionist-type workaholic may become heavily focused on control, leading to rigid behavior and strained interpersonal relationships. However, some people who work long and hard are classified as achievement-oriented workaholics who thrive on hard work and are usually highly productive.[7]

WORK HABITS AND SKILLS THAT
ENHANCE PERSONAL PRODUCTIVITY

Overcoming procrastination and developing the right attitudes contribute to personal productivity. Effective work habits and skills are also essential for high productivity. Five key work habits and skills are described next. They represent a mixture of traditional productivity boosters and those geared toward information technology.

Prepare a To-Do List and Set Priorities

At the heart of every time-management system is list making, whether the list is placed on an index card, in a leather-bound planner, or in a palm-size computer. As already described, the to-do list is the basic tool for achieving your daily goals, which in turn helps you achieve bigger goals and your mission. Almost every successful person in any field composes a list of important and less important tasks that need to be done. Before you compose a useful list, you need to set aside a few minutes of quiet time every day to sort out the tasks at hand. This is the most basic aspect of planning.

As is well known, it is helpful to set priorities for items on the to-do list. A typical system is to use A to signify critical or essential items, B to signify important items, and C for the least important ones. Although an item might be regarded as a C (for example, emptying the wood shavings from the electronic pencil sharpener), it still makes a contribution to your management of time and sense of well-being. Accomplishing anything reduces some stress. Also, many people obtain satisfaction from crossing off an item on their list, however trivial. If you are at all conscientious, small, unaccomplished items will come back to interfere with your concentration.

Streamline Your Work and Emphasize Important Tasks

As companies continue to operate with fewer workers than in the past despite prosperity, more unproductive work must be eliminated. Getting rid of unproductive work is part of *reengineering*, in which work processes are radically redesigned and simplified. Every employee is expected to get rid of work that does not contribute to productivity or help customers.

In general, to streamline or reengineer your work, look for duplication of effort and waste. An example of duplication of effort would be to routinely send people e-mail and fax messages covering the same topic. An example of waste would be to call a meeting for disseminating information that could easily be communicated by e-mail.

Emphasizing important tasks means that you make sure to take care of A items on your to-do list. It also implies that you search to accomplish a few work activities that, if done well, would make a big difference in your job performance. Although important tasks may take less time to accomplish than many routine tasks, they can represent the difference between success and failure. Five minutes of telephone conversation with a major customer might do more good for your company than three hours of arranging obsolete inventory in the warehouse.

Stay in Control of Paperwork and Electronic Work

Although it is fashionable to complain about paperwork in responsible jobs, the effective career person does not neglect paperwork. (Paperwork includes electronic work such as electronic mail and voice mail.) Paperwork involves taking care of administrative details such as correspondence, invoices, human resource reports, and inventory forms. Unless paperwork and electronic work are attended to, a person's job may get out of control. A small amount of time should be invested in paperwork every day. Nonprime time (when you are at less than your peak of efficiency but not overfatigued) is the best time to take care of paperwork.

Time management specialist Odette Pollar recommends that you sort and handle the papers in your in-basket twice a day. Decide what you will do with every piece of paper and put it in its proper location, not back in the basket.[8] A similar process can be used for e-mail. Respond quickly to high-priority messages, and permanently delete those you will mostly not need to refer to again. Avoid the hazard of making a hard copy of every message and filing it in your in-basket.

Work Productively from Your Home Office or Virtual Office

A growing segment of the workforce spends full or part time working either from home or from a **virtual office**. Such an office is a place of work without a fixed physical location from which the worker or workers communicate their output electronically. A virtual office might be in a car, train, airplane, or hotel room; on a park bench; or wherever the worker happens to be at the time. Many people adapt well to working at home and from virtual offices because they are self-starters and self-disciplined. Many other workers lack the self-discipline and effective work habits necessary to be productive outside a traditional office. Following is a list of representative suggestions for being productive while working independently:[9]

➤ Act as if you work in a traditional office. Set specific working hours, get dressed, go outside the house for a few minutes, then return and get to work. Also, close your office at home or virtual office at some regular time. Otherwise, you are open for business all the time. If you work at home, establish a clear workspace and let your family and friends know when you cannot be disturbed.

➤ Stay in touch with teammates to enhance your team player skills and not lose out on important information that could lower your effectiveness (such as missing an appointment at the traditional office).

➤ Minimize conducting your personal life at the same time as working (for example, such as watching television, talking to neighbors, or shopping over the Internet).

➤ Schedule regular times for meals and snacks, otherwise you will lose many minutes and gain many pounds taking food and beverage breaks.

➤ Use whatever information technology your employer offers to send and receive output. For example, software like *Hot-Office* acts as a command center for a virtual team. Members can place objects such as documents, images, and spreadsheets into a common location for review; retrieve files; and share ideas.

The practice of working at home or from virtual offices is increasing, so these suggestions merit careful consideration. Several of the productivity ideas also fit the conventional office.

Enhance Your Internet Search Skills

For many workers, an important job skill is searching the Internet for various information. It follows that if you develop your Internet search skills you will be more productive by obtaining the results you need within a reasonable time. The example given earlier about finding the Internet mutual fund illustrates the value of having effective Internet search skills. A few more suggestions follow.

First, it is important to rely on several search engines to seek needed information. Several metasearch engines claim to be so comprehensive that no other engine is required. Such claims are exaggerated, because the same search word entered into several different comprehensive engines will reveal a different list of sources. Second, give careful thought to the search word or phrase you use. The more specific the better. Assume that you wanted to find software to enhance your productivity, and that you enter the word "software" into a search engine. You will probably receive a message indicating that 3,500,000 entries have been located in response to your personal inquiry. You are better advised to use the search phrase "Software for increasing personal productivity."

Third, for many searches, framing the query as a phrase by enclosing it in quotation marks refines the number of hits (or sites) returned.[10] Simply place quotation marks before and after the search word, such as "Software for improving work habits." Fourth, if you don't find what you want in your initial search, reframe your question in another way or change the terms. How about, "Software for time management" or "Computer programs for increasing personal efficiency"?

Skill-Building Exercise 14-2 will help you make better use of the Internet to enhance your personal productivity.

OVERCOMING TIME WASTERS

Another basic thrust to improve personal productivity is to minimize wasting time. Many of the techniques already described in this chapter help save time, such as eliminating nonessential work. Whether or not an activity is a time waster depends on the purpose of the activity. Suppose you play computer solitaire for 10 minutes to reduce stress and then return to work refreshed. In contrast, another worker who spends 10 minutes playing solitaire just for fun is wasting time. Figure 14-1 presents a list of common time wasters. Being aware of time wasters will help sensitize you to the importance of minimizing them.

Internet Skill-Building Exercise 14-2

PRODUCTIVITY BOOSTING ON THE INTERNET

The number of people online continues to grow rapidly, with thousands of people around the world getting started every day. Gather into small teams or work individually to identify 10 ways in which the Internet can increase personal productivity, either on the job or at home. To supplement your own thinking, you might search the Internet for ideas on how the Internet is supposed to boost productivity. I look forward to being informed of your most creative ideas.

Happy surfing.
ajdubrin@frontiernet.net

Even if you saved just 10 minutes per work day, the productivity gain over a year could be enormous.

UNDERSTANDING AND MANAGING STRESS

A major challenge facing any worker who wants to stay healthy and have good interpersonal relationships is to manage stress effectively. Although *stress* is an everyday term, a scientific definition helps clarify its meaning. **Stress** is an adaptive response that is the consequence of any action, situation, or event that places special demands on a person. Note that stress refers to a *reaction* to the situation, not the situation or force itself. A **stressor** is the external or internal force that brings about the stress.

Individual differences play a key role in determining what events are stressful. Giving a presentation to management, for example, is stressful for some people but not for others. The term *special demands* is also critical, because minor adjustments, such as a pencil point that breaks, are usually not perceived as stressful.[11] Yet a piling on of minor adjustments, such as having 10 small things go wrong in one day, is stressful. This is true because stress is additive: A series of small doses of stress can create a major stress problem.

Our approach to understanding stress centers around its symptoms and consequences, personality and job factors that contribute to stress, and methods and techniques for stress management. Managing stress receives more emphasis because the same techniques can be used to combat a variety of stressors.

SYMPTOMS AND CONSEQUENCES OF STRESS

The physiological changes that take place within the body in response to stress are responsible for most stress symptoms. These physiological changes are almost identical for both positive and negative stressors. Ski racing, romantic attraction, and being downsized can make you feel about the same physically.

Wasted time is a major productivity drain, so it pays to search for time wasters in your work activities. The following list includes ways to minimize some of the major time wasters in the workplace. Most people can add a personal list of time leaks to this list.

1. Use a time log for two weeks to track time wasters.

2. Minimize daydreaming on the job by forcing yourself to concentrate.

3. Avoid the computer as a diversion from work, such as sending jokes back and forth to network members, playing video games, and checking out recreational Web sites during working hours.

4. Batch together tasks such as returning phone calls or responding to e-mail messages. For example, in most jobs it is possible to be polite and productive by reserving two or three 15-minute periods per day for taking care of e-mail correspondence.

5. Socialize on the job just enough to build your network. Chatting with coworkers is a major productivity drain and one of the reasons so many managers work at home part of the time when they have analytical work to get done.

6. Be prepared for meetings by, for example, having a clear agenda and sorting through the documents you will be referring to. Make sure electronic equipment is in working order before attempting to use it during the meeting.

7. Keep track of important names, places, and things to avoid wasting time searching for them.

8. Set a time limit for tasks after you have done them once or twice.

9. Prepare a computer template for letters and computer documents that you send frequently. (The template is essentially a form letter, especially with respect to the salutation and return address.)

10. When you only have to provide routine information by voice mail, telephone people before and after normal working hours, leaving a message on their voice mail. (This saves conversation time.)

11. Avoid perfectionism, which leads you to keep redoing a project. Let go and move on to another project.

12. Make use of bits of time—for instance, 5 minutes between appointments. Invest those 5 minutes in sending a business e-mail or revising your to-do list. (Note the exception to the batch principle.)

13. Minimize procrastination, the number one time waster for most people.

14. Avoid spreading yourself too thin by doing too many things at once, such as having one project too many to handle. When you are overloaded, time can be wasted because of too many errors.

Figure 14-1 Ways to Prevent and Overcome Time Wasting

Source: Suggestions 4, 5, and 6 are based on Stephen R. Covey with Hyrum Smith, "What If You Could Chop an Hour from Your Day for Things That Matter Most?" *USA Weekend,* January 22–24, 1999, pp. 4–5.

The experience of stress helps activate hormones that prepare the body to run or fight when faced with a challenge. This battle against the stressor is referred to as the **fight-or-flight response**. It helps you deal with emergencies.

An updating of the fight-or-flight response theory explains that, when faced with stress, the brain acts much like a thermostat. When outside condi-

tions deviate from an ideal point, the thermostat sends a signal to the furnace to increase heat or air conditioning. The brain senses stress as damage to well-being and therefore sends out a signal to the body to cope. The purpose of coping is to modify the discrepancy between the ideal (low-stress) and actual (high-stress) conditions.[12] The brain is thus a self-regulating system that helps us cope with stressors.

Physiological Reactions

The activation of hormones when the body has to cope with a stressor produces a short-term physiological reaction. Among the most familiar reactions are an increase in heart rate, blood pressure, blood glucose, and blood clotting. To help you recognize these symptoms, try to recall your internal bodily sensations the last time you were almost in an automobile accident or heard some wonderful news. Less familiar changes are a redirection of the blood flow toward the brain and large muscle groups and a release of stored fluids from places throughout the body into the bloodstream.

If stress is continuous and accompanied by these short-term physiological changes, annoying and life-threatening conditions can occur. Damage occurs when stress levels rarely subside. A stressful life event usually leads to a high cholesterol level (of the unhealthy type) and high blood pressure. Other conditions associated with stress are cardiac disease, migraine headaches, ulcers, allergies, skin disorders, and cancer. To make matters worse, stress can hamper the immune system, thereby increasing the severity of many diseases and disorders. For example, people whose stress level is high recover more slowly from colds and injuries, and they are more susceptible to sexually transmitted diseases. Stress symptoms vary considerably from one person to another. A general behavioral symptom of intense stress is for people to exaggerate their weakest tendencies. For instance, a person with a strong temper who usually keeps cool under pressure may throw a tantrum under pressure. Some common stress symptoms are listed in Figure 14-2.

Job Performance Consequences

Despite all the problems just mentioned, stress also plays a positive role in our lives. The right amount of stress prepares us for meeting difficult challenges and spurs us on to peak intellectual and physical performance. An optimum level of stress exists for most people and most tasks.

In general, performance tends to be best under moderate amounts of stress. If the stress is too great, people become temporarily ineffective; they may freeze or choke. Under too little stress, people may become lethargic and inattentive. Figure 14-3 depicts the relationship between stress and performance. An exception to this relationship is that certain negative forms of stress are likely to lower performance even if the stress is moderate. For example, the stress created by an intimidating supervisor or worrying about radiation poisoning—even in moderate amounts—will not improve performance.

The optimum amount of stress is a positive force that is the equivalent of finding excitement and challenge. Your ability to solve problems and deal with challenge is enhanced when the right amount of adrenaline flows in your

Mostly Physical and Physiological	
Shaking or trembling	Mouth dryness
Dizziness	Upper and lower back pain
Heart palpitations	Frequent headaches
Difficulty breathing	Low energy and stamina
Chronic fatigue	Stomach problems
Unexplained chest pains	Constant craving for sweets
Frequent teeth grinding	Increased alcohol or cigarette consumption
Frequent nausea	Frequent need to eliminate
Mostly Emotional and Behavioral	
Difficulty concentrating	Anxiety or depression
Nervousness	Forgetfulness
Crying	Restlessness
Anorexia	Frequent arguments with others
Declining interest in sex	Feeling high strung much of the time
Frequent nail biting or hair tugging	

Figure 4-2 A Variety of Stress Symptoms

blood to guide you toward peak performance. In fact, highly productive people are sometimes said to be hooked on adrenaline.

Burnout and Stress

One of the major problems of prolonged stress is that it may lead to **burnout**, a condition of emotional, mental, and physical exhaustion in response to long-term stressors. Burned-out people are often cynical. Burnout is a complex phenomenon, but it often occurs when people feel out of control. Other critical

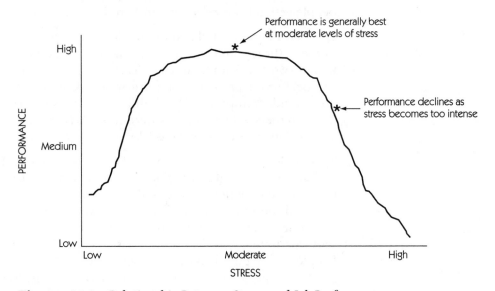

Figure 14-3 Relationship Between Stress and Job Performance

factors that contribute to burnout are insufficient recognition and reward, a lack of emotional support in the workplace, or an absence of fairness. Christina Maslach observes that "When the workplace does not recognize the human side of work, then the risk of burnout grows, carrying with it a high price and hurting all the parties involved."[13]

The key feature of burnout is the distancing that occurs in response to work overload. Burnout sufferers shift into a mode of doing the minimum as a way of protecting themselves. They start leaving work early and dehumanizing their clients, patients, or customers. People experiencing burnout may do their jobs, but their heart is not in it any more.[14]

PERSONALITY AND JOB FACTORS CONTRIBUTING TO STRESS

Workers experience stress for many different reasons, including personal predispositions, factors stemming from the job, or the combined influence of both. If a person with an extreme negative predisposition has to deal with irate customers, he or she is most likely to experience substantial stress. Here we describe a sampling of important individual and organizational factors that contribute to job stress.

Personality Factors Predisposing People Toward Stress

Individuals vary considerably in their susceptibility to job stress based on their personality traits and characteristics. Four such factors are described next.

Low Perceived Control. A key factor in determining whether workers experience stress is how much they believe they can control a given adverse circumstance. **Perceived control** is the belief that an individual has at his or her disposal a response that can control the negative aspects of an event. A survey of over 100 studies indicated that people with a high level of perceived control had low levels of physical and psychological symptoms of stress. Conversely, people with low perceived control are more likely to experience work stress.[15]

Low Self-Efficacy. Related to the idea of low perceived control, workers with low self-efficacy tend to experience more emotional strain and physical strain than do workers with high self-efficacy. In short, people who are confident they can perform a particular task are more likely to either avoid stress of have much milder symptoms. The finding about self-efficacy was based on a study of 2,273 soldiers whose stressors were long work hours and work overload. The average age of the soldiers was 24.[16]

Type A Behavior. A person with **Type A behavior** is demanding, impatient, and overstriving and is therefore prone to negative stress. Type A behavior has two main components. One is the tendency to try to accomplish too many things in too little time. This leads the Type A individual to be impatient and demanding. The other component is free-floating hostility. Because of this sense of urgency and hostility, these people are irritated by trivial things. People with Type A behavior are aggressive and hard working.

Type A personalities frequently have cardiac diseases, such as heart attacks and strokes, at an early age, but only certain features of the Type A personality

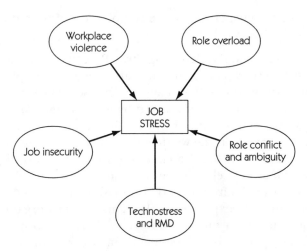

Figure 14-4 Five Major Sources of Job Stress

pattern may be related to coronary heart disease. The heart attack triggers are hostility, anger, cynicism, and suspiciousness, as contrasted to impatience, ambition, and being work driven.[17] Note that the heart attack triggers also make for strained interpersonal relationships.

Negative Affectivity. A major contributor to being stress prone is **negative affectivity**, a tendency to experience aversive emotional states. In more detail, negative affectivity is a pervasive disposition to experience emotional stress that includes feelings of nervousness, tension, and worry. The same disposition also includes such emotional states as anger, scorn, revulsion, guilt, self-dissatisfaction, and sadness.[18] Such negative personalities seem to search for important discrepancies between what they would like and what exists. Poor interpersonal relationships often result from the frequent complaining of people with negative affectivity.

Job Sources of Stress

Almost any job situation can act as a stressor for some employees, but not necessarily for others. As just described, certain personality factors make it more likely that a person will experience job stress. Furthermore, other personal life stressors may spill over into the workplace, making it more likely that a person will experience job stress. Here we describe five frequently encountered job stressors, as outlined in Figure 14-4.

Role Overload. Having too much work to do, **role overload**, can create negative stress in two ways. First, the person may become fatigued and thus be less able to tolerate annoyances and irritations. Second, a person subject to unreasonable work demands may feel perpetually behind schedule, a situation that is itself a powerful stressor. Downsizing often creates overload because fewer people are left to handle the same workload as previously. (If work is carefully streamlined, role overload is minimized.) The widespread problem of role overload was suggested by a Harris Research study of 5,300 adults in 16 coun-

tries. Fifty-four percent of the respondents indicated that the leading cause of stress was overwork.[19]

Role Conflict and Role Ambiguity. Role conflict, described in Chapter 7 as an important workplace conflict, is also a major workplace stressor. People experience stress when they have to choose between two sets of expectations. Suppose an accountant is asked by her manager to state company earnings in a way that conflicts with the professional norms of accountants. If she complies with her manager, she will feel that she is betraying her profession. If she does not comply with her manager, she will enter into dispute with the manager. The woman is likely to experience job stress.

 Role ambiguity is a condition in which the job holder receives confusing or poorly defined expectations. Workers in many organizations are placed in situations in which they are unsure of their true responsibilities. Some workers who are placed on a self-managing work team experience role ambiguity because they are asked to solve many problems by themselves. It is less ambiguous to have the manager tell you what to do. Many people experience stress symptoms when faced with role ambiguity.

Technostress and Repetitive Motion Disorder. The computerization of the workplace, especially in information technology, has created a significant stressor labeled **technostress**. This condition refers to stress caused by an inability to cope with computer technologies in a constructive manner.[20] One contributor to technostress is the demand for continuous learning as software changes so rapidly. At the same time, software problems surface at unpredictable times, often leaving the computer operator feeling incompetent and helpless. Another contributor to technostress is that computer work can become so consuming that the person loses interest in human interaction. As a result, interpersonal relationships suffer.

 Technostress also comes in the form of a repetitive motion disorder as a consequence of prolonged keyboarding. The repetitive motion disorder most frequently associated with keyboarding is **carpal tunnel syndrome**. The syndrome occurs when repetitive flexing and extension of the wrist causes the tendons to swell, thus trapping and pinching the median nerve. Carpal tunnel syndrome creates stress because of the pain and misery, and it sometimes makes it necessary to change jobs. Repetitive motion disorders are a major cause of worker compensation claims.

Job Insecurity. Worrying about losing your job is a major stressor. Even when jobs are plentiful, having to search for another job and facing the prospect of geographic relocation are stressors for many people. Downsizing and corporate mergers (which usually result in downsizing) have contributed to job insecurity. The anticipation of layoffs among employees can increase negative stress and lower job performance. In addition, the survivors of a downsizing often experience pressure from fear of future cuts, loss of friends, and worry about a sudden increase in workload.[21]

Workplace Violence. As DeFrank and Ivancevich observe, the issue of violence and stress is complex because violence may be both the cause and the

result of stress. Workplace violence alarms many workers, with an average of 20 people murdered at work each week in the United States. Seventy-five percent or more of these murders occur during a robbery or other crime. Furthermore, 1 million workers are assaulted annually.[22] Workers who are victims of workplace assaults, or who watch a coworker being assaulted, experience intense negative stress. Worrying about being assaulted is also a stressor.

METHODS AND TECHNIQUES FOR STRESS MANAGEMENT

Unless stress is managed properly, it may lead to harmful long-term consequences, including disabling physical illness and career retardation. Managing stress refers to controlling stress by making it a constructive force in your life. Managing thus refers to both preventing and reducing stress. However, the distinction between methods of preventing and reducing stress is not clear cut. For example, physical exercise not only reduces stress, it also contributes to a relaxed lifestyle that helps you prevent stress.

Coping with, or managing, stress includes hundreds of activities, with substantial individual differences in which technique is effective. Running is a case in point. For many people running or jogging is an excellent method of stress reduction. Others find running creates new stressors, such as aching knees, shin splints, dizziness from breathing in vehicle exhausts, and worry about being hit by vehicles. In general, coping efforts involve cognitions and behaviors aimed at managing the stressor and its associated emotions. For example, you might have to decrease the troublesome elements in your job (such as role overload) and also deal with the tension generated by overwork. Here we describe six representative methods for managing stress, including a list of everyday stress busters.

Eliminate or Modify the Stressor. The most potent method of managing stress is to eliminate or modify the stressor giving you trouble. One value of relaxation techniques and tranquilizing medication is that they calm down a person enough so that he or she can deal constructively with the stressor. A helpful way to attack the cause of stress is to follow the steps in problem solving and decision making. You clarify the problem, identify the alternatives, weight the alternatives, and select one alternative. One difficulty, however, is that your evaluation of the real problem may be inaccurate. There is always a limit to self-analysis. For example, a person might think that work overload is the stressor when the true stressor is low self-efficacy.

Get Appropriate Physical Exercise. A moderate amount of physical exercise is a cornerstone of managing stress and achieving wellness. To manage stress it is important to select an exercise program that is physically challenging but does not lead to overexertion and muscle and bone injury. Competitive sports, if taken too seriously, can actually increase stress. Aerobic exercises are most beneficial because they make you breathe faster and raise your heart rate. A major mental and emotional benefit of physical exercise stems from endorphins produced in the thalamus portion of the brain. The endorphins are

associated with a state of euphoria referred to as a "runner's high." Endorphins also work like painkillers, adding to their stress-reduction value.

Rest Sufficiently. Rest offers benefits similar to those of exercise, such as stress reduction, improved concentration, improved energy, and better tolerance for frustration. Achieving proper rest is closely linked to getting proper exercise. The current interest in adult napping reflects the awareness that proper rest makes a person less stress prone and enhances productivity. A growing number of firms have napping facilities for workers, and many workers nap at their desks or in their parked vehicles during lunch breaks. *Power naps,* those of about 15 minutes duration taken during the work day, are used both as energizers and as stress reducers.[23] To keep the effectiveness of power napping in perspective, workers who achieve sufficient rest during normal sleeping hours have less need for a nap during working hours.

Build a Support Network. A **support network** is a group of people who can listen to your problems and provide emotional support. These people, or even one person, can help you through your difficult episodes. Members of your network can provide you with a sense of closeness, warmth, and acceptance that will reduce your stress. Also, the simple expedient of putting your feelings into words can be a healing experience. The way to develop this support network is to become a good listener yourself so that the other person will reciprocate. A support network is therefore a method of stress management based squarely on effective interpersonal skills.

Practice Visualization. Perhaps the most effortless and enjoyable relaxation technique for managing stress is to visualize a pleasant experience, as explained in Skill-Building Exercise 14-3. Visualization, like so many stress-reduction techniques, including meditation, requires concentration. Concentrating helps slow down basic physiological processes such as the heart beat and dissipates stress. Forcing yourself to concentrate is also valuable because a key stress symptom is difficulty in concentration.

Practice Everyday Methods of Stress Reduction. The simple expedient of learning how to relax is an important method of reducing the tension and anxiety brought about by both positive and negative stress. Visualization of a pleasant experience is one such method. A sample of everyday suggestions for relaxation and other methods of stress reduction are presented in Figure 14-5. If you can accomplish these you are less likely to need tranquilizing medication to keep you calm and in control. Your stress symptoms will ordinarily return, however, if you do not eliminate and modify the stressor. If the stress is an emotional conflict you do not see or understand, assistance from a mental health professional is recommended.

SUMMARY

Achieving high personal productivity on the job is more in demand than ever. A starting point in improving productivity is to minimize procrastination, an

Skill-Building Exercise 14-3

VISUALIZATION FOR STRESS REDUCTION

A standard, easy-to-use method for reducing stress symptoms is to visualize a pleasant and calm experience. If you are experiencing stress right now, try the technique. Otherwise, wait until the next time you perceive your body to be experiencing stress. In this context, visualization means to picture yourself doing something that you would like to do. Whatever fantasy suits your fancy will work, according to the advocates of this relaxation technique. Visualizations that work for some people include smiling at a loved one, floating on a cloud, caressing a baby, petting a kitten or puppy, and walking in the woods. Notice that all of these scenes are relaxing rather than exciting. What visualization would work for you?

To implement the technique, close your eyes and bring the pleasant image into focus in your mind. Think of nothing else at the moment. Imagine that a videotape of the pleasant experience is playing on the television screen in your brain. Breathe softly and savor the experience. Slowly return to reality, refreshed, relaxed, and ready to tackle the challenges of the day.

➤ Give in to your emotions. If you are angry, disgusted, or confused admit your feelings. Suppressing your emotions adds to stress.

➤ Take a brief break from the stressful situation and do something small and constructive, such as washing your car, emptying a wastebasket, or getting a haircut.

➤ Get a massage, because it can loosen tight muscles, improve your blood circulation, and calm you down.

➤ Get help with your stressful task from a coworker, supervisor, or friend.

➤ Concentrate intensely on reading, surfing the Internet, a sport, or a hobby. Contrary to common sense, concentration is at the heart of stress reduction.

➤ Have a quiet place at home and have a brief idle period there every day.

➤ Take a leisurely day off from your routine.

➤ Finish something you have started, however small. Accomplishing almost anything reduces some stress.

➤ Stop to smell the flowers, make friends with a young child or elderly person, or play with a kitten or puppy.

➤ Strive to do a good job, but not a perfect job.

➤ Work with your hands, doing a pleasant task.

➤ Find somebody or something that makes you laugh, and have a good laugh.

➤ Minimize drinking caffeinated or alcoholic beverages, and drink fruit juice or water instead. Grab a piece of fruit rather than a can of beer.

➤ Help somebody less fortunate than yourself. The flood of good feelings will act like endorphins.

Figure 14-5 Stress Busters

enormous problem for many people that can be approached as follows: Calculate the cost of procrastination; use the worst in, first out (WIFO) principle; break the task into manageable chunks; make a commitment to other people; remove some clutter from your mind; and satisfy your stimulation quota in constructive ways.

Developing good work habits and time-management practices is often a matter of developing the right attitudes toward your work and toward time, as follows: (a) Begin with a mission statement and goals; (b) work smarter, not harder; (c) value orderliness and cleanliness; (d) value good attendance and punctuality; and (e) attain a balance in life and avoid being a workaholic.

Effective work habits and skills are essential for high productivity, including the following: (a) Prepare a to-do list and set priorities; (b) streamline your work and emphasize important tasks; (c) stay in control of paperwork and electronic work; (d) work productively from your home office or virtual office; and (e) enhance your Internet search skills.

Another basic thrust to improved personal productivity is to minimize time wasting. Whether or not an activity is a time waster depends on its purpose. Being aware of time wasters such as those presented in Figure 14-1 will sensitize you to the importance of minimizing them.

A major challenge facing any worker who wants to stay healthy and have good interpersonal relationships is to manage stress effectively. Individual differences play a big role in determining whether an event will lead to stress. The physiological changes that take place within the body in response to stress are responsible for most of the stress symptoms. The fight-or-flight response is the battle against the stressor.

The activation of hormones when the body has to cope with a stressor produces short-term physiological reactions, including an increase in heart rate and blood pressure. When stress levels rarely subside, the physiological changes create damage. However, the right amount of stress prepares us for meeting difficult challenges and improves performance. An optimum level of stress exists for most people and most tasks. In general, performance tends to be best under moderate amounts of stress.

One of the major problems of prolonged stress is that it may lead to burnout, a condition of emotional, mental, and physical exhaustion in response to long-term stressors. Burnout also creates cynicism and a distancing from tasks and people.

Four personality factors predisposing people toward stress are low perceived control, low self-efficacy, Type A behavior, and negative affectivity. The heart attack triggers associated with Type A behavior are hostility, anger, cynicism, and suspiciousness. Five frequently encountered job stressors are role overload, role conflict and ambiguity, technostress and repetitive motion disorder, job insecurity, and workplace violence.

Managing stress refers to controlling stress by making it become a constructive force in your life. Coping with, or managing, stress includes hundreds of activities, with substantial individual differences in which technique is effective. Six representative stress-management methods are to eliminate or modify

the stressor, get appropriate physical exercise, rest sufficiently, build a support network, practice visualization, and use everyday methods of stress reduction.

QUESTIONS FOR DISCUSSION AND REVIEW

1. Provide an example from your own or somebody else's life of how having a major goal in life can help a person be better organized.

2. Describe any way in which you have used information technology to make you more productive.

3. Use information in this chapter to explain how a person might be well organized yet still not get very far in his or her career.

4. If you wanted to streamline your work as a student, what low-value activities could you eliminate?

5. Ask an experienced high-level worker to identify his or her most effective method of time management.

6. Some researchers have suggested that the term *challenge* be substituted for the term *stressor*. What do you think of the merit of their suggestion?

7. A student told his instructor, "You have to give me a deadline for my paper. Otherwise, I can't handle it." What does this statement tell you about (a) the stressor he was facing and (b) how pressure influences his work performance?

8. Why might having your stress under control improve your interpersonal relationships?

9. What are you going to do to prevent burning out in the next five years?

10. Interview a person in a high-pressure job in any field. Find out whether the person experiences significant stress and what method he or she uses to cope with it.

An Interpersonal Relations Case Problem

NOT GETTING IT DONE

Carol Winchester sat nervously outside the office of Daniel Delvin, a time-management consultant and personal coach. She kept thinking about how self-conscious she felt about seeking professional help just because she had a little trouble getting started on projects or finishing projects she had started. Carol said to herself, "This counselor is going to think there's something really wrong with me just because I have a small procrastination problem."

Winchester's thought pattern was interrupted by a warm welcome from Daniel Delvin, a neatly dressed, middle-age counselor. With a smile and an extended hand, Delvin said, "Hi. You must be Carol Winchester. I'm Dan Delvin. Come in and have a seat near the coffee table. That's where we'll be talking. Delvin sat in a chair a few feet away from Winchester.

"What kind of help do you want from me?" asked Delvin.

"The reason I'm here," answered Winchester, "is that both my boss and my boyfriend think I'm a procrastinator. Big Time. I don't disagree entirely, but I don't think I'm quite the basket case they do."

Delvin replied, "I doubt you're a basket case, but I don't think you would be here if you weren't experiencing a little pain. Hurting a little bit and admitting that you have a problem are the beginning points for overcoming your problem. Let's get started, Carol, by telling me about some of the ways in which you procrastinate."

"I've got a few horror stories to tell you," said Winchester with a nervous laugh. "A recent example is that it took me four months to make this appointment with you. [They both laugh.] I kept looking at my calendar and saying to myself that I was too busy to get help. I would pick up the phone to make an appointment. Then I would think of all the other things I needed to do. I finally set April 1 as an absolute firm date to call you. Then I realized I only had two more weeks to prepare my income tax forms for last

year. I guess you could say that I even procrastinated on my income tax. But I finally did get it in April 30, and the penalty only amounted to about $45. Those are two examples for you."

"Yes, they are two good examples. But I need more examples of your procrastination so I can better understand your problem."

"Okay, you asked for it," responded Winchester. "Lance, my boyfriend, whom I love very much, proposed to me one year ago. We were in a beautiful Greek restaurant called Acropolis. He pulled a ring out of the box. The group at the table across from us were watching intently. They were ready to clap when I said yes. Lance just assumed I would say yes. I didn't say yes, but I didn't say no. I just said I wasn't ready to make a decision that night.

"Two months later, when the engagement came up for about the tenth time in conversation, I did say yes. I know that by delaying my decision I took some of the romance out of Lance's proposal. His feelings are still a little hurt, but it didn't change his mind about wanting to marry me."

"Hold on a second," said Delvin. "Have you two agreed upon a wedding date yet?"

"Lance has been pressing me a little, but I'm just not ready to be that specific about getting married."

"Let's switch channels now," said Delvin. "What about on the job? What has prompted your boss to think you have a major procrastination problem?"

"It would be fair to say that I need more time than most people to get my projects done. I'm the assistant sales promotion manager. I have to do things like make some of the arrangements for trade shows and work with printers to have brochures ready. My boss says that I wait so long to make arrangements for booking hotels that we often have to pay premium rates. I think he exaggerates that problem. I'm very thorough, and that can be a big asset.

(Continued)

"A few times I have been late in getting computer disks ready for the printer so they can do their job on time. Yet since we're supposed to be the customer, I think they should be adapting to our schedule. I can think of another recent example. We were going to hire a new assistant for the office. We all agreed she was the right person to do the job. My boss had to go out of town for an important sales meeting. So he told me to contact this woman and tell her about the job offer.

"I got so busy with other stuff that I didn't call her for a week. By that time she had accepted another job. My boss was upset and blamed losing her on my procrastination. My take on it is a little different. If that woman really wanted to work for us, she could have waited for the job offer instead of taking another position."

Delvin asked, "Carol, why do you think you procrastinate so much?"

Carol replied, "You're a little bit like my boss and my boyfriend. You assume that every time I delay doing something, it's procrastination. Sometimes something else very important comes up that prevents me from going down a particular path. At other times I might be just a little forgetful, like filing the taxes on time."

Case Questions

1. What do you see as some of the reason behind Winchester's procrastination?

2. What evidence do you find that Winchester might be defensive about her problem (or denying its reality)?

3. What advice can you offer Carol Winchester for overcoming her procrastination problem?

Chapter 15

Job Search and Career Management Skills

John Cirello is chief executive of MP Water Resources Group, the largest private water-supply utility company in Florida. His company has used adversity training extensively. For example, his company irrigates lawns for golf courses, hotels, and other businesses. A big problem occurs when it rains five times as much as average and demand for irrigation dries up.

Adversity training helped MP employees cope by focusing on the things over which they have control. Cirello said that after the training, "My people knew they couldn't control the weather, but they could control the cost." The employees cut power costs and other extras. The company has been using adversity training seminars for close to three years, and Cirello says he has seen a major change. The employees are more able to come up with innovative ways to solve problems.[1]

As the experience of the company just described suggests, leaning to cope with adversity is an important behavioral skill for performing well in your career. This final chapter of the book focuses on career success, including a description of strategies and tactics that will help you gain advantage. Learning to cope with adversity is but one such tactic.

Our approach to achieving career success is divided into four major segments: conducting a job campaign, understanding two major types of career paths, using career advancement strategies and tactics, and overcoming career barriers. The previous 14 chapters also deal with topics and skills that facilitate success. However, the information presented in this chapter is more specifically about managing your career.

CONDUCTING A JOB SEARCH

A relatively small number of people are sought out by employers because they possess skills in short supply, or they are invited by family members or friends to join an existing firm. However, the vast majority of workers have to conduct a job search at various times in their career. Job searches are conducted to find employment in a firm the job hunter is not already working for, or sometimes to find a new position within one's own firm. Even during the most prosperous of times, when jobs are in ample supply, learning more about conducting a job search is useful. It can help you land an excellent position. Included in the job search are job-hunting tactics and preparing a résumé and cover letter.

JOB-HUNTING TACTICS

Most people already have usable knowledge about how to find a job. Some of the ideas discussed next will therefore be familiar; some will be unfamiliar. We recommend using this list of tactics as a checklist to ensure that you have not neglected something important. It is easy to overlook the obvious when job hunting, because your emotions may cloud your sense of logic.

Identify Your Job Objectives

An effective job search begins with a clear perception of what kind of position (or positions) you want. If you express indecision about the type of work you seek, the prospective employer will typically ask in a critical tone, "What kind of work are you looking for?" Your chances of finding suitable employment increase when several different types of positions will satisfy your job objectives. Assume that one person who majored in business administration is only willing to accept a position as an office manager in a corporation. Another person with the same major is seeking a position as (a) an office manager; (b) a management trainee in a corporation; (c) an assistant manager in a retail store, restaurant, or hotel; (d) a sales representative; (e) an assistant purchasing agent; or (f) a management analyst. The second person has a much better chance of finding a suitable position.

Be Aware of Qualifications Sought by Employers

What you are looking for in an employer must be matched against what an employer is looking for in an employee. If you are aware of what employers are seeking, you can emphasize those aspects of yourself when applying for a position. For example, applicants for almost any type of position should emphasize their computer skills. Job interviewers and hiring managers do not all agree on the qualifications they seek in employees. Nevertheless, a number of traits, characteristics, skills, and accomplishments are important to many employers.[2] Self-Assessment Quiz 15-1 summarizes these qualifications in a way that you can apply to yourself as you think about your job hunt.

Identify Your Skills and Potential Contribution

Today's job market is skill based. Employers typically seek out job candidates with tangible skills (including interpersonal skills) that can be put to immediate use in accomplishing work. Job-relevant skills you might identify include computer skills, written communication skills, oral communication skills, math skills, and listening skills. A successful candidate for a help-desk position at a telecommunications company told the interviewer, "I know I can help your customers with their software and hardware problems. I worked on the help desk at college, and my friends and family members are forever coming to me with their computer problems. I even get long-distance calls for help. Give me a chance to help your customers." (Notice that this candidate implied good listening skills.)

Develop a Comprehensive Marketing Strategy

A vital job-finding strategy is to use multiple approaches to reach the right prospective employer. This is particularly true when the position you seek is in short supply. Among the many approaches employers use to recruit candidates are employee referrals, newspaper ads, online recruiting, college and professional school recruitment, job fairs, temporary help firms, walk-ins, unsolicited résumés and phone calls, and government employment services. Some people looking for a highly specialized job place a position-wanted ad in a newspaper or on the Internet. Such ads receive many inquiries from career agents who offer to help you find a suitable position.

Self-Assessment Quiz 15-1

QUALIFICATIONS SOUGHT BY EMPLOYERS

Following is a list of qualifications widely sought by prospective employers. After reading each qualification, rate yourself on a 1 to 5 scale on the particular dimension. 1 = very low; 2 = low; 3 = average; 4 = high; 5 = very high.

1. Appropriate education for the position under consideration and satisfactory grades	1	2	(3)	4	5
2. Relevant work experience	1	2	3	4	(5)
3. Communication and other interpersonal skills	1	2	3	(4)	5
4. Motivation and energy	1	2	3	4	(5)
5. Problem-solving ability (intelligence) and creativity	1	2	3	4	(5)
6. Judgment and common sense	1	2	3	4	(5)
7. Adaptability to change	1	2	3	4	(5)
8. Emotional maturity (acting professionally and responsibly)	1	2	3	(4)	(5)
9. Teamwork (ability and interest in working in a team effort)	1	2	3	(4)	5
10. Positive attitude (enthusiasm about work and initiative)	1	2	3	(4)	5
11. Emotional intelligence (ability to deal with own feelings and those of others)	1	2	3	4	(5)
12. Customer service orientation (wanting to meet customer needs)	1	2	3	4	(5)
13. Computer skills	1	2	3	4	(5)
14. Willingness to continue to study and learn about job, company, and industry	1	2	3	4	(5)
15. Likableness and sense of humor	1	2	3	4	(5)
16. Dependability, responsibility, and conscientiousness (including good work habits and time management)	1	2	3	(4)	5
17. Willing and able to work well with coworkers and customers from different cultures.	1	2	3	4	(5)

Interpretation: Consider engaging in some serious self-development, training, and education for items on which you rated yourself low or very low. If you accurately rated yourself as 4 or 5 on all the dimensions, you are an exceptional job candidate.

Use Networking to Reach Company Insiders

An estimated 80 percent of successful job campaigns stem from personal contacts. Employers rely heavily on referrals from employees to fill positions. Positions that have not been filled by word of mouth are then publicly announced, for example, through Internet listings. In regard to job hunting, **networking** is contacting friends and acquaintances and building systematical-

➤ Coworkers and previous employers
➤ Friends and neighbors
➤ Faculty and staff
➤ Graduates of any schools you have attended
➤ Former employers
➤ Present employers (assuming you hold a temporary position)
➤ Professional workers such as bankers, brokers, and clergy
➤ Political leaders at the local level
➤ Members of your club or athletic team
➤ Community groups, churches, temples, and mosques
➤ Trade and professional associations
➤ Student professional associations
➤ Career fairs
➤ People met in airports and on airplanes
➤ People met in aerobic classes and health clubs
➤ People you get to know through Internet chat rooms

Figure 15-1 Potential Sources of Network Contacts

ly on these relationships to create a still wider set of contacts who might lead to employment. Figure 15-1 presents a list of potential network contacts. In addition, a skill-building exercise about networking as a method of career enhancement, including a job search, is presented toward the end of this chapter.

The networking technique is so well known today that it suffers from overuse. It is therefore important to use a tactful, low-key approach with a contact. For example, instead of asking a person in your network to furnish you a job lead, ask that person how a person with qualifications similar to yours might find a job. And guard against taking up a large portion of a busy person's work day, for instance, by insisting on a luncheon meeting.

Another way of reaching company insiders is to write dozens of letters to potential employers. A surprisingly large number of people find jobs by contacting employers directly. Many company Web sites have a section allocated to inviting job inquiries as part of the employee recruitment program. Prepare a prospective employer list, including the names of executives to contact in each firm. The people who receive your letters and e-mail messages become part of your network. A variation of this approach is to develop a 30-second telephone presentation of your background. After you have researched firms that may have opportunities for you, call them and make your pitch.

Use the Internet and Résumé Database Services

The Internet is a standard avenue for job hunting, even for middle-management and executive positions. For little or no cost, the job seeker can post a résumé or scroll through hundreds of job opportunities. The Career Mosaic

TABLE 15-1 Popular Job Search Web Sites

100 Hot Most Popular Job Sites	www.100hot.com/directory/business/jobs.html
Career Magazine	www.careermag.com
Career Mosaic	www.careermosaic.com
Career Path	www.careerpath.com
Hot Jobs	www.hotjobs.com
JOBTRAK	www.jobtrak.com
Monster Board	www.monster.com
PeopleSoft	www.peoplesoft.com
Recruiting on the Web	www.recruitersnetwork.com
Yahoo!	www.jobs.yahoo.com
America's JobBank	www.ajb.dni.us
CareerWeb	www.cweb.com
NationJob Network	www.nationjob.com
JOB HUNT: ONLINE JOB META-LIST	www.job-hunt.org
EuroJobs	www.eurojobs.com
The Career Crossroads	www.careerxroads.com (job seekers can scan as many as 50 databases with one search engine)

Web site alone receives about 35 million hits per month, from both job seekers and recruiters. Web sites such as Career Mosaic and E-Span are résumé database services because they give employers access to résumés submitted by job hunters. The organizers of E-Span explain to employers that the service provides access to millions of qualified candidates through the World Wide Web, the Internet, and more than 10 online networks and bulletin boards.

Many position announcements on the Internet require the job seeker to send a résumé by attached file, or an electronic résumé (described later in this chapter). Others request that the résumé by sent by fax or paper mail. Technical positions such as computer programmer, engineering technician, or accountant are more likely to be found on the Internet than general positions. The Internet is also a source of job openings for working on the Internet, including jobs such as *cybersmith* (creates and edits information in cyberspace) and *cybernaut* (navigates through cyberspace to locate data and information). Thousands of nontechnical positions are also listed on the Internet, even some at very high income levels. Job hunting on the Internet is menu driven, as you will discover if you visit the Web sites listed in Table 15-1.

Job hunting on the Internet can lead to a false sense of security. Using the Internet, a résumé is cast over a wide net, and hundreds of job postings can be explored. As a consequence, the job seeker may think that he or she can sit back and wait for a job offer to come through e-mail. In reality, the Internet is just one source of leads that should be used in conjunction with other job-finding methods. Remember also that thousands of other job seekers can access the same job opening, and many of the positions listed have already been filled.

An important danger in placing your résumé on the Internet is that is will be accessed by a third party and passed along to thousands of other prospective employers. Your résumé may wind up on the computer of your present employer, much to your embarrassment. Pam Dixon, an Internet job search

Skill-Building Exercise 15-1

JOB HUNTING ON THE WEB

Job hunting on the Web can be a rewarding or frustrating experience, depending on your skill in navigating job search Web sites and the availability of positions for a person with your qualifications. Use several job search Web sites to locate a position opening for the following three persons:

Position 1: You. Find a position listed on the Web that would appear to be an excellent fit for you at this time in your career.

Position 2: Sales representative, fluent in English and Japanese. Attempt to find an opening for an industrial sales representative or retail sales position that requires the applicant to be fluent in English and Japanese.

Position 3: Sports administrator. Attempt to find an opening for a sports administrator, typically a person who does administrative work for a professional sports team.

Set a time limit for your surfing, perhaps 60 minutes. If you are working in a team, each team member can search for one position. Share with each other your approaches and Web sites that appear to achieve the best results.

specialist, says "I get a minimum of two messages a week from readers saying they've lost their job from posting on the Net."[3] Yet Dixon also notes that some companies appoint a human resource specialist to search the Internet looking for résumés posted by present employees. The specialist then brings in the job seeker to attempt to *salvage,* or find ways to prevent the employee from leaving.[4] (Perhaps you will be offered more money and a nicer cubicle!)

Skill-Building Exercise 15-1 will give you an opportunity to learn first hand about job hunting on the Web.

Smile at Network Members and Interviewers

Assuming that you have the right qualifications, the simple act of smiling can be an effective job-hunting technique. According to career specialist James Challenger, "People would rather work with people who have pleasant dispositions. If you have been looking for a job for three months with no success, it may be hard to smile, but make yourself do it. It works."[5]

Smooth Out Rough Spots in Your Background

About 95 percent of employers routinely conduct background investigations of prospective employees. A background investigation by a firm hired for the purpose could include speaking to neighbors and coworkers about your reputation. In addition, the investigator may delve into your driving record, check for criminal charges or convictions, survey your credit record, and find out whether you have had disputes with the government about taxes. The infor-

mation just mentioned is used to supplement reference checks because so many employers are hesitant to say anything negative about past employees.

Any job seeker who has severe negative factors in his or her background cannot readily change the past. Yet the job seeker can receive copies of a credit bureau report to make sure it is fair and accurate. If inaccuracies exist, or certain credit problems have been resolved, the credit report might be changed in the applicant's favor. It might also be possible to obtain a more favorable reference from an employer by making a polite request. A third step can be to request a copy of the *consumer report,* which is a report of your reputation based on interviews with coworkers, neighbors, and others. A person might be able to negotiate a deletion of damaging information that is incorrect or exaggerated.[6]

THE JOB RÉSUMÉ AND COVER LETTER

No matter what method of job hunting you choose, inevitably somebody will ask you for a résumé. Sometimes you will be asked to complete a job application form instead of, or in addition to, a résumé. Résumés are also important for job hunting within your own firm. You may need one to be considered for a transfer with a large firm, or to be assigned to a team or project.

Résumé Purpose

Regard your résumé as a marketing tool for selling your skills and potential to handle new responsibilities. The most specific purpose of a résumé is to help you obtain an interview that can lead to a job. Your résumé must therefore attract enough attention for an employer to invite you for an interview. Recognize that you are competing against many carefully prepared résumés, some of which have been prepared with assistance from others. If the demand for your skills is high enough, it is conceivable that you will be hired without an interview.

Résumé Length and Format

Opinions vary about the desirable length for a résumé. For a recent graduate with limited work experience, a one-page résumé may be acceptable. For more experienced people, it would seem too short. Employers today demand considerable detail in résumés, particularly about the candidate's skills, accomplishments, and teamwork and leadership experience. Nevertheless, a four-page or longer résumé may irritate an impatient reader. Two pages is therefore recommended for early stages in your career.

A general-purpose hard-copy résumé is presented in Figure 15-2. Recognize that hiring managers and human resource professionals have widely different perceptions of what constitutes an effective résumé. Check at least two résumé guides before preparing a final version of your résumé.

A current development in résumé construction is to prepare one primarily for electronic databases. Many companies store résumés electronically, making it important to prepare one that is suitable for an electronic database. Should you prepare an electronic résumé, remember to create a file for your hard drive and a disk. If a job search Web site calls for an electronic résumé, it

Scott Wayland
170 Glenview Drive
Dallas, Texas 75243
Phone/Fax (312) 555-3986
swayland@frontiernet.net

Qualification Summary	Experience in selling industrial machinery. Education in business administration, combined with apprenticeship in tool and die making. In one year sold $375,000 worth of excess machine inventory. Received letter of commendation from company president.
Job Objective	Industrial sales, handling large, complex machinery. Willing to work largely on commission basis. Want to help my employer earn more profit.
Job Experience	
2000–present	Industrial account representative, Bainbridge Corporation, Dallas. Sell line of tool and die equipment to companies in Southwest. Responsibilities include servicing established accounts and canvassing new ones. Served on team establishing E-commerce capability.
1998–2000	Inside sales representative, Bainbridge Corporation. Answered customer inquiries. Filled orders for replacement parts. Trained for outside sales position. Served as sales team representative on company quality-improvement team.
1994–1998	Tool and die maker apprentice, Texas Metals, Inc., Dallas. Assisted senior tool and die makers during four-year training program. Worked on milling machines, jigs, punch presses, computer-assisted manufacturing, computer-assisted design (CAD/CAM).
Formal Education	
1994–2000	Madagascar College, Dallas, Texas. Associate Degree in Business Administration; graduated with 3.16 grade point average. Courses in marketing, sales techniques, human relations, accounting, and statistics. President of Commuter's Club.
1990–1994	Big Horn High, Dallas. Honors student; academic major with vocational elective. Played varsity football and basketball. Earned part of living by selling magazine subscriptions.
Job-Related Skills	Professional sales representative. Able to size up customer manufacturing problem and make recommendations for appropriate machinery. Precise in preparing call reports and expense accounts. Good skill in gathering input from the field for market research purposes. Can contribute to development of E-commerce site.
Personal Interests and Hobbies	Information technology enthusiast (developed and installed own Web site), scuba diving, recreational golf player, read trade and business magazines. Auto enthusiast, including restoring a 1972 Corvette.
References	On file with placement office at Madagascar College.

Figure 15-2 A General Purpose Résumé

can be entered into the right place on the Web page. At other times an electronic résumé is printed and mailed to the employer, who in turn uses an optical scanner to enter the résumé in the company database. A distinguishing feature of an electronic résumé is that it contains key words that fit the requirements of a keyword search. The job seeker should isolate keywords (nouns and adjectives) by placing them right under the individual's name, address, and telephone numbers. Zane K. Quible recommends that key words be selected from among the following information:[7]

➤ Titles of jobs held by applicant

➤ Names of job-related tasks performed by the applicant

➤ Industry jargon such as "zero defects," "customer delight," or "just-in-time inventory management." Also use acronyms such as JIT for "just in time."

➤ Special skills or knowledge possessed by the applicant such as knowledge of enterprise software, including SAP and Oracle

➤ Degrees earned

➤ High school program or college major (For college graduates, information about the high school program can be deleted.)

➤ High schools or colleges attended

➤ Special awards or honors received

➤ Nature of interpersonal skills the applicant possesses

Most of this information, of course, should also be included in a conventional printed résumé. Figure 15-3 illustrates an electronic résumé.

In preparing either a print or electronic résumé, keep in mind that certain key words or references attract the attention of managers and specialists who scan résumés. In today's market these are as follows: *languages, computer, experience, achievement, hard working, overseas experience, flexible, task-oriented, Internet,* and *E-commerce.*[8] A sensible tactic would be to mention those words that apply to you. Except for *languages* and *overseas experience*, these terms are widely applicable.

The Cover Letter

A résumé should be accompanied by a cover letter explaining who you are and why you are applying for this particular position. The cover letter customizes your approach to a particular employer, whereas the résumé is a more general approach. Sometimes it is helpful to prepare an attention-getting cover letter in which you make an assertive statement about how you intend to help the employer deal with an important problem. A person applying for a credit manager position might state, "Let me help you improve your cash flow by using the latest methods for getting customers to pay on time, or even early."

Employment specialist Richard H. Beatty recommends a slightly different version of the attention-getting cover letter. He explains that an effective cover

Sara L. Adams
123 Elmwood Terrace
Framingham, MA 01701
(617) 555-1485 FAX (617) 555-4587
SLAdams@hmp.aol

Keywords: Accountant. Bookkeeper. Accounts receivable ledger. Accounts payable ledger. Financial reports. Business Administration. Lotus 1-2-3. Excel. Windows 95. Windows 2000. French. Supervision. President's Honor Roll. Superior oral communication skills. Superior written communication skills. Self-starter. Quick learner. Conscientious. Detail oriented. Reliable. Top 5 percent of class. IBM-compatible computers. Lakeville College, Framingham, MA.

Job objective: To work as accountant or bookkeeper for private or public business, with eventual goal of becoming supervisor of bookkeeping or accounting or office manager.

Education:	Lakeville College, Framingham, MA, 1999–2001
	Accounting major. Associate's degree in Business Administration with High Honors.
	East Framingham High School, National Honor Society, 1995.
Experience:	London's Department Store, Framingham, MA, 1995–present.
	Full time for four years, part time while attending college. Performed bookkeeping and cashier activities. Maintained accounts receivable and accounts payable ledgers. Prepared variety of financial reports.
Key Accomplishment:	Developed a system of prompt payments that saved employer approximately $60,000 per year.
College Activities and Honors	President of Accounting Club for two years. Team Leader of Student Misconduct Committee. President's Honor Roll, each semester 1999–2001. Delta Phi Kappa Honorary, 1999–2001

Figure 15-3 Electronic Résumé

letter has five parts: an attention-grabbing introduction, a paragraph selling your value to the employer, a background summary paragraph, a compelling follow-up action statement, and an appreciative close. Beatty recommends mentioning a personal contact as part of the attention grabber.[9] An example: "John Kowolski, your computer operations manager, mentioned that you are looking for a talented person to manage your Web site. I would very much like to talk to you about this position."

PERFORMING WELL IN A JOB INTERVIEW

After a prospective employer has reacted favorably to your cover letter and résumé, the next step is a telephone screening interview or a more comprehensive job interview. The purpose of the telephone screening interview is gen-

erally to obtain some indication of the candidate's oral communication skills. Such an interview is most likely when one applies for a customer contact position or one that requires knowledge of a second language. Having passed the screening interview, the candidate is invited for an in-person job interview. Another type of screening interview is to respond to computerized questions, including a sample job problem. Your answers are printed for the interviewer to review. Candidates who get through the computer-assisted interview get to be interviewed by a company representative.[10]

Typically the applicant is interviewed by one person at a time, yet team interviews are becoming more commonplace. In this format, members of the team or department with whom you would be working take turns asking you questions. One justification for team interviews is to observe how the candidate fits in with the team.

A general guide for performing well in the job interview is to present a positive but accurate picture of yourself. Your chances of performing well in a job increase if you are suited for the job. Tricking a prospective employer into hiring you when you are not qualified is therefore self-defeating in terms of your career. Outright deception, such as falsifying one's educational or employment record, is widely practiced during interviews, on résumés, and in cover letters. If the person is hired and the deception is discovered later, he or she is subject to dismissal. Following is a list of some key points to keep in mind when being interviewed for a job you want:

1. *Be prepared, look relaxed, and make the interviewer feel comfortable.* Coming to the interview fully prepared to discuss yourself and your background and knowing key facts about the prospective employer will help you look relaxed. Many people today use company Web sites to gather background information about the prospective employer.

2. *Establish a link between you and the prospective employer.* A good way to build rapport between you and the prospective employer is to mention some plausible link you have with that firm. To illustrate, if being interviewed for a position at a Kmart, one might say, "It's fun to visit the office part of Kmart. Our family has been shopping here for years. In fact, I bought a CD player here last month. It works great."

3. *Ask perceptive questions.* The best questions are sincere ones that reflect an interest in the content of the job (intrinsic motivators) and job performance, rather than benefits and social activities. A good question to ask is "What would you consider to be outstanding performance in this job?" If the issue of compensation is not introduced by the interviewer, ask about such matters after first discussing the job and your qualifications.

4. *Be prepared to discuss your strengths and developmental opportunities.* Most interviewers will ask you to discuss your strengths and developmental opportunities. (These and other frequently asked questions are presented in Figure 15-4.) Knowledge of strengths hints at how good your

An effective way of preparing for job interviews is to rehearse answers to the types of questions you will most likely be asked by the interviewer. The following questions are a sampling of the types found in most employment interviews. Rehearse answers to them prior to going out on job interviews. One good rehearsal method is to role play the employment interview with a friend who asks these typical questions or to videotape yourself.

1. Why did you apply for this job?
2. What are your career goals?
3. What salary are you worth?
4. What new job skills would you like to acquire in the next few years?
5. Give me an example of how you displayed good teamwork.
6. Describe how you have shown leadership on the job or off the job.
7. What are your strengths (or good points)?
8. What are your weaknesses (or areas for needed improvement)?
9. Why should we hire you instead of other candidates for this position?
10. How well do you work under pressure?
11. What positions with other companies are you applying for?
12. What makes you think you will be successful in business?
13. What do you know about our firm?
14. Here is a sample job problem. How would you handle it?
15. What questions do you have for me?

Figure 15-4 Questions Frequently Asked of Job Candidates

potential job performance will be. If you deny having areas for improvement you will appear uninsightful or defensive. Some candidates describe developmental opportunities that could be interpreted as strengths. A case in point: "I have been criticized for expecting too much from myself and others." Do you think this approach is unethical?

5. *Be prepared to respond to behavioral interview questions.* A *behavioral interview* asks questions directly about the candidate's behavior in relation to an important job activity. The job candidate is expected to give samples of important job behaviors. The behavioral interview is therefore more applicable to candidates with substantial work experience. Two behavioral inquiries are "Tell me about a time in which your ability to work well on a team contributed to the success of a project" and "Give me an example of a creative suggestion you made that was actually implemented. In what way did it help the company?" To prepare for such questions, think of some examples of how you handled a few difficult job challenges. The idea is to document specific actions you took or behaviors you engaged in that contributed to a favorable outcome.

6. *Show how you can help the employer.* A prospective employer wants to know whether you will be able to perform the job well. Direct much of your conversation toward how you intend to help the company solve problems and get important work accomplished. Whatever the question, think about what details of your skills and experiences will be useful to the employer.

Skill-Building Exercise 15-2

THE JOB INTERVIEW

As described in Figure 15-4, a good way to prepare for a job interview is to rehearse answers to frequently asked questions. In this role play, one student will be the interviewer and one the interviewee (job applicant). The job in question is that of property manager for a large apartment complex in Phoenix, Arizona. Assume that the applicant really wants the job. The interviewer, having taking a course in human resource management, will ask many of the questions in Figure 15-4. In addition, the interviewer will ask at least one behavioral question, perhaps about teamwork. The interviewer might also have other questions, such as "Why do you want to live in Phoenix?"

Before proceeding with the role play, both people should review the information in this chapter about the job interview and in Chapter 3 about listening.

7. *Send a follow-up letter.* Mail a courteous follow-up letter several days after the interview, particularly if you want the job. A follow-up letter is a tip-off that you are truly interested in the position. You should state your attitudes toward the position, the team, and the company and summarize any conclusions reached about your discussion.

Now do Skill-Building Exercise 15-2 to practice the job interview.

THE VERTICAL AND HORIZONTAL CAREER PATHS

Career planning can begin at any point, including a kindergarten child saying, "I want to be an astronaut." Many other people think about developing their career after they have worked in a full-time professional position for several years. Planning and developing your career involves some form of goal setting. If your goals are laid out systematically to lead to your ultimate career goal, you have established a **career path**, a sequence of positions necessary to achieve a goal. Here we look at the more traditional career path with an emphasis on moving upward, along with the more contemporary path that emphasizes acquiring new skills and knowledge.

THE VERTICAL (TRADITIONAL) CAREER PATH

The vertical, or traditional, career path is based on the idea that a person continues to grow in responsibility with the aim of reaching a target position, such as becoming a top-level manager. The vertical career path is synonymous with "climbing the corporate ladder." The same path is based somewhat on the unwritten contract that a good performer will have the opportunity to work for one firm for a long time and receive many promotions in the process. However, a vertical career path can be spread out over several employers.

As the year 2000 approached, many employers had returned to the old-fashioned idea of cultivating corporate loyalty by emphasizing promotions for good performers. The reason for the change in attitude by top management was a shortage of workers to fill many positions. After an era of frequent downsizings, executives are now trying to send a new message to employees: "Don't leave. We need you. Work for us—you can build a career here."[11] Inducements for staying include helping workers develop skills to advance their careers and making it easier to change jobs with the company. Employees who are downsized in one unit of a firm are often transferred to another unit.

A career path should be related to the present and future demands of one firm or the industry. If you aspire toward a high-level manufacturing position, it would be vital to know the future of manufacturing in that firm and in the industry. Many U. S. firms, for example, plan to conduct more of their manufacturing in the Pacific Rim and Mexico. If you were really determined, you might study the appropriate language and ready yourself for a foreign position.

While laying out a career path, it is also helpful to list your personal goals. They should mesh with your work plans to avoid major conflicts in your life. Some life-styles, for example, are incompatible with some career paths. It would be difficult to develop a stable home life (spouse, children, friends, community activities, sports team, and garden) if a person aspired toward holding field positions in international marketing. Contingency ("what if") plans should also be incorporated into a well-designed career path. For instance, "If I am not promoted within two years, I will pursue an advanced degree."

Mary Gonzalez, an ambitious 20-year-old, formulated the career path shown in Figure 15-5 prior to receiving an associate degree in business management. After she presented her tentative career path to her classmates, several accused Mary of aiming too high. Mary's career goals are high, but she has established contingency plans.

A career path laid out in chart form gives a person a clear perception of climbing steps toward his or her target position. As each position is attained, the corresponding step can be shaded in color or cross-hatched. The steps, or goals, include a time element, which is helpful for sound career management even in work environments that are less predictable than they used to be. Your long-range goal might be clearly established in your mind (such as become regional manager of a hotel chain). At the same time, you must establish short-range (get any kind of job in a hotel) and intermediate-range (be manager of a hotel by age 27) goals. Goals set too far in the future that are not supported with more immediate goals may lose their motivational value.

THE HORIZONTAL CAREER PATH

In many organizations, the hope of staying for a long time and receiving a long series of promotions has vanished. Instead of climbing the ladder, the person is placed on a jungle gym in which he or she makes a series of moves in different directions. Each position in the company represents a rung on the jungle gym. Managers and others make their careers by scrambling over the frame or moving between positions.[12]

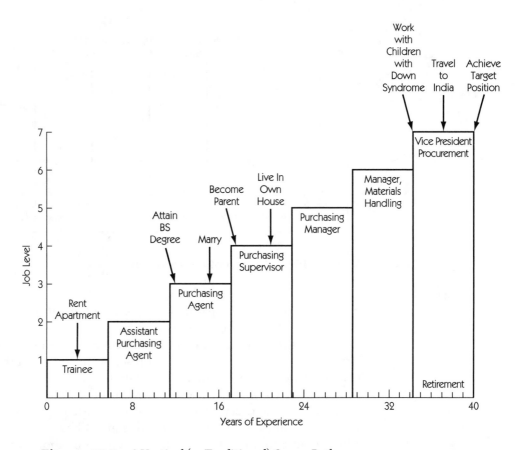

Figure 15-5 A Vertical (or Traditional) Career Path

Typically these moves in the modern organization are horizontal rather than vertical. A significant feature of the horizontal career path is that people are more likely to advance by moving sideways than by moving up. Or at least people who get ahead will spend a considerable part of their career working in different positions at or nearly at the same level. In addition, they may occasionally move to a lower-level position in order to gain valuable experience. With a horizontal career path, the major reward is no longer promotion, but the opportunity to gain more experience and increase job skills.

The horizontal career path is closely linked to the new employment contract that offers shared responsibility for career growth. The old employment contract was lifetime employment in exchange for corporate loyalty. Instead, today employees get a chance to develop new technical and professional skills. Instead of being offered job security, they become more employable because of the diversity of skills they acquire. The company provides the environment for learning, and the employees are responsible for developing their skills. (As mentioned earlier, many employers are reverting to the old promises of an opportunity to climb the organizational ladder. Furthermore, it is not unusual for workers to aspire toward holding higher-level, higher-paying positions.)

Figure 15-6 A Horizontal Career Path

A horizontal career path, as well as a traditional (or vertical) career path, does not necessarily mean the person stays with the same firm. For example, a worker might spend three years in one company as an electronics technician, three years in another as a sales representative, and then three years as a customer service specialist in a third company. All three positions would be approximately at the same level. The third company then promotes the individual to a much-deserved position as the marketing team leader. Figure 15-6 illustrates a horizontal career path for Larry Chang, a career school graduate who did attempt to make long-range predictions about his career. Notice that all the positions through year 17 are at the first level, and the positions for year 22 and beyond are at the second level. Chang's career contingency plans are as follows:

(1) If cannot obtain experience as a market research analyst, customer service rep, or sales rep, will continue to develop as electronics technician. (2) If cannot find employment as a sales manager, will attempt to become supervisor of electronic technicians. (3) If do not raise sufficient funds for starting own business, will continue in corporate job until retirement.

USING CAREER ADVANCEMENT STRATEGIES AND TACTICS

The many ways of improving interpersonal relationships described in this book can help advance and enhance a person's career. People who enhance their relationships with others are laying a foundation for career advancement. Here we will describe 12 other key strategies and tactics for career advancement, whether the advancement be vertical, horizontal, or a combination of the two. The first seven of the methods described deal more with controlling your own

characteristics and behaviors, whereas the remaining five deal more with interacting with the environment.

Be Passionate About Your Work

Successful people in all fields are passionate about their work. Without passion, you rely too heavily on external rewards to sustain effort. Passion contributes to both your career growth and company productivity.[13] Effective leaders and business owners are usually passionate about their work. Being passionate is also important because it is linked to developing expertise and high job performance.

The surest path to career success is to identify your area of expertise and then build a career around it. The more passionate you are about your area of expertise, the better. Becoming wealthy and achieving recognition are by-products of making effective use of your talents. Expertise combined with passion helps you attain high job performance. Consistently good job performance is the foundation on which you build your career. Job competence is still the major success ingredient in all but the most political organizations (those where favoritism outweighs merit).

Develop a Code of Professional Ethics

Another solid foundation for developing a career is to establish a personal ethical code. An ethical code determines what behavior is right or wrong, good or bad, based on values. The values stem from cultural upbringing, religious teachings, peer influences, and professional or industry standards. As implied in Chapter 13, a code of professional ethics helps a worker deal with such issues as accepting bribes, backstabbing coworkers, and sexually harassing a work associate.

Develop a Proactive Personality

If you are an active agent in taking control of the forces around you, you stand a better chance of capitalizing on opportunities. Also, you will seek out opportunities such as seeing problems that need fixing. A **proactive personality** is a person who is relatively unconstrained by situational forces and who brings about environmental change. People who are highly proactive identify opportunities and act on them, show initiative, and keep trying until they bring about meaningful change. A health and safety specialist with a proactive personality, for example, might identify a health hazard others had missed. She would identify the nature of the problem and urge management to supply funding to control the problem. Ultimately her efforts in preventing major health problems would be recognized.

A study conducted with close to 500 men and women workers in diverse occupations examined the relationship between career success and a proactive personality. Proactive personality, as measured by a test, was related to salary, promotions, and career satisfaction.[14]

It may not be easy to develop a proactive personality, but a person can get started by taking more initiative to fix problems and attempt to be more self-

starting. A proactive personality is close in meaning to having high perceived control over situations.

Keep Growing Through Continuous Learning and Self-Development

Given that continuous learning is part of the new employment contract, engaging in regular learning can take many forms, including formal schooling, attending training programs and seminars, and self-study, including using the Internet. It is particularly important to engage in new learning in areas of interest to the company, such as developing proficiency in a second language if the company has customers and employees in other countries. Many companies support continuous learning because they perceive themselves to be *learning organizations*. It may therefore be easy for you to implement the tactic of growth through continuous learning.

Document Your Accomplishments

Keeping an accurate record of what you have accomplished in your career can be valuable when being considered for reassignment, promotion, or applying for a position outside your company. The same log of accomplishments is useful for résumé preparation. It is preferable to point to tangible, quantifiable accomplishments than to another person's subjective impression of your performance. Let's assume that a retail store manager reduced inventory shrinkage by 30 percent in one year. It would be better to state that fact than to record a statement from the manager saying that "Kelly shows outstanding ability to reduce inventory shrinkage."

Documenting your accomplishments in a business field is similar to a person in the arts such as a photographer, interior designer, or architect developing a portfolio of work. When the person applies for a job or assignment, he or she carries along the portfolio of representative work.

Documentation enables you to promote yourself in a dignified, tactful way. When discussing work with key people in the company, let them know of your good deeds without taking too much credit for team accomplishments. If you distinguish yourself in the community, for example, by fundraising for a shelter for the homeless, let your manager know of your activities. The rationale is that most companies want their workers to be responsible community members.

Project a Professional Image

Your clothing, desk and work area, speech, and general knowledge should project the image of a professional, responsible person if you seek career advancement. Good grammar and sentence structure can give you the edge because so many people use highly informal patterns of speech. Being a knowledgeable person is important because today's professional businessperson is supposed to be aware of the external environment. Also, as noted by a human relations specialist, projecting a professional image hastens the development of trust and rapport in business relationships.[15]

A challenge in projecting a professional image is to figure out what constitutes a professional image in your particular environment. The information

technology field in Silicon Valley, for example, is extremely informal. A programmer who wore a tank top and running shoes and brought a parrot to the office might be considered to project a professional image. Yet a marketing specialist for a health insurance provider behaving in the same way in Boston would be perceived as unprofessional.

Perceive Yourself as a Provider of Services

A useful perspective for upgrading your professional self-image and enhancing your feelings of job security is to perceive yourself as something other than a traditional employee. According to career specialist John A. Thomson, everyone should see himself or herself as a *personal service business entity*. Basically you are a business, offering the company (also your client from this perspective) a valuable service. You keep offering the service so long as the company keeps you on the payroll and you enjoy the work. Note the similarity to a high-level professional such as a dentist or information technology consultant. You are offering a service that many people need. Part of the same perception is that you own your skills, and that these are the service your business (you) offer to others.[16]

Another way of perceiving yourself as different from a traditional employee is to think of yourself as a professional-level temporary employee. Sometimes you will have a long stay with one employer, acting like a permatemp. At other times, you will move on to another company where your skills are more in need.

Develop Depth and Breadth

A continuing concern about career management is whether to acquire substantial depth in a specialty or to obtain broader experience. Is it better to be a specialist or a generalist? In general it pays to have good depth in one area of expertise, yet also acquire broad experience. A distribution specialist who helped set up shipping systems in an automobile supply company, an office supply company, and a hospital supply company would have excellent credentials. Yet some career specialists would argue that knowing one industry well has its merits.

If your goal is to become an executive, broadening your experience is a career enhancer. A person who held positions in sales and manufacturing would have broad experience. Breadth could come about also by experience in different industries, such as retailing and mining, or by holding positions in different companies. Being assigned to different teams, projects, and committees is another natural broadening experience. Another approach to broadening is to self-study different aspects of the business.

Rely on a Network of Successful People

Networking has already been described as a major assist to finding a job. Members of your network can also help you by assisting with difficult job problems, providing emotional support, buying your products or services, and offering you good prices on their products or services. The starting point in networking is to obtain an ample supply of business cards. You then give a card to any person you meet who might be able to help you now or in the future.

While first developing your network, be inclusive. Sandy Vilas says, "Remember the 3-foot rule—anyone within three feet of you is someone you can network with."[17] Later, as your network develops, you can strive to include a greater number of influential and successful people. Skill-Building Exercise 15-3 provides suggestions for systematically building your network.

Work with a Mentor

In Chapter 10 mentoring was presented as a way of helping people grow and develop. Mention also was made that minority group members who advanced in their careers attributed some of their success to mentors. Here we reemphasize that having a mentor can facilitate career advancement. Ideally a person should develop a small network of mentors who give advice and counsel on different topics such as job advancement opportunities and how to solve a difficult problem.

Many people who receive exceptional promotions within their own firms, or receive excellent job offers from other companies, are chosen by their mentors. At the root of mentoring is the ability to attract and build a relationship with a person who is more experienced and talented than yourself.

Find a Good Person–Organization Fit

Assuming that you have the luxury of selecting among different prospective employers, it is best to work for a company where your personality and style fit the organization culture. A **person–organization fit** is the compatibility of the individual and the organization. Job interviews represent a good opportunity for evaluating a person–organization fit for both the applicant and the employer.[18]

The compatibility often centers around the extent to which a person's major work-related values and personality traits fit major elements of the organization culture. Following this idea, a person who is adventuresome and risk taking would achieve highest performance and satisfaction in an organization in which adventuresome behavior and risk taking are valued. Conversely, a methodical and conservative individual should join a slow-moving bureaucracy. How much an organization emphasizes individual effort versus teamwork is another important area for person–organization fit. Workers who enjoy teamwork would fit better in a teamwork-oriented culture.

Person–organization fit can also include superficial aspects of behavior such as physical appearance and dress. For example, a person who dressed like a Wall Street investment banker might not feel comfortable working in a high-tech firm in California where jeans and sandals were standard work attire. As a consequence of not feeling comfortable in your work environment, you might not perform at your best.

Take Sensible Risks

People who make it big in their careers usually take sensible risks on their journey to success. Among these risks would be to work for a fledgling company that offers big promises but a modest starting salary, or to take an overseas assignment with no promise of a good position when you return. Purchasing stock in start-up companies is *sometimes* a sensible risk, if you do not absolutely

Skill-Building Exercise 15-3

BUILDING YOUR NETWORK

Networking can be regarded as the process of building a team that works with you to achieve success. You can start the following exercise now, but it will probably take your entire career to implement completely. To start networking, or make your present networking more systematic, take the following steps:

Step 1: Jot down your top three goals or objectives for the following three months, such as obtaining a new job or promotion, starting a small business, or doing a field research study.

1. _____

2. _____

3. _____

Step 2: List family members, friends, or acquaintances who could assist you in meeting your goals or objectives. Prepare a contact card, or database entry, for each person on your list, including as many details as you can about the person, the person's family, friends, employers, and contacts.

Step 3: Identify what assistance you will request of your contact, or contacts. Be realistic in light of your prior investment in the relationship. Remember, you have to be a friend to have a friend.

Step 4: Identify how you will meet your contact or contacts during the next month. Could it be for lunch, at an athletic field, night club, sports club, recreational facility on campus, cafeteria, and so forth? Learn more about your contacts during your face-to-face meetings. In some cases you may have to use the telephone or e-mail to substitute for an in-person meeting. Look for ways to mutually benefit from the relationship. At the beginning of each week, verify that you have made a small investment in building these relationships.

Step 5: Ask for the help you need. A network must benefit you. Thank the contact for any help given. Jot down on your planner a reminder to make a follow-up call, letter, or e-mail message to your contacts. In this way you will have less work to do before you make another request for help.

Step 6: For each person in your network, think of a favor, however small, you can return to him or her. Without reciprocity, a network fades rapidly.

Source: Adapted and expanded from Cheryl Kitter, "Taking the Work Out of Networking," Success Workshop, supplement to *The Pryor Report*, March 1998, pp. 1–2.

need the funds for living expenses. Industrial relations manager Michael Oliver offers this advice:

> If you want to achieve something really creative, thus enhancing your profession, then try a little risk taking. This doesn't mean you should pick up a lance and seek out a windmill. Balance your risk taking with good sense so you will be able to reach a new comfort level somewhere between the

role of a bureaucratic follower and leaper of tall buildings. The goal should be to develop credibility without perpetrating a maverick reputation.[19]

OVERCOMING CAREER BARRIERS

Another major aspect of career management is to be able to overcome career barriers or hurdles, as recognized in the chapter opener about adversity training. You may also recall from Chapter 8 that resiliency is an important leadership characteristic. People who are reslilient, or *psychologically hardy,* have developed the skills to overcome problems. They are able to overcome the emotional hurt associated with setback. After dealing with their emotions, they tackle the hurdle with a problem-solving approach.[20] Two representative barriers that many people face are overcoming the loss of employment and coping with hidden barriers to advancement.

COPING WITH JOB LOSS

Much has been written and said in recent years about coping with job loss because of the many downsizings in business, government, and education. Even during prosperous times, job loss can be a big emotional hurt and a major inconvenience. The best strategy for coping with job loss is to have good credentials, including a good reputation, and marketable skills. In addition, the following suggestions are in order:[21]

1. *Avoid panic.* Work hard at avoiding panic, because panic is a natural response to trauma that often immobilizes a person. The danger is that the person will run in the wrong direction such as grabbing a lower-paying job that does not fit his or her career plan. Talking over your job loss with a confidant (or confidante) will sometimes help control panic.

2. *Do a reality check.* Attempt to uncover what you might have done wrong that could have contributed to the job loss. Take stock of your assets and what you can offer prospective employers. Investigate the job market for a person of your background. Think through whether the network you have established will be helpful in finding new employment.

3. *Guard against depression and stay physically healthy.* Again we emphasize talking about your problems with one or two confidants. Get ample exercise and rest so you look your best when making contacts or going out on job interviews.

4. *Avoid bitterness and making angry statements about your past employer—especially to prospective employers.* Rehearse making whatever positive statements you can about your most recent employment, and practice smiling. Here is an example of a positive statement about a negative situation: "Although my job was eliminated, I am proud of what I accomplished during my stay. I am also thankful for how much I learned. My

only regret is that I was not able to continue contributing and learning."

5. *Give full-time attention to conducting a job campaign.* When unemployed your job is finding a job, and it should be a full-time, energetic activity including all the steps described in this chapter. A major mistake many job searchers make is to slow down or stop their efforts when the first warm job lead surfaces. Keep searching until you have reached an employment agreement. And don't discard the leads your job search has created until you are secure in your new position.

DEALING WITH THE GLASS CEILING

Many women and minority-group members complain that they may get off to a good start in their careers, but at some point the promotions stop. Outright discrimination may not be evident, but somehow a subtle barrier to further growth emerges despite all the progress women and minority-group members have made in business. A **glass ceiling** is an invisible but difficult-to-penetrate barrier to promotion based on subtle attitudes and prejudices. For example, less than 3 percent of senior executive positions in business are occupied by women and minorities combined.

Although the glass ceiling is difficult to crack, many women and minority-group members are making progress. A survey of Fortune 1000 CEOs, and the highest-ranking women in their companies, identified career-advancement strategies and tactics used by women to rise to the top.[22] (Notice that these women pursued a traditional career path.) The seven most effective strategies the women used are shown in Table 15-1. You will observe that the strategies chosen by the glass-ceiling breakers are similar to the career-advancement tactics described in this chapter. A later study by the career-research firm Catalyst investigated why minority-group women managers were not able to penetrate the glass ceiling. Nearly 50 percent of the women surveyed cited the lack of an influential mentor, in comparison to 29 percent of white women.[23]

An important conclusion is that workers in professional-level jobs who want to overcome hidden barriers to success should make effective use of sensible career-advancement strategies and tactics. Evidence presented here and in Chapter 10 emphasizes the importance of finding the right mentor to enhance your career.

SUMMARY

Recommended job-hunting tactics include the following:

1. Identify your job objectives.

2. Be aware of qualifications sought by employers.

3. Identify your skills and potential contribution.

4. Develop a comprehensive marketing strategy.

TABLE 15-1 Percentage of Women Using Seven Leading Strategies to Break the Glass Ceiling

Strategy	Critical	Fairly Important	Not Important	Did Not Use
Consistently exceed performance expectations	77	22	1	0
Develop style that men are comfortable with	61	35	3	1
Seek difficult or high-visibility assignments	50	44	2	4
Have an influential mentor	37	44	9	9
Network with influential colleagues	28	56	9	6
Gain line management experience	25	29	11	33
Move from one functional area to another (gain breadth)	23	34	20	22

Note: Not all percentages add to 100 because of rounding errors by researchers.

Source: Excerpted from Belle Rose Ragins, Bickely Townsend, and Mary Mattis, "Gender Gap in the Executive Suite," *Academy of Management Executive,* February 1998, p. 29.

5. Use networking to reach company insiders.

6. Use the Internet and résumé database services.

7. Smile at network members and interviewers.

8. Smooth out the rough spots in your background.

Job hunting almost always requires a résumé, with two pages in length recommended. A frequent requirement is to construct a résumé for an electronic database. Résumés should emphasize skills and accomplishments. A résumé should almost always be accompanied by a cover letter explaining how you can help the organization and why you are applying for this particular job.

Screening interviews, including computer-assisted ones, precede a full job interview. A general guide for performing well in an interview is to present a positive but accurate picture of yourself. More specific suggestions include the following:

1. Be prepared, look relaxed, and make the interviewer feel comfortable.

2. Establish a link between you and the employer.

3. Ask perceptive questions.

4. Be prepared to discuss your strengths and developmental opportunities.

5. Be prepared to respond to behavioral (examples of job behaviors) interview questions.

6. Show how you can help the employer.

7. Send a follow-up letter.

The vertical, or traditional, career path is based on the idea that a person continues to grow in responsibility with the aim of reaching a target position,

such as becoming a top-level manager. A vertical path is based on the traditional employment contract. A vertical career path should be related to the present and future demands of one firm or the industry. The horizontal career path is less predictable; it resembles a jungle gym. A horizontal career path emphasizes lateral moves with an opportunity to gain more experience and increase job skills. A horizontal path is closely linked to the new employment contract that offers shared responsibility for career growth. Career paths should have contingency plans.

Improving interpersonal relationships assists career advancement. In addition, the following strategies and tactics are relevant:

1. Be passionate about your work.

2. Develop a code of professional ethics.

3. Develop a proactive personality.

4. Keep growing through continuous learning and self-development.

5. Document your accomplishments.

6. Project a professional image.

7. Perceive yourself as a provider of services.

8. Develop depth and breadth.

9. Rely on a network of successful people.

10. Work with a mentor.

11. Find a good person–organization fit.

12. Take sensible risks.

Another important aspect of career management is to be able to cope with barriers or problems. Being a resilient, or psychologically hardy, person is helpful. Two key career barriers are coping with job loss and, for some people, dealing with invisible barriers to promotion (the glass ceiling).

QUESTIONS FOR DISCUSSION AND REVIEW

1. Identify four situations in a career in which conducting a job campaign would be necessary.

2. Why do many employers look for signs of emotional intelligence when hiring candidates for professional-level positions?

3. As part of recruiting on the Internet, some human resource specialists hunt through the files of other companies to find résumés of employees who have certain key skills. (They gain access through a process called "flipping a Web site.") What is your opinion of the ethics of this approach to recruiting?

4. What is your evaluation of the ethics of a company firing a present employee when a company representative finds the employee's résumé on the Internet?

5. Why is a horizontal career path referred to as a *jungle gym?*

6. Give an example from your own life in which you behaved as if you were a proactive personality.

7. In the field you are in, or intend to enter, what are some of the characteristics of a professional image?

8. How would you rate the effectiveness of sending e-mail messages to people as a method of sustaining a network?

9. In your own words, what really is a *glass ceiling?* Why the choice or words, *glass ceiling?*

10. What is the most useful idea you picked up from this chapter about either conducting a job campaign or managing your career?

A Interpersonal Relations Case Problem

WHY ISN'T MY RÉSUMÉ GETTING RESULTS?

Billy Joe Wentworth was working in the family business as a manufacturing technician while he attended career school. Although he got along well with his family members, Billy Joe wanted to find employment elsewhere so he could build a career on his own. Billy Joe's job objective was a position in industrial sales. He compiled a long list of prospective employers. He developed the list from personal contacts, classified ads in newspapers, and job openings posted on the Internet. Billy Joe clipped a business card with a brief handwritten noted to each résumé. The note usually said something to the effect, "Job sounds great. Let's schedule an interview at your convenience." The résumé is shown in the accompanying exhibit.

After mailing out 200 résumés, Billy Joe still did not have an interview. He asked his uncle and mentor, the owner of the family business, "Why isn't my résumé getting results?"

Case Questions

1. What suggestions can you make to Billy Joe for improving his résumé? Or does it require improvement?

2. What is your evaluation of Billy Joe's approach to creating a cover letter?

(Continued)

Exhibit 1

RÉSUMÉ OF BILLY JOE WENTWORTH

BILLY JOE WENTWORTH
275 Birdwhistle Lane
Cleveland, Ohio 44131
(216) 555-7512(Please call after 7 PM weekday nights)
Billyjoe@wentworth.com

Objective

Long-range goal is Vice President of sales of major corporation. For now, industrial sales representative paid by with salary and commission.

Job Experience

Five years experience in Wentworth industries as manufacturing technician, tool crib attendant, shipper, and floor sweeper. Voted as "employee of the month" twice. Two years experience in newspaper delivery business. Distributed newspapers door to door, responsible for accounts receivable and development of new business in my territory.

Education

Justin Peabody Career College, business administration major with manufacturing technology minor. Expect degree in June 2001. 2.65 GPA. Took courses in sales management and selling. Received a B+ in professional selling course.
Cleveland Heights High School, business and technology major, 1994–1998. Graduated 45th in class of 125. 82% average.

Skills and Talents

Good knowledge of manufacturing equipment; friends say I'm a born leader; have been offered supervisory position in Wentworth Industries; real go getter.

References

Okay to contract present employer except for my immediate supervisor Jill Baxter with whom I have a personality clash.

Glossary

action plan A series of steps to achieve a goal.

active listener A person who listens intensely, with the goal of empathizing with the speaker.

aggressive personality A person who verbally, and sometimes physically, attacks others frequently.

assertiveness Being forthright in expressing demands, opinions, feelings, and attitudes.

behavior modification An attempt to change behavior by manipulating rewards and punishments.

brainstorming A group problem-solving technique that promotes creativity by encouraging idea generation through noncritical discussion.

brainwriting Brainstorming by individuals working alone.

burnout A condition of emotional, mental, and physical exhaustion in response to long-term stressors.

business etiquette A special code of behavior required in work situations.

career path A sequence of positions necessary to achieve a goal.

carpal tunnel syndrome A condition that occurs when repetitive flexing and extension of the wrist causes the tendons to swell, thus trapping and pinching the median nerve.

casual time orientation A cultural characteristic in which people view time as an unlimited and unending resource and therefore tend to be patient.

character trait An enduring characteristic of a person that is related to moral and ethical behavior that shows up consistently.

charisma A special quality of leaders whose purposes, powers, and extraordinary determination differentiate them from others. (However, people besides leaders can be charismatic.)

coaching A method of helping workers grow and develop and improve their job competence by providing suggestions and encouragement.

cognitive factors The collective term for problem-solving and intellectual skills.

cognitive restructuring Mentally converting negative aspects into positive ones by looking for the positive elements in a situation.

cognitive style Mental processes used to perceive and make judgments from situations.

collectivism A feeling that the group and society should receive top priority, rather than the individual.

communication The sending, receiving, and understanding of messages.

complementary transactions An exchange of words between two people that reduces tension and moves the two people toward a positive resolution.

compromise Settlement of differences by mutual concessions.

concern for others An emphasis on personal relationships and a concern for the welfare of others.

conflict A situation in which two or more goals, values, or events are incompatible or mutually exclusive.

conflict of interest A situation that occurs when a person's judgment or objectivity is compromised.

consensus General acceptance by the group of a decision.

cross-functional team A work group composed of workers from different specialties.

cultural fluency The ability to conduct business in a diverse, international environment.

cultural sensitivity An awareness of and willingness to investigate the reasons why people of another culture act as they do.

cultural training A set of learning experiences designed to help employees understand the customs, traditions, and beliefs of another culture.

cycle-of-service chart A method of tracking the moments of truth with respect to customer service.

defensive communication The tendency to receive messages in such a way that self-esteem is protected.

defining moment Choosing between two or more ideals in which one deeply believe.

denial The suppression of information a person finds uncomfortable.

developmental need A specific area in which a person needs to change or improve.

difficult person An individual who creates problems for others, even though he or she has the skill and mental ability to do otherwise.

disability A physical or mental condition that substantially limits an individual's major life activities.

diversity training (or valuing-differences training) Training that attempts to bring about workplace harmony by teaching people how to get along better with diverse work associates.

effort-to-performance expectancy The probability assigned by the individual that effort will lead to performing the task correctly.

electronic brainstorming Method of generating ideas with the aid of a computer. Group members simultaneously and anonymously enter their suggestions into a computer, and the ideas are distributed to monitors of other group members.

emotional intelligence Qualities such as understanding one's own feelings, empathy for others, and the regulation of emotion to enhance living.

empathy In communication, imagining oneself in the receiver's role, and assuming the viewpoints and emotions of that individual.

empowerment The process of managers transferring, or sharing, power with lower-ranking employees.

ethical screening Running a contemplated decision or action through an ethics test.

ethics The moral choices a person makes.

expectancy theory A motivation theory based on the premise that the effort people expend depends on the reward they expect to receive in return.

extinction Decreasing the frequency of undesirable behavior by removing the desirable consequence of such behavior.

feedback In communication, messages sent back and forth to the sender.

feeling-type individuals People who have a need to conform and adapt to the wishes of others.

femininity In the study of cultures, an emphasis on personal relationships and a concern for others.

fight-or-flight response The body's physiological and chemical battle against a stressor in which the person tries to cope with the adversity head-on or tries to flee from the scene.

formality A cultural characteristic of attaching considerable importance to tradition, ceremony, social rules, and rank.

frame of reference The fact that people perceive words and concepts differently because their vantage points and perspectives differ.

g (general) factor A factor in intelligence that contributes to the ability to perform well in many tasks.

glass ceiling An invisible but difficult-to-penetrate barrier to promotion based on subtle attitudes and prejudices.

group decision making The process of reaching a judgment based on feedback from more than one individual.

group norms The unwritten set of expectations for group members.

groupthink A deterioration of mental efficiency, reality testing, and moral judgment in the interest of group solidarity.

groupware Technology designed to facilitate the work of groups.

high-context culture A culture that makes extensive use of body language.

image exchanging A technique for resolving conflict in which two antagonists make it clear that they each understand the other person's point of view.

impression management A set of behaviors directed at enhancing one's image by drawing attention to oneself.

individual differences Variations in how people respond to the same situation based on personal characteristics.

individualism A mental set in which people see themselves first as individuals and believe that their own interests take priority.

informal learning The acquisition of knowledge and skills that take place naturally outside of a structured learning environment.

informality A cultural characteristic of a casual attitude toward tradition, ceremony, social rules, and rank.

intelligence The capacity to acquire and apply knowledge, including solving problems.

intermittent reward A reward that is given for good performance occasionally, but not always.

internal customers The people with whom a person interacts on the job.

interpersonal relations The technical term for relationships with people.

interpersonal skill training The teaching of skills in dealing with others so they can be put into practice.

intuitive-type individuals People who prefer an overall perspective, or the big picture.

job discrimination An unfavorable action brought against another person because of a characteristic unrelated to job performance.

law of effect Behavior that leads to a positive consequence for the individual tends to be repeated, whereas behavior that leads to a negative consequence tends not to be repeated.

leader-exchange model A theory explaining that group leaders establish unique working relationships with group members, thereby creating in-groups and out-groups.

leadership The ability to inspire support and confidence among the people who are needed to achieve common goals.

long-term orientation A cultural characteristic of maintaining a long-term perspective.

masculinity In the study of cultures, an emphasis on assertiveness and the acquisition of money and material objects.

materialism An emphasis on assertiveness and the acquisition of money and material objects.

mentor An individual with advanced experience and knowledge who is committed to giving support and career advice to a less experienced person.

message A purpose or idea to be conveyed.

metacommunicate To communicate about your communication to help overcome barriers or resolve a problem.

mirroring Subtly imitating someone.

moments of truth Situations in which a customer comes in contact with a company and forms an impression of its service.

moral intensity In ethical decision making, how deeply others might be affected by the decision.

motivation An internal state that leads to effort expanded toward objectives; an activity performed by one person to get another to accomplish work.

motivational state Any active needs and interests operating at a given time.

multiple intelligences A theory of intelligence contending that people know and understand the world in distinctly different ways and learn in different ways.

negative affectivity A tendency to experience aversive emotional states.

negative reinforcement (avoidance motivation) Rewarding people by taking away an uncomfortable consequence of their behavior.

negotiating Conferring with another person to resolve a problem.

networking Developing contacts with influential people, including gaining their trust and confidence.

noise Anything that disrupts communication, including the attitudes and emotions of the receiver.

nominal group technique (NGT) A group problem-solving technique that calls people together in a structured meeting with limited interaction.

nonverbal communication The transmission of messages through means other than words.

nurturing person One who promotes the growth of others.

organizational politics Gaining power through any means other than merit or luck.

paradigm A model, framework, viewpoint, or perspective.

participative leadership Sharing authority with the group.

perceived control The belief that an individual has at his or her disposal a response that can control the negative aspects of an event.

performance-to-outcome expectancy The probability assigned by the individual that performance will lead to outcomes or rewards.

personal productivity How much resources, including time, you consume to achieve a certain level of output.

personality Persistent and enduring behavior patterns that tend to be expressed in a wide variety of situations.

personality clash An antagonistic relationship between two people based on differences in personal attributes, preferences, interests, values, and styles.

person–organization fit The compatibility of the individual and the organization.

person–role conflict The situation that occurs when the demands made by the organization clash with the basic values of the individual.

positive gossip Unofficial information that does not attack others, is based on truth, and does not leak confidential information.

positive reinforcement Increasing the probability that behavior will be repeated by rewarding people for making the desired response.

power The ability or potential to control anything of value and to influence decisions.

power distance The extent to which employees accept the idea that members of an organization have different levels of power.

proactive personality A person who is relatively unconstrained by situational forces and who brings about environmental change.

procrastination Delaying action for no good reason.

protégé The less experienced person in a mentoring relationship who is helped by the mentor.

punishment The presentation of an undesirable consequence or the removal of a desirable consequence because of unacceptable behavior.

Pygmalion effect The phenomenon that people will rise (or fall) to the expectations that another person has of them.

role ambiguity A condition in which the job holder receives confusing or poorly defined expectations.

role conflict The situation that occurs when a person has to choose between two competing demands or expectations.

role overload Having too much work to do.

s (special) factors Specific components of intelligence that contribute to problem-solving ability.

self-efficacy The confidence in your ability to carry out a specific task.

self-managing work team A small group of employees responsible for managing and performing technical tasks to deliver a product or service to an external or internal customer.

sensation-type individuals People who prefer routine and order.

sexual harassment Unwanted sexually oriented behavior in the work place that results in discomfort and/or interference with the job.

short-term orientation A cultural characteristic characterized by a demand for immediate results.

social loafing Shirking individual responsibility in a group setting.

stress An adaptive response that is the consequence of any action, situation, or event that places special demands on a person.

stressor The external or internal force that brings about stress.

summarization The process of summarizing, pulling together, condensing, and thereby clarifying the main points communicated by another person.

support network A group of people who can listen to your problems and provide emotional support.

synergy A situation in which the group's total output exceeds the sum of each individual's contribution.

team A small number of people with complementary skills who are committed to a common purpose, set of performance goals, and approach for which they hold themselves mutually accountable.

technostress Stress caused by an inability to cope with computer technologies in a constructive manner.

thinking-type individuals People who rely on reason and intellect to deal with problems.

toxic person One who negatively affects others.

training The process of helping others acquire a job-related skill.

triarchic theory of intelligence An explanation of mental ability holding that intelligence is composed of three different subtypes: analytical, creative, and practical.

Type A behavior A behavior pattern in which the individual is demanding, impatient, and overstriving and therefore prone to negative stress.

uncertainty avoidance The extent to which people accept the unknown and tolerate risk and unconventional behavior.

universal training need An area for improvement common to most people.

urgent time orientation A cultural characteristic of perceiving time as a scarce resource and tending to be impatient.

valence The value, worth, or attractiveness of an outcome.

value The importance a person attaches to something.

virtual office A place of work without a fixed physical location, where the output is communicated electronically.

virtual team A small group of people who conduct almost all of their collaborative work by electronic communication rather that face-to-face meetings.

win-win The belief that after conflict has been resolved both sides should gain something of value.

workaholism An addiction to work in which not working is an uncomfortable experience.

References

CHAPTER 1

1. James C. Georges, "The Hard Reality of Soft-Skills Training," *Personnel Journal*, April 1989, p. 41.

2. The model presented here is an extension of the one presented in Thomas V. Bonoma and Gerald Zaltman, *Psychology for Management* (Boston: Kent Publishing Company, 1981), pp. 88–92.

3. Nancy Day, "Informal Learning Gets Results," *Workforce*, June 1998, pp. 30–36.

4. Morgan W. McCall, Jr., *High Flyers: Developing the Next Generation of Leaders* (Boston: Harvard Business School Press, 1998).

CHAPTER 2

1. Such is the theme of Kevin R. Murphy, *Individual Differences and Behavior in Organizations* (San Francisco: Jossey-Bass, 1996).

2. J. Madeline Nash, "The Personality Genes," *Time*, April 27, 1998, pp. 60–61; Dean Hamer, Living with Our Genes (New York: Doubleday, 1998).

3. Margaret A. McManus and Mary L. Kelly, "Personality Measures and Biodata: Evidence Regarding Their Incremental Predictive Value in the Life Insurance Industry," *Personnel Psychology*, Spring 1999, pp. 137–148; Murray R. Barrick and Michael K. Mount, "The Big Five Personality Dimensions and Job Performance: A Meta-Analysis," *Personnel Psychology*, Spring 1991, p. 11.

4. Jesus F. Salgado, "The Five Factor Model of Personality and Job Performance in the European Community," *Journal of Applied Psychology*, February 1997, pp. 30–43.

5. Adapted from John R. Schermerhorn, Jr., James G. Hunt, and Richard N. Osburn, *Managing Organizational Behavior*, 5th ed. (New York: John Wiley & Sons, 1994), p. 119.

6. Arthur R. Jensen, *The g Factor: The Science of Mental Ability* (Westport. CT: Praeger, 1998).

7. Robert J. Sternberg, *Beyond IQ: A Triarchic Theory of Human Intelligence* (New York: Cambridge University Press, 1985); Bridget Murray, "Sparking Interest in Psychology Class," *APA Monitor*, October 1995, p. 51.

8. Howard Gardner, *Leading Minds: An Anatomy of Leadership* (New York: Basic Books, 1996); www.funderstanding.com/multipleint.htm.

9. Daniel Goleman, "What Makes a Leader?" *Harvard Business Review*, November–December 1998, p. 95; Bridget Murray, "Does 'Emotional Intelligence' Matter in the Workplace?" *APA Monitor*, July 1998, p. 21.

10. Paul G. Stoltz, *Adversity Quotient—Turning Obstacles into Opportunities* (New York: Wiley, 1997).

11. David C. McClelland, "How Motives, Skills, and Values Determine What People Do," *American Psychologist*, July 1985, p. 815.

12. John B. Miner, *Organizational Behavior: Performance and Productivity* (New York: Random House, 1988), p. 83.

CHAPTER 3

1. Albert Mehrabian and M. Weiner, "Decoding of Inconsistent Communications," *Journal of Personality and Social Psychology*, 6, 1967, pp. 109–114.

2. Frederick Golden, "Lying Faces Unmasked," *Time*, April 5, 1999, pp. 52–53.

3. Jeffrey Jacobi, *The Vocal Advantage* (Upper Saddle River, NJ: Prentice Hall, 1996).

4. Roberta H. Krapels and Vanessa D. Arnold, "Speaker Credibility in Persuasive Work Situations," *Business Education Forum*, December 1997, p. 25.

5. Irene Hanson Frieze, Josephine E. Olson, and June Russell, "Attractiveness and Business Success: Is It More Important for Women or Men?" Paper presented at the Academy of Management, Washington, D.C., August 1989.

6. Suzette Haden Elgin, *Genderspeak* (New York: Wiley, 1993).

7. Mark Henricks, "Can We Talk? Speaking Up About the Value of Dialogue," *Entrepreneur,* January 1998, p. 82.

8. Sharon Lund O'Neil, "An Empowered Attitude Can Enhance Communication Skills," *Business Education Forum,* April, 1998, pp. 28–30.

9. Jimmy Calano and Jeff Salzman, "Persuasiveness: Make It Your Power Booster," *Working Woman,* October 1988, pp. 124–125; Krapels and Arnold, "Speaker Credibility," pp. 24–26; Gayle Theiss, "Say It Smart," *Aspire,* November–December 1998, pp. 3–4.

10. Jean Mausehund and R. Neil Dortch, "Communications—Presentation Skills in the Digital Age," *Business Education Forum,* April 1999, pp. 30–32.

11. Barry L. Reece and Rhonda Brandt, *Effective Human Relations in Organizations,* 5th ed. (Boston: Houghton Mifflin, 1993), p. 250.

12. Deborah Tannen, *Talking from 9 to 5* (New York: William Morrow, 1994); Tannen, *You Just Don't Understand* (New York: Ballantine, 1990); John Gray, *Men Are from Mars, Women Are from Venus* (New York: HarperCollins, 1992).

13. Deborah S. Roberts, "Communication + Stress = Breakdown," *Dartnell's Communication at Work,* sample issue, undated.

CHAPTER 4

1. Deborah Fineblum Raub, "Chief Mankiller to Talk Here on Power, Women," Rochester, New York, *Democrat and Chronicle,* May 1, 1994, p. 1F.

2. Jon R. Katzenbach and Douglas K. Smith, "The Discipline of Teams," *Harvard Business Review,* March–April 1993, p. 112.

3. Deal E. Yeatts and Cloyd Hyten, *High Performing Self-Managed Work Teams: A Comparison of Theory and Practice* (Thousand Oaks, CA: Sage, 1998), p. xiii.

4. Carla Johnson, "Teams at Work," *HR Magazine,* May 1999, p. 30.

5. James L. Creighton and James W. R. Adams, "The Cybermeeting's About to Begin," *Management Review,* January 1998, pp. 29–31.

6. Johnson, "Teams at Work," p. 32.

7. "When Committees Spell Trouble: Don't let Individuals Hide Within a Group," *WorkingSMART,* August 1998, p. 1.

8. Irving L. Janus, *Victims of Groupthink: A Psychological Study of Foreign Policy Decisions and Fiascos* (Boston: Houghton Mifflin, 1972); Glen Whyte, "Groupthink Reconsidered," *Academy of Management Review,* January 1989, pp. 40–56.

9. Martha A. Peak, "Treating Trauma in Teamland," *Management Review,* September 1997, p. 1.

10. Glenn M. Parker, *Team Players and Teamwork: The New Competitive Business Strategy* (San Francisco: Jossey-Bass, 1990), pp. 61–98; Thomas L. Quick, *Successful Team Building* (New York: AMACOM, 1992), pp. 40–52.

11. Pamela Lovell, "Healthy Teams Display Strong Vital Signs," *Teamwork,* sample issue, the Dartnell Corporation, 1997.

12. Glenn M. Parker, *Cross-Functional Teams: Working with Allies, Enemies, & Other Strangers* (San Francisco: Jossey-Bass, 1994), p. 170.

CHAPTER 5

1. Ryan K. Lahti, "Group Decision Making within the Organization: Can Models Help?" www.work-teams.unt.edu/reports/lahti.htm. Copyright 1996, University of North Texas. Accessed June 3, 1999.

2. Andrew E. Schwartz and Joy Levin, "Better Group Decision Making," *Supervisory Management,* June 1990, p. 4.

3. R. Brente Gallupe, William H. Cooper, Mary-Liz Grise, and Lana M. Bastianutti, "Blocking Electronic Brainstorms," *Journal of Applied Psychology,* February 1994, pp. 77–78;

4. R. Brent Gallupe and Associates, "Electronic Brainstorming and Group Size," *Academy of Management Journal,* June 1992, p. 352; R. Brent Galuppe, Lana M. Bastianutti, and William H. Cooper, "Unblocking Brainstorms," *Journal of Applied Psychology,* February 1991, pp. 137–142.

5. Keng L. Siau, "Electronic Brainstorming," *Innovative Leader,* April 1997, p. 3.

6. Allen C. Bluedorn, Daniel B. Turban, and Mary Sue Love, "The Effects of Stand-Up and Sit-Down Meeting Formats on Meeting Outcomes," *Journal of Applied Psychology,* April 1999, pp. 277–285.

7. Howard Baker, "Promoting Interaction and Teamwork with Electronic Mail," *Business Education Forum,* October 1994, pp. 30–31.

8. "Introduction to Groupware," www.usabilityfirst. com/groupware/intro.html. Accessed June 3, 1999.

CHAPTER 6

1. Adapted and excerpted from Rene Blank and Sandra Slipp, "Manager's Diversity Workbook," *HRfocus,* July 1998, p. S7.

2. Personal communication, January 1995.

3. Joan Crockett, "Winning Competitive Advantage Through a Diverse Workforce," *HRfocus,* May 1999, p. 9.

4. Arvind V. Phatak, *International Dimensions of Management* (Boston: Kent, 1983), p. 167.

5. Gillian Flynn, "White Males See Diversity's Other Side," *Workforce,* February 1999, p. 52.

6. Charlene Marmer Solomon, "Global Operations Demand That HR Rethink Diversity," *Personnel Journal,* July 1994, p. 50.

7. Geert Hofstede, *Culture's Consequences: International Differences in Work Related Values* (Beverly Hills, Calif.: Sage, 1980); updated and expanded in "A Conversation with Geert Hofstede," *Organizational Dynamics,* Spring 1993, pp. 53–61; Jim Kennedy and Anna Everest, "Put Diversity in Context," Personnel Journal, September 1991, pp. 50–54.

8. "Koreans Pitch In to Help In Crisis," Associated Press, syndicated story December 2, 1997.

9. Rick Borelli, "A Worldwide Language Trap," *Management Review,* October 1997, pp. 52–54.

10. The etiquette suggestion is from "Letitia Baldrige: Arbiter of Business Manners and Mores," *Management Review,* April 1992, p. 50.

11. Roger E. Axtell, *Gestures: The Do's and Taboos of Body Language around the World* (New York: Wiley, 1990).

12. Chris Sandlund, "There's a New Face to America," *Success,* April 1999, p. 42.

13. Marcia Forsberg, "Cultural Training Improves Relations with Asian Clients," *Personnel Journal,* May 1993, pp. 79–89. The quotes are from the same source.

14. Valerie Frazee, "Culture & Language Training: Send Your Expats Prepared for Success," *Global Workforce,* March 1999, p. 7. (The list of facts was compiled from 10 different sources by Frazee.)

15. R. Roosevelt Thomas, Jr., *Beyond Race and Gender: Unleashing the Power of Your Total Work Force by Managing Diversity* (New York: AMACOM, 1991), p. 25.

16. Gillian Flynn, "The Harsh Reality of Diversity Programs," *Workforce,* December 1998, p. 29.

CHAPTER 7

1. Richard J. Mayer, *Conflict Management: The Courage to Confront* (Columbus, Oh.: Batelle Press, 1990).

2. Dominic A. Infante, *Arguing Constructively* (Prospect Heights, Ill.: Waveland Press, 1992).

3. Survey reported in Jessica Guynn, "Bullying Behavior Affects Morale as Well as the Bottom Line," Knight Ridder, syndicated story November 2, 1998.

4. Michael D. Kelleher, *Profiling the Lethal Employee: Case Studies of Violence in the Workplace* (Westport, CT: Praeger, 1997), p. 112.

5. Kenneth Thomas, "Conflict and Conflict Management," in Marvin D. Dunnette (ed.), *Handbook of Industrial and Organizational Psychology* (Chicago: Rand McNally College Publishing, 1976), pp. 900–902.

6. Simon, cited in Mark Liu, "You Can Learn to Be Less Accommodating—If You Want To," Rochester, New York, *Democrat and Chronicle,* April 25, 1999, p. 1C.

7. Catherine Tinsley, "Models of Conflict Resolution in Japanese, German, and American Cultures," *Journal of Applied Psychology,* April 1998, p. 317.

8. Robert R. Blake and Jane S. Mouton, *The Managerial Grid III* (Houston: Gulf Publishing, 1985), p. 101.

9. The first three suggestions are from Connirae Andreas and Steve Andreas, *Heart of the Mind* (Moab, Ut.: Real People Press, 1991).

10. Kenneth Kaye, *Workplace Wars and How to End Them: Turning Personal Conflicts into Productive Teamwork* (New York: AMACOM, 1994).

11. Kimberly T. Schneider, Suzanne Swan, and Louise F. Fitzgerald, "Job-Related and Psychological Effects of Sexual Harassment in the Workplace: Empirical Evidence from Two Organizations," *Journal of Applied Psychology,* June 1997, p. 406; Joanne Cole, "Sexual Harassment: New Rules, New Behavior," *HRfocus,* March 1999, p. 1.

12. Jennifer Laabs, "What You're Liable For Now," *Workforce,* October 1998, pp. 34–42; Gillian Flynn, "Sexual Harassment Interpretations Give Cause for New Concerns," *Workforce,* May 1999, pp. 105–106.

13. Schneider, Swan, and Fitzgerald, "Job-Related and Psychological Effects," pp. 412–413.

14. Theresa M. Glomb, Liberty J. Munson, and Charles L. Hulin, "Structural Equation Models of Sexual Harassment: Longitudinal Explorations and Cross-Sectional Generalizations," *Journal of Applied Psychology*, February 1999, pp. 14–28.

15. Kathleen Neville, *Corporate Attractions: An Inside Account of Sexual Harassment with the New Sexual Roles for Men and Women on the Job* (Reston, Va.: Acropolis Books, 1992; Joanne Cole, "Sexual Harassment: New Rules, New Behavior," *HRfocus*, March 1999, pp. 1, 14–15.

16. Robert McGarvey, "Hands Off! How Do the Latest Supreme Court Decisions On Sexual Harassment Affect You?" *Entrepreneur*, September 1998, p. 86; Cole, "Sexual Harassment: New Rules," p. 14.

CHAPTER 8

1. Bill Bradley, "Whatever the Score—Bounce Back," *Parade Magazine*, October 18, 1998, p. 6.

2. Shelley A. Kirkpatrick and Edwin A. Locke, "Leadership: Do Traits Matter?" *The Executive*, May 1991, pp. 26–27; Nathaniel Brandon, *Self-Esteem at Work: How Confident People Make Powerful Companies* (San Francisco: Jossey-Bass, 1998).

3. Dale E. Zand, *The Leadership Triad: Knowledge, Trust, and Power* (New York: Oxford University Press, 1997).

4. Reported in "Developing Trust Pays Off," *Managers Edge*, April 1999, p. 9.

5. Richard Mullins, "Big Job—Fast Track," *Rochester, New York, Democrat and Chronicle*, April 18, 1999, p. 1E.

6. Anthony Bianco, "The Rise of a Star," *Business Week*, December 21, 1998, p. 63.

7. Bruce J. Avolio, Jane M. Howell, and John J. Sosik, "A Funny Thing Happened on the Way to the Bottom Line: Humor as a Moderator of Leadership Style Effects," *Academy of Management Journal*, April 1999, pp. 219–227.

8. Zand, *The Leadership Triad*, p. 8.

9. Keith Bradsher, "Saturn's New Boss Rose to the Top from the Factory Floor," *The New York Times*, syndicated story, December 27, 1998.

10. Daniel Goleman, "What Makes a Leader?" *Harvard Business Review*, November–December 1998, p. 92.

11. Jay A. Conger, *The Charismatic Leader: Behind the Mystique of Exceptional Leadership* (San Francisco: Jossey-Bass, 1989).

12. Elizabeth Weil, "Every Leader Tells a Story," www.fastcompany.com/online/15/rftf.html. (Accessed May 6, 1999).

13. Suggestions 7, 9, and 10 are from Roger Dawson, *Secrets of Power Persuasion* (Upper Saddle River, N.J.: Prentice-Hall, 1992), pp. 181–183.

14. Jon R. Katzenbach and Douglas K. Smith, "The Discipline of Teams," *Harvard Business Review*, March–April 1993, p. 118.

15. Terri A. Scandura and Chester A. Schrieisheim, "Leader-Member Exchange and Supervisor Career Mentoring as Complementary Constructs in Leadership Research," *Academy of Management Journal*, December 1994, pp. 1588–1602; George Graen and J. F. Cashman, "A Role Making Model of Leadership in Formal Organizations: A Developmental Approach," in J. G. Hunt and L. L. Larson (eds.), Leadership Frontiers (Kent, Ohio: Kent State University Press, 1975), pp. 143–165.

16. Francis J. Yammarino, Alan J. Dubinsky, Lucette B. Comer, and Marvin A. Jolson, "Women and Transformational and Contingent Reward Leadership: A Multiple-Levels-of-Analysis Perspective," *Academy of Management Journal*, February 1997, pp. 205–222.

17. Jon R. Katzenbach and Jason A. Santamaria, "Firing Up the Front Line," *Harvard Business Review*, May–June 1999, pp. 116–117.

18. William D. Hitt, *The Model Leader: A Fully Functioning Person* (Columbus, Oh.: Battelle Press, 1993).

19. Michael E. McGill and John W. Slocum, Jr., "A *Little* Leadership Please?" *Organizational Dynamics*, Winter 1998, p. 48.

CHAPTER 9

1. Gerald Kushel, *Reaching the Peak Performance Zone: How to Motivate Yourself and Others to Excel* (New York: AMACOM, 1994), p. 66.

2. Research summarized in "One of These Seven Things Will Motivate Any Employee in the Company," *The Motivational Manager*, sample issue, 1998 (Lawrence Ragan Communications, Inc.)

3. Jennifer J. Laabs, "Targeted Rewards Jump-start Motivation," *Workforce*, February 1998, p. 90.

4. cited in Shari Caudron, "Motivating Creative Employees Calls for New Strategies," *Personnel Journal,* May 1994, p. 105.

5. Fred Luthans and Alexander D. Stajkovic, "Reinforce for Performance: The Need to Go Beyond Pay and Even Rewards," *Academy of Management Executive,* May 1999, p. 52.

6. Steven Kerr, *Ultimate Rewards: What Really Motivates People to Achieve* (Boston: Harvard Business School Publishing, 1997).

7. Jennifer Laabs, "Satisfy Them with More Than Money," *Workforce,* November 1998, p. 43.

8. The original version of expectancy theory applied to work motivation is Victor Vroom, *Work and Motivation* (New York: Wiley, 1964).

9. Alexander D. Stajkovic and Fred Luthans, "Social Cognitive Theory and Self-Efficacy: Going Beyond Traditional Motivational and Behavioral Approaches," *Organizational Dynamics,* Spring 1998, p. 66.

CHAPTER 10

1. Jeffrey Keller, "Associate with Positive People," A Supplement to the *Pryor Report,* 1994.

2. Ibid.

3. Erik J. Van Slyke and Bud Van Slyke, "Mentoring: A Results-Oriented Approach," *HRfocus,* February 1998, p. 14.

4. Based mostly on Kathy E. Kram, *Mentoring at Work: Developmental Relationships in Organizational Life* (Glenview, Ill.: Scott, Foresman, 1985), pp. 22–39; Van Slyke and Van Slyke, "Mentoring," 1998, p. 14.

5. Jerry Langdon, "Minority Executives Benefit from Mentors," Gannett News Service, December 7, 1998. See also Letty C. Hardy, "Mentoring: A Long-term Approach to Diversity," *HRfocus,* July 1998, p. S11.

6. Hal Rosenbluth and Diane McFerrin Peters, *Good Company: Caring as Fiercely as You Compete* (Reading, MA: Addison Wesley, 1998).

7. "Coach with 'Could,' not 'Should,'" *Executive Strategies,* April 1998, p. 1.

8. Ian Cunningham and Linda Honold, "Everyone Can Be a Coach," *HRMagazine,* June 1998, pp. 63–66.

9. *Career Track* seminar, How to Deal with Difficult People, 1995; Kenneth Kaye, *Workplace Wars and How to End Them: Turning Personal Conflicts into Productive Teamwork* (New York: AMACOM, 1994);

"Tame the Best Within You: How to Cope with Mood Swings in Yourself and Others," *WorkingSMART,* April 1999, p. 1.

10. Quoted in Jessica Guynn, "Bullying Behavior Affects Morale as Well as the Bottom Line," Knight Ridder syndicated story, November 2, 1998.

CHAPTER 11

1. Andrew J. DuBrin, "Sex Differences in the Use and Effectiveness of Tactics of Impression Management," *Psychological Reports,* 1994, 74, pp. 531–544.

2. William L. Gardner III, "Lessons in Organizational Dramaturgy: The Art of Impression Management," *Organizational Dynamics,* Summer 1992, p. 45.

3. Jim Rucker and Jean Anna Sellers, "Changes in Business Etiquette," *Business Education Forum,* February 1998, p. 45.

4. This section of the chapter is based on Annette Vincent and Melanie Meche, "It's Time to Teach Business Etiquette," *Business Education Forum,* October 1993, pp. 39–41; "Business Etiquette: Teaching Students the Unwritten Rules," *Keying In,* January 1996, pp. 1–8; Rucker and Sellers, "Changes in Business Etiquette," pp. 43–45; "Culture Shock?" *Entrepreneur,* May 1998, p. 46. The quotes are from the same source.

5. "Hardball Office Politics," *WorkingSMART,* September 1993, p. 5.

6. Research reported in Laura Lippman, "The Age of Obsequiousness: Flattering Your Way Up the Corporate Ladder," Baltimore, Maryland, *The Sun,* October 24, 1994.

7. Unpublished research reported in Kathleen Kelleher, *Los Angeles Times,* February 24, 1997.

8. Quoted in Mildred L. Culp, "Work Productively: Buddy-Up with Tech Fixers," *WorkWise®,* a syndicated column, January 10, 1999.

CHAPTER 12

1. Mike Miller, "Customer Service Drives Reengineering Effort," *Personnel Journal,* November 1994, pp. 87–91.

2. Anthony J. Rucci, Steven P. Kirn, and Richard T. Quinn, "The Employee-Customer-Profit Chain at Sears," *Harvard Business Review,* January–February 1998, pp. 82–97.

3. Barry M. Stow and Jerry Ross, "Stability in the Midst of Change: A Dispositional Approach to Job Attitudes," *Journal of Applied Psychology*, August 1985, p. 471.

4. Adrian J. Slywotzky and David J. Morrison, "Forget the Product: Focus on the Customer," *Leadership* (Newsletter of the American Management Association International), February 1999, p. 2.

5. Karl Abrecht, *The Only Thing That Matters* (New York: HarperCollins, 1992).

6. Susan Okula, "Customer Service: New Tools for a Timeless Idea," *Business Education Forum*, December 1998, p. 7; Robert F. Gault, "Managing Customer Satisfaction for Profit," *Management Review*, April 1993, p. 23.

7. Okula, "Customer Service," p. 9.

8. Joyce E. Santora, "Alamo's Drive for Customer Service," *Personnel Journal*, April 1991, p. 43.

9. Dot Yandle, "Helping Your Employees Give Customers What They Want," *Success Workshop* (A supplement to *Managers Edge*), November 1998, p. 1.

10. "Supermarket Smiles Misread in the Aisles," Associated Press, September 3, 1998.

11. Research cited in "Service Facts," *Customer Service Professional*, October 1997, p. 1.

12. Donna Deeprose, "Helping Employees Handle Difficult Customers," *Supervisory Management*, September 1991, p. 6; Chip R. Bell and Ron Zemke, "Service Breakdown-The Road to Recovery," in *Service Wisdom: Creating and Maintaining the Customer Service Edge* (Minneapolis, Minn.: Lakewood Books, 1992).

13. "Customer Problem Clinics," in *Making . . . Serving . . . Keeping Customers*, published by Dartnell, 4660 Ravenswood Avenue, Chicago, IL 60640.

14. Excerpted and paraphrased from Scott Hays, "Exceptional Customer Service Takes the 'Ritz' Touch," *Workforce*, January 1999, pp. 99–102.

CHAPTER 13

1. Linda K. Treviño and Katherine A. Nelson, *Managing Business Ethics: Straight Talk About How to Do It Right* (New York: Wiley, 1995), pp. 24–35; "Why Have a Code of Ethics?" *The Fact Finder*, January 1995, p. 3; Ralph Estes, *Tyranny of the Bottom Line: Why Corporations Make Good People Do Bad Things* (San Francisco: Berrett-Koehler, 1996).

2. Thomas M. Jones, "Ethical Decision Making by Individuals in Organizations: An Issue Contingent Model," *Academy of Management Review*, April 1991, p. 391.

3. Samuel Greengard, "50% of Your Employees Are Lying, Cheating, and Stealing," *Workforce*, October 1997, pp. 44–53.

4. Treviño and Nelson, *Managing Business Ethics*, pp. 47–64.

5. The concept of the game is from Karen Ireland, "The Ethics Game," *Personnel Journal*, March 1991, p. 74. The scenarios are original.

6. Joseph L. Badaracco, Jr., "The Discipline of Building Character," *Harvard Business Review*, March–April 1998, pp. 114–124.

7. Michael S. Josephson, "Does Character Still Count?" *USA Weekend*, September 23–25, 1994, p. 20.

8. "Extolling the Virtues of Hot Lines," *Workforce*, June 1998, pp. 125–126. For the original article, go to: www.depaul.edu/ethics/inter1.html.

9. Treviño and Nelson, *Managing Business Ethics*, pp. 71–75.

10. Daniel J. Brass, Kenneth D. Butterfield, and Bruce C. Skaggs, "Relationships and Unethical Behavior: A Social Network Perspective," *Academy of Management Review*, January 1998, pp. 14–31.

CHAPTER 14

1. Daniel Eisenberg, "Offices by the Hour," *Time*, February 1, 1999, p. 40.

2. Robert Boice, *Procrastination and Blocking: A Novel, Practical Approach* (Westport, CT: Greenwood Publishing Group, 1996).

3. The term *WIFO* has been contributed by Shale Paul, as cited in "Tips to Keep Procrastination Under Control," Gannett News Service syndicated story, November 9, 1998.

4. Dru Scott, *How to Put More Time in Your Life* (New York: New American Library, 1980), p. 1.

5. Mildred L. Culp, "Looking for Harmony? Swat the Clutter Bug for Greater Efficiency," syndicated column, Passage Media, 1998.

6. Meni Koslowky and Abraham Sagie, "Correlates of Employee Lateness: Some Theoretical Considerations," *Journal of Applied Psychology*, February 1997, pp. 79–88.

7. Mildred L. Culp, "Working Productively with Workaholics While Minimizing Legal Risks," Passage Media syndicated story, 1997.

8. Odette Pollar, "Tame Your In-Basket Once and for All," *Managers Edge*, September 1998, p. 11.

9. Amy Dunkin, "Saying 'Adios' to the Office," *Business Week*, October 12, 1998, p. 153; Heather Page, "Remote Control," Entrepreneur, October 1998, p. 148; Jenny C. McCune, "Telecommuting Revisited," February 1998, p. 14; E. Jeffrey Hill, Brent C. Miller, Sara P. Weiner, and Joe Colihan, "Influences of the Virtual Office on Aspects of Work/Life Balance," *Personnel Psychology*, Autumn 1998, pp. 667–683.

10. John J. Fried, "Be a Sharp Web Detective," Knight Ridder syndicated story, June 27, 1999.

11. Richard S. DeFrank and John M. Ivancevich, "Stress on the Job: An Executive Update," *Academy of Management Executive*, August 1998, pp. 55–56.

12. Jeffrey R. Edwards, "A Cybernetic Theory of Stress, Coping, and Well-Being in Organizations," *Academy of Management Review*, April 1992, p. 248.

13. Quoted in "An Ounce of Prevention Beats Burnout," *HRfocus*, June 1999, p. 1.

14. Christina Maslach, *The Truth About Burnout* (San Francisco: Jossey-Bass, 1997). See also Dirk van Dierendonck, Wilmar B. Schaufeli, and Bram P. Buunk, "The Evaluation of an Individual Burnout Intervention Program: The Role of Equity and Social Support," *Journal of Applied Psychology*, June 1998, pp. 392–407.

15. M. Afalur Rahim, "Relationships of Stress, Locus of Control, and Social Support to Psychiatric Symptoms and Propensity to Leave a Job: A Field Study with Managers," *Journal of Business and Psychology*, Winter 1997, p. 159.

16. Steve M. Jex and Paul D. Bliese, "Efficacy Beliefs as a Moderator of the Impact of Work-Related Stressors," *Journal of Applied Psychology*, June 1999, pp. 349–361.

17. Jeffrey R. Edwards and A. J. Baglioni, Jr., "Relationships between Type A Behavior Pattern and Mental and Physical Symptoms: A Comparison of Global and Component Measures," *Journal of Applied Psychology*, April 1991, p. 276.

18. Peter Y. Chen and Paul E. Spector, "Negative Affectivity as the Underlying Cause of Correlations between Stressors and Strains," *Journal of Applied Psychology*, June 1991, p. 398.

19. "Too Much Work Causes Stress," *Management Review*, March 1995, p. 6.

20. Craig Bond, *Technostress: The Human Cost of the Computer Revolution* (Reading: Mass.: Addison-Wesley, 1984), p. 16.

21. DeFrank and Ivancevich, "Stress on the Job," pp. 56–57.

22. DeFrank and Ivancevich, "Stress on the Job," pp. 57–58.

23. Harriet Johnson Brackey, "Snoozing Studies Alarm Experts," Knight Ridder syndicated story, July 6, 1998; Donald J. McNerney, "Napping at Work: You Snooze, You Win!" *HRfocus*, March 1995, p. 3.

CHAPTER 15

1. "Turn Passive Workers into 'Climbers'" *The Washington Post* syndicated story, June 29, 1998.

2. "CEOs Speak Out: What Is Needed to Work in Today's Ever-changing Business World," *Keying In*, November 1996, pp. 1–2; Brien N. Smith, Carolee Jones, and Judy Lane, "Employers' Perceptions of Work Skills," *Business Education Forum*, April 1997; Claudio Fernandez-Araoz, "Hiring without Firing," *Harvard Business Review*, July–August 1999, p. 113.

3. Quoted in Jerry Useem, "Cyberspace Is a Job Jungle: Read This Before You Put a Résumé Online," *Fortune*, May 24, 1999, p. 290.

4. Cited in Anitia Bruzzese, "Dangers Lurk for Job Hunters Online," Gannett News Service syndicated story, January 11, 1999.

5. Quoted in "Job Hunt," *Business Week Careers*, February 1987, p. 77.

6. Edward A. Robinson, "Beware—Job Seekers Have No Secrets," *Fortune*, December 29, 1997, p. 285.

7. Zane K. Quible, "Job Seeking Process," in *The Changing Dimensions of Business Education* (Reston, Va.: National Business Education Association, 1997), p. 176.

8. Quoted and updated July 1999 from Carol Kleiman, "Key Words Bosses Seek When Scanning Résumés," *Chicago Tribune* syndicated story, October 27, 1997.

9. Richard H. Beatty, *The Perfect Cover Letter* (New York: Wiley, 1997).

10. Linda Thornburg, "Computer-Assisted Interviewing Shortens Hiring Cycle," *HRMagazine*, February 1998, pp. 73–79.

11. Aaron Bernstein, "We Really Want You to Stay, Really," *Business Week*, June 22, 1998, p. 68.

12. Hugh P. Gunz, R. Michael Jalland, and Martin G. Evans, "New Strategy, Wrong Managers? What You Need to Know about Career Streams," *Academy of Management Executive,* May 1998, p. 22.

13. Such is the theme of James R. Lucas, *The Passionate Organization: Igniting the Fire of Employee Commitment* (New York: AMACOM, 1999).

14. Scott E. Seibert, Michael Crant, and Maria L. Kraimer, "Proactive Personality and Career Success," *Journal of Applied Psychology,* June 1999, pp. 416–427.

15. Philip L. Hunsaker, "Projecting the Appropriate Image," *Supervisory Management,* May 1989, p. 26.

16. "Taking Charge in a Temp World," *Fortune,* October 21, 1998, pp. 247–248.

17. Quoted in "Network Your Way Up," *WorkingSMART,* February 1997, p. 4.

18. Daniel L. Cable and Timothy A. Judge, "Interviewers' Perceptions of Person–Organization Fit and Organizational Selection Decisions," *Journal of Applied Psychology,* August 1997, pp. 546–561.

19. Michael Oliver, "Taking Risks Will Get You Moving," *Personnel Journal,* April 1983, p. 319.

20. This theme pervades Manuel London, *Career Barriers: How People Experience, Overcome, and Avoid Failure* (Mahwah, N.J.: Lawrence Erlbaum, 1998).

21. Gloria Dunn, "What to Do After You've Lost Your Job," *Workforce Extra* (supplement to the April 1999 *Workforce*), April 1999, pp. 2–3.

22. Belle Rose Ragins, Bickley Townsend, and Mary Mattis, "Gender Gap in the Executive Suite: CEOs and Female Executives Report on Breaking the Glass Ceiling," *Academy of Management Executive,* February 1998, pp. 28–42.

23. "Advancement for Minority Women Slow," The Associated Press syndicated story, July 14, 1999.

Index